PENGUIN SHAKESPEARE LIBRARY
GENERAL EDITOR: T. J. B. SPENCER

SHAKESPEARE'S LATER COMEDIES

David Palmer was born in Manchester in 1935, and educated at Kettering Grammar School and New College, Oxford. He left Oxford in 1960 to teach at the University of Hull, where he is now a Senior Lecturer in the English Department. He is the author of *The Rise of English Studies* (1965) and Co-General Editor of 'Stratford-upon-Avon Studies'. During 1968/69 he was Visiting Professor of English in the University of Rochester, New York.

D0242792

David Hume was born in Rochester in 1631
and educated at ... Grammar School and
... He ...
... the University of ... Where he was
... lecturer in the English Department. He
is the author of *... College English Studies* (1957),
and *Shakespeare's Father* (1963), and *The
Shorter* ... During ... he was Visiting Professor ... at the University of ...,
New York.

SHAKESPEARE'S
LATER COMEDIES

AN ANTHOLOGY
OF MODERN CRITICISM

Edited by D. J. Palmer

PENGUIN BOOKS

Penguin Books Ltd, Harmondsworth, Middlesex, England
Penguin Books Inc., 7110 Ambassador Road, Baltimore, Maryland 21207, U.S.A.
Penguin Books Australia Ltd, Ringwood, Victoria, Australia

———

First published 1971
This selection copyright © D. J. Palmer, 1971

———

Made and printed in Great Britain by
Hazell Watson & Viney Ltd
Aylesbury, Bucks
Set in Monotype Fournier

This book is sold subject to the condition
that it shall not, by way of trade or otherwise,
be lent, re-sold, hired out, or otherwise circulated
without the publisher's prior consent in any form of
binding or cover other than that in which it is
published and without a similar condition
including this condition being imposed
on the subsequent purchaser

CONTENTS

'PERICLES'

'CYMBELINE'

'THE WINTER'S TALE'

'THE TEMPEST'

ACKNOWLEDGEMENTS

THANKS are due to the following for permission to reprint the contents of this anthology:

The author, Chatto & Windus Ltd, and Oxford University Press (New York) for pages 162–70 from *Shakespeare and Elizabethan Poetry* (1951) by M. C. Bradbrook.

Columbia University Press for pages 103–13 and 126–31 from *Shakespeare and the Comedy of Forgiveness* (1965) by Robert Grams Hunter; and for 'Parolles' by G. P. Krapp, from *Shaksperian Studies by Members of the Department of English and Comparative Literature in Columbia University* (1916), edited by Brander Matthews and Ashley Thorndike.

The author and the Athlone Press of the University of London for pages 97–104 and 108–13 from *Shakespeare's 'Measure for Measure'* (1953) by Mary Lascelles.

Longmans, Green & Co. Ltd and Theatre Art Books (New York) for pages 152–69 from *Angel with Horns* (1961) by A. P. Rossiter.

The author, Routledge & Kegan Paul Ltd, and Schocken Books (New York) for pages 96–112 from *The Problem Plays of Shakespeare* (1963) by Ernest Schanzer.

The authors and Edward Arnold Ltd for extracts from 'Shakespeare and Romance' by Stanley Wells, and for '*The Tempest*: Conventions of Art and Empire' by J. P. Brockbank, from *Later Shakespeare* (Stratford-upon-Avon Studies 8, 1966), edited by J. R. Brown and Bernard Harris; and for '*The Tempest* on the Stage' by David William, from *Jacobean Theatre* (Stratford-upon-Avon Studies 1, 1960), edited by J. R. Brown and Bernard Harris.

The authors and Cambridge University Press for an extract from 'Shakespeare and the Blackfriars Theatre' by G. E. Bentley, from *Shakespeare Survey 1* (1948), pages 40–49; and for 'History and Histrionics in *Cymbeline*' by J. P. Brockbank, from *Shakespeare Survey 2* (1958), pages 42–8.

The author and Quelle & Meyer (Heidelberg) for 'Shakespeare and the Court Masque' by Allardyce Nicoll, from *Shakespeare Jahrbuch* 94 (1958), pages 51–62.

ACKNOWLEDGEMENTS

The author and Faber & Faber Ltd for pages 83–103 from *Poets on Fortune's Hill* (1952; revised title: *Elizabethan and Jacobean Poets*) by J. F. Danby.

The author and Swets & Zeitlinger (Amsterdam) for 'Themes and Variations in Shakespeare's *Pericles*' by G. A. Barker, from *English Studies* 44 (1963), pages 401–14.

Methuen & Co. Ltd for pages lxxxviii–xci from the Introduction to *Pericles* (new Arden Shakespeare, 1963), edited by F. D. Hoeniger; and for pages 146–63 from *Shakespeare's Wordplay* (1957) by M. M. Mahood.

Princeton University Press and B. T. Batsford Ltd for an extract from *Prefaces to Shakespeare* (1965 edition, Volume 2; *Cymbeline*) by Harley Granville-Barker, pages 77–87. Copyright (1963) by the Trustees of the author.

The author, the editor and the publisher of *Essays in Criticism* for an extract from 'Stuart *Cymbeline*' by Emrys Jones, from *Essays in Criticism* 11 (1961), pages 84–99.

The author, the editor of *ELH*, and the Johns Hopkins Press for '*Cymbeline* and Coterie Dramaturgy' by Arthur C. Kirsch, from *ELH: A Journal of English Literary History* 34 (1967), pages 285–306.

The author and the University of Iowa for '*Pandosto* and the Nature of Dramatic Romance' by John Lawlor, from *Philological Quarterly* 41 (1962), pages 96–113.

The author for 'The Triumph of Time in *The Winter's Tale*' by Inga-Stina Ewbank, from *A Review of English Literature* 5 (1964), pages 83–100.

The author and the University of Missouri Press for 'Recognition in *The Winter's Tale*' by Northrop Frye, from *Essays on Shakespeare and Elizabethan Drama in Honor of Hardin Craig* (1962), edited by Richard Hosley, pages 235–46.

Professor T. M. Raysor, J. M. Dent & Co. Ltd, and E. P. Dutton & Co. (New York) for an extract from *Coleridge's Shakespearian Criticism* (2 volumes, Everyman's Library, 1960), edited by T. M. Raysor, Volume 2, pages 130–40.

Oxford University Press (New York) for pages 95–122 from *The Fields of Light* (1951) by Reuben A. Brower.

INTRODUCTION

SPEAKING of Shakespeare's comedies, we often mean only those plays written during the 1590s, culminating in the poise and perfection of *Twelfth Night* (this, for instance, is the scope of Laurence Lerner's companion volume, *Shakespeare's Comedies*, Penguin Shakespeare Library, 1967). The later comedies are usually disguised under their description as 'problem plays' and 'last plays, or romances'. The orthodox account of the comedies belonging to the first half of Shakespeare's career stresses their wit and lyricism, their light-hearted 'romantic' qualities, in contrast to the more searching 'realism' of the 'problem plays'; the latter group is commonly characterized by its stronger ethical concerns, its deeper ironies, and more resonant rhetoric; while the 'last plays' are shown to represent an almost visionary remoteness from reality, as serious as the 'problem plays' in their tragi-comic treatment of the destructive and creative forces, and as self-consciously artificial as the earlier comedies in their courtly pastoralism.

Yet the diversity within each of these groups is also remarkable, and attempts to formulate a single pattern for each type of comedy encounter the awkward truth that Shakespeare constantly varied and remoulded the forms he worked with. Thus the differences between *Twelfth Night* and *The Merchant of Venice*, between *All's Well That Ends Well* and *Measure for Measure*, or between *The Winter's Tale* and *The Tempest*, are just as obvious and as important as their similarities. Moreover none of these groups is really self-contained; the 'problem plays' are commonly related to the tragedies composed during the same years, while anticipation of the 'last plays' has often been noted in *King Lear* and *Antony and Cleopatra*. Shakespeare frequently echoes his own work, and the restoration of Hero at the end of *Much Ado About Nothing* foreshadows the increasingly spectacular and 'miraculous' reappearances of Helena in *All's Well That Ends Well* and of Hermione in *The Winter's Tale*, no less than Oberon's manipulation of events in *A Midsummer Night's Dream* invites comparison with the Duke's role in *Measure for Measure* and with that of Prospero in *The Tempest* (*Pericles*, it might be added, is based upon the tale of Apollonius of Tyre which Shakespeare had first used in *The Comedy of Errors*).

Any classification of groups within the comedies is therefore bound to be arbitrary in some degree. A conception of Shakespearian comedy as a whole, based upon its thematic interests rather than its astonishingly variable forms, would find that its constant preoccupation is with the power of love. The comedies of the 1590s are plays of courtship, while the 'problem plays' probe more deeply into the moral conflicts generated by sexual passion, and the 'last plays' celebrate the regenerative power of love over time and mutability. From another point of view, an awareness of those qualities of style and structure which are the general properties of the age, rather than uniquely Shakespeare's, suggests that the comedies of the 1590s might be described as 'Elizabethan', and the 'problem plays' and 'last plays' as characteristically 'Jacobean'. The language and attitudes of the sonneteers are used and abused by the affected postures of the lovers in the 'Elizabethan' comedies, which are also imbued with the spirit of sweet and witty Ovid; while typical aspects of 'Jacobean' taste are reflected both in the analytical, sceptical mood of the 'problem plays' and in the heightened mannerism and virtuoso technique of the 'last plays', with their spectacular effects.

Another 'Jacobean' feature of the later comedies is the social orientation of the typical comic movement from misfortune to happiness. For the lovers in Shakespeare's 'Elizabethan' comedies this movement was principally if not entirely a personal affair. But Helena's 'miraculous' cure of the King in *All's Well That Ends Well* widens the scope of the comedy, prefiguring her ultimate redemption of Bertram and also representing that renewal of society which is associated with the younger generation in this play and in the 'last plays'. The social concerns of *Measure for Measure* are obvious enough, and like *All's Well That Ends Well* the comedy contains a double movement, the first part leading to a collapse of personal and social values, the second working towards their re-establishment: in this respect they may be compared with the structures of *Cymbeline* and *The Winter's Tale* (*The Tempest* represents the destructive movement in the shipwreck of the opening scene, with its emblematic recollection of past events). The striking elaborateness of the recognition scenes which conclude these later comedies is directly related to the wider contexts in which the personal fortunes of their characters are involved.

Therefore, although I have preserved the chronological division between the 'problem plays' and the 'last plays' represented in this volume, the larger concept of the later comedies as a whole is more than a mere portmanteau term for two distinct groups of plays. The principle on which I have selected the critical pieces is a very simple one: to bring together the most perceptive and best-informed writings on these plays known to me. Several of the essays are well-known and influential; others, usually more recent, have a quality, interest, and breadth of appeal that deserve a wider audience than they find in the scholarly publications where they first appeared. There are doubtless some obvious omissions: the work of E. M. W. Tillyard, for instance, and that of G. Wilson Knight have not been reprinted, because they are readily available and frequently anthologized elsewhere. But the selection is obviously intended to be eclectic; the criticism one admires is not always that which one agrees with.

On a more defensive note, I have to explain my decision to exclude *Troilus and Cressida*, which is conventionally, in modern times at least, placed among the 'problem plays'. To appeal to the editors of the first Folio, who also had doubts about its status as a comedy, would provide an obvious alibi, if I had not flouted their authority by including *Cymbeline* (which they classified as a tragedy) and *Pericles* (which they left out altogether, doubtless because they knew it was not entirely Shakespeare's work). Properly speaking, *Troilus and Cressida* is neither comedy nor tragedy: it is 'a thing *per se*, and stands alone'.*

* Among recent studies suggesting that *Troilus and Cressida* should be dissociated from *Measure for Measure* and *All's Well That Ends Well* are Brian Morris, 'The Tragic Structure of *Troilus and Cressida*', *Shakespeare Quarterly* 10 (1959); Ernest Schanzer, *The Problem Plays of Shakespeare* (1963), Appendix; and Geoffrey Bullough's indispensable *Narrative and Dramatic Sources of Shakespeare*, where *Troilus and Cressida* is represented in Volume 6 (1966) among the miscellaneous '*Other "Classical" Plays*'.

Notes indicated by numbers in the text are printed at the end of each extract. Quotations from Shakespeare are normally cited according to editions of the New Penguin Shakespeare available at the time of going to press; otherwise the text is that of *The Complete Works*, edited by Peter Alexander (1951).

1969   D. J. PALMER

Part One: 1602–4

'ALL'S WELL THAT ENDS WELL'

ONE

The Theme of Honour in *All's Well That Ends Well*

M. C. Bradbrook

HOVERING uncertainly in date between early and late nineties, *All's Well That Ends Well* is a play which is of its age rather than for all time.[1] It might have as sub-title 'Two plays in one', for the reason of its neglect – and the reason why in spite of the title, all did not end well, and it is not a successful play – is that a personal and an impersonal theme are here in conflict. It began by being a 'moral play', a grave discussion of the question of what constituted true nobility, and the relation of birth to merit. This was *the* great topic of the courtesy books, and in a court that included such a high proportion of self-made men as Elizabeth's did, the question was not without practical consequences. Such questions were the equivalent of a political discussion today. But in *All's Well* the 'social problem' – to give it the modern term – of high birth, exemplified in Bertram, and native merit, exemplified in Hellen,[2] is bisected by a human problem of unrequited love. The structural centre of the play is the King's speech on nobility, by which he justifies Hellen's marriage: the poetic centre is Hellen's confession of her love to the Countess. Few readers would deny that this speech is different in kind from anything else in the play:

> I know I love in vain, strive against hope,
> Yet in this captious and intenable sieve
> I still pour in the water of my love
> And lack not to lose still. Thus, Indian-like,
> Religious in mine error, I adore
> The sun that looks upon his worshipper
> But knows of him no more.   I.3.196–202

This is the voice of Juliet.

> My bounty is as boundless as the sea,
> My love as deep. The more I give to thee,
> The more I have, for both are infinite.   II.2.133–5

Seen through Hellen's eyes, Bertram is handsome, brave, the glass of fashion and the mould of form: seen through older and wiser eyes, he is a degenerate son, an undutiful subject, a dishonourable seducer. The two images blend in the action as he sinks from irresponsibility to deceit, but makes a name for himself in the wars. He ends in an abject position: no other hero receives the open condemnation that Bertram does. Modern taste may disrelish Claudio, Bassanio, or Orsino; but Shakespeare does not ratify it.

Here all the harsh words are spoken upon the stage: all but Hellen condemn Bertram. After suffering rebukes from his elders, his contemporaries, and even his inferiors, he ends unable to plead any excuses,[3] in danger of the law. The characters of the Countess and Lafew were invented by Shakespeare, and the King's role much expanded, in order that judgement might be passed on Bertram. By these three, who have an equal share of blood and merit and are therefore impartial judges, he is compared with Hellen throughout the play, to his increasing disadvantage.[4] In the end she alone can restore the honours he has lost.

Bertram is very young, perhaps seventeen or eighteen at most, left without a father's direction and highly conscious of his position. He is handsome, courageous, winning in manners; but also an inveterate liar. Yet the Elizabethan code of honour supposed a gentleman to be absolutely incapable of a lie. To give the lie was the deadliest of insults, not to be wiped out but in blood. Honour was irretrievably lost only by lies or cowardice; a gentleman, as Touchstone remembered, swore by his troth, as a knight by his honour. Crimes of violence were less dishonourable: the convicted liar was finished socially. Bassanio, though he thinks of a lie at the end, to get himself out of an awkward situation, does not utter it.

Bertram's fall is due to ill company: Parolles, or Words, another character of Shakespeare's own invention, is perceived in the end by Bertram himself to be the Lie incarnate, a fact which everyone else has known from the beginning.[5] He is that principal danger of noble youth, the flatterer and misleader, the base companion against whom all books of behaviour issued lengthy warning. The relation of Bertram and Parolles resembles that which everyone except Prince Hal takes to exist between himself and Falstaff. Parolles claims to be both courtier and soldier but his courtship is entirely speech, as his soldiership is entirely dress. Even the clown calls him knave and fool to his face; he is ready to play the pander, and at the end he crawls to the protection of old Lafew, the first to detect and, with provocative insults, to 'uncase' him.

The model of a perfect courtier is set before the young man by the King, in a 'mirror' or portrait of his father.

His father's 'moral parts' are what the King wishes for Bertram: their physical likeness has already been commented on. The elder Rossillion was a soldier first of all, but also a courtier.

> In his youth
> He had the wit which I can well observe
> Today in our young lords, but they may jest
> Till their own scorn return to them unnoted
> Ere they can hide their levity in honour.
> So like a courtier, contempt nor bitterness
> Were in his pride or sharpness; if they were,
> His equal had awaked them, and his honour,
> Clock to itself, knew the true minute when
> Exception bid him speak, and at this time
> His tongue obeyed his hand. Who were below him
> He used as creatures of another place,
> And bowed his eminent top to their low ranks ....
>
> I.2.31–43

Such is Bertram's inheritance of conduct, and he had a duty to live up to it. Hellen's miraculous cure of the King, which is proffered by her and accepted by him and the court as an act of Heaven,[6] makes her a candidate for nobility, though she is only the daughter of a poor gentleman belonging to the least dignified of the professions.[7] The recognized causes for ennobling the simple were headed by 'virtue public', that is, some great public service. Sir Thomas Elyot had declared that nobility is 'only the prayse and surname of virtue' and set forth the eleven moral virtues as the model for his Governor. Desert for virtue is Hellen's claim, and this, all but Bertram allow her.

By making his social climber a woman Shakespeare took a good deal of the sting out of the situation. The question of blood and descent versus native worth was an ancient subject of debate on the stage: indeed the first secular play to survive, *Fulgens and Lucres*, deals with precisely this matter. Here the lady's verdict was given for the worthy commoner against the degenerate nobleman. Though noble descent was prized as giving a disposition to virtue, and the opportunity of good education and good examples, yet 'one standard commonplace on nobility took shape; that lineage was not enough, but that the son of a noble house should increase and not degrade the glory of his ancestors'.[8]

Hellen has been conscious throughout of her humble station, and has urged the Countess that though she loves Bertram she would not have him till she should deserve him (I.3.194). Before and after marriage she thinks of Bertram as her 'master' as well as her lord, a title Parolles will not give him. It was within the power of the King to confer honour where he chose; and Hellen had already been ennobled in a superior way by being marked out as the instrument of Heaven towards the King's recovery.

When therefore she is offered her choice of a husband, none save Bertram think of refusing her. The 'lottery' is like a reversal of Portia's caskets, for here the lady makes her choice, sure to win. In bestowing a wife upon his ward, the King was certainly doing no more than Elizabeth or any other monarch might do. Yet Bertram's cry, 'A poor physician's daughter my wife!', would not sound so outrageous to an Elizabethan ear as it does today, for marriage out of one's degree was a debasing of the blood which blemished successive generations. The King, in his great central speech, whose formality is marked by the couplet form, replies and sets out to Bertram the causes why he should not disdain merit. This speech contains the germ of the play – or one of the two plays which together make up this story.

> 'Tis only title thou disdainest in her, the which
> I can build up. Strange is it that our bloods,

Of colour, weight, and heat, poured all together,
Would quite confound distinction, yet stands off
In differences so mighty. If she be
All that is virtuous, save what thou dislikest –
A poor physician's daughter – thou dislikest
Of virtue for the name. But do not so.
From lowest place when virtuous things proceed,
The place is dignified by th'doer's deed.
Where great additions swell's and virtue none,
It is a dropsied honour. Good alone
Is good, without a name: vileness is so;
The property by what it is should go,
Not by the title. She is young, wise, fair;
In these to nature she's immediate heir,
And these breed honour; that is honour's scorn
Which challenges itself as honour's born
And is not like the sire. Honours thrive
When rather from our acts we them derive
Than our foregoers. The mere word's a slave,
Debauched on every tomb, on every grave
A lying trophy, and as oft is dumb
Where dust and damned oblivion is the tomb
Of honoured bones indeed. . . .

II.3.116–40

This is doctrine of a kind which ought to convince Bertram. It is
only after he has objected, 'I cannot love her, nor will strive to
do't', that the King exercises his power to compel submission.

The customary formula when presenting young people to each
other in such circumstances was, 'Can you like of this man?', 'Can
you like of this maid?', in other words, can you make a harmonious
marriage? Love was not expected. If Bertram is thought to show
peculiar delicacy in demanding passion as the basis of marriage, he
removes all such notions at the end of the play by his alacrity in
accepting Lafew's daughter, a match which the King had planned
since their childhood. In the original story, Beltramo protests his
unwillingness but he does not defy the King, nor does he recant as
Bertram so abjectly does under the King's threats, protesting that
he now sees Hellen to be ennobled by the royal choice. The King's
fury, far more reasonable than old Capulet's when Juliet exercises a

right of rejection, depends on his, and everyone else's conviction that Hellen is 'virtuous' and the special favourite of heaven. Not only his king but his mother accepts it. That Bertram should misprize her is not in keeping with the decorum of the play. This is not *Romeo and Juliet*; it is written upon quite different premises, the social premises which that play so pointedly omits. And Bertram has no precontract; for his vamped-up excuse in the fifth act that he was really in love with Mademoiselle Lafew is patently one of his fibs. He dislikes Hellen on social, not personal grounds. He is being wilful; and in running away after the marriage ceremony, he is evading obligations which are imposed by the Church as well as the State, as Diana does not fail to recall to him (IV.2.12–13).

His rejection of Hellen must be seen then not in isolation but as linked with his choice of Parolles. The first dialogue of Hellen and Parolles, the Liar and Virtue as she herself designates them, must be seen as the encounter of Bertram's good and evil angels, who, if this were a Morality play, would contend for his soul in open debate.[9]

The exposure of Parolles's cowardice and lies precedes but foreshadows the exposure of Bertram. The last scene, which is Shakespeare's improvement of his source, is a 'judgement', like those which conclude so many of Chapman's comedies. The most extraordinary stratagems are practised by Diana and Hellen to extract Truth from the Accused. The jewels which are bandied about have symbolic significance; they stand for a contract and an estate of life. The King's gem derived from him to Hellen, and Bertram neither knows nor cares what it is. His own monumental ring symbolizes all he has thrown away,

> an honour 'longing to our house,
> Bequeathèd down from many ancestors,
> Which were the greatest obloquy i'th' world
> In me to lose. IV.2.42–5

This jewel, with which he had taunted Hellen, is found at the end to be in her keeping. Hellen too is a 'jewel' (V.3.1) which Bertram has thrown away. In this scene the King appears as the fount of justice, as earlier he had been the fount of honour: he deprives

Bertram of all honour (V.3.180–82) and the rapidity with which he jumps to thoughts of murder is prompted as much by his affection for Hellen as his well-merited distrust of her lord. Lafew and the Countess also recall Hellen's memory with sorrow. The likeness with the later play of *Measure for Measure*,[10] which was evidently modelled in part on *All's Well*, is particularly strong in this judgement scene, with charge and countercharge piled up in bewildering succession till they are resolved as if by magic in the appearance of the central figure. The ingenuities of Hellen, like those of the Duke, are not to modern taste but their purpose is conversion.

Bertram's conversion must be reckoned among Hellen's miracles. It is notable that on the fulfilment of the bargain she turns to seek, not her husband, but the King. What is achieved is public recognition of her right, which he concedes her. She has been acknowledged by her lord; that her personal happiness is simply irrelevant, and the ending neither hypocritical nor cynical, can be granted only if the play is seen as a moral debate on the subject: Wherein consists true honour and nobility?

This is a grave subject: more lofty than that of *Romeo and Juliet*, for example. But such a subject needed to remain upon the level of debate. An Elizabethan audience might have been quite willing to see it worked out as a species of Morality play, without taking the personal aspect into account. What is now called 'the love interest' is generally overweighted in the modern view of Shakespearean comedy. His audience would be well accustomed to see a love-intrigue provide the spring of the action without providing any of the interest or body of the play, as it does in the comedies of Jonson or Chapman, where it is like the love interest in a detective story, strictly subordinate to the disguisings. But here the nature of the story makes it extremely difficult to insulate the marriage as a social and religious contract.

Two incompatible 'species' are mingled because the personal aspect awakened to life. The play is a genuine hybrid, one of the few examples of Shakespeare's failure to master and control his form. Bertram is magnificently drawn: his petulance, his weakness, his cub-like sulkiness, his crude and youthful pride of rank. His charm has to be accepted because Hellen loves him, but there is little other evidence for it. Hellen's love, as expressed in her three great speeches, is a devotion so absolute that all thought of self is obliterated; yet her action cannot but make her appear, however much more modestly to an Elizabethan than to us, a claimant, and a stickler for her bond.[11] The parallels between her love speeches and the Sonnets (especially 35, 67, 82, 84, 95, 96), something in common between the lineaments of Bertram and those of Adonis, Bassanio, and Proteus, suggest that the theme of high birth versus native merit, first approached impersonally, had touched off reactions which could not properly be related to the story as it originally stood. The figure of Bertram, so radically changed from that of Boccaccio's Beltramo, is drawn with a fullness, a kind of uncynical disillusion which makes Hellen as a person still more unsatisfactory. She is a voice of despair breaking into the play; at other times a pliant lay-figure on which the characters drape their admiration. No crude and direct personal equation can be thought of; Shakespeare would certainly not wish to unlock his heart on the public stage. But here for once the poet and the dramatist are pulling different ways. He set out to start a discussion on the fashioning of a gentleman, and found himself impelled to draw the likeness of one whom Lafew called an 'ass' and Hellen the god of her 'idolatrous fancy', but whose portrait stands out clearly as something more complex than either.

NOTES

1. In the following pages I have summarized my article 'Virtue is the true Nobility', *Review of English Studies*, N.S. Volume 1, Number 4 (1950). Those who are interested will find there a more extended account of the background of courtesy literature, and in particular the relation of civil nobility to Christian nobility as it is treated by the writers of courtesy books, and books of nobility.

[Many scholars believe that the play belongs to a slightly later date than Miss Bradbrook suggests here. G. K. Hunter, for instance, places it in the years 1603–4, closer to *Measure for Measure*, in the Introduction to his edition in the new Arden Shakespeare (1959), page xxv. – Ed.]

2. Her name is so spelt throughout the Folio text. There is only one occasion on which the metre requires Helena. Shakespeare evidently took great care over his proper names; consider the way in which the diminutives Harry and Kate are used (like Jane Austen, he seems to think only the best people worthy to be called Henry): the beauty of his new forms, Desdemona and Cordelia. James Joyce erected a considerable biographic speculation upon Shakespeare's aversion from the name Richard.

3. For example, IV.2.12–30 where Diana rebukes him; IV.3.1–35 where the young Lords criticize him. Parolles's sonnet to Diana, 'Dian, the Count's a fool', contains some nasty home truths. In the last scene the King and Lafew are quite uncompromising. Bertram's word is no longer of the slightest value (V.3.182–4).

4. The Countess is convinced of Hellen's virtue in the first scene (I.1.38–44), but not so fully of Bertram's. She loves Hellen as her own child (I.3.97, 137–9) and after Bertram's flight disclaims him for her son and takes Hellen as her only child (III.2.67–8). Lafew's view of Bertram is never very high (II.3.98–100). In IV.5 he and the Countess unite in praise of Hellen's memory and at the beginning of V.3 the King laments her and accuses Bertram's 'mad folly' in which he is heartily seconded by Lafew, who joins his condemnation with still more praise of Hellen.

5. For example the Countess (III.2.87–9), Hellen (I.1.99–102). Parolles is meant to be representative of the evils of the court, which are much stressed in the opening scenes. It is no longer the fount of good manners, exclusively, as it had been in *The Two Gentlemen of Verona*.

6. The formal couplets in which Hellen, after making ready to retire, suddenly returns and announces herself as a minister of Heaven mark the portentousness of the occasion. See Hardin Craig, 'Shakespeare's Bad Poetry', *Shakespeare Survey 1* (1948). The automatic writing down of such passages as 'first draft fossils' is not justified. Hellen's 'miracle' is discussed at length by Lafew (II.3.1–37); it is 'A showing of a heavenly effect in an earthly actor', as Hellen confirms (II.3.63) to the court.

7. For those younger sons of the nobility who were obliged to take to the professions, Law was considered the noblest study: the profession of arms was of course the oldest and most honourable, but it notoriously failed to supply means of livelihood. The physician was concerned with base matters, and approximated too

nearly to the barber-surgeon and the apothecary to receive much honour.

8. John E. Mason, *Gentlefolk in the Making* (1935), page 8. This book is the most comprehensive account known to me of the doctrine of gentility.

9. Parolles, it should be noted, is a character entirely of Shakespeare's own invention. His alterations of his source (ultimately Boccaccio, *Il Decamerone*, 3.9) are highly significant, tending to greater humility, and dependence on Hellen's part – in the original she has a fortune – and greater perfidy, weakness, and youthfulness on Bertram's. I do not wish to suggest that *All's Well* is a Morality disguised, but it is a moral play which, like *The Merchant of Venice*, depends on a central theme of ethical significance.

10. *Measure for Measure* has in common the rejection of a devoted bride for insufficiency, and a marriage compelled by the ruler: the substitution of one woman for another: the false self-accusation of the chaste woman followed by denial from the culprit and culminating in his exposure through the arrival of an absent person. The similarity between the themes is also noticeable: both plays deal with what Bacon called 'Great Place', the problems of authority, and both are moral plays; that is to say, they are concerned with general truths explicitly handled, though handled in human terms. But *Measure for Measure* seems to me to belong to a much later period: the close resemblances in plot, far from suggesting that the two plays were written close together, imply that Shakespeare returned to his earlier material when he returned to a similar theme.

11. Hellen's three great speeches (I.1.78–97, I.4.186–212, III.2.99–129) have a number of parallels with the Sonnets. The picture of her as a canny fortune-hunter is entirely twentieth-century, and may lead critics so far as to see in her careful disclaimer of any ambition to match with the 'royal blood of France' a vulgar foresight, rather than a due sense of rank. Elizabeth's sense of what constituted suitable matches was extremely strict: the Earl of Essex was considered to have committed a shocking impropriety by marrying the widow of Philip Sidney.

from *Shakespeare and Elizabethan Poetry* (1951)
by M. C. Bradbrook, pages 162–70

TWO

All's Well That Ends Well as a Comedy of Forgiveness

Robert Grams Hunter

I

In *All's Well That Ends Well*, the world of comedy is threatened not so much by strife as by mutability. Change, the second great enemy of love, beauty, and happiness, has brought the once charmed worlds of Rossillion and Paris to the point of final dissolution. Within the first fifteen lines of the play we learn that the fathers of this world are dead and that its king is near death, the victim of an incurable disease, against which he refuses to struggle. Constantly throughout the first part of the play, the old – the Countess, Lafew, the King – remember and lament the past. They remember the nobility and honour of the dead Count Rossillion, the wisdom and skill of Helena's father, Gerard de Narbon, and their memories communicate the sense that irreplaceable virtues are in danger of passing from the world. The elegiac, autumnal tone of these opening scenes is close to that of the quatrains of Sonnet 73 with their images of bare boughs, twilight, and dying fire, and the effect of this beauty in *All's Well* is that described in the couplet of the sonnet: we love that best which we must leave ere long. Like all autumnal beauty, it has a double force. It reminds us simultaneously that it will soon disappear, and that its decay will one day be our own.

All's Well presents us with a dying world and if, as has been suggested, it is a problem play, its problem is a basic one – how do you rejuvenate a constantly dying race? The answer is one that we all know, and one that is suggested at the play's very opening when we discover, on stage, not only an old man and an old lady, but a young man and a girl. Here, then, is our solution, and being members of the audience at a comedy, we recognize it. In romantic comedy, boy and girl mean love, love means marriage, marriage means sexual intercourse, means procreation, means the re-creation of an always dying world. And, of course, we are right. No sooner is the beautiful girl left alone than she confesses to us her passionate love for the handsome young man:

> My imagination
> Carries no favour in't but Bertram's.
> I am undone: there is no living, none,
> If Bertram be away.   I.1.81-4

If we are not surprised by this news, however, we are no more startled to learn that there are obstacles in the way of this love's fulfilment. In Act I, scene 1 of a comedy, how could it be otherwise? Bertram and Helena are separated by more than Bertram's imminent departure:

> 'Twere all one
> That I should love a bright particular star
> And think to wed it, he is so above me.
> In his bright radiance and collateral light
> Must I be comforted, not in his sphere.
> Th'ambition in my love thus plagues itself:
> The hind that would be mated by the lion
> Must die for love.   I.1.84-91

With remarkable economy, in little more than a hundred lines, Shakespeare has established his basic comic situation: a noble but dying world stands in need of the rejuvenating force of sexual love. That love is potentially present in Bertram and Helena, but, as always in romantic comedy, a barrier exists between boy and girl – in this case, the barrier of a great disparity in social position. As members of the audience, we appear to know where we are and we can settle ourselves to enjoy the destruction of the barrier and the vicarious pleasures that attend the fulfilment of love and the artistic creation of happiness. Though the heroine despairs of the possibility of achieving her desires, though she seems content, with Viola's mythical sister, to sit like patience on a monument, smiling at grief, we know better. Love, in romantic comedy, will find out the way.

It is at this moment in the play that Shakespeare, for the first time, does something slightly odd. It will not be the last time, for of all Shakespeare's comedies, this is certainly the oddest, the most uncomfortable, perhaps the least popular, and it is probable that in those elements that cause its oddity and discomfort, the clues to its special significance are to be found.

As amateurs of the various forms of literary romance, any audience, whether Elizabethan readers of chivalric or pastoral narrative, or moderns with an experience of Victorian fiction or Hollywood movies, would have, I should imagine, a not wholly formed but nonetheless definite expectation at this point in the play's action. We are expecting, surely, some sort of sign from the hero, some indication of the state of his emotions – the declaration of a passion that he, too, realizes to be hopeless, perhaps. Or even better, an expression of his determination to defy the prejudices of society, followed, of course, by the heroine's refusal to let him make the sacrifice. But instead of '*Enter Bertram*', the stage direction at this point reads, '*Enter Parolles*'. Instead of the *jeune premier* we are presented with the parasite, with one who is immediately identified for us as a liar, a fool, and a coward, and instead of a tender passage between hero and heroine, we are treated to some fifty lines of bawdy on the absurdity of remaining a virgin. It is not surprising that Shakespeare has been strongly reprehended for creating the scene. Quiller-Couch would like to cut it (and 'the whole Parolles business') right out of the play, 'like a wen'. He finds it offensive and worse: '. . . such chat is more than offensive; it is pointless lacking a listener; and as we wish Helena to be, and as Boccaccio conceives Helena, she would have dismissed Parolles by a turn of the back. Shakespeare degrades her for us by allowing her to remain in the room with this impertinent.'[1]

A shift in taste since Quiller-Couch's time has made it easier for the modern reader to enjoy Shakespeare's jokes about sex and tempts us to regard Edwardian attitudes toward them as quaint if not neurotic. We should not be too quick to dismiss Quiller-Couch's objections as absurd, however. They are absurd, but the absurdity they demonstrate is common to a great deal of the adverse criticism

'ALL'S WELL THAT ENDS WELL'

of *All's Well*. Again and again in the critical remarks on this comedy (and in one's own reactions to it) one notices the unconscious assumption that *All's Well* should really be another play altogether, and that Shakespeare wrote the one we have either by mistake or through a combination of perversity and incompetence. *We*, the argument appears to run, know perfectly well what should happen in the play, but Shakespeare seems to be unable to get it through his head what it is that we want him to do. *We* know what Helena is like but the author fails to provide us with a Helena who is 'as we wish Helena to be'. *All's Well* obstinately refuses to be as we like it.

Our expectations are consistently disappointed, our hopes are frustrated, and the romantic comedy that, after the first hundred lines, we had settled down comfortably to enjoy is again and again pulled out from under us in the most annoying and awkward way. So consistently does this occur that one must end, finally, by entertaining the suspicion that in writing *All's Well* Shakespeare had something other than our undisturbed comfort in mind, and by acknowledging the fact that an understanding of the play can be arrived at only through an attempt to deal with it on its own terms, as Shakespeare wrote it.

Parolles's bawdy is a case in point. His interchange with Helena is an odd and unexpected incident, but its reasons for being in the play are clear enough. Parolles tells some home truths, none of which Helena gives the slightest sign of ever having doubted. 'Virginity', he tells her and us, is 'too cold a companion'. It is unnatural, self-consuming suicidal, and, finally, unattractive:

Loss of virginity is rational increase, and there was never virgin got till virginity was first lost. . . . your virginity, your old virginity, is like one of our French withered pears: it looks ill, it eats drily; marry, 'tis a withered pear; it was formerly better; marry, yet 'tis a withered pear.

I.1.126–7, 157–61

Helena does more than tolerate this 'offensive chat'. She listens to it and she clearly allows it to influence her state of mind. As G. K. Hunter points out, this dialogue

is a free and frothy play upon the ideas which are fermenting . . . in Helena's (or rather Shakespeare's) mind, and the topic it turns upon –

28

the use of virginity and the manner in which it can be laid out to best advantage – is obviously germane to the situation of a virgin yearning for honest marriage to a young nobleman.[2]

Its obvious effect upon Helena is to make her stop merely yearning and begin planning how she may lose her virginity, as she puts it, 'to her own liking' – to Bertram and in marriage. She casts off the hopeless melancholy of her first soliloquy and substitutes for it the self-confidence of her second:

> Our remedies oft in ourselves do lie,
> Which we ascribe to heaven. The fated sky
> Gives us free scope, only doth backward pull
> Our slow designs when we ourselves are dull.   I.1.212–15

This change from despair to determination is entirely in keeping with the comic spirit. Comedy, traditionally, is anything but dedicated to the preservation and exaltation of virginity, and Helena's desire to lose hers lawfully entirely befits a comic heroine. And yet her determination to marry Bertram unquestionably makes Helena something of an oddity among the usual heroines of romance. It is the function of the lady, ordinarily, to appear, at least, to be the pursued rather than the pursuer in a romantic narrative. According to Andrew Lang, 'Everyone would prefer the worm in the bud to feed on the damask cheek rather than to see "Vénus toute entière à sa proie attachée", as Helena attaches herself to Bertram.'[3] Again, Shakespeare appears to have failed or refused to write this comedy as we would like it. An instructive example of how Lang's 'everyone' expects a heroine like Helena to behave can be found in Trollope's *Framley Parsonage*. There, too, the heroine, Lucy Robarts, is the daughter of a poor and recently deceased physician. There, too, the hero, Lord Lufton, is a great aristocrat of proud family. Lucy loves Lufton, but Lufton also loves Lucy, and far from pursuing him, Lucy refuses Lufton when he proposes and continues to refuse him until, in Volume III, his heretofore recalcitrant mother proposes for him.

In fact, *All's Well* is not a romantic comedy in the usual sense of the term. If we look to this play to gratify the expectations commonly raised by romantic comedy, we will be disappointed and our frustration will make an understanding of the play impossible. It has been suggested that these frustrated expectations are a largely modern phenomenon and that the Elizabethan audience for whom the play was intended would have accepted it, with little discomfort, as a perhaps slightly odd but still quite satisfactory romantic drama. This is the argument of W. W. Lawrence in his excellent essay on the play, and by an intelligent examination of Shakespeare's source in Boccaccio and of analogous medieval stories, Professor Lawrence certainly manages to demonstrate the absurdity of objecting to Helena's 'indelicacy' in pursuing Bertram, or to her use of the bed trick in catching him.[4] It is, however, in the play's departure from the traditional story that the argument from narrative and dramatic convention breaks down. Boccaccio's *novella* tells the story of a 'clever wench' (to use Lawrence's term) who by curing the King gets herself married to a tough, unwilling aristocrat, who is nonetheless 'rather a good fellow'.[5] The new husband refuses to sleep with his low-born wife and tells her that he will not do so until she has a child by him. His wife accepts the challenge and proves herself worthy of her husband by fulfilling the condition he has imposed upon her. When the clever wench reveals how clever she has been, the aristocrat accepts her as his wife. It is, as a matter of fact, a good story, and, straightforwardly dramatized, it could have made an amusing play. Shakespeare, however, did not choose to dramatize it straightforwardly. 'The blackening of the character of Bertram is one of the most sweeping changes made by Shakespeare in the story as a whole'.[6] Indeed, by turning Bertram 'into a thoroughly disagreeable, peevish, and vicious person',[7] Shakespeare has altered his story in a very basic way. Instead of a clever wench who must prove herself worthy of an aristocratic husband, we have an unworthy husband who must be made worthy of his wife. Shakespeare has chosen to transform his hero into an erring mortal in need of regeneration and forgiveness. Like the anonymous author of *Calisto and Melebea*, Shakespeare has changed his narrative source into a play of forgiveness, and it is as a comedy of forgiveness rather than as a purely romantic comedy that *All's Well* should be examined and judged. *All's Well* was never meant to please in the way that *As You Like It* or *Twelfth Night* please.

Though the comedy of forgiveness is a subspecies of the genre romantic comedy, it is different enough in its conventions and in the expectations which it is designed to arouse and fulfil, to require that it be examined critically on the basis of criteria slightly but distinctly different from those by which we ordinarily judge purely romantic comedy. As a purely romantic comedy, *All's Well* is unquestionably a failure; as a comedy of forgiveness it may be only partially successful, but the successes it does achieve are frequently of a high order.

That we should mistake *All's Well* for a purely romantic comedy is not entirely our fault, for Shakespeare only gradually reveals to us that it is not. Indeed, one could say that for the first act and a half, the characters themselves are under the impression that they are appearing in an almost typical boy/girl romance. Helena and the Countess, who learns of her love, believe that the barrier to love and happiness is the disparity in rank between Helena and Bertram. With her future mother-in-law's blessing, Helena sets about to destroy that barrier. In Elizabethan terms, Helena is the victim of Fortune, who has assigned her a worldly position which is inappropriate to her deserts. Helena's project in the first half of the play is to raise herself in Fortune to a position of equality with Bertram. Mark Van Doren has pointed out that one of Helena's favourite words is 'nature',[8] and well it might be, for if the goddess Fortuna has been niggardly in her gifts to Helena, the goddess Natura has been abundantly generous, and it is through the gifts of Nature that Helena means to overcome the opposition of Fortune. The King says of her:

> She is young, wise, fair;
> In these to nature she's immediate heir,
> And these breed honour. . . . II.3.130–32

Though she does not name them, Helena is clearly thinking of the power of her youth, intelligence, and beauty when she contemplates her chances of winning Bertram:

> The mightiest space in fortune nature brings
> To join like likes, and kiss like native things. I.1.218–19

But, as Helena realizes, she must have a means by which to show her merit. That means is a symbolically powerful one – the King's disease. . . .

2

Helena has cured the King and, by obtaining Bertram's ring and becoming pregnant by him, she has fulfilled the tasks which her husband imposed upon her. The dying world of the play's opening scene has been restored to health and fertility. It now remains for Helena to restore Bertram to that state of honour which, we are told, is naturally his. This she can do only by forcing self-knowledge upon him.

The method by which this end is achieved is both predicted and explained by the analogous action of Parolles's unmasking. The two French Lords undertake this project specifically in the hope that it will force Bertram to confront the true nature, not so much of Parolles, as of himself:

> I would gladly have him see his company anatomized, that he might take a measure of his own judgements wherein so curiously he had set this counterfeit.
>
> IV.3.30–33

Their hopes, for the time being, prove fruitless, for Bertram's self-esteem needs harsher methods for its correction than the revelation of someone else's weakness. The plot of the drum does, however, provide Shakespeare with a method of demonstrating how a man may be forced to act in accordance with his own nature.

The basic difference between the unmasking of Parolles here and the unmasking of Bertram in the last act is that Parolles learns nothing about himself because he has never been the victim of any illusions about what he is. He, like everyone else in the play, except Bertram, is perfectly well aware that Parolles is a coward and a knave. In order to profit by Bertram's credulity, Parolles is willing to pretend to be what he is not, but he knows that he is playing a role and he curses himself when he begins playing it too realistically:

> What the devil should move me to undertake the recovery of this drum, being not ignorant of the impossibility, and knowing I had no such purpose?
>
> IV.1.33–5

Again the comments of the French Captains underline the point: 'Is it possible he should know what he is, and be that he is?' It is, indeed, possible, though, unlike Parolles, most of us manage to prevent ourselves from knowing what we are. There is, however, nothing immoral about ignobility so long as one cannot be and does not pretend to be noble. Pretensions to nobility can be dangerous to society for they may lead to misplaced trust. In deflating Parolles's pretensions, the French Lords are performing a public service, and the way in which they go about it has a strong resemblance to the way in which Helena goes about the cure of Bertram. Like Bertram in his desire for Diana, Parolles, in his desire for life, is ready to promise anything, compromise anything, betray anyone. Like Bertram, the blindfolded Parolles is caught in the dark, and just as Bertram commits adultery with his wife, Parolles betrays his comrades to his comrades. When the blindfold is removed from his eyes, Parolles realizes that he has revealed his true nature beyond hope of concealment or excuse. His reaction is to accept that nature and decide to live by it:

> Rust, sword; cool, blushes; and Parolles live
> Safest in shame; being fooled, by foolery thrive.
> There's place and means for every man alive.
> I'll after them.
> IV.3.327–30

By becoming a tame toady to Lord Lafew, he discovers the place in the world that is proper to him.

It is necessary to keep the unmasking of Parolles in mind when one approaches the last scene of the play – a highly uncomfortable piece of theatre which has been generally held to result in the failure of the comedy as a whole. Parolles thinks he is safe in defaming his fellow soldiers – Captain Dumaine, for example:

> I know him: 'a was a botcher's prentice in Paris, from whence he was whipped for getting the shrieve's fool with child, a dumb innocent that could not say him nay.
> IV.3.182–5

By doing so, he hopes to save his life. Bertram thinks he is safe in defaming Diana:

33

She's impudent, my lord,
And was a common gamester to the camp.   V.3.187–8

By doing so, he hopes to save his reputation. When the truth dawns upon Parolles, he has no choice but to become himself and to turn to the charity of his fellow men in the hope that they will accept him as he is. The truth which dawns upon Bertram is more complex. He realizes, first that the girl whom he thinks he has seduced and whom he has had no compunction about slandering, is, in fact, innocent, and has revealed to the King, the Countess, and the court of France that Bertram is a lying, promise-breaking seducer. Like Parolles when the blindfold is removed, Bertram must face the fact that the truth about him is irretrievably known, but we have also the sense that for the first time the truth about Bertram has been revealed to Bertram himself.

In Bertram's case, then, the blindfold is removed from the inner eye of conscience, and *humanum genus* is able, as a result, finally to see the evidence of his own corruption. That revelation is no more fortuitous than the unmasking of Parolles. The French Lords have played a socially valuable practical joke which results in the return of Parolles to his appropriate station in the world. Like them, Helena has arranged a salutary discomfiture – that of her erring husband. In doing so, she has once again served as the instrument of God's grace. As Clifford Leech puts it, 'Helena, in her curing of the King, is a dispenser of divine grace, and in her definitive subjection of Bertram she is setting his foot on the path of Christian virtue.'[9] For Bertram, the descent of grace equals the access of self-knowledge, and because 'the turning of the heart unto God is of God,'[10] the means by which that 'turning' is achieved must be of God, too. Helena is the instrument which heaven has employed in working out its designs:

Whatsoever God doeth, he bringeth it about by his instruments ordained thereto. He hath good angels, he hath evil angels; he hath good men, and he hath evil men; he hath hail and rain, he hath wind and thunder, he hath heat and cold; innumerable instruments hath he, and messengers. . . .[11]

Helena is such an instrument and messenger.

34

The Old Countess, reflecting on her son's flight to Italy, asks:

> What angel shall
> Bless this unworthy husband?   III.4.25–6

The answer, of course, is Helena, as the Countess goes on to explain in the lines that follow:

> He cannot thrive,
> Unless her prayers, whom heaven delights to hear
> And loves to grant, reprieve him from the wrath
> Of greatest justice.   III.4.26–9

These lines describe Helena, but they do so in terms that inevitably suggest the Virgin Mary. The Arden editor believes that 'a straight-forward reference to the Virgin as intercessor is too Popish to be probable,'[12] but a more 'Popish' activity than a barefoot pilgrimage to Santiago da Compostella is difficult to imagine, and yet Helena has just left on such an errand when these lines are spoken of her. Shakespeare evokes the Virgin here because Helena's function in the play is similar to that of the Mother of God in the 'Popish' scheme of things. Both serve as means through which the grace of God can be communicated to man. Nor is this similarity surprising, for, considered historically, the charitable heroines of the comedy of forgiveness are literary descendants of the Virgin in the medieval narrative and dramatic 'Miracles of Our Lady'. Ordinarily their function is simply to be sinned against and to forgive, but unlike Hero, Imogen, and Hermione, Helena is called upon to serve as the active agent in the regeneration of the erring hero.

Two main objections, largely inspired by that regeneration, have been raised to the happy ending of *All's Well*. The first of these sees the forgiveness of Bertram as a violation of poetic justice. For Dr Johnson, Bertram's felicity is not deserved. Bertram is merely 'dismissed to happiness',[13] after a series of sneaking profligacies, and Dr Johnson cannot, therefore, reconcile his heart to him. Against this objection no defence is possible except a very basic one. Poetic justice is *not* served by the comedies of forgiveness. It is not meant to be served, because these comedies celebrate another virtue – charity. The second objection is more complicated in its implications. Critics of this play have felt (as far as I know, without exception) that the final scene of the play fails because Bertram's regeneration is unconvincing. There can be no doubt that, indeed, the scene does so fail for a modern audience. We do not believe in the regeneration. It is not communicated to us.

The reasons for that failure of communication need careful consideration, however. The general feeling seems to be that Shakespeare fell back on a rather shallow theatrical convention for the denouement of this play. According to Quiller-Couch, 'All's Well has no atmosphere save that of the stage. . . . It is a thing "of the boards"'[14] and such a 'thing', we assume, does not deserve the name of great drama and is unworthy of a great dramatist. Robert Y. Turner, in a recent essay, has shown how common a theatrical event such arbitrary regenerations were in the drama of Shakespeare's time, but, as Turner points out, this use of a literary commonplace 'will not justify Shakespeare's workmanship. It merely tells us that All's Well is a failure of one kind and not another.'[15] And yet, theatrical conventions of this sort are not simply arbitrary or purely formal. They succeed because they refer to and draw upon the shared beliefs of an audience.

The final scene of All's Well draws upon and refers to a belief in the reality of the descent of grace upon a sinning human. The Elizabethan audience believed in such an occurrence not as a theological abstraction, but as an everyday psychological possibility. What happens to Bertram would, I think, have been clear to Shakespeare's contemporaries. The scales fall from Bertram's eye, he sees what he has done, and he is filled with shame and a sense of the necessity for pardon:

We have a common experience of the same in them which, when they have committed any heinous offence or some filthy and abominable sin, if it once come to light, or if they chance to have a through feeling of it, they be so ashamed, their own conscience putting before their eyes the filthiness of their act, that they dare look no man on the face, much less that they should be able to stand in the sight of God.[16]

Out of such an experience, a new man is born:

> After his repentance he was no more the man that he was before, but was clean changed and altered.[17]

A Renaissance audience would not, I think, have considered even Bertram incapable of that alteration.

By referring the characters and events of *All's Well* to the Christian concepts which help to explain them, I am not, I hope, maintaining that this comedy is a Christian allegory, a Christian parable, or a Christian homily. It is a secular comedy concerned with this world and with the relationships between men and women in this life. It was, however, written for a Christian audience and it draws naturally upon a Christian view of the world. It is, furthermore, cast in a traditionally Christian dramatic form – that of the play of forgiveness.

NOTES

1. *All's Well That Ends Well* (New Cambridge Shakespeare, 1929), edited by Sir Arthur Quiller-Couch and J. Dover Wilson, Introduction, page xxv.
2. *All's Well That Ends Well* (new Arden Shakespeare, 1959), edited by G. K. Hunter, Introduction, page xlii.
3. '*All's Well That Ends Well*', *Harper's Magazine* 85 (1892), page 216.
4. *Shakespeare's Problem Comedies* (1931; Penguin Shakespeare Library 1969).
5. op. cit., Penguin Shakespeare Library edition, page 66.
6. op. cit., page 67.
7. ibid.
8. *Shakespeare* (1939), page 215.
9. 'The Theme of Ambition in *All's Well That Ends Well*', *ELH* 21 (1954), page 20.
10. *Certain Sermons or Homilies Appointed to be Read in Churches in the Times of Queen Elizabeth*, edited by J. Griffiths (1908), page 571.
11. op. cit., page 516.
12. New Arden Shakespeare edition, page 82.
13. *Dr Johnson on Shakespeare*, edited by W. K. Wimsatt (1960; Penguin Shakespeare Library 1969), page 113.

14. New Cambridge Shakespeare edition, page xxxiv.
15. 'Dramatic Conventions in *All's Well That Ends Well*', *Publications of the Modern Language Association of America* 75 (1960), page 502.
16. *Certain Sermons*, page 584.
17. op. cit., page 580.

from *Shakespeare and the Comedy of Forgiveness* (1965)
by Robert Grams Hunter, pages 106–13 and 126–31

THREE

Parolles

G. P. Krapp

PAROLLES enjoys the bad eminence of being one of the least likeable of all Shakespeare's characters. Other persons in the plays stir deeper feelings of aversion or of uncertain admiration, but Parolles is one of those obnoxious creatures who make themselves too conspicuous to be disregarded and yet must be scorned and despised. The critics are at one in finding *All's Well* one of the least agreeable of Shakespeare's plays, and Parolles one of the least agreeable of the persons in the play. And yet it is not probable that Shakespeare set himself the task of writing an unpleasant play in *All's Well*, or that he conceived Parolles as merely a horrid example of all that is mean and contemptible. If that were so, it is doubtful if Shakespeare would have thought the character worth putting into a play. Parolles is bad enough, but he is not altogether without excuse to offer for his existence. For one thing, we note that he seems to be held in higher esteem by some of the characters in the play than he has been by later readers of it. Perhaps it is no high commendation to be patronized by Bertram, but to be endured by Helena is something. He would be a rash advocate who should attempt a eulogy of Parolles, but there may be a word of explanation to be said in placing him more precisely in the social group where we find him than his critics have sometimes done.

One consideration has been almost universally drawn into the critical discussion of Parolles which seems quite irrelevant. This is the endeavour to connect him with the genesis of the character of Falstaff. It has often been assumed that Parolles is a kind of preliminary and unsuccessful Falstaff, 'the first slight sketch for Falstaff', as Brandes describes him,[1] and that, having Falstaff, we may neglect Parolles. Now this assumption rests in the first place upon several doubtful chronological hypotheses. It is by no means certain that *All's Well* is the same play, in a revised form, as the lost *Love's Labour's Won*, and consequently by no means certain that the first composition of *All's Well* antedates the composition of *Henry IV*. But granting that *All's Well* and *Love's Labour's Won* are the titles of one and the same play, there is nothing to prove that Parolles was in the earlier version of the play, or, if there, that it was the same character as we find it in the extant version. Parolles does not appear in the source from which the main fable of *All's Well* was derived, and how or when he came into the play is entirely a matter of guess-work. So far as the chronological evidence goes, one might as reasonably argue that Falstaff was a preliminary study for Parolles.

And this assumption, in a way, has also been made. For it has been asserted that Parolles is merely the dregs of the character of Falstaff, fashioned out of the left-over materials of Shakespeare's imagination and thus betraying weakness and lassitude of invention. He has been characterized by Professor Brander Matthews, for example, as 'only a variant of the braggart', 'a diminished replica of Falstaff, done without gusto or unction'.[2] But is not the resemblance between Parolles and Falstaff mainly one of externals? The flavour of the personality of Parolles is different from that of Falstaff, less full-bodied perhaps and certainly more pungently satirical. And one may reasonably refuse to believe that Shakespeare repeated characters as mechanically as this identification of Parolles and Falstaff implies. By the same argument, Falstaff himself would be a replica, even though an enlarged one, of Don Adriano, for Falstaff and Don Adriano have the same characteristics in common as Falstaff and Parolles. But assuredly neither Parolles nor Falstaff is cast in the same mould as this more conventionally typical boasting soldier.

With all allowance for the significance of chronological groupings and for conventional dramatic types of character, it seems that, such as they are, Parolles is capable of standing on his own legs. The traits he has in common with Falstaff, and also with Don Adriano, are very general. All three are soldiers, are cowards, are braggarts, and each is the victim of a practical joke. But there are various ways of being a soldier, a coward, and a braggart, just as there are various ways of being the victim of a practical joke. The differences between Parolles and Falstaff, at least, are as great as one usually finds them between two persons of a generally similar class in real life. Don Adriano seems the most literary and least real of the three. Parolles may not be a minutely faithful photograph of contemporary reality, he may owe something to the traditional comedy character of the boastful soldier, but at the same time there can be little doubt that he suggested to Elizabethan audiences more intimate associations than with a general literary tradition or with other characters of the Shakespearian drama.

Externally, there is one important difference between Parolles and Falstaff to be noted. By birth at least, Falstaff is a gentleman, but there is nothing in the play to indicate that Parolles is anything but a climber. He is a follower of Bertram, not a companion or associate. The gentlemen in the play do not joke and play with him as do Hal and his friends with Falstaff. He is merely the victim of their pranks, not a participant in them. He seems to be endured among gentlemen for certain qualities that make him entertaining but he has no prescriptive right to the enjoyment of such society. As soon as he ceases to be amusing, he is cast aside and easily disgraced out of existence. One might question whether this treatment of Parolles is to be regarded as indicative of that aristocratic attitude towards his characters which in other instances has been noted in Shakespeare's plays. The treatment which Parolles receives is certainly hard and unsympathetic, but under the circumstances could it well have been otherwise? It is not merely that the fate of Parolles is true enough to life, since it has been the portion of many a hanger-on to the fringes of gentility. Shakespeare might easily have given the character a somewhat more pleasing aspect if the conventions of his subject had permitted. But in *All's Well* Shakespeare was not writing a picaresque romance in glorification of roguish wit and ingenuity. What he was writing was a formally constructed play in which royalty and high nobility occupy the chief places and in which the unsympathetic portrayal of an ignoble, pretentious character was an almost necessary consequence. One must hesitate, therefore, to look upon the treatment which Parolles receives too much in the light of a personal condemnation or expression of opinion. If it were, Shakespeare might be open to the accusation of fouling his own nest, for Parolles is just the sort of person he might be supposed to understand and to sympathize with. Shakespeare was probably neither a soldier, a coward, nor a braggart, but was he not, at the time this play was written, rising in the world by his wit, just as Parolles was endeavouring to do? And in the world in which Shakespeare lived, is it likely that a rogue, if witty, would be disposed of as harshly as Parolles is in the play? It should not be forgotten that Parolles, also, is a poet (IV.3.218), and if we may be allowed to guess a little as to what would have been consistent with his character, of the same school as Shakespeare. In the sonnet which he 'writ to Diana in behalf of the Count Rossillion', it would have been quite in keeping if he had practised the same fashionable devices of style as Shakespeare had employed in his own sugared sonnets. For there is no question that Parolles was just such another lover of aureate diction and the ornamental poetic style as Shakespeare.

An equally important difference between Parolles and Falstaff lies in the fact that the latter enjoys a joke upon himself as much as anyone else. He sheds a practical joke as easily as a duck sheds water. But Parolles succumbs under similar treatment. He is made of quite different stuff, and nothing short of an entire re-creation could make a Falstaff out of him. It is impossible to think of Parolles mellowing into Falstaff, because he is entirely lacking in humour, that invaluable preservative of old age and corrective of the false judgements of youth. When he falls into decay, to put it mildly, he smells 'somewhat strong' of Fortune's displeasure. The quality which makes him temporarily entertaining is not humour, but a kind of intellectual briskness and smartness which does well enough for the diversion of an idle moment, but which makes little appeal to sympathy and a poor foundation for a solid structure of character. You cannot laugh with Parolles – at times you can scarcely laugh at him. Both Parolles and Falstaff know they are cowards, but the knowledge does not worry Falstaff. Parolles, however, tries to reason away his cowardice. This defect in his nature is a queer puzzle, even to himself, and he endeavours to make himself extraordinarily brave and effective by thinking himself into an honourable situation. His fatal error arises when he tries to realize this intellectual ambition in action, and he thus deceives himself in a way of which Falstaff would never be capable.

Helena is fully aware of the weaknesses of Parolles, and yet she declares that these 'fixed evils' in him are so apt to the man that they take precedence over 'virtue's steely bones'. In plain English, Parolles is a light weight, even worse, but he knows how to dress himself up in a way which makes you overlook the fundamental defects of his character. He is like a French novel, vicious but tolerated for its style. And he suggests again the old courtly theme of debate as to the relative merits of nature and nurture. Not born to virtue, it is by nurture that Parolles is endeavouring to lift himself by his boot-straps, but the play takes the courtly point of view that nurture alone is but a feeble support.

The particular virtue which Parolles cultivates is one of manner. In the text of the play it appears as vivacity and novelty of phrase, sometimes shallow, sometimes genuinely witty. Parolles is a soldier only because gentlemen usually were soldiers, but in truth his tongue is mightier than his sword. He is a soldier-wit, like George Pettie, Barnabie Riche, Gascoigne, and dozens of others in Elizabethan days. He first appears upon the scene in a wit combat with Helena, the subject matter of which is supposedly 'smart', but to most readers now is merely revolting. It should be judged, however, not for its matter, but its manner. Parolles is here 'a great way fool', but an acute fool. Pompous words are not his stock in trade, as with the traditional boasting soldier. He speaks a courtly idiom, which by Shakespeare's day had ceased to be learned and pedantic. A 'snipped-taffeta fellow' in speech as well as dress, he knows how to use the language of the smart set of his day. Perhaps what he says is not more witty than most smart talk, which depends largely for its effect upon its freshness and its superiority to contemporary morals. The reader a few generations from now will perhaps equate it with discussions of divorce and similar topics as they appear in present-day high society novels. The level of taste seems to be about the same.

The relations of Bertram to Parolles are those of student and mentor. Bertram is young and ignorant of the ways of the world, and he believes in Parolles's assumption of wide human experience and of knowledge of the proprieties of worldly conduct. It is not a hopeful situation for Bertram, but after all, what Parolles is to teach his pupil is not virtuous action, but the exterior ornament and dress of action. When Bertram says good-bye to his comrades in arms abruptly, Parolles directs him how to take a more 'dilated farewell'. The plain and honest phrase of the old Lafew he translates into an elegant style befitting the gallant courtier. Lafew is the cloth-breeches of Greene's allegory, and Parolles the velvet breeches. 'Will this capriccio hold in thee?' he asks Bertram in a fine Italianated phrase. Bertram, being a young spark, and not too penetrating, accepts Parolles at his surface valuation. But Lafew immediately starts a quarrel by questioning Parolles's gentility. The soul of this man is his clothes, he tells Bertram, with a great show of interest in Parolles's tailor. A fine manner, in Lafew's opinion, does not make Parolles a fit companion of counts. 'You are more saucy with lords and honourable personages', he tells him, 'than the commission of your birth and virtue gives you heraldry' (II.3.259–61). But Parolles insists that his virtue does not lie in his birth, that he is fit companion for Bertram or any count – for all that is man. A higher claim than this no up-start courtier could make.

The reader has long been prepared for the final undoing of Parolles in the fourth act. Only Bertram has been blind to the innate viciousness of his follower, but Helena, Lafew, and Bertram's comrades in arms have seen through him. What little sympathy one may have had for him flies to the winds when we learn in the third act that he has been reporting 'but coarsely' of Helena in Florence (III.5.56). As an act of mercy, Bertram's friends finally decide that his eyes also must be opened. They tell him that Parolles is the 'owner of no one good quality worthy your lordship's entertainment', but only an ocular demonstration will suffice to redeem Bertram. The practical joke is accordingly planned and carried out with such perfect success that the bright bubble of Parolles's courtly pretensions is for ever exploded. But he remains the same Parolles as before. He had set for himself the task of achieving a place among gentlemen by his wit. He had failed, 'crushed with a plot'. He therefore puts aside his sword, cools his blushes, and sets out in search of a new world where he can thrive by foolery. 'There's place and means for every man alive.' He has not been wounded in any vital spot, only convicted, as he thinks, of an error in judgement. One is not surprised to find, however, that he thrives but meanly in his new world. He runs the regular progress of the witling from presumption to decay. He is sure that his merits have never received their deserts, that he has been 'cruelly scratched' by fortune, but in the end he is glad to accept a meal at the hands of his old enemy Lafew.

If we may judge from contemporary reports and other evidence, the character of Parolles found many counterparts among the young wits of the day. In the last quarter of the sixteenth century, a new type of character appeared in English life. The way to eminence for those who were not born to distinction had hitherto been along the road of serious scholarship, especially theological scholarship, supported of course by solid morality. The Reformation, however, had destroyed the old ecclesiastical system, and the State had helped itself so generously to the treasury of the Church that little was left with which to reward aspiring scholars. The Renaissance had also emphasized many non-theological activities; and now brilliance, a dash, a fine manner, came to be so highly esteemed that they often took the place of the more substantial virtues. Young university graduates thronged to the city with the intent of coining their brains into gold. They had an extravagant belief in the sufficiency of genius, and genius they considered to be only distantly related to morality. Nor did they clearly distinguish genius from ingenuity. Conventional morality, indeed, often remained, and was converted into an ornament of style. The heroes of Lyly's novels, model fine gentlemen, always have a neat moral at the tip of their tongues. It is astonishingly easy for them, however, to recover from a violation of honourable principle. And ingenuity as a substitute for genius is illustrated on every page of the writings of the fine stylists of the school of Pettie and Lyly. It was a natural enough survival from humanist theory, which had made a good Ciceronian style of sufficient virtue to save in this world and the next. At bottom what the Elizabethan painters of contemporary high life cultivated was a certain liveliness of fancy and phrase, an expression that had point and finish. The prime requisite of the fashionable hero was to be clever, to be animated, and interesting, and above all, not too precise. One of the most commonly expressed opinions among the Elizabethan wits was that the genius is free, that he must taste of both the good and evil fruit of the tree of knowledge and must follow wherever his star might lead him. Greene's *Vision* contains an instructive comparison of Chaucer with Gower, the latter standing for the learned and well-regulated moralist, the former for the expansive genius who sometimes forgets the demands of common decency. A perfunctory approval is given to Gower, but the defence of the free wit of Chaucer, as Chaucer was conceived by the Elizabethans, comes more directly from Greene's heart. And similar ideals of conduct we find illustrated elsewhere, not only in Elizabethan fiction, but also in real life. A philosophy of behaviour which took so little account of the judgement of society was bound often to result in sordid failure, for genius, even when real, has always been of uncertain value and never sure of its reward. The biographies of Marlowe, Nashe, Greene, and many others all point the lesson of the final disaster of wit that is hoist with its own petard. Shakespeare has justified the fate of Parolles by emphasis upon his lack of honourable principle and substantial character. Poetic justice demanded this of him. But would he have justified the fate of Marlowe, Nashe, and Greene in the same way?

The conflict of ideals as it was exemplified in the Elizabethan literary world is well illustrated in the correspondence between Nashe and Harvey. The latter continually insists upon moderation, learning, and serious elevation of tone as essential to good style. The solid morality of Cheke and Ascham and the chivalric honour of Sidney he looks upon as the ideals of conduct to be cultivated. Nashe, on the contrary, finds the old morality stupid. He pins his faith to natural quickness of perception and ability to strike off the novel and interesting phrase. Too much study, he concludes, throttles genius, which must follow its bent at any cost and above all must never be 'soft and mediocre'. Harvey returns with the objection that the 'new-new writers' depend merely upon 'a knacke of dexterity', that they ignore art and discipline. He complains that people no longer respect the painful student. And he declares that if you seek out the arch-mystery of 'the busiest Modernistes', of whom Nashe is his dread example, you shall find it 'nether more or lesse then a certayne pragmaticall secret, called Villany.' Scholars, he continues ironically, are fools for labouring over their compositions – 'the book-worme was never but a pickgoose.' It is the villainist who knocks the nail on the head and goes farther in a day 'then the quickest artist in a weeke' – almost a repetition of Helena's comment on Parolles. The defence of himself which Harvey puts into the mouth of the villainist is that he takes life as he finds it. 'Life is a gaming, a iugling, a scoulding, a lawing, a skirmishing, a warre, a Comedie, a Tragedy, the sturring witt, a quintenessence of quicksiluer; and there is noe deade fleshe in affection or courage.' Stability and solid virtues, continues this ironical defence, are of little avail; what counts is ingenuity, wit, and vivacity. 'Try, when you meane to be disgraced; and neuer giue me credit if Sanguine witt putt not Melancholy Arte to bedd.'³ With such sentiments as these, Parolles is in complete accord. 'Simply the thing I am', he says, 'Shall make me live' (IV.3.323–4). The world is his orange; and if he cannot make a hole in one place, he can in another; for are there not place and means for every man alive?

To the Elizabethan audience witnessing a performance of *All's Well*, it seems probable that the comparison which the character Parolles suggested was not with any Miles Gloriosus or with Falstaff, but with those villainist and modernist time-servers who walked the streets of London in gaudy splendour. If so, Parolles may not be regarded as merely an echo of the braggart soldier of Renaissance comedy or a weak reproduction of Falstaff. He seems rather a transcript from Elizabethan life. He has his virtues, for after all his distinction of style in itself is not without merit. He really has the gift of phrase, as so many Elizabethan wits had. And his style seems meretricious only when it is measured by a different standard from its own, by the standard of the downright simplicity of the blunt English style. By the same test, however, the most highly prized Elizabethan literature would suffer. There was a reason for enduring Parolles, even for finding him interesting. The question, however, how far his accomplishments justify his existence goes back to deep questions of art and morality. So far as *All's Well* is concerned, the moral of the character of Parolles, if there is one, seems to be that style is not enough to procure the salvation of a man.

NOTES

1. Georg Brandes, *William Shakspere, A Critical Study* (2 vols., 1898), Volume 2, page 67.
2. Brander Matthews, *Shakspere as a Playwright* (1913), page 225.
3. *Elizabethan Critical Essays*, edited by Gregory Smith (2 vols., 1904), Volume 2, pages 254–5.

from *Shaksperian Studies by Members of the Department of English and Comparative Literature in Columbia University* (1916), edited by Brander Matthews and Ashley Thorndike, pages 291–300

SUGGESTIONS FOR FURTHER READING

All's Well That Ends Well, edited by G. K. Hunter (new Arden Shakespeare, 1959). The most useful edition for a close study of the play, containing a full discussion of the play in the editor's Introduction, ample notes to the text, and the principal source, 'Giletta of Narbona', from Painter's *The Palace of Pleasure* (1575 edition). This and other source material may be found in G. Bullough, *Narrative and Dramatic Sources of Shakespeare*, Volume 2 (1958); it is also reprinted (from the 1566 edition) in *Elizabethan Love Stories*, edited by T. J. B. Spencer (Penguin Shakespeare Library, 1968). The play has been edited for the New Penguin Shakespeare by Barbara Everett (1970), with an excellent introductory essay and a full commentary.

W. W. LAWRENCE: *Shakespeare's Problem Comedies* (1931; Penguin Shakespeare Library 1969). An important work which attempts to clarify some of the problems in the 'problem plays' by examining Shakespeare's use of the conventional motifs of folk-tale and romance. Helena is thus related to the traditional figure of 'the clever wench', and less odium attaches to the 'bed-trick' (inelegant term!) by which she wins her husband. Whether or not one agrees with the interpretation, the book is full of fascinating and suggestive material on the popular narrative traditions which Shakespeare exploited so well.

E. M. W. TILLYARD: *Shakespeare's Problem Plays* (1950; Penguin Books 1965). A well-known study, in which the chapter on *All's Well That Ends Well* discusses the play as an attempt to inject serious Christian themes and realistic characterization into the folk-lore elements of the plot. The book qualifies W. W. Lawrence's emphasis upon the wholly conventional nature of the dramatic situations.

G. WILSON KNIGHT: 'The Third Eye', in *The Sovereign Flower* (1958). This interpretation deals with the theme of honour in the play in terms of its masculine and feminine counterparts, martial prowess and chastity, represented by Bertram and Helena. Helena's 'miracle' introduces a supernatural plane of meaning, and, as he pursues this, Professor Wilson Knight leaves the play somewhat beneath him.

SUGGESTIONS FOR FURTHER READING

JOSEPH G. PRICE: *The Unfortunate Comedy: A Study of 'All's Well That Ends Well' and its Critics* (1968). An account of the stage history and critical reputation of *All's Well That Ends Well*, relating the wide range of interpretations to the play's mixture of diverse elements, its lack of a unifying mood.

'MEASURE FOR MEASURE'

FOUR

An Appreciation of
Measure for Measure

Walter Pater

IN *Measure for Measure*, as in some other of his plays, Shakespeare has remodelled an earlier and somewhat rough composition to 'finer issues', suffering much to remain as it had come from the less skilful hand, and not raising the whole of his work to an equal degree of intensity. Hence perhaps some of that depth and weightiness which make this play so impressive, as with the true seal of experience, like a fragment of life itself, rough and disjointed indeed, but forced to yield in places its profounder meaning. In *Measure for Measure*, in contrast with the flawless execution of *Romeo and Juliet*, Shakespeare has spent his art in just enough modification of the scheme of the older play to make it exponent of this purpose, adapting its terrible essential incidents, so that Coleridge found it the only painful work among Shakespeare's dramas, and leaving for the reader of today more than the usual number of difficult expressions; but infusing a lavish colour and a profound significance into it, so that under his touch certain select portions of it rise far above the level of all but his own best poetry, and working out of it a morality so characteristic that the play might well pass for the central expression of his moral judgements. It remains a comedy, as indeed is congruous with the bland, half-humorous equity which informs the whole composition, sinking from the heights of sorrow and terror into the rough scheme of the earlier piece; yet it is hardly less full of what is really tragic in man's existence than if Claudio had indeed 'stooped to death'. Even the humorous concluding scenes have traits of special grace, retaining in less emphatic passages a stray line or word of power, as it seems, so that we watch to the end for the traces where the nobler hand has glanced along, leaving its vestiges, as if accidentally or wastefully, in the rising of the style.

The interest of *Measure for Measure*, therefore, is partly that of an old story told over again. We measure with curiosity that variety of resources which has enabled Shakespeare to refashion the original material with a higher motive; adding to the intricacy of the piece, yet so modifying its structure as to give the whole almost the unity of a single scene; lending, by the light of a philosophy which dwells much on what is complex and subtle in our nature, a true human propriety to its strange and unexpected turns of feeling and character, to incidents so difficult as the fall of Angelo, and the subsequent reconciliation of Isabella, so that she pleads successfully for his life. It was from Whetstone, a contemporary English writer, that Shakespeare derived the outline of Cinthio's 'rare history' of *Promos and Cassandra*, one of that numerous class of Italian stories, like Boccaccio's *Tancred of Salerno*, in which the mere energy of southern passion has everything its own way, and which, though they may repel many a northern reader by a certain crudity in their colouring, seem to have been full of fascination for the Elizabethan age. This story, as it appears in Whetstone's endless comedy, is almost as rough as the roughest episode of actual criminal life. But the play seems never to have been acted, and some time after its publication Whetstone himself turned the thing into a tale, included in his *Heptameron of Civil Discourses*, where it still figures as a genuine piece, with touches of undesigned poetry, a quaint field-flower here and there of diction or sentiment, the whole strung up to an effective brevity, and with the fragrance of that admirable age of literature all about it. Here, then, there is something of the original Italian colour: in this narrative Shakespeare may well have caught the first glimpse of a composition with nobler proportions; and some artless sketch from his own hand, perhaps, putting together his first impressions, insinuated itself between Whetsone's work and the play as we actually read it. Out of these insignificant sources Shakespeare's play rises, full of solemn expression, and with a profoundly designed beauty, the new body of a higher, though sometimes remote and difficult poetry, escaping from the imperfect relics of the old story, yet not wholly transformed, and even as it stands but the preparation only, we might think, of a still more imposing design. For once we have in it a real example of that sort of writing which is sometimes described as *suggestive*, and which, by the help of certain subtly calculated hints only, brings into distinct shape the reader's own half-developed imaginings. Often the quality is attributed to writing merely vague and unrealized, but in *Measure for Measure*, quite certainly, Shakespeare has directed the attention of sympathetic readers along certain channels of meditation beyond the immediate scope of his work.

Measure for Measure, therefore, by the quality of these higher designs, woven by his strange magic on a texture of poorer quality, is hardly less indicative than *Hamlet* even, of Shakespeare's reason, of his power of moral interpretation. It deals, not like *Hamlet* with the problems which beset one of exceptional temperament, but with mere human nature. It brings before us a group of persons, attractive, full of desire, vessels of the genial, seed-bearing powers of nature, a gaudy existence flowering out over the old court and city of Vienna, a spectacle of the fullness and pride of life which to some may seem to touch the verge of wantonness. Behind this group of people, behind their various action, Shakespeare inspires in us the sense of a strong tyranny of nature and circumstance. Then what shall there be on this side of it – on our side, the spectators' side, of this painted screen, with its puppets who are really glad or sorry all the time? what philosophy of life, what sort of equity?

Stimulated to read more carefully by Shakespeare's own profounder touches, the reader will note the vivid reality, the subtle interchange of light and shade, the strongly contrasted characters of this group of persons, passing across the stage so quickly. The slightest of them is at least not ill-natured: the meanest of them can put forth a plea for existence – *Truly, sir, I am a poor fellow that would live!* – they are never sure of themselves, even in the strong tower of a cold unimpressible nature: they are capable of many friendships and of a true dignity in danger, giving each other a sympathetic, if transitory, regret – one sorry that another 'should be . . . foolishly lost at a game of tick-tack'. Words which seem to exhaust man's deepest sentiment concerning death and life are put on the lips of a gilded, witless youth; and the saintly Isabella feels fire creep along her, kindling her tongue to eloquence at the suggestion of shame. In places the shadow deepens: death intrudes itself on the scene, as among other things 'a great disguiser', blanching the features of youth and spoiling its goodly hair, touching the fine Claudio even with its disgraceful associations. As in Orcagna's fresco at Pisa, it comes capriciously, giving many and long reprieves to Barnardine, who has been waiting for it nine years in prison, taking another thence by fever, another by mistake of judgement, embracing others in the midst of their music and song. The little mirror of existence, which reflects to each for a moment the stage on which he plays, is broken at last by a capricious accident; while all alike, in their yearning for untasted enjoyment, are really discounting their days, grasping so hastily and accepting so inexactly the precious pieces. The Duke's quaint but excellent moralizing at the beginning of the third act does but express, like the chorus of a Greek play, the spirit of the passing incidents. To him in Shakespeare's play, to a few here and there in the actual world, this strange practical paradox of our life, so unwise in its eager haste, reveals itself in all its clearness.

The Duke disguised as a friar, with his curious moralizing on life and death, and Isabella in her first mood of renunciation, a thing 'enskied and sainted', come with the quiet of the cloister as a relief to this lust and pride of life: like some grey monastic picture hung on the wall of a gaudy room, their presence cools the heated air of the piece. For a moment we are within the placid conventual walls, whither they fancy at first that the Duke has come as a man crossed in love, with Friar Thomas and Friar Peter, calling each other by their homely, English names, or at the nunnery among the novices, with their little limited privileges, where

> if you speak, you must not show your face,
> Or, if you show your face, you must not speak. I.4.12–13

Not less precious for this relief in the general structure of the piece than for its own peculiar graces is the episode of Mariana, a creature wholly of Shakespeare's invention, told, by way of interlude, in subdued prose. The moated grange, with its dejected mistress, its long, listless, discontented days, where we hear only the voice of a boy broken off suddenly in the midst of one of the loveliest songs of Shakespeare, or of Shakespeare's school,[1] is the pleasantest of many glimpses we get here of pleasant places – the field without the town, Angelo's garden-house, the consecrated fountain. Indirectly it has suggested two of the most perfect compositions among the poetry of our own generation. Again it is a picture within a picture, but with fainter lines and a greyer atmosphere: we have here the same passions, the same wrongs, the same continuance of affection, the same crying out upon death, as in the nearer and larger piece, though softened, and reduced to the mood of a more dreamy scene.

Of Angelo we may feel at first sight inclined to say only *guarda e passa!* or to ask whether he is indeed psychologically possible. In the old story, he figures as an embodiment of pure and unmodified evil, like 'Hyliogabalus of Rome or Denis of Sicyll'. But the embodiment of pure evil is no proper subject of art, and Shakespeare, in the spirit of a philosophy which dwells much on the complications of outward circumstance with men's inclinations, turns into a subtle study in casuistry this incident of the austere judge fallen suddenly into utmost corruption by a momentary contact with supreme purity. But the main interest in *Measure for Measure* is not, as in *Promos and Cassandra*, in the relation of Isabella and Angelo, but rather in the relation of Claudio and Isabella.

Greek tragedy in some of its noblest products has taken for its theme the love of a sister, a sentiment unimpassioned indeed, purifying by the very spectacle of its passionlessness, but capable of a fierce and almost animal strength if informed for a moment by pity and regret. At first Isabella comes upon the scene as a tranquillizing influence in it. But Shakespeare, in the development of the action, brings quite different and unexpected qualities out of her. It is his characteristic poetry to expose this cold, chastened personality, respected even by the worldly Lucio as 'a thing enskied and sainted', and almost 'an immortal spirit', to two sharp, shameful trials, and wring out of her a fiery, revealing eloquence. Thrown into the terrible dilemma of the piece, called upon to sacrifice that cloistral whiteness to sisterly affection, become in a moment the ground of strong, contending passions, she develops a new character and shows herself suddenly of kindred with those strangely conceived women, like Webster's Vittoria, who unite to a seductive sweetness something of a dangerous and tigerlike changefulness of feeling. The swift, vindictive anger leaps, like a white flame, into this white spirit, and, stripped in a moment of all convention, she stands before us clear, detached, columnar, among the tender frailties of the piece. Cassandra, the original of Isabella in Whetstone's tale, with the purpose of the Roman Lucretia in her mind, yields gracefully enough to the conditions of her brother's safety; and to the lighter reader of Shakespeare there may seem something harshly conceived, or psychologically impossible even, in the suddenness of the change wrought in her, as Claudio welcomes for a moment the chance of life through her compliance with Angelo's will, and he may have a sense here of flagging skill, as in words less finely handled than in the preceding scene. The play, though still not without traces of nobler handiwork, sinks down, as we know, at last into almost homely comedy, and it might be supposed that just here the grander manner deserted it. But the skill with which Isabella plays upon Claudio's well-recognized sense of honour, and endeavours by means of that to insure him beforehand from the acceptance of life on baser terms, indicates no coming laxity of hand just in this place. It was rather that there rose in Shakespeare's conception, as there may for the reader, as there certainly would in any good acting of the part, something of that terror, the seeking for which is one of the notes of romanticism in Shakespeare and his circle. The stream of ardent natural affection, poured as sudden hatred upon the youth condemned to die, adds an additional note of expression to the horror of the prison where so much of the scene takes place. It is not here only that Shakespeare has conceived of such extreme anger and pity as putting a sort of genius into simple women, so that their 'lips drop eloquence', and their intuitions interpret that which is often too hard or fine for manlier reason; and it is Isabella with her grand imaginative diction, and that poetry laid upon the 'prone and speechless dialect' there is in mere youth itself, who gives utterance to the equity, the finer judgements of the piece on men and things.

From behind this group with its subtle lights and shades, its poetry, its impressive contrasts, Shakespeare, as I said, conveys to us a strong sense of the tyranny of nature and circumstance over human action. The most powerful expressions of this side of experience might be found here. The bloodless, impassible temperament does but wait for its opportunity, for the almost accidental coherence of time with place, and place with wishing, to annul its long and patient discipline, and become in a moment the very opposite of that which under ordinary conditions it seemed to be, even to itself. The mere resolute self-assertion of the blood brings to others special temptations, temptations which, as defects or over-growths, lie in the very qualities which make them otherwise imposing or attractive; the very advantage of men's gifts of intellect or sentiment being dependent on a balance in their use so delicate that men hardly maintain it always. Something also must be conceded to influences merely physical, to the complexion of the heavens, the skyey influences, shifting as the stars shift; as something also to the mere caprice of men exercised over each other in the dispensations of social or political order, to the chance which makes the life or death of Claudio dependent on Angelo's will.

The many veins of thought which render the poetry of this play so weighty and impressive unite in the image of Claudio, a flower-like young man, whom, prompted by a few hints from Shakespeare, the imagination easily clothes with all the bravery of youth, as he crosses the stage before us on his way to death, coming so hastily to the end of his pilgrimage. Set in the horrible blackness of the prison, with its various forms of unsightly death, this flower seems the braver. Fallen by 'prompture of the blood', the victim of a suddenly revived law against the common fault of youth like his, he finds his life forfeited as if by the chance of a lottery. With that instinctive clinging to life, which breaks through the subtlest casuistries of monk or sage apologizing for an early death, he welcomes for a moment the chance of life through his sister's shame, though he revolts hardly less from the notion of perpetual imprisonment so repulsive to the buoyant energy of youth. Familiarized, by the words alike of friends and the indifferent, to the thought of death, he becomes gentle and subdued indeed, yet more perhaps through pride than real resignation, and would go down to darkness at last hard and unblinded. Called upon suddenly to encounter his fate, looking with keen and resolute profile straight before him, he gives utterance to some of the central truths of human feeling, the sincere, concentrated expression of the recoiling flesh. Thoughts as profound and poetical as Hamlet's arise in him; and but for the accidental arrest of sentence he would descend into the dust, a mere gilded, idle flower of youth indeed, but with what are perhaps the most eloquent of all Shakespeare's words upon his lips.

As Shakespeare in *Measure for Measure* has refashioned, after a nobler pattern, materials already at hand, so that the relics of other men's poetry are incorporated into his perfect work, so traces of the old 'Morality', that early form of dramatic composition which had for its function the inculcating of some moral theme, survive in it also, and give it a peculiar ethical interest. This ethical interest, though it can escape no attentive reader, yet, in accordance with that artistic law which demands the predominance of form everywhere over the mere matter or subject handled, is not to be wholly separated from the special circumstances, necessities, embarrassments, of these particular dramatic persons. The old 'Moralities' exemplified most often some rough-and-ready lesson. Here the very intricacy and subtlety of the moral world itself, the difficulty of seizing the true relations of so complex a material, the difficulty of just judgement, of judgement that shall not be unjust, are the lessons conveyed. Even in Whetstone's old story this peculiar vein of moralizing comes to the surface: even there, we notice the tendency to dwell on mixed motives, the contending issues of action, the presence of virtues and vices alike in unexpected places, on 'the hard choice of two evils,' on the 'imprisoning' of men's 'real intents.' *Measure for Measure* is full of expressions drawn from a profound experience of these casuistries, and that ethical interest becomes predominant in it: it is no longer *Promos and Cassandra*, but *Measure for Measure*, its new name expressly suggesting the subject of *poetical justice*. The action of the play, like the action of life itself for the keener observer, develops in us the conception of this poetical justice, and the yearning to realize it, the true justice of which Angelo knows nothing, because it lies for the most part beyond the limits of any acknowledged law. The idea of justice involves the idea of rights. But at bottom rights are equivalent to that which really is, to facts; and the recognition of his rights therefore, the justice he requires of our hands, or our thoughts, is the recognition of that which the person, in his inmost nature, really is; and as sympathy alone can discover that which really is in matters of feeling and thought, true justice is in its essence a finer knowledge through love.

> 'Tis very pregnant,
> The jewel that we find, we stoop and take't,
> Because we see it; but what we do not see
> We tread upon, and never think of it.   II.1.23–6

It is for this finer justice, a justice based on a more delicate appreciation of the true conditions of men and things, a true respect of persons in our estimate of actions, that the people in *Measure for Measure* cry out as they pass before us; and as the poetry of this play is full of the peculiarities of Shakespeare's poetry, so in its ethics it is an epitome of Shakespeare's moral judgements. They are the moral judgements of an observer, of one who sits as a spectator, and knows how the threads in the design before him hold together under the surface: they are the judgements of the humorist also, who follows, with a half-amused but always pitiful sympathy, the various ways of human disposition, and sees less distance than ordinary men between what are called respectively great and little things. It is not always that poetry can be the exponent of morality; but it is this aspect of morals which it represents most naturally, for this true justice is dependent on just those finer appreciations which poetry cultivates in us the power of making, those peculiar valuations of action and its effect which poetry actually requires.

NOTE

1. Fletcher, in *The Bloody Brother*, gives the rest of it.

from *Appreciations* (*Works*, Volume 5, 1901)
by Walter Pater, pages 170–84

FIVE

Shakespeare's Treatment of his Materials in *Measure for Measure*

Mary Lascelles

I

The Duke

CRITICISM has for some while inclined towards the opinion that here is one of those persons in Shakespearian drama who should be regarded as important in respect rather of function than of character, and are to be interpreted as we should interpret the principal persons in allegory.[1] Now, the language of allegory is at least approximately translatable. These persons, therefore, must stand for something that can be expressed in other than allegorical terms, and the concept for which the Duke stands be capable of formulation in such terms as criticism may employ. What is this concept?

This is not an easy question to answer, nor are the answers so far proposed easy to discuss. Since those that suggest a religious allegory, and hint at a divine analogy, are shocking to me, and cannot be anything of the sort to those who have framed them, it must follow that my objections are all too likely to shock in their turn. This offence is apt to be mutual; for, where reverence is concerned, there is even less hope of reaching agreement by argument than in matters of taste. I would not willingly offend; but there is not room for compromise.

Let me recall the burden of the popular tale of the monstrous ransom: the situation in which the woman, the judge, and the ruler confronted one another signified power, exerted to its full capacity against weakness, and weakness (reduced to uttermost misery) gathering itself up to appeal beyond power to authority. Expressed thus, in simple and general terms, it seems indeed analogous with that allegory of divine might invoked to redress abuse of human inequality which is shadowed in Browning's *Instans Tyrannus*. But it should be remembered that such simplification obliterates one particular which, if fairly reckoned with, might forbid religious analogy: in the old tale, the ruler was distant, ignorant, brought to intervene only by uncommon exertion on the part of those whom his absence had exposed to oppression[2]; and none of the amplifications designed to make the tale more acceptable had done anything to shift or reduce this untoward circumstance. Indeed, by magnifying the whole, they made the part more obvious.

Lupton's *Siuqila* beyond the rest develops that element in the story which draws us to think about the maintenance of justice, not merely in the version it gives of this tale but also in the similar tales surrounding it. And it is notable that, whereas this one tale is told by the wretched Siuqila to show that even in his own country one who has no longer anything to lose will tell all and thus bring about retribution, Omen's tales are told to illustrate the happier state of Mauqsun. The theme of three of them is the success of the good ruler who goes about his domain incognito to discover and redress wrong. In one, a judge who waylays and interrogates suitors is able to rescue a woman from oppression. In both of the others, the King himself is shown using disguise and similar subterfuge, not only to obtain truth but also to make it publicly apparent. In one, he learns by means of his 'privie Espials', who ride about the country at his command in the character of private gentlemen, the plight of a woman who has been ill used by her stepson. He hides her at court and lets it be rumoured that she is dead; and, after much handling of witnesses, confronts the offender with his victim, and delivers sentence. The other tells how he 'changed his apparell, making himselfe like a Servingmã, and went out at a privie Posterngate, and so enquired in the prisons, what prisoners were there', and was able to confute the cunning oppressor by bringing him face to face with the oppressed.

Now, in all these variations on a single theme, the activity of some magistrate or ruler – going about or sending out his agents, in disguise – *assists* in bringing smothered truth to light. Reflecting on opportune intervention in one, Siuqila sums up the moral of all: 'It was only the Lords working, that putte it into his heart' to speak with the woman who was secretly oppressed, and into hers to tell this stranger what she has hitherto forborne to utter; for 'God works al this by marvellous means, if we would consider it, for the helping of the innocent and godly'. Even under an ideal system of justice, that is, the discovery of wrong might well be impossible were it not for the intervention of divine providence, which, on some particular occasion, puts it into the heart of this or that human agent to make a pertinent inquiry. Now, this is in keeping with popular thought, which comes very near to supposing an element of caprice in divine government,[3] because it does not look ahead, but complacently descries pieces of pattern in particular events, without considering the ugly unreason of the total design which such parts must compose. But how fearfully the distance between this false start and its logical conclusion diminishes, if the ruler is regarded not as agent but as emblem of divine providence! It is difficult to believe that those who would have us interpret the Duke's part so can have followed the implied train of thought all the way.

The centre of gravity for this interpretation is the passage in which Angelo capitulates to the alliance of knowledge and power in the reinstated Duke:

> O my dread lord,
> I should be guiltier than my guiltiness
> To think I can be undiscernible,
> When I perceive your grace, like power divine,
> Hath looked upon my passes.   V.1.363–7

On this Professor Wilson Knight comments:

Like Prospero, the Duke tends to assume proportions evidently divine. Once he is actually compared to the Supreme Power.[4]

So to argue is surely to misunderstand the nature and usage of imagery – which does not liken a thing to itself. Yet this argument has been widely accepted; if not unreservedly, yet with reservations which do not reach the real difficulty. To suggest that the comparison may have been made 'unconsciously' by Shakespeare, and to admit that 'both the Duke in *Measure for Measure*, and Prospero, are endowed with characteristics which make it impossible for us to regard them as direct representatives of the Deity, such as we find in the miracle plays . . . Prospero, at least, [having] human imperfections'[5] – this is not enough. There will, of course, be human imperfections in any human representation, most plentiful where least desired, for what we ourselves are is most evident when we declare what we would be, in the endeavour to represent ideal beings. But observe where the prime fault occurs, in the character of this ruler: he is to blame in respect of the performance of that very function in virtue of which he is supposedly to be identified with Divine Providence. Read the sentence

> I perceive your grace, like power divine,
> Hath looked upon my passes

as the figurative expression which its syntax proclaims it – that is, as a comparison proposed between distinct, even diverse, subjects in respect of a particular point of resemblance – and it yields nothing at odds with the accepted idea of a ruler who, despite the utmost exertion of human good will, must still be indebted to a power beyond his own for any success in performance of that duty which is entailed on him as God's vice-regent, and who, when such success visits his endeavours, will transiently exemplify the significance of that vice-regency. But, exact from that same sentence more than figurative expression has to give, and you are confronted with the notion of a divine being who arrives (like a comic policeman) at the scene of the disaster by an outside chance, and only just in time.

Treat the whole story as fairy-tale, and you are not obliged to challenge any of its suppositions. Treat it as moral apologue, expressed in terms proper to its age, and it will answer such challenge as may fairly be offered. The Duke's expedients will then serve to illustrate the energy and resources of a human agent. But, suppose him other than human,[6] and the way leads inescapably to that conclusion which Sir Edmund Chambers reaches, when he reflects on this play: 'Surely the treatment of Providence is ironical.'[7] Unless

Measure for Measure is to be accepted, and dismissed, as simple fairy-tale – and what fairy-tale ever troubled so the imagination? – the clue to this central and enigmatic figure must be sought in representations of the good ruler as subjects of a Tudor sovereign conceived him; above all, in those illustrative anecdotes which writers (popular and learned alike) were glad to employ, and content to draw from common sources.

A number of these are to be found associated with the name and reputation of the Emperor Alexander Severus.[8] Developing on a course similar to that taken by Guevara's Marcus Aurelius romance, this curious legend was for a spell popular in England. Its fullest, most circumstantial, and most influential exemplar I take to be Sir Thomas Elyot's *Image of Governance*.[9] Here the salient features of the ideal portrait are these: inheriting a legacy of disorder and corruption, the good emperor is zealous in the reform of manners by means of social legislation and the careful appointment and assiduous supervision of his ministers of justice. To ensure a just outcome he will intervene in a case by subterfuge, not merely employing spies but acting in that capacity himself, and, when he has detected wrong-doing, not content merely to bring the accused to trial, he will handle the witnesses, cause false information to be put about, and trick the culprit into pronouncing his own sentence.[10] One after another, Tudor and Stuart sovereigns were addressed obliquely through anecdotes of Alexander Severus, congratulated on resemblance to him in respect of those virtues which the writer most desired in a ruler, and delicately invited to put to opportune employment those powers and qualities of which the country stood in need.[11] These pseudo-historical anecdotes, of which more than one bears a resemblance to those in Lupton's *Siuqila*, are many of them commonplaces of popular fiction; but, used by writers whose main intention was not to tell a story (either historical or fictitious), they illustrate an idea of the business of government which could then be seriously canvassed by men involved in that very business, or eager to advise those so involved. They chart the tides and currents that a writer for an Elizabethan audience must have reckoned with, and remind us how far the direction of these habitual sympathies and antipathies has since altered: thus removing some of the obstacles to a fair estimate of the Duke's conduct.

Another part of time's obstruction may be loosened by a close comparison at particular points of *Measure for Measure* with Middleton's *Phoenix*. This again is a disguise-story. Now, the man present in disguise is the man left out of the reckoning by everyone else. The situation his presence creates is charged with that sort of irony which the stage can use to fullest effect. Moreover, the difference between what he knows and may communicate to us, and what the rest of the people in the play suppose, can be broad comedy for the simpler part of the audience, yet take on a finer edge for quick and reflective minds.

When Phoenix proposes to find out the true state of affairs under his father's rule, he obtains leave to depart without ceremony, attended only by a chosen friend:

> For that's the benefit a private gentleman
> Enjoys beyond our state, when he notes all,
> Himself un-noted.   I.1.59–61

Evil can evade a prince's scrutiny:

> if I appear a sun,
> They'll run into the shade with their ill deeds,
> And so prevent me.   I.1.66–8

Alone with the companion of his travels, Fidelio, he explains that he holds it best,

... since my father is near his setting, and I upon the eastern hill to take my rise, to look into the heart and bowels of this dukedom, and, in disguise, mark all abuses ready for reformation or punishment. I.1.99–102

There is thus both likeness and difference between these two, the man left out of the reckoning in either play. They are alike in what they undertake. But, whereas the Duke accepts responsibility for the suspected evil both seek to uncover, Phoenix can attribute it to his father's enfeebled state and injudicious lenity. This certainly smooths the way to the happy ending; but it may perhaps explain why the acquisition of wisdom on which his father congratulates him when he finally abdicates in his favour has to be taken on trust. His sententious observations in the course of his discoveries have marked no advance on his original confidences to Fidelio. What he has acquired is in fact merely information – worth not a farthing beyond its value to the intrigue.

It is in this context, of traditional and popular stories which essay (with more or less seriousness) *of government the properties to unfold*, that we have to understand the eleven couplets which the Duke delivers to the audience at the close of Act III: before that scene at the moated grange, which alone relieves the succession of prison episodes stretching from the failure of Isabel's appeal to the eve of the trial. The substance of these lines is appropriate to the speaker and the occasion: the first four are general and sententious, advancing a proposition which is upheld elsewhere in the play[12] – that personal rectitude is the most important qualification for a magistrate; the next two bring this generalization to bear on Angelo; of the remaining five, the first two are obscure, but – taken in conjunction with those that follow – suggest that ill designs may be thwarted by corresponding 'craft' directed to good ends; the last three particularize – the Duke intends to turn the tables on Angelo, using the means which he has already mentioned to Isabel.

The form, however, of these twenty-two lines is obviously questionable. They have been called octosyllabics, which is surely misleading, and likened to the Gower choruses in *Pericles*, from which they differ signally. Those, while they sustain their initial impulse,[13] are a spirited imitation of fourteenth-century octosyllabic verse – as it were, a Rowley-poem before its time; these go to another tune. The staple is a line of seven syllables, which proceeds with a rocking motion from a strong beat in the opening to a strong beat in the close – 'Pattern in himself to know'.[14] It is capable of easy expansion, in any of three ways: by a light syllable at the end, giving a disyllabic rhyme ('More nor less to others paying'); by a light syllable at the beginning, giving a regular octosyllabic line ('To weed my vice and let his grow'); by a heavy syllable at the beginning, leading to a ripple of light syllables before the rhythm re-establishes itself ('Craft against vice I must apply').

Now, the closest metrical counterpart to these couplets, within the compass of Shakespeare's plays, is the epilogue to *The Tempest*, spoken by Prospero[15]; and the only place where verse of this sort would be proper is prologue or epilogue – or, where its substance forbids either supposition, as it does here, a formal pause midway. For a play in ten acts, such as Whetstone's, it would indeed be necessary, as prologue to the second part; we cannot, however, suppose it a survival from a lost play closely modelled on Whetstone's, because it requires an active ruler, a feigned submission by the woman, and another end than his in view. One conjecture remains permissible; at some performance,[16] Shakespeare's play was given in two parts, a pause intervening, and on this occasion it was judged prudent to remind[17] the audience, on renewal of the performance, of the theme and situation. For such a pause, this, the resolution of a train of episodes in which the Duke has had opportunity to assess his undertaking, would be appropriate enough. . . .

2

Barnardine

If the author of *Measure for Measure* should ever come to learn of the theory that he designed to recommend himself to the new sovereign by presenting his Duke as a flattering emblem of royal wisdom and benignity, he would need to call but one witness – Barnardine. It is neither here nor there that Lucio attempts to bring the Duke's name in disrepute, and achieves something – we are to understand that every public name is at the mercy of idle calumny – nor, that he is punished for it. So likewise Proditor speaks ill of Phoenix and the old Duke his father, and is punished. These reversals, comic or ironic, are proper to the intrigue; they are not felt beyond it. But the repercussions of what Barnardine does to the Duke are felt, not merely throughout the rest of the play, but beyond. For, while Lucio impinges on the Duke by what he says, Barnardine's impact is charged with the peculiar shock of what he is. Barnardine is the old soldier by the Scottish crossroads; he is the poacher in the shadow of an English spinney; the man who will always, without effort or apparent intention, make constituted authority appear ridiculous – especially in the person of his interlocutor. Escalus and Elbow would have fared alike with him. To express a sense of the ludicrous change that independence works in the aspect of authority is by no means to call authority in question; but to represent that incongruity in a conversation-piece, juxtaposing a Barnardine, or an Edie Ochiltree, with authority personified – this is to produce a picture in which one would not wish a royal patron to discover his own likeness. Judged as flattery, such a representation could only be ironical – or uncommonly off-hand. Favourable acceptance might be hoped from a man very dense, very vain, reared in the softest circumstances: without these three to blunt discernment, the charm will never work. The newly come King was not such a man. As to the dramatist, his well-wishers at court had never reason to say of him:

> I love not to see wretchedness o'ercharged,
> And duty in his service perishing.

It is surely time that we heard the last of that supposed connexion between the Duke's sagacity, and *Basilikon Doron*[18]; and with it the notion of a dramatist deeply disquieted by the corrupting influence of power, yet intent on flattering, in the person of his patron, the highest representative of that power.

It is time to trace Barnardine's short, erratic, but ineffaceable course. When Claudio enters, in response to the Provost's summons,[19] the names of the two men have been coupled and Barnardine's associated with a crime which sets him in antithesis to Claudio: condemned, not by Angelo but by common opinion. Claudio's first reference to him, and the Provost's rejoinder, develop the contrast in a way which becomes fully intelligible only when Angelo's letter is under discussion between the Provost and the Duke.[20] His name having here been joined, yet again, with Claudio's, the Duke (whom Angelo's precipitancy has compelled to review his own plan) seizes upon it and asks: 'What is that Barnardine who is to be executed in th'afternoon?' Having learnt something of the case (though nothing of the crime), he continues, in his assumed character: 'Hath he borne himself penitently in prison? How seems he to be touched?' – and gets this answer: 'A man that apprehends death no more dreadfully but as a drunken sleep; careless, reckless, and fearless of what's past, present or to come; insensible of mortality, and desperately mortal'.[21] Except for an echo, which I must suppose unintended and unlucky, of the Duke's recent attempt to persuade Claudio that sleep and death are one, this passage seems to complete deliberately the impression we are to receive of Barnardine as Claudio's opposite: where Claudio thinks with too vivid and particular imagination on what it will be like to be dead, Barnardine is incapable of imagining that state at all. 'Conscience' makes a coward of Claudio; the want of it makes Barnardine a brute. Thus, I find so far no hint of after-thought or improvisation, no perfunctory provision of a nonentity demanded by the exigencies of a recalcitrant intrigue, but rather the fashioning of a character who, even before his first appearance, is recognized as integral to the play's design. It is indeed when Barnardine appears that the perplexity about him begins.

The Duke has obtained that ascendancy over the Provost which the plot now requires, first by the proffer of *stage proofs*, then by the spell of poetry. On the withdrawal of these two figures, the prison wakens: the former night-references[22] give place to those of dawn.[23] Pompey presents himself in a passage of commonplace fooling with which any clown might be furnished by any dramatist, or might even furnish himself. Presently Abhorson joins him, and they bend their attention to the business of Barnardine; so, indeed, does everyone in the prison – to little apparent effect. If Barnardine was really created for no other purpose than to do Claudio *a present and a dangerous courtesy*, it is surely odd that the whole resources of authority in the prison should be engaged in obtaining his compliance; odder still that it should prove unobtainable, and that a character called into being only to die, should survive. The situation captured Hazlitt's imagination.[24] It prompted Raleigh to tease dull readers with the pleasant suggestion that 'Barnardine, a mere detail of the machinery, comes alive, and so endears himself to his maker, that his execution is felt to be impossible. Even the murderer of Antigonus has not the heart to put Barnardine to death.'[25]

Now, this is *very gracious fooling*; but it fails, or perhaps refuses, to take into account one fact. Whetstone's compassionate gaoler had explained, after dismissing Andrugio to refuge:

> ... See how God hath wrought for his safety?
> A dead mans head, that suffered th'other day,
> Makes him thought dead, through out the citie.[26]

It seems unlikely that Shakespeare, with this way open before him, chose a rougher course – that of making the man destined to suffer in Claudio's stead a living character in the play – that he proceeded some distance along it, only to change his mind belatedly, and hurry back to the road Whetstone had taken, leaving at a very loose end this now unwanted character. This is so extravagant a hypothesis that I think we could hardly do worse if we were to approach the problem from the opposite end. Suppose we consider Barnardine as created for survival. Would not that first audience, who *knew their Shakespeare* in the double sense in which we can never know him, receive the fooling between Pompey and Abhorson as an assurance that the happy ending was to be complete? Even if they were momentarily disconcerted by the Duke's insistence that Barnardine is to die as soon as he is fit for death, they might recollect that no sooner was the Duke satisfied of Claudio's readiness for death, than he began to take measures for preserving his life. The Provost's tale, of having tried to bring Barnardine to a fit state by feigned preparations for his execution, would trouble them not at all.

When he beganne to reigne, the people were abandoned to dissolute manners: for which cause he made some rigorous lawes, and other milde and pittifull: but, when he commaunded them to be proclaimed openly, he gave advertisement unto his ministers, to execute them in secrete. Consider not so much what I commaund you, as the intent wherewith I commaund you, which is to weete, that rigorous lawes are not, but to terrifie: but lawes which are pitifull, to be executed, because we make not lawes, to take away mennes lives, but to roote and weede vices out of our common wealthes.[27]

That is a representative passage from a 'life' of Alexander Severus, one of some importance in the development of that legend to which I have referred. It reflects the contemporary idea of the penal code as (in one aspect at least) didactic; and it reminds us that Shakespeare's contemporaries were accustomed to think in extremes: the extreme penalty, for example, or else free pardon. It is surely probable that his original audience awaited confidently the emergence of the real victim, and were not surprised when (true to Whetstone's precedent, and the established customs of tragi-comedy) he proved to be merely a name, without so much as a body to excite sympathy. But they may not have guessed, before the end, Shakespeare's purpose in making nature, not Angelo, pronounce sentence on this bodiless Ragozine.

To all this I see no serious objection, unless it were the gravity of the crime on Barnardine's charge-sheet; and of this we have but the one indication – a single word in that difficult and doubtful couplet of the Provost's: murderer. If this indeed represents the dramatist's final intention, it is surely odd that the Duke should know nothing of it; odder, perhaps, that he, who makes so many inquiries about Barnardine's case, should – as the text stands – not ask for what crime he has been condemned. That Barnardine was never intended to die in the play, I am certain. But whether the qualities that have made him deathless in the imagination of many readers[28] were part of Shakespeare's design, or came from that bounty which he could hardly deny any of his creatures – here lies no certainty, nor the hope of any.

NOTES

1. This opinion is shared by those who find in the play an explicitly Christian meaning.
2. For this absence, a reason is usually given – seemingly, to forestall censure.
3. This is well exemplified by the speech of Whetstone's compassionate gaoler, after he has released Andrugio (*1 Promos and Cassandra*, IV.5).
4. *The Wheel of Fire* (1930), page 79.
5. S. L. Bethell, *Shakespeare and the Popular Dramatic Tradition* (1944), pages 106–7. See also F. R. Leavis, 'The Greatness of *Measure for Measure*', and Derek Traversi, '*Measure for Measure*' (*Scrutiny* 10 and 11, January and Summer 1942). V. K. Whitaker

('Philosophy and Romance in Shakespeare's "Problem" Comedies', in *The Seventeenth Century* by R. F. Jones and others (1951), page 353) suggests that this passage approaches as nearly to a reference to God 'as Shakespeare could come under the law of 1605 against stage profanity' – an explanation which raises many more questions than it answers.

6. For the extreme form of this supposition, see Roy Battenhouse, '*Measure for Measure* and Christian Doctrine of the Atonement', *Publications of the Modern Language Association of America* 61 (1946).

7. *Shakespeare: a Survey* (1925), page 215.

8. For an account of this legend, its development in England and range of application, see my article 'Sir Thomas Elyot and the Legend of Alexander Severus', *Review of English Studies*, N.S. Volume 2, (October 1951).

9. *The Image of Governance Compiled of the Actes and Sentences notable, of the moste noble Emperour Alexander Severus* (1541). This purports to be a translation from a Greek work by the Emperor's secretary, supplemented from other sources.

10. See particularly Chapters 8–19, 24, 38, and 39.

11. For an illustration of the adaptability of Elyot's anecdotes, see Whetstone's *Mirour for Magestrates of Cyties*, apparently a free version of those that Whetstone found congenial to his own times, and temper.

12. For example, at IV.2.76–82. Here, admittedly, the *application* is ironical, but there is no reason for supposing the proposition so.

13. They presently subside into lame decasyllabics.

14. It is possible that more lines were once of this sort, for example:

> Who the sword of heaven would bear
> Should be holy as severe.

15. Though this has no light ending nor disyllabic rhyme, it contains the other three types of line, and fluctuates easily between seven and eight syllables.

16. Probably, part of some festival, at court or great house; perhaps, on the original occasion, the Christmas revels of 1604.

17. Remind, not inform; the manner is allusive.

18. See L. Albrecht, *Neue Untersuchungen zu Shakespeares Mass für Mass* (1914). I find nothing in James I's political writings to support the view that Shakespeare intended any echo of the King's opinions to be recognized in this play.

19. IV.2.57.
20. IV.2.116–24.
21. IV.2.125–42.
22. "'Tis now dead midnight . . .' (IV.2.61). 'The best and whole-som'st spirits of the night . . .' (IV.2.70). 'As near the dawning . . . as it is . . .' (IV.2.91). Notice also the Provost's consternation at every knock, and the business of 'calling up' the officer, to open the gate.
23. 'Look, th'unfolding star calls up the shepherd' (IV.2.196–7).
24. He recurs to Barnardine, even when writing on another play (*The Tempest*). Hazlitt permits himself an occasional critical escapade: Lucio, for tweaking a duke's nose, becomes very nearly a hero to him.
25. *Shakespeare* (1907), page 148. See also R. W. Chambers, *The Jacobean Shakespeare and 'Measure for Measure'* (1937), page 55.
26. *1 Promos and Cassandra*, IV.5.
27. Antonio de Guevara, *Décades de las vidas de los x Césares* (Vallado-lid, 1539), translated by E. Hellowes as *A Chronicle, conteyning the lives of tenne Emperours of Rome* (1577), page 441.
28. Readers rather than auditors. The audience too often sees him smothered in farcical stage business.

from *Shakespeare's 'Measure for Measure'* (1953)
by Mary Lascelles, pages 97–104 and 108–13

SIX

Justice on Trial in *Measure for Measure*

A. P. Rossiter

Oh, wearisome condition of Humanity!
Born under one law, to another bound;
Vainly begot, and yet forbidden vanity;
Created sick, commanded to be sound;
What meaneth Nature by these diverse laws?
Passion and Reason, self-division's cause.

Is it the mark or majesty of power
To make offences that it may forgive?
Nature herself doth her own self deflower
To hate those errors she herself doth give.
But how should man think what he may not do,
If Nature did not fail, and punish too?

Tyrant to others, to herself unjust,
Only commands things difficult and hard.
Forbids us all things which it knows we lust,
Makes easy pains, impossible reward.
If Nature did not take delight in blood,
She would have made more easy ways to good.

We that are bound by vows and by promotion,
With pomp of holy sacrifice and rites,
To lead belief in good and still devotion,
To preach of heaven's wonders and delights;
Yet when each of us in his own heart looks,
He finds the God there far unlike his books.

(Fulke Greville, Lord Brooke)

UNDERSHAFT You have learnt something. That always feels, at
first, as if you had *lost* something.

(Bernard Shaw, *Major Barbara*)

I HAVE presented tragi-comedy[1] as an inquisition into human nature and humanism; and that implies an inquiry into what controls human nature: into 'institutions' such as the principles of order, the essences of honour or virtue, etc. I have insisted that these inquiries are 'sceptical', in the sense of relying on empirical observation, not on *a priori* hypotheses: in the same way that Donne's inquiries into love are empirical – and sceptical.

In drama, this means investigating (in the frame of a play) things as they are, as distinct from 'seemings'; and as deceit is human, this means the unmasking of Man. I have (I hope) firmly rejected the term 'cynical' for that. Cynics do not ask questions: they know the answers. 'Pessimistic' I refuse to argue about: beyond saying that to call the empirical observation of Man (or anything else) 'pessimistic' is only the emotive expression of a preference for some kind of delusion.

Tragi-comedy found this inquisitorial field through the critical use of the comic in 'serious' plots: 'serious' (rather than 'tragic'), because in them the sceptical contemplation of Man checks approach to tragic greatness, even if the pseudo-hero is not presented as too pinched by *circumstance* to have the necessary degree of freedom. In the pseudo-heroes Troilus and Bertram, a critical and intellectual detachment checks or denies sympathy; and that is what makes their plays inquisitions. Jonson's intellectual-critical comedies differ only in degree.

Expert inquisitors manipulate circumstances so that the truth is extracted from men undistorted. They do it by playing on weaknesses; and all men are weak before unknowns. In dramatic inquisitions, highly improbable circumstances are used (the Trojan War is a fantastic one, and Bertram's a fairy-tale marriage); but out of these 'possible improbabilities' are wrung implications about human fundamentals: about action, passion, pride, honour, love, justice. This gives the plays the air of being highly developed Moralities: with this difference, that the accepted *code* itself may be on trial. Order is, I think, in *Troilus and Cressida*; in *Measure for Measure* nobody questions that justice is on trial. In *All's Well* it is virtue, mainly examined as masculine honour.

How all these intertwist is shown by a passage in Montaigne which Shakespeare used in *All's Well*.[2]

> We taste nothing purely. ... When I religiously confess myself unto myself, I find the best good I have hath some vicious taint ... if Plato in his purest virtue had listened to it ... he would have heard therein some harsh tune, of human mixture, but an obscure tune, and only sensible to himself. ... Man all in all is but a botching and party-coloured work. The very Laws of Justice, can not subsist without some commixture of Injustice ...
>
> *Essays*, II.20

Now sex is a human fundamental: it is also a theme where the web of life is a highly mingled yarn, and man most plainly a 'botching and party-coloured work', if you look clear-sightedly and empirically at all the facts. But as it is a theme too on which human hypocrisy (self-defensive masking) is highly developed, the inquisitor needs ingenuity in manipulating his circumstances. It would be hard to devise a more shrewdly searching situation than one in which a nun and a pimp comment on an unwanted pregnancy; yet Shakespeare's ingenuity adds to the discussion-group a severely chaste male Puritan and a gentlemanly whore-monger, a good-natured worldly magistrate and the expectant father. That is only one aspect of *Measure for Measure*: yet one in which human nature must inevitably give itself away a lot, in the opinion that each of the six expresses. (There is something almost prophetic in staging the play in Freud's own city of Vienna.)

The situation is twisted tighter still by making the sex-mishap truly a matter of life and death: through a law which is completely Gilbertian. Like the 'wise Mikado (virtuous man)', the Duke is

> Resolved to try
> A plan whereby
> Young men might best be steadied.
> So he decreed, in words succinct,
> That all who flirted, leered or winked
> (Unless connubially linked)
> Should forthwith be beheaded

— only, *he* has an old dead-letter law which can be recalled to operation. Angelo's task is to do this: to make men chaste by Act of Parliament; and this brings in not only the unchaste Claudio, but the brothel-world as well. To them too

> This stern decree, you'll understand
> Caused wide dismay . . . .

The point of my analogy is that, unless the persons are presented very realistically, the Gilbertian absurdity will make the whole thing a fantasy; and that this kind of flippant badinage on sex is a normal (if also hypocritically denied) human attitude towards 'getting into trouble'. You may say 'not normal to *me*': I congratulate you. For others (who do not see life with that clear-eyed empiricism), I may add that such flippancy is partly a defence-reaction – 'denying the importunity of the blood' by making sex a base jest – and partly the index of a potential or real hardness of sensibility. Lucio and his fellow Gentlemen stand for both. They are a chorus of *je m'en fiche*, the voices of shallowness of mind and feeling; yet their jesting has a serious implication, since all turns on the incongruity of men's dignified pretensions and their animal behaviour; and on the latter's usual consequences: sexual scandal and venereal disease (as a kind of cruel practical joke which makes the sufferer ridiculous). Lucio is an entirely human being: if very low, he is also very funny. And though he 'stands for' sex intellectualized as witty smuttiness, stripped of emotion and there-fore debased, he is a mingled yarn; for there are touches in him of good sense in a 'low' mind which is denied to his betters. 'Why, what a ruthless thing is this in him, for the rebellion of a cod-piece to take away the life of a man!' (III.2.108–9); and (earlier in the same scene): 'but it is impossible to extirp it quite, friar, till eating and drinking be put down'. The humane (and respectable) Provost agrees:

> All sects, all ages smack of this vice, and he
> To die for it! II.2.5–6

The comic part of the play ('very natural and pleasing': Johnson!) acts as a commentary on the difficulty of applying *law* (a reasoned thing) to matters of *instinct*. It supports the serious part, which results in a damaging analysis of the shortcomings of law

and justice as social institutions. It also has its own farcical sidelight
to throw on law in the persons of its officers (Elbow versus Pompey). And it presents aspects of sex which reflect on the sexual side
of the main plot: so that lust – like law – is subjected to an inquisitorial cross-questioning. The worlds of Mrs Overdone and
Pompey, of Claudio and Julietta, and of Isabella and Angelo,[3]
all meet – in *prison*. One might say, 'In human bondage' (in the
sense in which Somerset Maugham took the title from Spinoza).

Lust is *disorder* and *confusion* of good and bad. I consider that
the Duke's absconding from office must be taken as symbolic
shorthand for the abrogation of 'degree' and order. He is not a
personification of the Gospel ethic (Wilson Knight[4]); nor a
peripatetic Providence performing a 'controlled experiment'
(F. R. Leavis[5]); much less 'the Incarnate Lord' in an allegory of
the Atonement (R. W. Battenhouse[6]). He is not a character who
moves in the same plane as the rest (the Arden editor, H. C. Hart,
went wildly astray here), and he does not 'stand for' Government
and 'the Prince's duty' (E. M. Pope[7]) in the over-all pattern;
though he is a shadowy figure, and his speech 'Be absolute for
death' is apart from the rest.[8]

What follows the Duke's abrogation of his office is the exposure
of a corrupted world. 'What Tiresias *sees*, in fact, is the substance of
the poem', Eliot wrote of *The Waste Land*. What the Duke sees is
inversion, topsyturveydom. The images in

> And liberty plucks justice by the nose;
> The baby beats the nurse, and quite athwart
> Goes all decorum   I.3.29–31

are not only paralleled by Ulysses and by Timon: they belong to
a European tradition – pictorial and literary – to the traditional
figure of *Die Verkehrte Welt*, *Le Monde Renversé*, the Inverted
World. (Bruegel painted it in his *Flemish Proverbs*. The *topoi* are
traced by E. R. Curtius from Virgil, *Ecl.* viii. 53 f.; and Bruegel's
picture shows humanity doing the opposite of all that traditional
wisdom – crystallized in Proverbs – says it should or should not
do.) I mentioned this, because (*a*) Peter Brook's production at
Stratford in 1950 appositely dressed the 'low-life' Flemishly and

from Bruegel: I.2. really proclaimed the vices. (*b*) This inversion-figure does symbolize the essential clash or disharmony in *Measure for Measure*: that things and people, 'realistically' seen and staged, indeed are like that (odd as they look); but by all the rights of things, they should not be. For example, the vice beneath the Judge's robe; the humanity of the Overdones and Pompeys – a sanity which is pearls in mud. The inverted world is the subject of 'Tired with all these, for restful death I cry' (Sonnet 66). It is the subject too of the 'cryptic' sentences of the Duke at III.2.211ff.:

ESCALUS What news abroad i'th'world?
DUKE None, but that there is so great a fever on goodness that the dissolution of it must cure it. Novelty is only in request, and it is as dangerous to be aged in any kind of course as it is virtuous to be constant in any undertaking. . . . Much upon this riddle runs the wisdom of the world.

With the development of the Angelo plot, this 'disorder' theme enwraps the whole. The Puritan has been specifically appointed Deputy to clean up a very dirty city; but when Claudio's life is in his hands and his sister comes to plead for it, lust determines him to rape the Nun, by blackmail. The conflict of sex and law, which *is* Vienna, erupts in him too – and law or justice itself becomes a mask:

> O place, O form,
> How often dost thou with thy case, thy habit,
> Wrench awe from fools, and tie the wiser souls
> To thy false seeming!   II.4.12–15

The Duke and Isabella express the same idea: 'the demigod Authority' is a *seeming* where

> Degree being vizarded,
> Th'unworthiest shows as fairly in the mask.
>   *Troilus and Cressida*, I.3.83–4

It is not only his robe which masks Angelo. 'Ha! little honour to be much believed', Isabella cries when he has revealed his 'most pernicious purpose'. 'Seeming, seeming!' But he meets her threat to expose him by showing her his other mask – his chilly reputation: 'my unsoiled name, th'austereness of my life.' Hardness of that *will* which is lust defeats her: just as the other hardness of will – a narrow self-righteousness – had turned aside the appeal of the tolerant, worldly-wise Escalus:

> Ay, but yet
> Let us be keen and rather cut a little
> Than fall, and bruise to death. . . .   II.1.5 ff.

But Isabella calls out for Christian charity, and truly speaks as 'a thing enskied and sainted':

> Why, all the souls that were were forfeit once,
> And He that might the vantage best have took
> Found out the remedy. How would you be,
> If He, which is the top of judgement, should
> But judge you as you are?   II.2.73–7

>   Go to your bosom,
> Knock there, and ask your heart what it doth know
> That's like my brother's fault.   II.2.136–8

There is a terrible irony here: he could answer nothing at the very moment when her beauty, her impassioned sense, had struck home to his heart. The two scenes with Isabella are unlike anything else in Shakespeare: and few, few indeed retain such power on the modern stage.

But exactly there – at the end of Act II – the difficulties begin: with the soliloquy which contains 'More than our brother is our chastity'. This and the subsequent hardness towards the terrified Claudio, who has come to see a dreadful ray of hope, turn some critical ink to gall at Isabella's expense. Other critics cling to her saintliness as if it were their own. Sir Arthur Quiller-Couch[9] calls the character inconsistent; Dr Tillyard[10] brings in Whetstone to explain. L. C. Knights[11] calls it 'ambiguity'; and Dr Leavis[12] says 'why assume it must be "either or"?' – 'chaste serenity' or 'self-regarding puritanism'. These critical contradictions are quite needless if you can entertain the concept of *ambivalence*. Isabella is a dramatic parallel to Angelo untempted. In both, the higher nature (of a Christian kind: Pauline Christianity) is taken too high; and by being too far from instinctive sympathy, approaches the un-natural. Lucio's very remarkable 'fertility' speech (I.4.39–44) is 'implied criticism' (F. R. Leavis) of Christian tradition. The apparent intention was to show Isabella first as the nun-elect (Johnson); then as exemplifying Langland's 'Chastity without Charity is chained in hell'; and, finally, as released – by a real conversion – to magnanimity. But the graph we read in the play is quite incoherent; hence the commentators' interpolations. They call the process 'interpretative criticism': in Bradley they damn it as invention (which it often is).

But 'More than our brother is our chastity' need trouble no one. The line makes sense – whatever Quiller-Couch, Una Ellis-Fermor and others may say – if you see that Isabella is just as terrified as Claudio is, and with an analogous cry of the reluctant flesh. As he fears death, so she fears the unknown violence and violation of lust ('. . . and go we know not where, | To lie . . . to rot . . . or to be worse than worst | Of those that lawless and incertain thought | Imagine howling'[13]). Hence her hysteria as she screams at Claudio 'O you beast! | O faithless coward! O dishonest wretch! . . . Die, perish'.[14] It makes 'More than our brother . . .' something very different from that tight-lipped, resolved, hard-principled, priggish utterance which the angry chastisers of Isabella apparently hear. Scared souls are small souls; and as she leaves Angelo, Isabella's soul is scared – to a tiny rod of iron principle which is all she can think. She is beyond despair. 'Who would believe me?' What irony there is in that line! There is not a soul in Vienna who would *not*, so far as we can judge: not even the eavesdropping Duke, who never for a moment believes what he tells Claudio – that it is only Angelo's 'practice' or a try-on to put her to the test, not meant.

Again:

> had he twenty heads to tender down
> On twenty bloody blocks, he'd yield them up,
> Before his sister should her body stoop
> To such abhorred pollution.   II.4.180–83

The hyperbole reveals her real doubts of Claudio: but she dare not think, dare not calculate; and so entertains the notion of this obliging hydra, rather than realize now a Claudio with only *one* head; for that way lies despair too.

Her fury at Claudio is the fury we feel at people made the centre of self-indulgent fantasy, when we find them mere humans. I am not 'against' Isabella: it is a very painful emotion. But brother and sister are of one family in lacking imagination (sympathetic insight); or their circumstances make them appear akin. And they are akin in selfishness; or in self-preservation, without insight into the cost – to another. Hence there is a hollowness in II.4.100 ff., Isabella's avowal that she would 'strip myself to death as to a bed': she is too ready for the rhetorical sacrifice which has not been asked for her. 'I would sooner die' is rhetoric unless you achieve your aim by dying; and her aim is to save Claudio's life – to which her readiness to be stripped and whipped does not contribute. But, again, she is scared there; and to take the lines as a programme ('greater love hath no man . . .') is to misread them.

But Isabella does not *end* as 'small-souled'. Her plea for Angelo[15] has a sufficient magnanimity, though Shakespeare has not built up to it, and it can be taken several ways. (*a*) We can see her speech as consistent with 'More than our brother . . .': chastity has not been lost, and if Claudio has – well, 'My brother had but justice', he deserved to die, and was the minor issue. On this view, Isabella is presumably a 'realist'? (*b*) 'Till he did look on me' opens awkward doors. 'I did all this wickedness for you' is a formula of seduction for a woman; and 'this man wanted *me*' is surely not a weak undermining – when there is no chance of his proceeding further? Is Isabella then mere woman? (*c*) She is – or ought to be – in love with the Friar-Duke; and therefore feels for Mariana. And what is the good of revenge *now*? (*d*) 'I partly think | A due sincerity governèd his deeds' marks her theoretical sympathy with the snow-broth frenzy. The official half of Angelo[16] is just such a hard man on lechery as she would admire, support, and aid ('There is a vice that most I do abhor . . .'[17]). She is still intellectually a Puritan.

Shakespeare's fault lies in giving Isabella no transitions. She ought to require some over-persuading before she permits Mariana to do rather more than Julietta had done by way of risking her soul. (Julietta is 'fast' Claudio's wife; Angelo has rejected Mariana

– and might refuse to marry her. She would then be – casuistically, I suppose, and legally, without doubt – worse off than the seduced Isabella: for Isabella would have submitted to Angelo without consent of the will, and presumably without falling into desire – lust – at all. But what Shakespeare thought here is anybody's guess.) Again, her plea for Angelo comes too suddenly, too like a Beaumont and Fletcher switch-over – without *thought*. Yet she is a thinking woman: hence intellectuals fall for her – as Angelo did ('She speaks, and 'tis | Such sense that my sense breeds with it', II.2.141–2). But though she twice needs to show hard thinking, and is entirely the woman for it, Shakespeare does not let her open her mind to us. This is worse than her silence for over eighty lines at the end of the play, before she declines coyly into the ex-Friar's bosom.

'Chastity' some critics call her: but what would St Paul have to say to this? Chastity should be in no such inner combustion as to fly from fire even to ducal arms. And she does it with no dramatic preparation either, making it hard on both actress and critics. The 'conventional' comedy ending is a weak plea. There is no need for either Duke or cloistress to marry to end the play – unless we are being pushed up to an allegorical plane, which is 'unconformable' with the realism and psychology of Acts I–III. Moreover, Shakespeare plots points on Isabella's curve which require a true conversion. At IV.3.133–5 the Friar offers her revenge on Angelo:

> And you shall have your bosom on this wretch,
> Grace of the Duke, revenges to your heart,
> And general honour.

Revenges do not go with the enskied and sainted object of the 'Christian' critics; and we equivocate much if, quoting Prospero or Scripture, we say that 'revenges' here means the opposite.

It is not only Isabella's character which is 'double'. The whole play is full of equivocal speeches, of a kind where there is no resolving the ambiguities, since both meanings 'belong' in the play-frame. Sometimes quite opposite value-judgements are involved:

CLAUDIO Fellow, why dost thou show me thus to th'world?
Bear me to prison, where I am committed . . . .
Thus can the demigod Authority
Make us pay down for our offence by weight
The words of heaven. On whom it will, it will;
On whom it will not, so; yet still 'tis just. I.2.115–16, 119–22

He alludes to Romans, 9.18: 'Therefore hath he mercy on whom
he will have mercy, and whom he will he hardeneth.' But 'yet still
'tis just' can equally be Claudio's bitter comment that Authority
can order these needless shames once you are in its hands: and 'it is
all called *just*'. No actor can play contrite resignation and angry
bitterness at once.

This same quality appears in the oddly frequent use of hendiadys
(seen in *Troilus and Cressida* and *Hamlet* too[18]): for example,
'leavened and preparèd choice' (I.1.52); 'the fault and glimpse of
newness' (I.2.157); 'a prone and speechless dialect' (I.2.182);
'rebate and blunt his natural edge' (I.4.60); 'nicety and prolixious
blushes' (II.4.162); 'abominable and beastly touches' (III.2.22);
'lawless and incertain thought' (III.1.130); 'stroke and line of his
great justice' (IV.2.77). It suggests a mind taken up with the
complexity – and contradictoriness – of experience: trying to force
as much as possible of it into double epithets or verbs with an
abrupt change of aspect. And we find a remarkable falling-off in
the use of this figure in the last two acts.

Something like doubleness of vision or aim is present in words,
situations (Claudio's), and characters. And the ethical subtleties
we are drawn into half *compel* a casuistic, fine-spinning attention
which, despite ourselves, runs beyond the warrant of the text.
Even Claudio's 'sin' and Angelo's application of the act are double.

Nearly all critics are agreed that there is a break in the play, and
that 'the last two acts, showing obvious signs of haste, are little
more than a drawing out and resolution of the plot' (L. C.
Knights[19]). Dr Leavis calls this view a 'casual and confident assumption', and says he finds it 'staggering'.[20] I find it staggering that he
is staggered. It is to me quite evident that the texture of the
writing – the tenseness of image and evocative quality – undergoes
an abrupt change when the Duke begins talking prose in III.1; and

that this change applies more or less to all the *serious* matter there-after. The commentators who are extracting or elaborating themes, of course, do not heed this: though it seems to me a quality that any *literary* critic *must* observe. But Dr Leavis's terms are evasive, and give the impression that only *theme* is under consideration.

I agree with him that 'what one makes of the ending . . . depends on what one makes of the Duke'. But I do not quite know what to make of the Duke; and I am confident that it is not the case that he 'has been very adequately dealt with by Wilson Knight'. Here is Wilson Knight[21] on the Duke: 'After rebuking Pompey the bawd very sternly but not unkindly, he concludes: "Go mend, go mend."' What is this 'not unkindly'?

> Fie, sirrah, a bawd, a wicked bawd!
> The evil that thou causest to be done,
> That is thy means to live. Do thou but think
> What 'tis to cram a maw or clothe a back
> From such a filthy vice. Say to thyself,
> From their abominable and beastly touches
> I drink, I eat, array myself, and live.
> Canst thou believe thy living is a life,
> So stinkingly depending? Go mend, go mend.
>
> III.2.17-25

'His attitude', Knight continues, 'is that of Jesus to the woman taken in adultery: "Neither do I condemn thee: go, and sin no more" (John, 8.11).' It is impossible to accept that comment as adequate.

The Jesus-figure of Wilson Knight breaks down in the final scene, where the Duke's treatment of *Lucio* is harsh and not far from spiteful. If you want a *charitable* attitude, read Montaigne, Book III, Chapter 5: '*Socrates* to one that told him he was railed upon and ill-spoken of; Tush (said he) There is no such thing in me. . . .' Montaigne comments: 'Likewise should any man call me traitour, theefe, or drunkard, I would deeme myself but little wronged by him' (*Upon Some Verses of* Virgil). It is a poor business if a Jesus-figure, or even Dr Leavis's 'Peripatetic Providence', must be sent to Montaigne to learn generosity of mind.

Finally, neither Wilson Knight nor the other interpreters of his group are adequate on the effect of the speech in III.1 ('Be absolute for death') on the Duke seen as a total character. It is full of Montaigne, but it is not his scepticism: rather the record of its emotional effects on a mind which wants to believe in human magnificence and the nobleness of life – and cannot. It enwraps a death-wish far profounder than 'Tired with all these'; yet is never a cynical dismissal of life as sour grapes, nor a self-dramatizing welcome of death with heroic, histrionic gesture. There is no touch here of 'encounter darkness as a bride'. It takes away all Man's proud additions, honours, titles, claims – even his selfhood and integrity; and the soul and after-life are not even dismissed as vain hopes. It cannot be the pseudo-Friar speaking Christian world-contempt: there is no redemption, no hint of immortality in the whole. The only certitudes are existence, uncertainty, disappointment, frustration, old age, and death. It mentions values only as delusions. It determines an attitude of mind in which tragedy is quite impossible; in its sombre light all odds is gone. Man is a quintessence of dust: Pompey Bum no more nor less than Isabella, nor the Duke above Claudio or Angelo, nor better than Froth, the fool of Mrs Overdone. Everything exists: nothing has value. We are in the Jacobean equivalent of E. M. Forster's Marabar Caves, of *A Passage to India*.

The Duke absconds from all this by the end of the play: returning as reinstated Justice (which, within this speech, is just another illusion). Meanwhile, Shakespeare has made us feel that there would perhaps be more humanity and kindliness in a world of Pompeys and Lucios, than in one of Isabellas and Dukes of dark corners. We do not know. In the complete and heart-aching doubt which is the world of that speech, the world (if it is a world) is one where the accommodated man is the magnificent and horrible *Barnardine*. He lies under sentence of death, and takes life as it comes – in prison ('Denmark's a prison') – content in his filthy straw, usually drunk, 'careless, reckless, and fearless of what's past, present, or to come' (IV.2.140–41). His sentence means nothing to him, not even fear of the law. He leaps into greatness with his blunt, unshakeable refusal to be executed to suit anybody's plans: 'I swear I will not die today for any man's persuasion.'

And back to his straw he goes, to sit in state like a judge and condescendingly listen to anything more they have to say.

In this world of tottering values and disordered will, Barnardine stands out as admirable. His will is single: mere will-to-live; and in him the will to be oneself, and to manage others in action by force of mind, reaches a limit. It is one which puts those other characters of action, Prince Henry, Ulysses, (?) Helena, and even Authority (the Duke) itself, in their right perspectives. I can but suppose he fascinated Shakespeare too; for at the end of the play, in flat defiance of justice and in shocking contrast to Lucio's harsh tit-for-tat treatment, Barnardine is let off scot-free:

> Sirrah, thou art said to have a stubborn soul,
> That apprehends no further than this world,
> And squar'st thy life according. . . .   V.i.477 ff.

He is sent off to learn to live – from a friar. Ridiculous. In the *Measure for Measure* world, he knows already. In the world of these Problem comedies, he is the one positive: man without a mask, entirely assured, unstrippable, 'complete'. All the rest are doubters and seemers. Develop Barnardine and the Duke's 'Be absolute for death', and you pass to Hobbes's picture of the world: where 'the nature of man is solitary, fearful, nasty, brutish and short'; a world where force and fraud are the only laws. Yet is not that exactly the world of Iago, that other Sirrah with 'a stubborn soul, | That apprehends no further than this world', and squares his life according?

It is only one of the many continuities between the Problem plays and *Othello*: a play about sex, much of it obscene in a nastier sense than most of *Measure for Measure*; a play too of *masks* and criss-cross patterns of *seeming* (Desdemona has but little 'character' yet there are three of her: ideal, real, and Othello's fantasy of her as a whore). And – as I have remarked of the Problem plays – where love is concerned, there is no standing-ground between the ideal and noble, and the base and vile or horrible.

To return to the Duke – and the play's ending. The earlier critics (the Arden editor, for example) are wrong in 'character' lines of approach: or if they are not, then the Duke is 'consis-

tently inconsistent'. Yet if we eschew these lines, and accept the
'symbolist/allegorical' interpretation, there is no integrating 'Be
absolute for death' with the Duke of the end (nor that Duke with
the one of earlier acts, such as offering Isabella 'revenges'). We
cannot get out of the difficulty by saying 'He speaks in the role of
Friar'; for to omit from Christianity 'the resurrection of the body
and the life of the world to come' destroys the Christianity: at all
events from any seventeenth-century viewpoint – and, I should
have thought, from any normal twentieth-century one too.

The *allegorical* reading gives two Dukes at least: the ideal
shadow of the end (flawed, for me, by lack of magnanimity) and
the realist of a pessimistically-contemplated world-order: and in
this mixture he is like the whole play, slipping or skidding from the
one to the other. The view that he is, like Prospero, an image of
Providence, operator of an apparatus for 'controlled experiments'
to test souls before forgiveness, suffers in the same way. That is
why its supporters side-step the 'Be absolute for death' speech,
and overlook the lack of charity and forgiveness towards Lucio. To
my mind, this interpretation very much depends on two things: (*a*)
on reading Shakespeare's works backwards, beginning with
twentieth-century interpretations of the Romances, especially *The
Tempest* and *The Winter's Tale*; and (*b*) on this syllogism: God
moves in a mysterious way: Duke Vincentio moves in a mysterious
way: therefore the Duke is God. There is a piece missing in the
syllogism: something missing in the play corresponds to it. Can we,
moreover, import into a seventeenth-century play the notions of
deity derived from the tormented Christianity of Kierkegaard? If
we *can*, then the 'Be absolute' lines are a *temptation* – to despair;
and Shakespeare ought to have made this clear to us. If what we
make of the ending depends on what we make of the Duke, then
all I can say is that the Duke (like everybody except Barnardine) is
ambiguous: therefore the ending is ambiguous too: and L. C.
Knights's essay wins on points.

I believe that *Measure for Measure* was *intended* to finish as a
play of a higher ethic, and that ethic 'Christian'. But this remains
largely an aim: achievable by manipulation of the plot (which is
why you can take out 'the moral fable' and talk about that), but

carried out neither by character-development, nor (more important) by the texture of the writing. It goes thin: the earlier tension and realized imagery are absent; and this quality marks a lack of inner conviction. It agrees with the *imposed* quality of the action. There is a solution there: but the 'problem' is on one plane, the 'solution' on quite another. It is like a wish-fulfilment; or like Ulysses's cosmic order. It ought to apply to existence absolutely: it does *not* apply to experience-as-observed.

The old 'Moralities' exemplified most often some rough-and-ready lesson. Here the very intricacy and subtlety of the moral world itself, the difficulty of seizing the true relations of so complex a material, the difficulty of just judgement, of judgement that shall not be unjust, are the lessons conveyed.

That is Pater on *Measure for Measure*.[22] I find it nearer to the theme of *justice* in Shakespeare's play than most modern interpretations get. Is it not perhaps odd that we had to wait for that singularly *Christian* century – our own – to see what Johnson and Coleridge never even noticed? But when I say that, remember that not even an Elizabethan 'atheist' could get his mind outside a 'Christian tradition'.

NOTES

1. See *Angel With Horns*, pages 116–28.
2. 'The web of our life is of a mingled yarn, good and ill together . . .' (IV.3.70 ff.).
3. Angelo's valuation of 'love' is no higher than that of the brothel-world: he thinks it can be gained by force; they, by sale and purchase.
4. '*Measure for Measure* and the Gospels', in *The Wheel of Fire* (1930).
5. 'The Greatness of *Measure for Measure*', *Scrutiny* 10 (1942).
6. '*Measure for Measure* and Christian Doctrine of the Atonement', *Publications of the Modern Language Association of America* 61 (1946).
7. 'The Renaissance Background of *Measure for Measure*', *Shakespeare Survey* 2 (1949).
8. Wilson Knight, in *The Wheel of Fire*, sees this and says so honestly: the other 'Christian' commentators take evasive action, or do not

mention the speech at all. And Knight forgets about it by the end of his essay, where the Duke becomes a kind of Jesus-figure: a type 'standing for' idealistic anarchism – that of the Millennium.

Many of the critics remind one of the 'sanctimonious pirate', mentioned by Lucio at I.2.7 ff. He 'went to sea with the Ten Commandments, but scraped one out of the table'. The Second Gentleman guesses right instantly: it was the inconvenient one about stealing. Commentators on *Measure for Measure* are no better. Sooner or later you find yourself saying: 'Ay, that he razed'; and you have but to read more commentary to find what X has scraped out restored by Y, and what Y enhanced and wrote *up* dismissed or written *off* by Z. The more a critic has a cause to push, the more of a sanctimonious pirate he is seen to be, only by taking into consideration the opinions of others not discoverably less sane. If nothing else refuted those who deny the 'problem' quality of the play, then this would; for the divergencies of opinion are hardly ever on the trifling or secondary points. Two obvious test-places – discussed later – are:

    (*a*) 'Be absolute for death . . .',
    (*b*) The ending and its meaning.

But (*b*) really implies also (*c*): Whether there is or is not an important change in the last 100 lines of III.1 (from line 150), affecting all the serious main-plot matter from then on, through Acts IV and V.

9. New Cambridge Shakespeare edition (1922), Introduction.
10. *Shakespeare's Problem Plays* (1949; Penguin Books 1965).
11. 'The Ambiguity of *Measure for Measure*', *Scrutiny* 10 (1942).
12. op. cit.
13. III.1.121 ff.
14. III.1.139 ff.
15. V.1.441–51.
16. Critics who say Angelo's actions were *tyranny* depart utterly from the text. To Escalus and the Provost, Claudio is simply 'a hard case' – not a case of illegality or wresting the law.
17. II.2.29 ff.
18. There are a few, but interesting occurrences in *All's Well*: 'On the catastrophe and heel of pastime' (I.2.57); 'captious and intenable sieve' (I.3.197: Dover Wilson would read 'inteemable', from French *intemible*); 'Into the staggers and the careless lapse | Of youth and ignorance' (II.3.162–3); 'inaudible and noiseless foot of time' (V.3.41). And a further and excellent example in *Othello*:

                                    Let her have your voice.
            Vouch with me, heaven, I therefore beg it not
            To please the palate of my appetite,
            Nor to comply with heat, the young affects
            In my defunct and proper satisfaction,
            But to be free and bounteous of her mind.
                    I.3.257-62 (Q1. Editors emend, and read *in me defunct*)

19. *Scrutiny* 10, page 232.
20. *Scrutiny* 10, page 243.
21. *The Wheel of Fire*, page 90.
22. See above, pages 53–62.

    from *Angel with Horns* (1961) by A. P. Rossiter, pages 152–69

SEVEN

The Problem of Isabel

Ernest Schanzer

LET us look next at Isabel, the most controversial figure in the play. There is perhaps no other Shakespeare character about whom critics have disagreed so violently, and female critics no less so than male, as the following specimens will illustrate. Here are Una Ellis-Fermor's comments on Isabel:

> Hard as an icicle she visits Claudio in prison and lays before him the terms and her decision. ... But because of her inhumanity she can watch unmoved while he faces the awful realization of immediate death, her pitilessness only growing with his pleading. Weak as he is, his self-indulgence cannot stand comparison with hers, with the pitiless, un-imaginative self-absorbed virtue which sustains her. ... We know from this moment that a nunnery contains no cure for Isabella's malady and we have a shrewd suspicion that she will not end there.[1]

And here are Mrs Jameson's comments upon her:

> Isabel is like a stately and graceful cedar, towering on some Alpine cliff, unbowed and unscathed amid the storm. She gives us the impression of one who has passed under the ennobling discipline of suffering and self-denial: a melancholy charm tempers the natural vigour of her mind: her spirit seems to stand upon an eminence, and look down upon the world as if already enskied and sainted. ... Upon what ground can we read the play from beginning to end, and doubt the angel-purity of Isabella, or contemplate her possible lapse from virtue?[2]

Faced with such antithetical views of the same character, Quiller-Couch, who, on his own admission, swings back and forth between them in the course of reading the play, declares:

> We do not set ourselves up for umpires in this dispute. Our point is that the dispute itself—the mere fact that intelligent readers can hold

such opposite views of a character which, on the face of it, should be simplicity itself – is proof that the play misses clearness in portraying its most important character.[3]

But is not this very assumption that the character of Isabel should be simplicity itself the great mistake made by many critics, who proceed from the notion that the character *should* be simple to the conviction that it *is* simple, and consequently paint it all black or all white? When Quiller-Couch goes on to say that 'our own sense of the play has to admit the perplexity of Isabella', he ought to have written 'complexity' instead. Once we admit the latter, the former vanishes. Isabel, like the other main characters in the play, is complex, while her critics have, all too often, been simple. 'The ready judgements which are often passed on Shakespeare's most difficult characters and situations', writes Sir Walter Raleigh apropos of this play, 'are like the talk of children. Childhood is amazingly moral, with a confident, dictatorial, unflinching morality. The work of experience, in those who are capable of experience, is to undermine this early pedantry and to teach tolerance, or at least suspense of judgement.'[4] Taking this wise piece of advice, and suspending our judgement a little, let us look at some of the issues raised by Shakespeare's depiction of Isabel.

Her detractors frequently use about her such words as 'icy' and 'glacial', when in reality she seems the most fiery of all Shakespeare's young women. At times this flame burns low, but most often it shoots up in a blaze of anger towards Angelo or Claudio or sinful man in general. The fierceness of Isabel's denunciation of her brother, however much it may pain us, therefore need not come as a surprise, in the face of similar outbursts by Isabel throughout the play. As R. W. Chambers, her ablest defender, remarks: 'For all her silence and modesty, Isabel has the ferocity of the martyr.'[5] That the outburst, unlike those directed at Angelo, *does* pain us, and was, I believe, intended by Shakespeare to do so, comes not so much from the vehemence or the nature of its invective as from the person at whom it is directed. Shakespeare has won our love and compassion for Claudio to such a degree that any except the gentlest of reproaches must jar upon us. Throughout the scene, as throughout the play, Shakespeare plays with our affection for Isabel, alternately arousing and chilling it. It is the technique discussed in the preceding chapter [*The Problem Plays of Shakespeare*, page 70] to which I have there given the name of 'dramatic coquetry'. Quiller-Couch's description of his vacillating reactions to the character bears witness to Shakespeare's successful use of it with at least one reader. He declares that 'to us, in our day, it looks as if this virgin "enskied and sainted" had saved herself by a trick which denudes her own chastity of all but chastity's conventional (or conventual) religious trappings; that she is chaste, even fiercely chaste, for herself, without quite knowing what chastity means. We tell ourselves this; anon, as we read, we repent having said it; and, a page or so later, we say it again – or at least that "We do not love thee, Isabel. The reason why we cannot tell. . . ."'[6] Such a sequence of opposed feelings towards Isabel is, I think, exactly what Shakespeare was trying to evoke. Earlier in this scene the girl whom her detractors declare to be lacking in human feeling has drawn us to her by declaring

> O, were it but my life,
> I'd throw it down for your deliverance
> As frankly as a pin.[7]   III.1.107–9

R. W. Chambers's comparison of her to the Christian martyrs is most apt. She has their eagerness for self-sacrifice in the cause of her ideals, their utter contempt for life. At this moment and in the following lines, when we are watching her growing agony at Claudio's surrender to the lure of life, we are drawn closer to Isabel than anywhere else in the play, and we divide our love and compassion between these two tormented souls. Then comes the flow of savage invective and most of us are inevitably repelled.

Isabel has not only the ferocity and the contempt for life of the Christian martyrs, but also, as has been remarked by F. R. Leavis, she is capable of experiencing a 'kind of sensuality of martyrdom'.[8] When asked by Angelo what she would do if confronted with the choice between her brother's death and the sacrifice of her virginity, she replies:

> As much for my poor brother as myself:
> That is, were I under the terms of death,
> Th'impression of keen whips I'd wear as rubies,
> And strip myself to death as to a bed
> That long I have been sick for, ere I'd yield
> My body up to shame.   II.4.99–104

Although she does not expressly call it a bridal bed, this seems implied by the context. The adornment of the bride ('Th'impression of keen whips I'd wear as rubies') is followed by her disrobing. The speech parallels Claudio's

> If I must die,
> I will encounter darkness as a bride,
> And hug it in mine arms.   III.1.86–8

There is a significant contrast between the note of strenuousness, of a kind of moral athleticism, which appears in this as in so many of Isabel's utterances, and the softer and more lyrical quality of Claudio's words.

The thought of sacrifice also evokes in Isabel something of the gaiety of the Christian martyrs, as is suggested, to me at least, by the couplet which has repelled so many readers:

> Then, Isabel, live chaste, and, brother, die.
> More than our brother is our chastity.[9]   II.4.184–5

Commentators have spoken of the callousness of these lines. But Isabel has just decided to sacrifice the person she loves most in this world rather than commit what she takes to be a deadly sin, and consequently can feel elated about her decision.

That Isabel could, apparently without a moment's hesitation, decide to sacrifice her brother rather than her virginity, has caused much offence among critics. Once we accept her postulate that the yielding to Angelo's demands would lead to the eternal damnation of her soul, it is impossible to quarrel with her decision or to be surprised that she reaches it instantly and unhesitatingly.

> Better it were a brother died at once
> Than that a sister, by redeeming him,
> Should die for ever.   II.4.106–8

But it is surely this very postulate that redemption of a brother under such circumstances would lead to eternal damnation which Shakespeare wishes us to question. Isabel takes as Pharisaical a view of the divine law as Angelo does of man-made law. In fact, she seems to imagine God as a kind of Angelo, a rigorous and legalistic judge, who will sentence her entirely according to the letter of the law rather than its spirit. It never occurs to her that it would be even more monstrous a perversion of justice for God to sentence her to eternal damnation for saving a brother's life by an act that has nothing whatever in common with the deadly sin of lechery except its outward form, than it is for Angelo to condemn Claudio to death for an act which can only in the most legalistic sense be said to fall within the law against fornication. Although Isabel eloquently stresses God's mercy when trying to move Angelo to imitate His example, when it comes to God's judgement of her own hypothetical sin she imagines Him as entirely rigorous and merciless. Her view of justice is indeed remarkably similar to that of Angelo: both seem to believe that the letter of the law and justice are synonymous. Her legalism is epitomized in her words to the Duke: 'I had rather my brother die by the law than my son should be unlawfully born' (III.1.191–3), a statement which tells us a lot about Isabel. She also shares Angelo's detestation of libertinism and his desire for a life of austerity and self-restraint. The Duke describes Angelo as 'A man of stricture and firm abstinence' (I.3.12), while Isabel in her opening words, always important with Shakespeare as an index to character, expresses her wish for 'a more strict restraint | Upon the sisterhood, the votarists of Saint Clare' (I.4.4–5), which she is about to join. And it is surely significant that, next to Angelo himself, she is the only person in the play who thinks the death-penalty a just punishment for fornication (II.2.41). It is this fact and her detestation of libertinism which make her plea for her brother's life at first so half-hearted an affair:

> There is a vice that most I do abhor,
> And most desire should meet the blow of justice,
> For which I would not plead, but that I must,
> For which I must not plead, but that I am
> At war 'twixt will and will not.   II.2.29–33

Isabel's inclination towards legalism is again shown in her exculpation of Angelo at the end of the play:

> My brother had but justice,
> In that he did the thing for which he died.
> For Angelo,
> His act did not o'ertake his bad intent,
> And must be buried but as an intent
> That perished by the way. Thoughts are no subjects,
> Intents but merely thoughts. V.1.445–51

One's spirit recoils at hearing this girl, who had not a word to say in excuse of her brother but rather admitted the justice of his doom, now plead, with all the finesse of a seasoned attorney, on the most purely legalistic grounds for her would-be ravisher and the judicial murderer of her brother. It is particularly startling when put against her own words earlier in the scene:

> That Angelo's forsworn, is it not strange?
> That Angelo's a murderer, is't not strange?
> That Angelo is an adulterous thief,
> An hypocrite, a virgin-violator,
> Is it not strange, and strange? V.1.38–42

Not as strange as that the person who has just called him these things should shortly afterwards plead that he is innocent in the eyes of the law and should therefore be pardoned. It is surely wrong to say with R. W. Chambers and others[10] that this is simply Christian forgiveness. We are not here concerned with private forgiveness, the duty of every Christian, but with a judicial pardon. The Duke clearly brings out the distinction when he tells Isabel that she must pardon Angelo 'For Mariana's sake', but that the law demands his death (V.1.397 ff.). Isabel may or may not have pardoned Angelo. We are not told (in contrast to Cinthio's play, where the heroine declares explicitly | 'io gli perdono | Qualunque offesa'[11]). Her prolonged silence in the face of Mariana's repeated appeals could certainly be taken to indicate that Isabel has not pardoned Angelo, and that she is torn by conflicting desires to see her enemy punished and to reciprocate Mariana's service to her by helping to save her husband – for this too is 'measure for measure' and thus a possible part of the complex meaning of the play's title. But all this is mere speculation. Indisputable is the fact that Isabel is here pleading for a judicial pardon, and not on the Christian grounds of the need to show mercy, as she does so eloquently in her first interview with Angelo, but on the legalistic grounds that Angelo is technically innocent of the crimes for which he is condemned to die. What repels us is not that Isabel should ask for Angelo to be pardoned. Had she done so on the same grounds on which she had pleaded for the pardon of her brother, we might have been surprised but we would not have been repelled. It is precisely the fact that her plea is *not* Christian but legalistic – 'a string of palpable sophistry', as Quiller-Couch justly calls it[12] – which antagonizes so many spectators. (Isabel is decidedly more unselfish in her plea for Angelo's life than her counterparts in the sources. Epitia pleads because she fears her reputation would suffer if she consented to her husband's execution, Cassandra because she has come to love him. Isabel's plea alone is prompted by entirely unselfish motives. But unselfishness is not a Christian monopoly.)

It is significant that R. W. Chambers's defence of Isabel's plea for Angelo, in spite of his emphasis on its supposedly Christian nature, is as legalistic as Isabel's own. Much of the passage – on which I may be allowed to insert some comments – is a mixture of the half-truths and specious reasoning which seem to me to mar much of his in many ways so admirable essay on the play. He writes[13]:

It is a postulate of our story that Claudio has committed a capital offence. Angelo has not committed a crime in letting the law take its course upon Claudio [that the Duke considers the promise-breach involved in 'letting the law take its course upon Claudio' as one of Angelo's two great crimes, his words make clear. Angelo, he tells Isabel, is

criminal, in double violation
Of sacred chastity, and of promise-breach,
Thereon dependent, for your brother's life[14]; V.1.401-3]

he has not committed a crime in his union with Mariana, to whom he has been publicly betrothed [in his union with Mariana Angelo has, in fact, committed fornication, and is thus as much subject to the death-penalty under the law which he has revived as Claudio had been. Whether his betrothal with Mariana was public or private is of no legal consequence]; those are assumptions on which the play is based. Angelo would be despicable if he put forward any such plea for himself, and he does not. But the fact remains that Angelo's sin has been, not in act, but in thought, and human law cannot take cognizance of thought: 'Thoughts are no subjects' [among Angelo's crimes in act, not thought, is his gross abuse of his judicial powers in his relations with Isabel, the worst crime which *qua judge* he could have committed]. Besides, Isabel is conscious that, however innocently, she herself has been the cause of Angelo's fall:

> I partly think
> A due sincerity governèd his deeds
> Till he did look on me. Since it is so,
> Let him not die.   V.I.442–5

[Chambers here confuses cause and occasion. A jeweller, by displaying his wares, is not the innocent cause of an attempted burglary.] And Angelo is penitent. There can be no doubt what the words of the Sermon on the Mount demand: 'Judge not, and ye shall not be judged.' That had been Isabel's plea for Claudio [like so many commentators on the play and like the early Anabaptists, Chambers here confuses public and private judgement. To prevent Anabaptist anarchy Protestant divines in the sixteenth century emphasized again and again that Christ's words merely applied to private judgement, and were by no means intended to abrogate the ruler's duty to pass judgement on all offenders.[15] Besides, Isabel had made no such plea for Claudio. She had not asked for an abstention from judgement but for the seasoning of Justice with Mercy]. It is a test for her sincerity, if she can put forward a plea for mercy for her dearest foe, as well as for him whom she dearly loves [by thus identifying the two pleas Chambers obscures the fact that, though they have the same object, they are utterly different in their nature: that for Claudio is predominantly Christian, while that for Angelo is purely legalistic].

This strain of legalism in Isabel has been remarked by Professor Charlton: 'Too frequently she seems to regard the letter as the fundamental thing in the law', he comments.[16] And Isabel's Puritanism – which also manifests itself at times in her diction, for example, 'I have spirit to do anything that appears not foul in the truth of my spirit' (III.1.207–9) – has also not gone unnoticed. Lascelles Abercrombie, in his excellent British Academy Lecture for 1930, says of it: 'When we come to Shakespeare's use of the feeling against puritanism in *Measure for Measure*, we find that the antagonist who brings into odium the popular idea of puritanism in Angelo is actually puritanism itself – the splendid and terrible puritanism of Isabella'.[17]

I am not suggesting that we should do what Quiller-Couch confesses he was once almost driven to do: to examine Isabel and Angelo 'as two pendent portraits or studies in the ugliness of Puritan hypocrisy'.[18] For Isabel is no hypocrite, nor is there anything ugly about her Puritanism. It is, as Abercrombie says, 'splendid and terrible'. I am merely maintaining that throughout the play Shakespeare is showing up certain likenesses between the two characters, that he is manipulating our feelings towards Isabel by alternately engaging and alienating our affection for her, and that he is doing all this mainly to make us question her decision to sacrifice her brother rather than her virginity. He makes us question it without forcing an answer upon us. The majority of critics have, in fact, felt that Isabel could have acted in no other way than she did. R. W. Chambers, who must speak for all these, declares that 'whether she remains in the Convent or no, one who is contemplating such a life can no more be expected to sell herself into mortal sin, than a good soldier can be expected to sell a stronghold entrusted to him'.[19] (By taking it for granted that it would be a mortal sin, Chambers begs the question. Hence the analogy with the soldier is a false one.) There have been others – a minority among critics, but much more numerous, I suspect, among those mute, inglorious Bradleys that constitute the bulk of Shakespeare's readers – who have thought that Cinthio's Epitia and Whetstone's Cassandra made the more admirable choice. The manner in which Shakespeare manipulates his material, as well as the evidence of his other plays, suggest to me very strongly that he, too, preferred Cassandra's choice. How he felt towards a legalistic conception of Divine Justice is suggested by his treatment of the churlish priest in *Hamlet*, who refuses Ophelia's body full burial rites because technically her death may come under the heading of suicide:

> Her death was doubtful;
> And, but that great command o'ersways the order,
> She should in ground unsanctified have lodged
> Till the last trumpet; for charitable prayers,
> Shards, flints, and pebbles, should be thrown on her ...

with Laertes's splendid reply:

> I tell thee, churlish priest,
> A ministering angel shall my sister be
> When thou liest howling.   *Hamlet*, V.1.221–5, 234–6

It is the kind of reply which one would like Isabel to have made when Angelo denounces the 'filthy vices' of her brother. Instead we get her

> My brother had but justice,
> In that he did the thing for which he died.   V.1.445–6

By depicting first the inhumanity of Angelo's legalism, followed by numerous parallels between Isabel's and Angelo's characters, and then showing Isabel's legalistic view of Divine Justice, Shakespeare is, it would seem to me, strongly suggesting his own attitude towards her choice. But he leaves it sufficiently unobtrusive to allow the audience to respond to it in an uncertain, divided, or varied manner.

Measure for Measure is thus seen to conform to the definition of the Problem Play given in the Introduction [*The Problem Plays of Shakespeare*, page 6]. We have found in it 'a concern with a moral problem which is central to it, presented in such a manner that we are unsure of our moral bearings, so that uncertain and divided responses to it in the minds of the audience are possible or even probable'. This view of the play is supported by Raleigh when he writes of it: 'Of all Shakespeare's plays, this one comes nearest to the direct treatment of the moral problem.'[20] It finds its sharpest opponent in E. E. Stoll, who declares that *Measure for Measure* is 'a tragi-comedy, still less than *All's Well* a problem play. No question is raised, no casuistry is engaged in, no "dilemma", whether intolerable or tolerable, is put. ... By his deviation from his source ... Shakespeare had made the play even less of the problem kind than it had been ... In fact, the moral rigour in the heroine – the want of a problem – is ... what some unsympathetic contemporary critics complain of.'[21] Professor Stoll fails to see that the moral rigour of the heroine, as Shakespeare presents it, is itself at the root of the problem. That Isabel's choice does not appear to her in any way problematic – that she is shown free from all inner conflict and doubt – in no way implies that Shakespeare presents it as unproblematic and that the same freedom from conflict and doubt is experienced by the audience. This truism – that the response of the audience and of the protagonist to a moral choice confronting him may be opposed and must be distinguished – can be most neatly illustrated by a comparison of Whetstone's presentation in his play of Cassandra's choice with Shakespeare's presentation of the choice of Isabel.

Like Epitia in Cinthio's *novella*, Cassandra, when faced with the judge's infamous proposal, is concerned solely about her 'honour', that is, her reputation in the eyes of the world, where Isabel is concerned solely about the salvation of her soul. Like Epitia, Cassandra declares that she would rather die than lose her honour: 'Honor farre dearer is then life, which passeth price of golde', she tells Promos (page 460). And in the scene with her brother she justifies this conviction:

> Yet honor lyves when death hath done his worst,
> Thus fame then lyfe is of farre more emprise: (page 462)

Andrugio replies that her honour will not suffer:

> Nay *Cassandra*, if thou thy selfe submyt,
> To save my life, to *Promos* fleashly wyll,
> *Justice* wyll say thou dost no cryme commit:
> For in forst faultes is no intent of yll.

(In Whetstone's *novella* he even argues: 'if this offence be known, thy fame will bee enlarged, because it will lykewise bee knowne, that thou receauedst dishonor to giue thy Brother lyfe'.[22]) Cassandra replies that

> *Dispite* wyll blase my crime, but not the cause:
> And thus although I fayne would set thee free,
> Poore wench, I feare the grype of slaunders pawes.

But out of love for her brother she consents to 'kill her credit' and to 'slay her honour'.

Cassandra never considers the action as sinful until after she has committed it. Then she speaks of 'my guilt' and 'my crime', and declares that 'my selfe, my conscience doth accuse'. But she is still primarily concerned about her reputation:

> And shall *Cassandra* now be termed, in common speeche, a stewes?
> Shall she, whose vertues bare the bell, be calld a vicious dame?
> O cruell death, nay hell to her, that was constraynd to shame!
>
> (page 469)

But immediately afterwards, upon deciding to complain to the King and make public her wrong, she declares:

> So doing yet, the world will say I broke *Dianas* lawes,
> But what of that? no shame is myne when truth hath showne my
> cause.   (page 470)

Cassandra's attitude towards her action is thus seen to be complex and divided. Fear that her fame will suffer, a feeling of guilt and shame, are mingled with the conviction that her action was honourable and her conduct irreproachable. Yet I do not think that there is anything in the least problematic in Whetstone's presentation of her choice. We are never made to question its rightness or to doubt that her act of self-sacrifice deserves our deepest admiration. We accept without questioning the King's description of it,

> Thy forced fault was free from evill intent,
> So long, no shame can blot thee any way ... (page 499)

which closely echoes Andrugio's words I have quoted:

> *Justice* wyll say thou dost no cryme commit:
> For in forst faultes is no intent of yll.

We find, then, a complete antithesis between Shakespeare's and Whetstone's presentation of their heroine's choice. To put it crudely and, perhaps, over-simply, but not, I think, unjustly: whereas Whetstone keeps his heroine divided and wavering but his audience single-minded and free from doubts, Shakespeare keeps his heroine single-minded and free from doubts but his audience divided and wavering. In other words, *Measure for Measure* is a problem play, whereas *Promos and Cassandra* is not.

Shakespeare made two main alterations in the story he took over from his sources. The first was to introduce the motif of the substituted bride, common in folk-tale and ballad, and used by himself probably only a few months earlier in *All's Well*. What made Shakespeare devise this 'bed-trick', as it is commonly referred to? Critics are apt to tell us that it was his desire to preserve his heroine's virginity, 'to make more gentle', as R. W. Chambers puts it, 'one of the quite horrible situations of the pre-Shakespearian drama'.[23] I do not believe that, had it suited his dramatic conception, Shakespeare would have hesitated to let Isabel follow Cassandra's course. But the whole conception for which I have argued, his desire to make us question Isabel's choice and to turn *Measure for Measure* into a problem play, demanded that she should persist in her refusal, and therefore a substitute had to be found if Angelo was fully to act out his villainy and yet a happy ending was to be contrived. And by means of the 'bed-trick' Shakespeare was able at the same time to avoid the one element which is most repugnant in what critics condescendingly like to call 'the barbarous old story' (though I find nothing barbarous in either Cinthio's or Whetstone's treatment of it): the heroine's forced marriage to the villain she hates in order to 'repair her crased honour', whether she continues to hate him after her marriage, as in Cinthio's two versions, or whether, as Whetstone, with much less psychological plausibility, has it, she is 'tyed in the greatest bondes of affection to her husband'[24] the moment she becomes his wife. Only through the 'bed-trick' is Shakespeare able to avoid this and to bring about a much more satisfying ending than was possible in any of the earlier versions.

One of the purposes of the 'bed-trick' seems explicable by a point of law which commentators have overlooked. Where, as we have seen, Claudio and Juliet were made husband and wife by a *de praesenti* contract, the marriage-contract between Angelo and Mariana seems to have been a case of sworn spousals *per verba de futuro* (in which the couple promise under oath to become husband

and wife at a future date).[25] Now any *de futuro* contract was turned into matrimony and became as indissoluble as a *de praesenti* contract as soon as cohabitation between the betrothed couple took place. This point of law seems to be basic to the Duke's substitution-plot, and appears to be alluded to when he declares, 'If the encounter acknowledge itself hereafter, it may compel him to her recompense' (III.1.251–3). And its recognition may make the expedient more acceptable to those who have been distressed by it and by Isabel's immediate consent to it.

The apparent contradiction between Isabel's condemnation of her brother's offence and her ready connivance in what would appear to be an identical transgression on the part of Mariana has often worried commentators, and has even been called by one scholar 'the central problem of *Measure for Measure*'.[26] His suggested solution is that her inconsistency in condemning the one and abetting the other 'exactly mirrors a national inconsistency. The Elizabethans recognized and acknowledged the ideal, but *Usus efficacissimus rerum omnium magister*, and they, a practical people, readily accepted the reality.' I should prefer to account for it in other ways. Isabel appears to be ignorant throughout of her brother's marriage-contract. Lucio fails to mention it in his report of Claudio's arrest, while the words he uses, 'He hath got his friend with child', 'Your brother and his lover have embraced' (I.4.29, 40), would, on the contrary, suggest that there was no matrimonial bond between them. But why did Shakespeare choose to keep Isabel ignorant of the marriage-contract? Because had she known of it her entire plea before Angelo would have had to be different, an appeal to equity rather than to mercy. And it would have much lessened her inner conflict, 'At war 'twixt will and will not'. For not even the 'enskied and sainted' Isabel could have called the consummation of a *de praesenti* contract 'a vice that most I do abhor' and have thought of it as justly deserving the death-penalty. It is apparently the situation of the saintly novice exculpating the seeming libertine which above all kindles Angelo's lust and gives him his opening in the seduction-scene. And all this Shakespeare would have had to forgo, had he made Isabel aware of the circumstances of Claudio's transgression.

To Isabel, therefore, her brother's 'vice' and Mariana's nocturnal encounter with Angelo, with its multiple benefits ('by this', the Duke tells her, 'is your brother saved, your honour untainted, the poor Mariana advantaged, and the corrupt deputy scaled'), would not have seemed by any means identical, or indeed to have much in common. And the fact that the scheme is put forward by the Friar-Duke as spokesman of the Church would have helped to counteract any possible scruples raised in her mind by the Church's commands in this matter.

And yet there remains a basic contradiction: not between Isabel's attitude to her brother's 'vice' and to the 'bed-trick', but rather between her ready acceptance of the scheme and her equally ready refusal to fulfil herself Angelo's demand. For Mariana is as much guilty of the deadly sin of fornication by her action as Isabel would have been. And the same legalistic view of Divine Justice which made Isabel assume that she would be eternally damned for it ought to have made her postulate the same about Mariana. It is difficult to see how Shakespeare could have avoided this inconsistency once he had decided on the 'bed-trick', for which Isabel's consent is needed. Shakespeare at this point required an Isabel with a liberal view of morality; elsewhere one with a narrowly legalistic view.

I do not believe that this inconsistency can be explained by postulating a change of outlook in Isabel. Several critics, notably Wilson Knight[27] and Donald A. Stauffer,[28] have seen her undergoing such a change in the course of the play. Wilson Knight, the only 'Christian' interpreter of the play who is among her detractors maintains that 'Isabella, like Angelo, has progressed far during the play's action: from sanctity to humanity'. He speaks of her 'self-centred saintliness', her 'ice-cold sanctity', and her lack of human feelings in the first part of the play. Then, towards the end, 'confronted by that warm, potent, forgiving human love, Isabella herself suddenly shows a softening, a sweet humanity'. Since I can see no lack of human feelings, nothing self-centred or ice-cold about the Isabel of the first part of the play, nor 'a sudden softening, a sweet humanity' in her plea for Angelo's life, it is not surprising that I cannot follow Professor Knight in this view. To me Isabel, like the other main *dramatis personae*, with the important exception of Angelo, seems essentially a static character. She possesses that remarkable integrity in the literal sense which would make any great change in her come as a surprise.

NOTES

1. *The Jacobean Drama* (1936), page 226.
2. *Shakespeare's Heroines* (1886), pages 66, 75.
3. *Measure for Measure* (New Cambridge Shakespeare, 1922), Introduction, pages xxix–xxx.
4. *Shakespeare* (1907), page 165.
5. *Man's Unconquerable Mind* (1939), page 293.
6. New Cambridge Shakespeare edition, page xxx.
7. Cassandra similarly declares in the corresponding scene [of *Promos and Cassandra*]:

   > O would my life would satisfie his yre,
   > *Cassandra* then, would cancell soone thy band.

8. 'The Greatness of *Measure for Measure*', *Scrutiny* 10 (1942), page 234.
9. One is reminded of that gay, dashing couplet in which Crashaw describes St Teresa setting off in search of martyrdom:

   > Farewell house, and farewell home!
   > She's for the Moors and Martyrdom.

10. Elizabeth Pope, for example, declares: 'it is sheer, reckless forgiveness of the kind Christ advocates in the Sermon on the Mount' ('The Renaissance Background of *Measure for Measure*', *Shakespeare Survey* 2 (1949), page 79).
11. *Epitia*, H2^v.
12. op. cit., page xxxii.
13. op. cit., pages 301–2.
14. In this formulation of Angelo's principal crimes Shakespeare was, no doubt, influenced by his sources, chiefly, it would seem, Cinthio's *novella*, where the Emperor tells Iuriste:

   > Due, sono stati i tuoi delitti, & ambidue molto graui: L'vno, l'hauer vituperata questa Giouane, con tale inganno, che si dee dire, che le habbi fatta forza; l'altro l'hauerle vcciso, contra la fede datale, il suo Fratello. . . . Però, poi che al primo peccato ho proueduto, con l'hauerti fatta sposare

la violata donna, in emenda del secondo voglio, che cosi sia a te tagliata la testa, come al suo fratello la facesti tagliare. *Hecatommithi*, Part II, R5ᵛ

Whetstone, in both his play and *novella*, follows Cinthio in making the King declare that Promos's forced marriage to Cassandra is 'to repayre her honour by thee violated' and that his subsequent execution is 'to make satisfaction for her Brother's death' (*Heptameron*, O2ᵛ; *Promos and Cassandra*, in *Narrative and Dramatic Sources of Shakespeare*, edited by G. Bullough, Volume 2 (1958), page 499).

15. For a valuable discussion of this point see page 69 of Miss Pope's article cited above, note 10.

16. *Shakespearian Comedy* (1938), page 254.

17. 'A Plea for the Liberty of Interpreting', in *Aspects of Shakespeare* (1933), page 236. Many years earlier Mary Suddard had written: 'In Isabella and Angelo Shakespeare not only embodies two main types of Puritan, but sets forth all the advantages and defects of Puritanic training. . . . Different as its results may seem on Angelo and Isabella, the two studies point to the same conclusion: Puritanism, in its present state, unmodified, is unfit to come into contact with society. To borrow the words of Lamb, "it is an owl that will not bear daylight"' (*Keats, Shelley, and Shakespeare Studies* (1912), p. 149).

18. New Cambridge Shakespeare edition, page xxx.

19. op cit., page 292.

20. op. cit., page 169.

21. '*All's Well* and *Measure for Measure*', in *From Shakespeare to Joyce* (1944), pages 259–60.

22. *Heptameron*, N4ᵛ.

23. op cit., page 279.

24. *Promos and Cassandra*, 'The Argument', page 445.

25. For arguments in support of this view see my article on 'The Marriage-Contracts in *Measure for Measure*', *Shakespeare Survey* 13 (1960), pages 84–6.

26. D. P. Harding, 'Elizabethan Betrothals and *Measure for Measure*', *Journal of English and Germanic Philology*, Volume 49 (1950), page 156.

27. *The Wheel of Fire* (1930), page 93.

28. *Shakespeare's World of Images* (1949), pages 152–6.

from *The Problem Plays of Shakespeare* (1963)
by Ernest Schanzer, pages 96–112

SUGGESTIONS FOR FURTHER READING

Measure for Measure, edited by J. W. Lever (new Arden Shakespeare, 1965). The most useful edition for a close study of the play, containing a full discussion of the play in the editor's Introduction, ample notes to the text, and extracts from the principal sources and analogues. These are available more fully in G. Bullough, *Narrative and Dramatic Sources of Shakespeare*, Volume 2 (1958). The play has been edited by J. M. Nosworthy for the New Penguin Shakespeare (1969), with a concise introductory essay and a full commentary. One of the possible sources not in Bullough, 'The Story of Promos and Cassandra' from George Whetstone's *An Heptameron of Civil Discourses* (1582), is included in *Elizabethan Love Stories*, edited by T. J. B. Spencer (Penguin Shakespeare Library, 1968).

G. WILSON KNIGHT: '*Measure for Measure* and the Gospels', in *The Wheel of Fire* (1930). A well-known and influential interpretation of the play as a Christian parable on the theme of judgement and mercy, in which the Duke is seen as a figure of Divine Providence.

W. W. LAWRENCE: *Shakespeare's Problem Comedies* (1931; Penguin Shakespeare Library 1969). An important work which attempts to clarify some of the problems in the 'problem plays' by examining Shakespeare's use of the conventional motifs of folk-lore and romance. On these grounds, Lawrence exonerates the Duke, Isabella, and Mariana from 'moral laxity' in the conspiracy of the 'bed-trick'. His chapter on the play has been somewhat superseded by Miss Lascelles's full-length study of Shakespeare's relation to other versions of the story, but his scepticism concerning the theory that the Duke is a compliment to King James's *Basilicon Doron* still makes its point in the context of D. L. Stevenson's recent revival of that theory (see below).

E. M. W. TILLYARD: *Shakespeare's Problem Plays* (1950; Penguin Books 1965). The chapter on *Measure for Measure* suggests that in treating his romantic materials seriously and realistically Shakespeare produced two splendid opening acts (especially the scenes between Isabella and Angelo), but that the second half represents a change in style, destroying the unity of the play.

DAVID LLOYD STEVENSON: *The Achievement of Shakespeare's 'Measure for Measure'* (1966). A scene-by-scene analysis of the play examining the 'undercurrents of suggestive moral ambiguity' that exist beneath the neat, schematic structure of the plot. Professor Stevenson also advances the theory that in Duke Vincentio Shakespeare intended a compliment to King James, whose treatise on kingship, *Basilicon Doron*, is proposed as a model for Shakespeare's presentation of the Duke.

THE SETTING OF THE LAST PLAYS

EIGHT

Shakespeare and Romance

Stanley Wells

I

THOUGH in Shakespeare's day the word 'romance' had been in the language for two centuries,[1] it occurs in none of his writings. The Elizabethans generally found little use for it, and so far as I know it was never used to describe a play. To the editors of the first Folio, *The Winter's Tale* and *The Tempest* were comedies, *Cymbeline* was a tragedy, and *Pericles* was – for reasons that we can only surmise – beyond the pale. Modern critics, discerning common characteristics in these plays, have grouped them together, sometimes non-committally as 'last plays', sometimes as 'romances' – and the term is genuinely descriptive. But it has been increasingly recognized that the final romances are in many ways directly descended from Shakespeare's earlier comedies. These are often called 'romantic' comedies; are they not, then, also romances? It depends, of course, what you mean by a romance. The very word is shadowy, having associations with literature of various kinds, forms, and periods; with modes of sensibility; with languages; and with love. It can be spoken with an auspicious or a dropping eye; with a sob, a sigh, or a sneer; with the aspiration to define or with a defiance of definition. It means so much that often it means nothing at all.

If the literary genre of romance can be defined – or described – it is not by formal characteristics. Rather perhaps is it a matter of certain recurrent motifs, and also a recognizable attitude towards the subject matter. Romancers delight in the marvellous; quite often this involves the supernatural; generally the characters are larger than life size. All is unrealistic; the logic of cause and effect is ignored, and chance or fortune governs all. Characteristic features vary somewhat from one sort of romance to another; and attempts at definition are bound to be circular – we can only decide what makes a romance by looking at works to which the label has been attached and seeing what they have in common. But it is fair to say that Shakespearian romance frequently includes the separation and disruption of families, followed by their eventual reunion and reconciliation; scenes of apparent resurrection; the love of a virtuous young hero and heroine; and the recovery of lost royal children. In this chapter it will be my purpose first to sketch the background of material such as this, then to say something of Shakespeare's use of it in certain of his earlier comedies, and finally to discuss the romantic characteristics of *The Winter's Tale* and *The Tempest*.

Elements of romance can be traced far back in the history of the world's literature. The *Odyssey* itself is (like *Pericles*) the story of a voyage and its hero's reunion with his wife. Oedipus, like Perdita, was cast away in infancy; and Euripides's *Alcestis* is often cited as an analogue of *The Winter's Tale* – both tell of a wife restored to her husband from apparent death. Romance elements are found in greater concentration in classical comedy – a form we are apt to think of as the antithesis of romantic. The common features of Greek New Comedy, we are told, are 'loss of children, far wanderings over many years, fortunate recognition at a moment of imminent peril, and final happy reunion of parents and children'.[2] Menander's *The Girl with Shorn Hair* tells – as do Plautus's *Menaechmi* and its derivative, *The Comedy of Errors* – of the reunion with each other and with their father of twins separated in infancy. That the plays of Plautus and Terence include this sort of material is the more interesting since, of course, they were standard text-books in Elizabethan schools. But it would not do to exaggerate their romantic characteristics, which in most of these plays are rather treated as plot-mechanism than elaborated for their own sake.

Far more important are the Greek romances, prose tales whose influence on later literature has been incalculable. They date from the post-classical period – most of them from the second and third centuries A.D. Perhaps the three most important are *Daphnis and Chloe*, by Longus; Heliodorus's *Aethiopica*; and *Clitophon and Leucippe*, by Achilles Tatius. Here the familiar motifs abound. *Daphnis and Chloe* tells of a pair of abandoned infants who are brought up together, tend flocks, and in adolescence fall in love with each other. Daphnis is captured by pirates, but escapes in circumstances of wild improbability. Chloe too is carried off, but is restored to Daphnis as a result of Pan's direct intervention. Finally their true identity is revealed, they are reunited with their families, and they marry. This is the most pastoral, and the least eventful, of the Greek romances.

Perhaps the most influential was the *Aethiopica*. Again the story centres on a pair of lovers – Theagenes and Chariclea. Many episodes could be paralleled at least in outline from Shakespeare's last plays. There is a wicked stepmother on the same pattern as the Queen in *Cymbeline*; there is more than one shipwreck; there are oracular dreams; insistence is placed on the heroine's virginity; the lovers are several times parted; and there is a scene of grief over a dead body mistakenly believed to be the beloved's – it is difficult not to think of Imogen with Cloten's body when we read how 'Theagenes, as though by violence one had thrust him down, fell on the dead body and held the same in his arms a great while without moving'.[3] Our memories of the same play must be still stronger when we read of the lovers' reunion; Chariclea

ran to him like a mad woman, and, hanging by her arms about his neck, said nothing, but saluted him with certain pitiful lamentations. He, seeing her foul face (belike of purpose beblacked) and her apparel vile and all torn, supposing her to be one of the makeshifts of the city, and a vagabond, cast her off and put her away, and at length gave her a blow on the ear for that she troubled him in seeing Calasiris. Then she spake to him softly: 'Pithius, have you quite forgotten this taper?' Theagenes was stricken with that word as if he had been pierced with a dart, and by tokens agreed on between them knew the taper and, looking steadfastly upon her, espied her beauty shining like the sun appearing through the clouds, cast his arms about her neck.[4]

In the final book there is a protracted reunion scene, as well as an episode in which the hero, under sentence of death, performs deeds of great valour – again one is reminded of the last act of *Cymbeline*.

Some of Heliodorus's comments, too, are interesting in relation to Shakespeare. Towards the end of the last book he describes the rejoicing at the satisfactory conclusion of events in terms that could be paralleled from a number of Shakespeare's plays, and that might indeed almost serve as an epigraph to the last plays:

The people in another place rejoiced and almost danced for joy, and with one consent were all glad of that which was done; marry, all they understood not, but gathered the most part of Chariclea. Perhaps also they were stirred to understand the truth by inspiration of the gods, whose will it was that this should fall out wonderfully, as in a comedy. Surely they made very contrary things agree, and joined sorrow and mirth, tears and laughter, together, and turned fearful and terrible things into a joyful banquet in the end; many that wept began to laugh, and such as were sorrowful to rejoice, when they found that they sought not for, and lost that they hoped to find; and to be short, the cruel slaughters which were looked for every moment were turned into holy sacrifice.[5]

The third Greek romance to have some importance in the Elizabethan period is *Clitophon and Leucippe*. Achilles Tatius, imitating Heliodorus, tells of a pair of lovers who pass through many dangers and narrow escapes from death to final reunion. Again the story includes features reminiscent of Shakespearian romance, such as oracular dreams, shipwreck, mourning over the wrong body, and scenes of apparent resurrection; and again the heroine's virginity is heavily emphasized.

The Greek romances were written well over a thousand years before Shakespeare's time. In the interim, many subspecies of romance developed and flourished – it is noticeable how often we need to qualify the noun. We hear of chivalric and heroic romance; epic and pastoral romance; courtly love romance; and even religious romance.[6] Malory's translation of French Arthurian cycles into the English *Morte D'Arthur* was known in late-Elizabethan England; so were chivalric romances such as those of the Palmerin cycle (written in Spanish in the sixteenth century) and the slightly earlier tales of Amadis de Gaule (also written in Spanish but probably based on lost French originals). And there was *Huon of Bordeaux*, the French *chanson de geste* of the thirteenth century which, translated by Lord Berners, suggested to Shakespeare at least the name of Oberon.

To compile a list of romances written up to Shakespeare's time would not of course take us far; but merely the widespread currency of romance in the period has significance. It is true that stories, especially plays, using this material were often scorned. Gosson attacked the artifices of recognition. Sir Philip Sidney (in a well-known passage of the *Apology for Poetry*) and Ben Jonson (in the Prologue to *Every Man in His Humour*) mocked at the violation of the neo-classical unities often necessitated by the adaptation of romance material. Nashe scorned those 'from whose idle pens proceeded those worn-out impressions of the feigned nowhere acts of Sir Arthur of the Round Table, Arthur of Little Britain, Sir Tristram, Huon of Bordeaux, the Squire of Low Degree, the Four Sons of Aymon, with infinite others'.[7] But the irritated utterances of literary and moral reformers should not suggest that romance was ever less than popular. Certain specimens went out of fashion, but others came in. It was during the later part of the sixteenth century that the Greek romances first began to be translated, and they immediately exercised a profound influence especially on the development of prose fiction. First came Heliodorus: a brief extract in 1567, and the full translation by Thomas Underdowne in 1569, with reprints in 1577, 1587, 1605, and 1622. Underdowne worked from the French of the invaluable Amyot, from whose version of *Daphnis and Chloe* Angel Day made the first English translation in 1587. Achilles Tatius was translated by William Burton in 1597.

We cannot prove that Shakespeare used these works directly; but the related tale of Apollonius of Tyre, on which *Pericles* is based, was of great importance to him. Though the earliest known version is a Latin manuscript of the tenth century, the original appears to have been another Greek romance. The story had a wide and long-lasting circulation – over a hundred medieval Latin manuscripts, in both prose and verse, are known – and was popular in many languages; it was translated, imitated, adapted, versified, and dramatized. (In Greece, we are told, it is still passed on by word of mouth.) Shakespeare of course can have known only a few of the versions extant in his time. He certainly knew Gower's (in *Confessio Amantis*), and also Lawrence Twine's (*The Pattern of Painful Adventures*). For the student of Shakespeare these obviously are the important versions; but it is helpful to be aware of the others – to know that Shakespeare was telling a story of great antiquity, familiar to many of his audience. The 'mouldy tale', as Jonson described it, must have seemed to his less censorious contemporaries rather to be part of their folklore; a tale they would no more consider rationally than we should question the motives of Cinderella or examine the psychology of the three bears.

Of Shakespeare's romances, only *Pericles* is wholly based on a traditional tale; but all the others employ equally conventional motifs. Obviously Shakespeare, in employing the material of romance, must have been well aware that many other writers of the time used similar conventions. Some (such as Greene and Lodge) we remember mainly for their connexions with Shakespeare; others (such as Emanuel Forde and Henry Roberts – both very popular in their day) we remember hardly at all. And a few survive with the status of 'classics'; Spenser's *The Faerie Queene* (much influenced by Italian romantic epic) and Sidney's *Arcadia* (on which Heliodorus was an important influence) have been declared 'outstanding epitomes of all that was most vital at the time in the romance tradition'.[8]

These two works no longer enjoy the popularity that was once their lot. 'The *Arcadia*', T. S. Eliot has said, 'is a monument of dulness';[9] and S. L. Wolff wrote 'one who reads for pleasure simply cannot understand the *Arcadia*'.[10] Scholars and critics have tried to help the modern reader to understand them, partly by assuring us how serious they are. The *Arcadia*, we are told, 'is as sage and serious as Spenser, or as anything Milton himself could have wished'. It is 'a study in Christian patience' – like *King Lear*.[11] This attitude can be overstressed. Undoubtedly many romances raise, or touch on, serious intellectual issues; at the same time they tend to resist intellectual schematization. The Elizabethans themselves, nervous lest their fictions be considered corrupting, tended to make exaggerated claims for their moral and ethical value. Defending romance, Sidney wrote: 'Truly I have known men that even with reading *Amadis de Gaule* (which God knoweth wanteth much of a perfect poesy) have found their hearts moved to the exercise of courtesy, liberality, and especially courage.' Clearly he expected moral benefits to come as a result of enjoyment and admiration rather than by any intellectual process induced by the work. No doubt he expected to confer similar benefits upon *Arcadia*'s readers. But no doubt either that he expected people (or at least his sister) to *read* his book, and to do so with enjoyment. And this happened: 'for a century and a half', writes John Buxton, it 'remained the best-loved book in the English language.'[12] Indeed, most prose romances, including some very poor specimens, were read much more widely than works for which the modern reader tends to have a higher regard. 'Today', we are told,[13] 'the most widely read work of Elizabethan fiction is *The Unfortunate Traveller*' of Thomas Nashe; a book which, though reprinted in the year of its publication (1594), had to wait till 1883 for its next edition. Of the far longer *Arcadia* on the other hand there were seventeen issues between 1590 and 1638. Clearly people read it – largely, we must assume, for pleasure, undeterred either by its great length or by the fact that parts of it are unfinished. Romances have a habit of being left unfinished; it is a symptom of their inclusive nature. Most of the motifs common in romance encourage copiousness, a virtue more admired perhaps in the Renaissance than at present. As Dr Johnson put it, 'In romance, when the wide field of possibility lies open to invention, the incidents may easily be made more numerous.' There is no real reason why romances should not go on for ever. This is not to say that romance material cannot be combined with a classical respect for form and economy, as certain of Shakespeare's plays clearly show. But the inclusive quality of the genre may warn us that to seek in examples of it for a single dominant purpose or theme is to risk denying its very nature. Spenser, in his letter to Raleigh printed with *The Faerie Queene*, says that most men 'delight to read ... an historical fiction ... rather for variety of matter than for profit of the example'. Readers expected variety as one of their rightful pleasures.

It is important, then, that the romances were written, not to be studied, but to be read primarily for enjoyment – or 'entertainment', if the word may be allowed. I quoted the remark that 'one who reads for pleasure simply cannot understand the *Arcadia*'. It would be truer to say that *until* we can read it for pleasure we cannot understand it. Sidney, Spenser, and Shakespeare all had serious purposes; but this does not necessarily imply that they were consciously didactic in any way. It is serious to create images of the joys of reunion after long parting, of the loneliness of the parted, of the fears that assail men to whom, as to Marina, the world is 'like a lasting storm, | Whirring me from my friends'. To construct a verbal or dramatic structure that can stimulate our imaginations to a keener apprehension of these matters requires no further justification. The full response to the works of the romancers comes only when we find ourselves reading for pure pleasure, caught up in the swirl of the story, rapt in wonder and tense with anticipation – reading in fact as children read. Sidney, Spenser, and Shakespeare appeal primarily to our imaginations, not our brains; and the standard motifs and conventions of romance were invaluable raw material to them. . . .

2

When we turn from Shakespeare's romantic comedies to his last plays, we find much similar material. There are, however, important changes of emphasis in the way it is treated. *The Winter's Tale* is perhaps best approached by way of its main source. Here, Shakespeare was working closely from a prose romance written a generation earlier – Robert Greene's *Pandosto* (1588). No single source of real importance has been found for *Pandosto*, though many have been proposed. There are many analogues, not necessarily because Greene knew or remembered any or all of those that have been put forward, but because he was a conventionally minded writer who picked up his material where he could find it, with no concern for originality. *Pandosto* is a fabric woven from the common stuff of romance literature: predominant in their influence upon it are the Greek romances.[14] The romance background to

Pandosto is relevant to a consideration of *The Winter's Tale* because it may remind us of some of the overtones that the play would have aroused in its own time, but that are no longer audible nowadays.

Although *Pandosto* is crudely constructed and on the whole badly written, it was popular for a phenomenally long time. It had been reprinted four times by the time Shakespeare wrote his play, and went on being read and reprinted regularly for at least a hundred and fifty years. It seems to have appealed especially to a not very highly educated class of reader. In Shakespeare's lifetime it was said that a typical chambermaid 'reads Greene's works over and over', and it is a girl of the same class who is shown reading it, a hundred and fifty years later, in Richardson's *Clarissa*. Probably no Elizabethan novel had as long a natural life as *Pandosto*.[15] Its popularity can be explained only on the assumption that its readers enjoyed its presentation of basic human situations in an undemanding manner. The same quality may well have recommended it to Shakespeare as a source. A fully realized work of art would have left him no room to work in. *Pandosto* is a collection of clichés, of the well-worn themes and stock situations of pastoral romance. Greene had done Shakespeare an initial service by organizing these stereotyped elements into a pattern. In taking them over Shakespeare was of course well aware of their unoriginal nature and improbable aspects. During the play we are reminded of the old-fashioned nature of the story we are watching. By a sort of alienation technique Shakespeare draws our attention to the nature of the fiction. Time the chorus says he will

> make stale
> The glistering of this present, as my tale
> Now seems to it;　　　　　　　　　IV.1.13–15

and within the play itself, especially towards the end when marvellous events crowd upon each other, we have such remarks as the comment upon Antigonus's death:

> Like an old tale still. . . .　　　　　　　　V.2.59

and Paulina's remark that the fact that Hermione is still alive would be 'hooted at | Like an old tale'. It appears not only that

Shakespeare was fully aware of the unrealities of the story, but that he deliberately played upon the audience's awareness too, inviting them to recall similar situations – even perhaps their memories of the source story itself, and also the centuries of tradition that lie behind it.

Shakespeare's handling of *Pandosto* is characterized at once by extreme freedom and by a remarkable willingness to turn to account even minute details of the original. He both takes over the episodic structure and draws attention to it in the long speech of Time as chorus. This emphasis seems designed to stress the romantic nature of the tale: in the non-dramatic romances, time is commonly the ally of chance and fortune in bringing about the changes of the actions. Time's speech is pivotal to the play. Shakespeare may have got the idea for it from Greene's sub-title, which is *The Triumph of Time*; and Greene's title-page bears the tag 'temporis filia veritas'. Certainly Shakespeare makes of the time element a poetic complex that helps in giving the play a richness of harmony without parallel in the novel. Showing how human beings can achieve at least the illusion of having triumphed over time, Shakespeare creates that illusion for us.

Leontes's comparatively unmotivated jealousy may be thought of as an intensification of the play's romance characteristics – motivation is not the strong point of most romancers; but the first scene is less than typical in the emotional intensity that it generates. Leontes's sexual obsession is portrayed as a self-consuming, almost fanatical state of mind; impervious to suggestion, completely incapable of admitting the possibility of error. This makes it appropriate that Shakespeare should have changed the business of the oracle. In Greene, the Queen asks her husband to send to the oracle, for the sake of their child. In the play Leontes sends of his own accord, merely to help to convince others of the truth of his suspicions:

> Though I am satisfied, and need no more
> Than what I know, yet shall the oracle
> Give rest to th'minds of others, such as he,
> Whose ignorant credulity will not
> Come up to th'truth.   II.1.189–93

Whereas Pandosto penitently accepts the oracle's pronouncement, Leontes at first denies it, pursuing his wilful course to the point of blasphemy:

> There is no truth at all i'th'oracle!
> The sessions shall proceed: this is mere falsehood.
>
> III.2.138–9

Immediately there arrives the report of his son's death from an illness that Leontes had earlier attributed to shame at hearing of Hermione's disgrace – which was as if Leontes blamed himself. The news strikes home. 'Apollo's angry,' he says, 'and the heavens themselves | Do strike at my injustice.' Thus Shakespeare greatly increases Leontes's implied responsibility for his son's death.

This emphasis on personal responsibility diminishes to some extent the part played in the action by those typical romance agents, chance, fate, fortune, etc. Shakespeare is humanizing his source, giving it greater relevance to normal life, making it a story of human beings rather than of puppets. To this extent the play is less of a romance than Pandosto. Shakespeare makes the baby Perdita's fate, too, less dependent on chance than in Greene, where she is simply left floating. Antigonus sails with the baby; we see him depositing her on the shore of Bohemia. But all evidence of where the baby is must be destroyed as otherwise it would be possible for the penitent Leontes to find his daughter. This no doubt is at least partly responsible for Shakespeare's introduction of the notorious bear that chases and devours Antigonus, and also for the less spectacular deaths of the sailors on his boat.

Shakespeare plays down too the element of chance in the matter of the lovers' return to Leontes's court. In Pandosto they are intent simply on getting away from the land ruled by the prince's father, who disapproves of their match; it is only because of a typical romance shipwreck that they land in Pandosto's country. In the play on the other hand the journey is carefully planned by Camillo, who suggests to Florizel that he may well be very welcome in Sicily, and says (in words that sound like a criticism of the lack of planning in Pandosto) that this is

> A course more promising
> Than a wild dedication of yourselves
> To unpathed waters, undreamed shores . . .
>
> IV.4.562–4

In such ways does Shakespeare give greater credibility to his original. 'There is a strong web of realism running through the warp of the romance.'[16] But 'realism' is an even more dangerous word than 'romance'. It could be argued that Shakespeare's love scenes are more realistic than Greene's. In another sense they are far more romantic; they are suffused by a passion that is real in a poetic, not an everyday, sense. Certainly the sheep-shearing scenes represent an almost total transformation of the original. Greene's lovers are largely preoccupied by social considerations: the prince constantly astounded that he can feel anything remotely resembling affection for a lowly shepherdess, the girl equally shocked by her presumption in loving a prince. In Shakespeare of course all is on a much higher plane; and it is all much more deeply related to the main plot. It is significant for instance that Florizel's admiration finds expression in a sense of the timelessness of Perdita's actions:

> When you speak, sweet,
> I'd have you do it ever; when you sing,
> I'd have you buy and sell so, so give alms,
> Pray so, and, for the ord'ring your affairs,
> To sing them too; when you do dance, I wish you
> A wave o'th'sea, that you might ever do
> Nothing but that – move still, still so,
> And own no other function.
>
> IV.4.136–43

We remember Polixenes's description of the time when he and Leontes, the fathers of this pair, were

> Two lads that thought there was no more behind
> But such a day tomorrow as today,
> And to be boy eternal.
>
> I.2.63–5

The lines look forward too to the illusion created by the last scene, that time the conqueror has been conquered: an illusion created partly by the presence of this same Perdita.

In the final episodes of Greene's novel, Pandosto is no different from his earlier self. He is violent and lustful; he throws the fugitives into prison and condemns all but the young prince to death. Leontes however is still penitent and intensely conscious of the wrong he did his wife. With terrible concentration he remembers her virtues and her beauty. This constancy of penitence may be regarded as a change in the direction of romance; certainly it is in line with, for instance, the inconsolable grief displayed by Pericles and by Posthumus. And it leads to the most important departures from the source. Greene has a tacked-on tragic ending – Pandosto, suddenly smitten once more with repentance, kills himself. Leontes of course remains alive, and, more important still, is reunited with his wife in the amazing statue scene, surely one of the most daring in Shakespeare. Here Shakespeare invests the familiar motifs of reunion and apparent resurrection with exceptional poetic and dramatic force. The scene is essentially of the theatre; the long wait before the statue moves is unfailing in its hold upon audiences. And Leontes's realization that Hermione lives, when art melts into nature, is one of those moments of silence in which in a sense Shakespeare leaves everything to the actor, yet in another sense has done everything for him. 'Silence', says Claudio, 'is the perfectest herald of joy'; and here (as in the *Alcestis*) husband and wife do not address each other. But there must be (as the First Gentleman says of the reunion of Leontes and Camillo) 'speech in their dumbness, language in their very gesture'. If one considered the scene in purely literary terms it might seem perfunctory, especially when Hermione tells Perdita that she has preserved herself in order to see whether the oracle was right in suggesting that Perdita might be alive (this does not suggest any great affection for Leontes). But there is no danger of this in the theatre, at any rate when Leontes is performed with the intensity with which, according to Helena Faucit, Macready played the scene:

At first he stood speechless, as if turned to stone; his face with an awe-struck look upon it. . . . Thus absorbed in wonder, he remained until Paulina said, 'Nay, present your hand.' Tremblingly he advanced, and touched gently the hand held out to him. Then, what a cry came with,

'O, she's warm!' It is impossible to describe Mr Macready here. He was Leontes' very self! His passionate joy at finding Hermione really alive seemed beyond control. Now he was prostrate at her feet, then enfolding her in his arms. I had a slight veil or covering over my head and neck, supposed to make the statue look older. This fell off in an instant. The hair, which came unbound, and fell on my shoulders, was reverently kissed and caressed. The whole change was so sudden, so overwhelming, that I suppose I cried out hysterically, for he whispered to me, 'Don't be frightened, my child! don't be frightened! Control yourself!' All this went on during a tumult of applause that sounded like a storm of hail. . . . It was such a comfort to me, as well as true to natural feeling, that Shakespeare gives Hermione no words to say to Leontes, but leaves her to assure him of her joy and forgiveness by look and manner only.[17]

It is appropriate to the suffering we have witnessed during the play that there should be a strongly elegiac tone here. Shakespeare's changes of his source have increased the marvellous – or the miraculous. There is joy in the scene; but it is pregnant with sorrow:

> in the very temple of delight
> Veiled Melancholy has her sovran shrine.

Deep emotions have been stirred, and will not be satisfied by a conventionally cheerful ending. In the romantic comedies we are accustomed to final scenes that stress the restoration of the social order, of which the dance or feast is an appropriate symbol. In *The Winter's Tale* there are no macrocosmic implications. Emphasis is placed not on the group but on individuals whose suffering we have closely followed. The ending is not a vision of ultimate unity, as that of *Cymbeline* might be considered. There is sobriety as Leontes in his closing lines suggests how each may heal the wounds 'Performed in this wide gap of time since first | We were dissevered'. It is not in fact a high romantic climax. The emphasis is not on the lovers, but on the older generation. We are reminded that Antigonus is dead, that Leontes has 'in vain said many | A prayer upon' Hermione's grave, and that he needs pardon from both Polixenes and Hermione. The individuals must salvage what they can.

A late-seventeenth-century edition of *Pandosto* is adorned with a crude woodcut illustrative of the story; one of the things represented is a cradle floating upon what appears to be a river but is presumably intended for the sea. It is a fitting emblem of the helplessness of humanity often implied in romance literature. Sometimes the forces against which mankind is helpless are external, sometimes internal. The baby Perdita is helpless in the face of her father's unreasonable passion; so is her mother; and so in a sense is Leontes himself – he is swept away by jealousy as a child might be swept away by the ocean. And the end of the play, focusing upon a few figures in their newly poised adjustments to each other, stresses the importance of human relationships as bulwarks against the forces of disaster. In his adaptation of *Pandosto* Shakespeare has produced a work that is far more powerful as a human document. He has done so not by denying the romance elements in Greene's book but by readjusting them – sometimes adding to them, sometimes toning them down with a modified realism, and always investing them with a poetic rather than a mundane reality.

That *The Tempest* employs basic romance material requires little demonstration. It begins with a shipwreck; Prospero and Miranda had themselves been cast up on this island after being exposed to wind and waves like the heroine of *Pandosto*; in the past Prospero had been separated from his brother; now Alonso is separated from his son and believes him dead; Miranda and Ferdinand are the handsome hero and pure heroine typical of romance; the supernatural plays its part; an air of deliberate unreality pervades the play; the story works towards reunion, reconciliation, and the happy conclusion of the love affair. But in form the play is very different from a typical romance. Shakespeare has chosen to begin his story at the end. The action is concentrated into a small space and a few hours. The sea-voyages and land-travels of *Pericles*, *Cymbeline*, and *The Winter's Tale* here can only be told in retrospect, or at most symbolized by the wanderings of the shipwrecked men around the island. Instead of being moved from a present which in the later acts becomes the past, we are throughout required to be conscious of the past in the present. The 'wide gap' of time in which we imagined the coming to maturity of Marina and

Perdita has here become 'the dark backward and abysm of time' into which Miranda gazes with her father. The method is closer to that of *The Comedy of Errors* than to that of the other last plays; but Prospero is the centre of this play, whereas Egeon is present only in the framework of the earlier one. The tension that results from this combination of romantic material with 'classical' form helps to give this play its peculiar dynamic. The characters, as well as the audience, are often bidden to remember the past; our minds move with theirs. The result is perhaps, paradoxically enough, a more consistent and deeper consciousness of the effects of time than in plays in which a wider time-span is directly presented.

By sacrificing the large dimensions of space and time common in romance, Shakespeare clearly gains much in concentration. Nevertheless, it is a sacrifice. The romancer, typically writing a story in which little attention is paid to the sequence of cause and effect, depends a good deal upon time, and also chance or fortune (sometimes conceived of as an active god-figure) in order to render plausible those turns of the action or changes of character for which no explanation is given. In *Cymbeline*, for instance, Iachimo's sudden last-act penitence goes psychologically uninvestigated but is the more easily accepted in that we last saw him some time ago and in a different country. The story of *The Tempest* demands similar changes. Alonso has to be shown in penitence for his usurpation; and the penitence has to come about as the direct result of his experiences on the island. Shakespeare can (and to some extent does) hint that the Alonso we see at the beginning of the action is not as objectionable as he was twelve years before, but the actual process of conversion has to take place within the brief time-span of the play. This is made convincing primarily by being made the result of a conscious purpose. In a normal romance story, chance would have caused the shipwreck that puts Prospero's enemies at his mercy. In this play, though fortune plays her part (and Shakespeare is most subtle in his constant shifting of responsibility), it is Prospero himself who by his 'art' brings about the shipwreck. He is partly dependent on fortune, partly master of it. In a sense he is the 'god of this great vast' on whom Pericles calls.

He has superhuman power, yet remains human. He is both god and man, a worker of miracles who finally accepts the full burden of humanity. At times it is difficult to distinguish him from a supernatural controlling force. It is partly by creating the wholly superhuman Ariel to act as the semi-independent agent of Prospero's will that Shakespeare has been able to keep Prospero human – perhaps the most remarkable technical feat of the play.

As the controlling agent of the play in which he has his being, Prospero himself resembles the narrator of a romance story. This is true not merely of the second scene, in which he tells Miranda of her childhood (with results, it would seem, resembling those of many romancers), but also of the methods by which he exercises his influence. Frequently and deliberately he tries to create a sense of awe, mystery, and wonder in the minds of those he is trying to influence. His use – generally through Ariel – of music is part of this. So is Ariel's tricksiness, such as his appearance to the mariners causing them to feel 'a fever of the mad', and the living drollery that reminds Gonzalo of the romantic travellers' tales he heard in boyhood. It is after the wonder induced by the appearance of the *'strange shapes, bringing in a banquet'* that Ariel makes his great speech of accusation against the courtiers; and in the last scene Prospero remarks:

> I perceive these lords
> At this encounter do so much admire
> That they devour their reason, and scarce think
> Their eyes do offices of truth, their words
> Are natural breath. But, howsoe'er you have
> Been justled from your senses, know for certain
> That I am Prospero.
> V.1.153–9

To justle them from their senses has been part of his aim; but not all are responsive to this – just as Antonio and Sebastian had not responded to Ariel's sleep-inducing music. The cynical pair deny the wonder expressed by the perhaps over-credulous Gonzalo (for example, II.1 *passim*).

If Prospero resembles a spinner of romance tales, his daughter is even more clearly the ideal audience for such tales. Belarius (in *Cymbeline*) describes such a person:

> When on my three-foot stool I sit and tell
> The warlike feats I have done, his spirits fly out
> Into my story; say 'Thus mine enemy fell,
> And thus I set my foot on's neck'; even then
> The princely blood flows in his cheek, he sweats,
> Strains his young nerves, and puts himself in posture
> That acts my words.   III.3.89–95

Miranda too has all the open-mindedness, the willingness to be impressed, the capacity for wonder, that a story-teller could desire. She is all sympathy and eagerness to believe the best:

> O, I have suffered
> With those that I saw suffer! A brave vessel,
> Who had, no doubt, some noble creature in her,
> Dashed all to pieces.   I.2.5–8

Her first sight of Ferdinand arouses similar awe:

> I might call him
> A thing divine, for nothing natural
> I ever saw so noble.   I.2.418–20

And the climax comes as Miranda looks up from her game of chess and sees the assembled group:

> O, wonder!
> How many goodly creatures are there here!
> How beauteous mankind is! O brave new world,
> That has such people in't!   V.1.181–4

By this time in the play we know a number of these people rather well, and Miranda's innocence has a deep pathos, all the more pointed by Prospero's quiet comment, ''Tis new to thee'. But though Prospero's words provide an implied criticism of Miranda's attitude, they do nothing to destroy it. It is one of Shakespeare's greatest achievements that he can show the co-existence of opposed attitudes, making us aware of the tension between them but not forcing us to decide in favour of one or the other. Miranda's naïve innocence and Prospero's mature wisdom are both part of the truth; to counterpoint one against the other is to create a harmony that more than doubles the effect of each alone.[18]

Another quality typical of romance that Shakespeare might appear to have sacrificed by his decision to cast his play in an approximation to classical form is discursiveness: the provision of that 'variety of mirth and pastime' that Elizabethan romancers were so fond of advertising in their wares. But in fact he manages to cram a remarkable amount of material into this, the second shortest of his plays. He does so not by the multiplication of incident, the copiousness, the sheer length of many of his predecessors, but rather by an extraordinary multiplicity of suggestiveness – his power of creating a structure which looks different from every angle – his myriad-mindedness, as Coleridge put it. The enchanted island reverberates with sounds hinting at tunes that never appear fully formed. We can follow one strand through the work, but only by shutting our ears to the others; what we gain in line we lose in depth. It is this of course that has made the play so happy a hunting ground for the symbol-seekers. 'Any set of symbols moved close to this play', wrote Mark van Doren, 'lights up as in an electric field.'[19] Prospero has frequently been seen as a self-projection of the author; the notion has been handled sensibly and persuasively by some, less so by others. Most critics find themselves driven to speak of Prospero in terms other than those in which Shakespeare has written of him. For some he is God; for others, the imagination. One sees him as Hymen or a masque-presenter; another as 'the genius of poetry'; yet another as both 'a close replica of Christ' and 'a matured and fully self-conscious embodiment of those moments of fifth-act transcendental speculation to which earlier tragic heroes, including Macbeth, were unwillingly forced'.[20]

Criticism of this play has its excesses; but we must recognize that the variety of available interpretations is the result of its extraordinary suggestiveness. The play invites consideration on different levels. Partly this comes from the resonance of the verse, which often takes us far beyond the immediate situation. Intimately connected is the fact that the characters lack the strong individuality of some – though by no means all – leading figures of the great tragedies. Depth of characterization is not a normal feature of romance. Generally this is because the emphasis is on event. The figures of the story are conventionalized. What happens to them is more important than what they are. In *The Tempest* there is less emphasis on event; there is indeed less event; but the characters also are representative rather than individual. They are comparatively little distinguished by variety of style. Miranda is not a Viola, a Rosalind, or an Imogen. But though she may lack these girls' vibrantly immediate impact, she gains in representativeness. Being less of a particular time and place, she becomes more of all time and everywhere. In this context, actions the more easily take on a symbolical value. It is not necessary to go outside the play to see Ferdinand's log-carrying as an expression of a theme that crops up at many points. On a realistic level, it is no hardship for a healthy young man to spend a few hours carrying firewood; but any hint of this attitude in performance is ruinous. Ferdinand's task must appear as one of the complex of actions and statements connected with the idea of control; a complex that begins in the first scene where the voyaging noblemen are seen powerless against the force of (as it seems) nature; which is further adumbrated in Prospero's control over nature, over Ariel, and over Caliban; in Caliban's failure to achieve self-control; in the falsely based power that Stephano and Trinculo achieve over Caliban; in their joint attempt to overcome Prospero's authority, which parallels Sebastian's and Antonio's plot to kill Alonso, which itself parallels Antonio's and Alonso's earlier usurpation of Prospero; in Prospero's ability to conjure up the masque, and in the explicit themes of the masque itself, which are clearly related to the self-control that Prospero regards as so important in his future son-in-law; and finally in Prospero's ultimate renunciation of power. By a variety of juxtapositions, hints, and poetic devices, Shakespeare makes his romance story a carrier of what might be regarded as a scheme of ideas on a philosophical topic.

And he even introduces contemporary matters. It is not fanciful to see in the play a whole set of correspondences to what for its original audience was a burning question of the day – the matter of colonization; it is no accident that among the few accepted minor sources are pamphlets on voyaging. There is little explicit reference to the topic; but there is enough for us to be sure that it was present in Shakespeare's consciousness. Caliban complains against Prospero's enslavement of him; and there is a kind of justice in his complaint. We are shown the totally irreconcilable situation that arises when civilizations clash. It is parallel to the situation of Shylock and Portia; and though we cannot but feel that Shylock and Caliban must be overcome, yet we feel too something of the anguish involved in a complex moral impasse.

While the unreality of *The Tempest* contributes towards the play's high suggestive power, it would be false to suggest that the total effect is unreal. The first scene is in prose so vivid and colloquial that with a few changes it could stand in a television script. But the opening lines of the next scene suspend reality as we learn that the storm was the effect of Prospero's art, and for the remainder of the play the alternation and balance between the palpably unreal and the illusion of reality is maintained. The romance is toughened by a strain of anti-romance. The unrealistic idealism of Gonzalo is countered by the callous cynicism of Antonio and Sebastian – just as, for instance, Autolycus adds astringency to the pastoral scenes of *The Winter's Tale*. The virtue of Ferdinand and Miranda is not taken for granted; it is thrown into relief by what we know of Caliban, by his suggestions that Stephano should make Miranda his queen, and by the care with which Prospero guards the lovers' virtue. Even Prospero's own virtue is not without its strains. It is easy to lay too much emphasis on the scene in which Ariel recommends him to have mercy on his enemies; the style does not suggest severe internal struggle. Nevertheless, we are reminded that he might have taken vengeance, that the travellers are in fact his enemies. He does not bear his responsibilities lightly; he is one of Shakespeare's worried rulers, for whom the burden of power is greater than the rewards.

In ways such as these the vicissitudes commonly undergone by inhabitants of the world of romance come to be seen, not so much as random happenings that they survive by the help of fortune, as events designed to test and, during the course of the action, to define them. The play has a moral seriousness uncommon in most romance literature – though least uncommon, perhaps, in Shakespeare's greatest immediate predecessors, Sidney and Spenser. *The Tempest* is a romance containing a built-in criticism of romance; not a rejection of it, but an appreciation both of its glories and of its limitations. Romance is associated with all that brings man nearer to Ariel than to Caliban. Responsiveness to nature and to art, the capacity for wonder, the ability to sympathize with those that suffer, the desire to shape experience in accordance with an imaginative and moral vision, the value of an attitude to life that denies cynicism even to the extent of creating a somewhat naïve credulity such as Gonzalo's – all these are included. When art guides nature, when the civilizing forces of self-control are dominant, then Gonzalo's vision may be realized – a vision that looks forward to the masque:

> Earth's increase, foison plenty,
> Barns and garners never empty,
> Vines with clust'ring bunches growing,
> Plants with goodly burden bowing;
> Spring come to you at the farthest
> In the very end of harvest.
> Scarcity and want shall shun you,
> Ceres' blessing so is on you.   IV.1.110–17

It is indeed 'a most majestic vision', and it is fitting that it should be celebrated in the form of a masque-like performance enacted by the spirits over whom Prospero has power. This was the great age of the masque – nothing could have been more suitable as an image of the results that man can achieve by the exercise of mind and imagination. The masque was at once a symbol of power and wealth – frequently used as such in the Jacobean game of power politics – and also of the highest achievements of civilization, in which the arts of music, dancing, painting, acting, and poetry combined in entertainments whose splendour was enhanced by their folly. Many thousands of pounds were lavished upon a single evening's entertainment by those who could not command unpaid spirits to enact their fancies. Thus the masque was an apt symbol too of the vanity of human greatness. The glittering bubble is easily pricked. The visions of a Prospero are at the mercy of the Calibans of this world. Power that can create can also destroy, and so, when Prospero learns of the evil being plotted against him, the vision vanishes, leaving not a rack behind. Prospero's famous reaction is one of acceptance rather than mourning. Though he is momentarily angered, he controls himself and consoles Ferdinand. The dream is recognized for what it is, but allowed the reality that belongs even to a dream – or to any other product of the imagination – a play, poem, or romance.

The Tempest takes the familiar material of romance but adopts to it an attitude firmly though sympathetically judicious. The creations of the fancy are subjected to the scrutiny of the imagination; and they do not emerge unscathed. The ending thus disappoints those who ask for a full romantic climax. It is true that Prospero's forgiveness, though nominally extended to all, lacks warmth at any rate when he speaks to his brother Antonio:

> For you, most wicked sir, whom to call brother
> Would even infect my mouth, I do forgive
> Thy rankest fault.   V.i.130–32

But perhaps we should have the right to be disappointed by this only if Prospero had been presented as wholly superhuman. Since Antonio is not shown as penitent, it is not easy to see why Prospero should be expected so soon to show any warmth towards the man who had behaved to him somewhat as Macbeth had to Duncan. *The Tempest* is austere, and its final moments are muted; but it is not harsh in its total effect. Antonio's impenitence is balanced by Alonso's contrition; Prospero's world-weary emotional exhaustion by Gonzalo's ebullient recognition of the good that has come out of these events and also, in the younger generation, by the satisfactory conclusion of the love affair of Ferdinand and Miranda. If Caliban remains in bondage, he is at least temporarily the wiser for his folly; and after Prospero has taken care to ensure that the royal party will have

> calm seas, auspicious gales,
> And sail so expeditious, that shall catch
> Your royal fleet far off . . .

Ariel is finally freed to the elements. One might even see a touch of humour in this reversal of the play's opening situation.

It would seem then that though the two 'last plays' on which I have concentrated make more use of the conventions of romance literature than do some of the romantic comedies, their total effect is by no means unqualifiedly romantic. In discussing romantic aspects of earlier plays I have had to omit much. These plays are of course more comic than the romances; but they are also more romantic, in the sense that their attitude towards the conventions of romance is less critical. Feste may cast his shadow over the bridal couples at the end of *Twelfth Night*, and Jaques has his sardonic contribution to make to *As You Like It*; but the mature Leontes, Hermione, and Prospero need no external safeguards against illusion; and the young lovers in both *The Winter's Tale* and *The Tempest* are surrounded by older and wiser friends and relatives. The world of romance is both tested against reality and itself shown to be part of reality. The realization of the romance vision has involved suffering, self-discipline, even death. There is here none of the irresponsibility with which romance literature is often charged. But neither is there any of that portentousness with which it is only too easy to invest these plays. They are entertainments; that is to say, the response they demand is primarily imaginative.

The mood most characteristic of Shakespeare's later handling of romance material is perhaps one that fuses extremes of emotion. It can be felt in plays that are not predominantly romantic – in Cordelia's 'smiles and tears' on hearing news of her father, in Menenius's

> I could weep
> And I could laugh   II.1.174-5

when he welcomes home the victorious Coriolanus. In the romances, Pericles has to call on Helicanus to

Give me a gash ...
Lest this great sea of joys rushing upon me
O'erbear the shores of my mortality;   V.1.190–92

when Leontes and Polixenes were reunited, 'their joy waded in tears'; and every third thought of Prospero, his purpose accomplished, will be his grave. But more important than such formulations is the pervasiveness of this mood in the climaxes. These plays suggest a Shakespeare who has been able with clear eyes to contemplate extremes of imaginative experience. At the same time, each play has its own uniqueness; there is great variety within each, and within the romances as a group. Nothing is more indicative of the total control that Shakespeare maintained over his inherited material.

NOTES

1. The adjective, however, is not recorded before 1659.
2. M. Doran, *Endeavors of Art* (1954), page 172.
3. *An Aethiopian History.* Translated by Thomas Underdowne (1569). Edited by Charles Whibley and W. E. Henley (Tudor Translations, 1895), page 47 (modernized spelling).
4. op. cit., pages 181–2.
5. op. cit., page 288.
6. In 1600 Robert Chambers, a Roman Catholic priest, published a most curious book called *Palestina*, which adapts the events of the Gospels to the conventions of romance.
7. *The Anatomy of Absurdity*, edited by R. B. McKerrow, I.11.
8. E. C. Pettet, *Shakespeare and the Romance Tradition* (1949), page 12.
9. *The Use of Poetry and the Use of Criticism* (1933), page 51.
10. S. L. Wolff, *The Greek Romances in Elizabethan Prose Fiction* (1912), page 352.
11. J. F. Danby, *Poets on Fortune's Hill* (1952), pages 71 and 72.
12. *Elizabethan Taste* (1963), page 246.
13. W. H. Allen, *The English Novel* (1954), page 25.
14. Wolff studies this influence in immense detail. He is somewhat inclined to attribute any parallel between the romances and *Pandosto* to direct influence, without consideration of other writings that exhibit the same features. But he demonstrates

beyond question that *Pandosto* has much in common with these works.

15. The scholars took over from the chambermaids in the middle of the eighteenth century; the last references to the book as popular reading coincide closely with the beginning of interest in it as a Shakespeare source.

16. *The Winter's Tale* (new Arden Shakespeare, 1963), edited by J. H. P. Pafford, Introduction, page lxvi.

17. *On Some of Shakespeare's Female Characters*, New and Enlarged Edition (1891), pages 389–90.

18. Compare F. R. Leavis: 'Shakespeare's power to present acceptingly and movingly the unironical vision (for us given in Miranda and Ferdinand) goes with his power to contemplate the irony at the same time' ('The Criticism of Shakespeare's Late Plays: A Caveat', in *The Common Pursuit* (1952; Penguin Books 1962), page 180).

19. *Shakespeare* (1941), page 323.

20. Enid Welsford, *The Court Masque* (1927), page 339. D. G. James, *Scepticism and Poetry* (1937), page 240. G. Wilson Knight, 'The Shakespearian Superman', in *The Crown of Life* (1947 etc.), page 208.

from *Later Shakespeare* (Stratford-upon-Avon Studies 8, 1966), edited by J. R. Brown and Bernard Harris, pages 49–56 and 63–79

NINE

Shakespeare and the Blackfriars Theatre

G. E. Bentley

... So far, it has been my contention that all we know of William Shakespeare has shown him to be above all else a man of the theatre, that during the twenty years of his creative maturity most of his time was spent in closest association with members of the Lord Chamberlain-King's company and in thought about their needs and their interests, and that therefore in the affairs of this company we should seek one of the principal influences in his creative life. I have mentioned six events which (so far as we can tell through the mists of 350 years) seem to have been important in the affairs of that theatrical organization. These events are not all of equal importance, but each of them, except possibly the Essex rebellion, must have had a marked effect on the activities of Shakespeare's company and therefore on the dramatic creations of Shakespeare himself. Each one, it seems to me, deserves more study than it has received in its relation to the development of Shakespeare's work.

Let me invite your attention now to a fuller consideration of one of the most important of these events in the history of the Lord Chamberlain-King's company, namely the acquisition of the Blackfriars Theatre. What did this event mean in the history of the company, and how did it affect the writing of William Shakespeare?

Probably we should note first the time at which the Blackfriars would have begun to influence the company and the writings of Shakespeare. All the dramatic histories say that the King's Men took over the Blackfriars Theatre in 1608, and this is true in a legal sense, for on 9 August 1608 leases were executed conveying the Blackfriars Playhouse to seven lessees: Cuthbert Burbage, Thomas Evans, and five members of the King's company – John Heminges,

William Sly, Henry Condell, Richard Burbage, and William Shakespeare.[1] The few scholars who have examined in detail the history of the King's company have noted, however, that Shakespeare and his fellows probably did not begin to act at the Blackfriars in August of 1608. The plague was rife in London at that time; fifty plague deaths had been recorded for the week ending 28 July, and for a year and a half, or until December 1609, the bills of mortality show an abnormally high rate from the plague.[2] Though specific records about the closing of the theatres are not extant, we have definite statements that they were closed for part of this period, and comparison with other years suggests that there must have been very little if any public acting allowed in London between 1 August 1608 and the middle of December 1609. Therefore, it has occasionally been said, the Blackfriars was not used by the King's Men much before 1610, and no influence on their plays and their productions can be sought before that year.

This conclusion of little or no influence before 1610 is, I think, a false one. It is based on the erroneous assumption that the actors and playwrights of the King's company would have known nothing about the peculiarities of the Blackfriars and that they would have had no plays prepared especially for that theatre until after they had begun performing in it. Actors are never so stupid or so insular as this in any time. The King's Men, we may be sure, were well aware of the Blackfriars and the type of performance it required, or specialized in, long before they came to lease the theatre. There must be many evidences of this, but three in particular come readily to mind.

Seven years before, in 1601, the King's Men had been involved in the War of the Theatres, which was in part a row between the public theatres and the private theatres. The chief attack on the public theatres and adult actors was made in Jonson's *Poetaster*, performed at the Blackfriars. Certain actors of the Lord Chamberlain's company, and possibly Shakespeare himself, were ridiculed in this Blackfriars play. The reply, *Satiromastix*, was written by Thomas Dekker and performed by Shakespeare's company at the Globe.[3] Certainly in 1601 at least, the company was well aware of the goings on at Blackfriars.

A second piece of evidence pointing to their knowledge of the peculiar requirements of the Blackfriars is the case of Marston's *Malcontent*. Marston wrote this play for the boys at the Blackfriars, who performed it in that theatre in 1604. The King's Men stole the play, as they admitted, and performed it at the Globe; the third edition, also 1604, shows the alterations they commissioned John Webster to make in order to adapt a Blackfriars script to a Globe performance, and in the induction to the play Richard Burbage, speaking in his own person, points out one or two of the differences between Blackfriars requirements and Globe requirements.[4]

Finally, and most familiar of all evidence that the King's Men were quite alive to what went on at Blackfriars, is the 'little eyases' passage in *Hamlet* and Shakespeare's rueful admission that, for a time at any rate, the competition of the Blackfriars was too much for the company at the Globe.

Clearly the King's Men did not have to wait until their performances of 1610 at the Blackfriars to know how their plays needed to be changed to fit them to that theatre and its select audience. They had known for several years what the general characteristics of Blackfriars performances were. Indeed, the leading member of the company, Richard Burbage, had a double reason for being familiar with all the peculiarities of the Blackfriars, for since his father's death in 1597 he had been the owner of the theatre and the landlord of the boy company that made it famous.[5] We can be perfectly sure, then, that from the day of the first proposal that the King's Men take over the Blackfriars they had talked among themselves about what they would do with it and had discussed what kinds of plays they would have to have written to exploit it. It is all too often forgotten that in all such discussions among the members of the King's company William Shakespeare would have had an important part. He had more kinds of connexions with the company than any other man: he was actor, shareholder, patented member, principal playwright, and one of the housekeepers of the Globe; even Burbage did not serve so many functions in the company. Few men in theatrical history have been so completely and inextricably bound up with the affairs of an acting troupe.

When would the King's Men have begun planning for their performances at the Blackfriars? We cannot, of course, set the exact date, but we can approximate it. There is one faint suggestion that consideration of the project may have started very early indeed. Richard Burbage said that Henry Evans, who had leased the theatre from him for the Children of the Queen's Revels, began talking to him about the surrender of his lease in 1603 or 1604.[6] These early discussions evidently came to nothing for we know that the boys continued in the theatre for three or four years longer. Burbage's statement about Evans does suggest the interesting possibility that the King's Men may have dallied with the project of leasing the Blackfriars Theatre as early as 1603 or 1604. This, however, is only the faintest of possibilities. The Blackfriars was tentatively in the market then, but all we know is that Burbage had to consider for a short time the possibility of getting other tenants for his theatre. Whether the King's Men came to his mind and theirs as possible tenants, we do not know.

We can be sure that active planning for performances at the Blackfriars did get under way when Burbage, who was both the leading actor of the King's Men and owner of the Blackfriars Theatre, knew for certain that the boy actors would give up their lease and that arrangements for a syndicate of King's Men to take over the theatre could be made. Conferences among these men– the Burbages, Heminges, Condell, Shakespeare, and Sly – and probably preliminary financial arrangements would have been going on before a scrivener was called in to draw up a rough draft of the lease. Such preliminaries, which must come before a lease can be formally signed, often consume months. We know that the leases were formally executed on 9 August 1608[7]; therefore discussions in June and July or even in April and May are likely enough. We know that the Blackfriars Theatre was available as early as March 1608, for in a letter dated 11 March 1608 Sir Thomas Lake officially notified Lord Salisbury that the company of the Children of Blackfriars must be suppressed and that the King had vowed that they should never act again even if they had to beg their bread. General confirmation of this fact is found in a letter written two weeks later by the French ambassador.[8] Thus it is evident that in

March of 1608 Richard Burbage knew his theatre was without a tenant. March to July 1608, then, are the months for discussions among the King's Men of prospective performances at the Black-friars.

What did this little group of Shakespeare and his intimate associates of the last fourteen years work out during their discussions in the months of March to July 1608? One of the things they must have considered was alterations of their style of acting. As Granville-Barker has pointed out,[9] the acting in the new Black-friars before a sophisticated audience would have to be more quiet than in the large open-air Globe before the groundlings. It would be easier to emphasize points in the quiet candlelit surroundings, and 'sentiment would become as telling as passion'. There must also have been extended discussions of what to do about the reper-tory: which of the company's plays would be suitable for the elegant new theatre and which should be kept for the old audience at the Globe? Some of their decisions are fairly obvious. *Muce-dorus*, which Rafe in *The Knight of the Burning Pestle* says he had played before the Wardens of his company and which went through fifteen editions before the Restoration, was clearly one of the Globe plays which might be laughed at by a Blackfriars audience. Similarly, *The Merry Devil of Edmonton* was not a good Blackfriars prospect. Certain other plays in the repertory might be expected to please at the Blackfriars; Marston's *Malcontent*, for instance, could easily be changed back to its original Blackfriars form, and Jonson's *Every Man in His Humour* and *Every Man out of His Humour*, though nine and ten years old, had been played by the company at court in the last three years and ought to be suitable for the Blackfriars.

These discussions of the old repertory, though no doubt important to the company then, are fruitless for us now. I know of no evidence as to their decisions. More important are the proposals for new plays for the Blackfriars, and I think we do have some evidence as to what these decisions were. The experienced members of the King's company were familiar with the fact so commonly recorded in the annals of the Jacobean theatre that new plays were in constant demand. With the acquisition of the new theatre they had an opportunity to claim for their own the most profitable audience in London. We know from the later Jacobean and Caroline records that this is just what they did.[10] It seems likely that one of the foundations of their later unquestioned dominance of the audiences of the gentry was their decision about plays and playwrights made in their discussions of March to July 1608.

One of their decisions, I suggest, was to get Jonson to write Blackfriars plays for them. He was a likely choice for three reasons. First, because he was developing a following among the courtly audience (always prominent at the Blackfriars) by his great court masques. At this time he had already written his six early entertainments for King James – those at the Coronation, at the Opening of Parliament, at Althorp, at Highgate, and the two at Theobalds. He had written for performance at Whitehall *The Masque of Blackness*, *The Masque of Beauty*, *Hymenaei*, and the famous *Lord Haddington's Masque*. The sensational success of these courtly entertainments made Jonson a most promising choice to write plays for the courtly audience which the King's Men did succeed in attracting to Blackfriars.

A second reason which would have led the King's Men to Jonson as a writer for their new theatre was his great reputation among the literati and critics. In this decade from 1601 to 1610 the literary allusions to him are numerous, more numerous than to Shakespeare himself. The poems to Jonson and the long prose passages about him in this time are far more frequent than to Shakespeare; quotations from his work occur oftener, and I find three times as many literary and social references to performances of his plays and masques as to Shakespeare's. Poems about him or references to his work are written in these years by John Donne, Sir John Roe, Sir Dudley Carleton, the Venetian ambassador, John Chamberlain, Sir Thomas Lake, Sir George Buc, Sir Thomas Salusbury.[11] This is just the kind of audience which might be attracted to the Blackfriars, and which, eventually, the King's Men did attract there.

There was a third reason which would have made Jonson seem to the King's Men a very likely bet for their new theatre: he had already had experience in writing plays for this theatre when it was occupied by boys. Before the conferences of the King's Men about their new project he had already had performed at Blackfriars *Cynthia's Revels*, *The Poetaster*, *The Case Is Altered*, and *Eastward Ho*. Possibly just before the time of the conferences of the King's Men he had been writing for the Blackfriars another play, *Epicoene*, for he says in the Folio of 1616 that the play was performed by the Children of Blackfriars, but the date he gives for performance comes after their expulsion from the Blackfriars Theatre. Not only had Jonson had the valuable experience of writing four or five plays for the Blackfriars, but the Induction to *Cynthia's Revels* and his personal statements about boys of the company, like Nathan Field and Salathiel, or Solomon, Pavy,[12] strongly suggest that he had directed them in their rehearsals. What valuable experience for the King's Men planning their first performance in this new theatre!

Now all these qualifications of Jonson as a prospect for the King's Men are, in sober fact, only speculations. Perhaps they simply show that if *I* had been participating in the conferences about the Blackfriars I should have argued long and lustily for Ben Jonson. Alas, I was not there! What evidence is there that they really did agree to secure his services for the company? The evidence is that before these conferences he had written only four plays for the Lord Chamberlain's or King's company – three, nine, and ten years before – nothing for the company in the years 1605–8. After these conferences, he wrote all his remaining plays for the company, with the exception of *Bartholomew Fair* six years later, a play which he gave to his good friend and protégé Nathan Field for the Lady Elizabeth's company at the Hope, and *A Tale of a Tub*, twenty-five years later, which he gave to Queen Henrietta's men. Jonson's first play after the reopening of Blackfriars was *The Alchemist*; it was written for the King's Men, and numerous allusions show clearly that it was written for Blackfriars. So were *Catiline*, *The Devil Is an Ass*, *The Staple of News*, *The New Inn*, and *The Magnetic Lady*. Of course we lack the final proof of recorded reference to a definite agreement, but the evidence is such as to suggest that one of the decisions reached by the King's Men in the reorganization of their enterprise to exploit the great advantages of their new theatre was to secure the services of Ben Jonson to write plays for the literate and courtly audience at Blackfriars.

Another decision, which I suggest the King's Men made at these conferences, was to secure for their new theatre the services of the rising young collaborators, Francis Beaumont and John Fletcher. These gentlemen were younger than Jonson by about ten years, and as yet their reputations were distinctly inferior to his, but they had already displayed those talents which were to make their plays the stage favourites at Blackfriars for the next thirty-four years,[13] and were to cause Dryden to say sixty years later that 'their plays are now the most pleasant and frequent entertainments of the stage'.

One of the great assets of Beaumont and Fletcher was social. In the years immediately before and after 1608, the London theatre audience was developing the social cleavage which is such a marked characteristic of the Jacobean and Caroline drama and stage. In Elizabeth's time the London theatre was a universal one, in which a single audience at the Globe could embrace Lord Monteagle, Sir Charles Percy, city merchants, lawyers, Inns of Court students, apprentices, servants, beggars, pickpockets, and prostitutes. The later Jacobean and Caroline audience was a dual one. The gentry, the court, the professional classes, and the Inns of Court men went to the Blackfriars, the Phoenix, and later to the Salisbury Court; the London masses went to the larger and noisier Red Bull and Fortune and Globe. This new state of affairs was just developing when the King's Men had their conferences about the Blackfriars in 1608. They evidently saw what was coming, however, for in the next few years they understood and exploited the situation more effectively than any other troupe in London. Indeed, the very acquisition of the Blackfriars and its operation in conjunction with the Globe was a device which had never been tried before in London and which is the clearest evidence that the King's Men knew just what was happening.

Under these circumstances, then, the social status of Beaumont and Fletcher was an asset for the company in their new house. Francis Beaumont came of an ancient and distinguished Leicester-shire family, with many connexions among the nobility. John

Fletcher was the son of a Lord Bishop of London and one-time favourite of Elizabeth. To a Blackfriars audience the social standing of these two young men would have been more acceptable than that of any other dramatist writing in London in 1608.

Another asset which made Beaumont and Fletcher valuable for the new enterprise of the King's Men was their private theatre experience. So far as we can make out now, all their plays before this time had been written for private theatres and most of them for the Blackfriars. *The Woman Hater* had been prepared for the private theatre in St Paul's, but *The Knight of the Burning Pestle*, *The Scornful Lady*, and *The Faithful Shepherdess* were Blackfriars plays. I think we can add to this list *Cupid's Revenge*. This play has been variously dated, but two forthcoming articles by James Savage[14] seem to me to offer convincing evidence that the play was prepared for Blackfriars about 1607 and that it displays a crude preliminary working out of much of the material which made *Philaster* one of the great hits of its time and one of the most influential plays of the seventeenth century. In any event, Beaumont and Fletcher were among the most experienced Blackfriars playwrights available in 1608. It is true that in 1608 none of their plays had been a great success; indeed the two best, *The Knight of the Burning Pestle* and *The Faithful Shepherdess*, are known to have been unsuccessful at first. The King's Men, however, were experienced in the ways of the theatre; it does not seem rash to assume that at least one of them knew enough about audiences and about dramatic talents to see that these young men were writers of brilliant promise – especially since that one was William Shakespeare.

Beaumont and Fletcher, then, because of their experience and social standing were very desirable dramatists for the King's Men to acquire in 1608 for their new private theatre. What is the evidence that they did acquire them? The evidence is that all the Beaumont and Fletcher plays of the next few years are King's Men's plays, several of them famous hits – *Philaster*, *The Maid's Tragedy*, *A King and No King*, *The Captain*, *The Two Noble Kinsmen*, *Bonduca*, *Monsieur Thomas*, *Valentinian*. The dating of many of the Beaumont and Fletcher plays is very uncertain because of their late publication, and it may be that two or three of the later plays were written for other companies, but at least forty-five plays by Beaumont and Fletcher were the property of the Jacobean and Caroline King's Men.[15] None of their plays before 1608, when Blackfriars was acquired, was, so far as we can find, written for the King's Men. It seems a reasonable assumption, therefore, that another of the policies agreed upon at the conferences of 1608 was to secure the services of Beaumont and Fletcher for the company in its new enterprise at the Blackfriars.

The third of these three important changes in policy which I think the King's Men agreed upon at their conferences about the new Blackfriars enterprise in 1608 is the most interesting of all to us, but it was the easiest and most obvious of them. Indeed, it may well have been assumed almost without discussion. It was, of course, that William Shakespeare should write henceforth with the Blackfriars in mind and not the Globe.

Why was this decision an easy and obvious one? The company could assume, of course, that he would continue to write for them, since he was a shareholder and a patented member of the company and a housekeeper in both their theatres. Since the formation of the company, fourteen years before, all his plays had been written for performance by them, always, in the last ten years, for performance at the Globe. All his professional associations as well as his financial ones were with this company, and probably no one in the group even considered his defection. Burbage, Shakespeare, Heminges, and Condell were the real nucleus of the organization.

This new enterprise at the Blackfriars was a very risky business. As we have noted, no adult company had ever tried to run a private theatre before. The King's Men not only proposed to make a heavy investment in this new departure, but they intended to continue running their old public theatre at the same time. Every possible precaution against failure needed to be taken. One such precaution would be the devotion of Shakespeare's full-time energies to the Blackfriars instead of the Globe. They could trust Shakespeare; he knew their potentialities and their shortcomings as no other dramatist did – indeed, few dramatists in the history of the English theatre have ever had such a long and intimate association with an acting company as William Shakespeare had had with these men. If anybody knew what Burbage and Heminges and Condell and Robert Armyn and Richard Cowley could do on the stage and what they should not be asked to do, that man was William Shakespeare. He could make them a success at the Blackfriars as they had been at the Globe if anyone could.

Another reason for the transfer of Shakespeare's efforts was the fact that the Globe could be left to take care of itself with an old repertory as the Blackfriars could not. For one thing, there was no old repertory for the Blackfriars, since the departing boys appear to have held on to their old plays. For another thing, it was the Blackfriars audience which showed the greater avidity for new plays; the public theatre audiences were much more faithful to old favourites. They were still playing *Friar Bacon and Friar Bungay* at the Fortune in 1630 and Marlowe's *Edward II* at the Red Bull in 1620 and *Dr Faustus* at the Fortune in 1621 and *Richard II* and *Pericles* at the Globe in 1631.[16] In the archives of the Globe at this time there must have been a repertory of more than a hundred plays, including at least twenty-five of Shakespeare's. Moreover, certain plays written for the Globe in the last few years, like Wilkins's *Miseries of Enforced Marriage* and the anonymous *Yorkshire Tragedy* and *The Fair Maid of Bristol* and *The London Prodigal*, had provided playwrights who might be expected to entertain a Globe audience with more of the same fare, but who could scarcely come up to the requirements of sophistication at Blackfriars. Altogether, then, the Globe repertory had much less need of Shakespeare's efforts in 1608 than did the Blackfriars repertory.

Why should Shakespeare have wanted to write for the Blackfriars, or at least have agreed to do so? The most compelling of the apparent reasons is that he had money invested in the project and stood to lose by its failure and gain by its success. He was one of the seven lessees of the new theatre; he had paid down an unknown sum and had agreed to pay £5 14s. 4d. per year in rent.[17] He had at least a financial reason for doing everything he could to establish the success of the Blackfriars venture, and what Shakespeare could do most effectively was to write plays which would insure the company's popularity with the audience in its new private theatre.

A third reason for this postulated decision of the King's Men in 1608 to have Shakespeare devote his entire attention to the Blackfriars and abandon the Globe was that the King's Men saw that the real future of the theatrical profession in London lay with the court and the court party in the private theatres. Their receipts for performances at court showed them this very clearly. In the last nine years of Elizabeth, 1594–1602, they had received from court performances an average of £35 a year; in the first five years of the reign of the new king, 1603–7, they had averaged £131 per year in addition to their new allowances for liveries as servants of the King.[18] The Blackfriars and not the Globe was the theatre where they could entertain this courtly audience with commercial performances. There is no doubt that in the next few years after 1608 the Blackfriars did become the principal theatre of the company. In 1612 Edward Kirkham said they took £1,000 a winter more at the Blackfriars than they had formerly taken at the Globe.[19] When Sir Henry Herbert listed receipts from the two theatres early in the reign of King Charles, the receipts for single performances at the Globe averaged £6 13s. 8d.; those for single performances at the Blackfriars averaged £15 15s., or about two and one half times as much.[20] In 1634 an Oxford don who wrote up the company simply called them the company of the Blackfriars and did not mention the Globe at all[21]; when the plays of the company were published in the Jacobean and Caroline period, the Blackfriars was mentioned as their theatre more than four times as often as the Globe was.[22] Such evidence proves that the Blackfriars certainly did become the principal theatre of the King's Men. I am suggesting that in the conferences of 1608 the King's Men had some intimation that it would, and accordingly they persuaded William Shakespeare to devote his attention to that theatre in the future instead of to the Globe.

So much for the reasons that Shakespeare might be expected to change the planning of his plays in 1608. What is the evidence that he did? The evidence, it seems to me, is to be seen in *Cymbeline*, *The Winter's Tale*, *The Tempest*, and *The Two Noble Kinsmen*, and probably it was to be seen also in the lost play, *Cardenio*. The variations which these plays show from the Shakespearian norm have long been a subject for critical comment. The first three of them in particular, since they are the only ones which have been universally accepted as part of the Shakespeare canon, have commonly been discussed as a distinct genre. Widely as critics and scholars have disagreed over the reasons for their peculiar characteristics, those peculiarities have generally been recognized, whether the plays are called Shakespeare's Romances, or Shakespeare's Tragi-Comedies, or his Romantic Tragi-Comedies, or simply the plays of the fourth period. No competent critic who has read carefully through the Shakespeare canon has failed to notice that there is something different about *Cymbeline*, *The Winter's Tale*, *The Tempest*, and *The Two Noble Kinsmen*.

When critics and scholars have tried to explain this difference between the plays of the last period and Shakespeare's earlier work, they have set up a variety of hypotheses. Most of these hypotheses have in common only the trait which I noted at the beginning of this paper – namely, they agree in considering Shakespeare as the professional poet and not the professional playwright. They turn to Shakespeare's sources, or to his inspiration, or to his personal affairs, or to the bucolic environment of his Stratford retirement, but not to the theatre which was his daily preoccupation for more than twenty years. Dowden called this late group in the Shakespeare canon 'On the Heights', because he thought the plays reflected Shakespeare's new-found serenity.[23] Such a fine optimism had, perhaps, something to recommend it to the imaginations of the Victorians, but to modern scholars it seems to throw more light on Dowden's mind than on Shakespeare's development. Dowden's explanation seemed utterly fatuous to Lytton Strachey, who thought that the plays of 'Shakespeare's Final Period' were written by a Shakespeare far from serene, who was really 'half enchanted by visions of beauty and loveliness and half bored to death'.[24] Violently as Dowden and Strachey differ, they agree in seeking subjective interpretations.

Best known of the old explanations of the peculiarities of the plays of this last period is probably Thorndike's[25]: the contention that the great success of *Philaster* caused Shakespeare to imitate it in *Cymbeline* and to a lesser extent in *The Winter's Tale* and *The Tempest*. In spite of the great horror of the Shakespeare idolaters at the thought of the master imitating superficial young whipper-snappers like Beaumont and Fletcher, no one can read the two plays together without noting the striking similarities between them. The difficulty is that although the approximate dates of the two plays are clear enough, their *precise* dates are so close together and so uncertain that neither Thorndike nor any subsequent scholar has been able to prove that *Philaster* came before *Cymbeline*, and the Shakespeare idolaters have been equally unable to prove that *Cymbeline* came before *Philaster*.

I suggest that the really important point is not the priority of either play. The significant and revealing facts are that both were written for the King's company; both were written, or at least completed, after the important decision made by the leaders of the troupe in the spring of 1608 to commission new plays for Black-friars, and both were prepared to be acted in the private theatre in Blackfriars before the sophisticated audience attracted to that house. It is their common purpose and environment, not imitation of one by the other, which makes them similar. Both *Philaster* and *Cymbeline* are somewhat like Beaumont and Fletcher's earlier plays, especially *Cupid's Revenge*, because Beaumont and Fletcher's earlier plays had all been written for private theatres and all but one for Blackfriars. Both *Philaster* and *Cymbeline* are unlike Shakespeare's earlier plays because none of those plays had been written for private theatres. The subsequent plays of both Beaumont and Fletcher and Shakespeare resemble *Philaster* and *Cymbeline* because they too were written to be performed by the King's Men before the sophisticated and courtly audience in the private theatre at Blackfriars.

So much I think we can say with some assurance. This explanation of the character of Shakespeare's last plays is in accord with the known facts of theatrical history; it accords with the bio-graphical evidence of Shakespeare's long and close association with all the enterprises of the Lord Chamberlain's-King's Men for twenty years; it is in accord with his fabulously acute sense of the theatre and the problems of the actor; and it does no violence to his artistic integrity or to his poetic genius.

May I add one further point much more in the realm of speculation? Since John Fletcher became a playwright for the King's Men at this time and continued so for the remaining seventeen years of his life, and since the activities of the King's Men had been one of Shakespeare's chief preoccupations for many years, is it not likely that the association between Fletcher and Shakespeare from 1608 to 1614 was closer than has usually been thought? Shakespeare was nearing retirement; after 1608 he wrote plays less frequently than before; Fletcher became his successor as chief dramatist for the King's company. In these years they collaborated in *The Two Noble Kinsmen*, *Henry VIII*, and probably in *Cardenio*. Is it too fantastic to suppose that Shakespeare was at least an adviser in the preparation of *Philaster*, *A King and No King*, and *The Maid's Tragedy* for his fellows? Is it even more fantastic to think that Shakespeare, the old public theatre playwright, preparing his first and crucial play for a private theatre, might have asked advice – or even taken it – from the two young dramatists who had written plays for this theatre and audience four or five times before?

Perhaps this is going too far. I do not wish to close on a note of speculation. My basic contention is that Shakespeare was, before all else, a man of the theatre and a devoted member of the King's company. One of the most important events in the history of that company was its acquisition of the Blackfriars Playhouse in 1608 and its subsequent brilliantly successful exploitation of its stage and audience. The company was experienced and theatre-wise; the most elementary theatrical foresight demanded that in 1608 they prepare new and different plays for a new and different theatre and audience. Shakespeare was their loved and trusted fellow. How could they fail to ask him for new Blackfriars plays, and how could he fail them? All the facts at our command seem to me to demonstrate that he did not fail them. He turned from his old and tested methods and produced a new kind of play for the new theatre and audience. Somewhat unsurely at first he wrote *Cymbeline* for them, then, with greater dexterity in his new medium, *The*

Winter's Tale, and finally, triumphant in his old mastery, *The Tempest*.

NOTES

1. E. K. Chambers, *The Elizabethan Stage* (4 vols., 1923), Volume 2, pages 509–10. Technically Richard Burbage leased one seventh of the theatre to each of the other six.

2. op. cit., Volume 4, page 351.

3. See J. H. Penniman, *The War of the Theatres* (1897), and R. A. Small, *The Stage Quarrel* (1899).

4. F. L. Lucas, *The Works of John Webster* (4 vols., 1927), Volume 3, pages 294–309.

5. J. Q. Adams, *Shakespearean Playhouses* (1917), pages 199–223.

6. The Answers of Heminges and Burbage to Edward Kirkham, 1612, printed by F. G. Fleay, *A Chronicle History of the London Stage* (1890), page 235.

7. E. K. Chambers, *William Shakespeare* (2 vols., 1930), Volume 2, pages 62–3.

8. *The Elizabethan Stage*, Volume 2, pages 53–4.

9. *Prefaces to Shakespeare*, Second Series (1930), pages 249–50.

10. See Bentley, *The Jacobean and Caroline Stage* (6 vols., 1941), Volume 1, Chapter 1 *passim*; Volume 2, pages 673–81.

11. See Bentley, *Shakespeare and Jonson* (2 vols., 1945), Volume 1, pages 38–41, 65–7, 73–9, 87–90, and J. F. Bradley and J. Q. Adams, *The Jonson Allusion-Book* (1922), *passim*.

12. See 'A Good Name Lost', *Times Literary Supplement* (30 May 1942), page 267.

13. *The Jacobean and Caroline Stage*, Volume 1, pages 29 and 109–14.

14. 'The Date of Beaumont and Fletcher's *Cupid's Revenge*', *ELH* 15 (1948), and 'Beaumont and Fletcher's *Philaster* and Sidney's *Arcadia*', *ELH* 14 (1947).

15. *The Jacobean and Caroline Stage*, Volume 1, pages 109–15.

16. op. cit., Volume 1, pages 156, 174, 157, 24, 129.

17. *Shakespearean Playhouses*, pages 224–5.

18. *The Elizabethan Stage*, Volume 4, pages 164–75.

19. C. W. Wallace, *University of Nebraska Studies* 8 (1908), pages 36–7, note 6.

20. *The Jacobean and Caroline Stage*, Volume 1, pages 23–4.

21. op. cit., Volume 1, page 26, note 5.

22. op. cit., Volume 1, page 30, note 1.
23. Edward Dowden, *Shakspere: His Mind and Art* (1875).
24. Lytton Strachey, 'Shakespeare's Final Period', in *Books and Characters* (1906).
25. Ashley H. Thorndike, *The Influence of Beaumont and Fletcher on Shakespeare* (1901).

from *Shakespeare Survey 1* (1948), pages 40–49

TEN

Shakespeare and the Court Masque

Allardyce Nicoll

SOME inquiries into literary problems, however significant their results may be, can possess no more than an academic interest: they are of importance to, and perhaps can be understood only by, specialists. Other inquiries are of more extensive appeal and value because they have a direct bearing upon matters affecting a more general public, and obviously within this sphere questions relating to the drama and the theatre, since the stage and what is presented on the stage are of peculiarly wide import, offer special opportunities for the exploration of themes likely to prove of both practical and academic significance.

I

Among the stage problems relating to Shakespeare one is especially important. During recent years the 'last' plays – *The Winter's Tale*, *The Tempest*, *Cymbeline*, even *Pericles* – have been attracting more and more public and specialist attention; during recent years in many countries productions of these dramas have become much more numerous than in the past. For the most part such productions have tended to be spectacularly magnificent, and it is quite clear that this magnificence has been inspired by a belief that in writing his final works Shakespeare had scenic adornments in mind. Even those who are prepared to admit that a *Hamlet* or a *Twelfth Night* may best be displayed on a simple set stage demand rich scenic spectacle in the romances, precisely because, they think or declare, the author planned them so. Inigo Jones's masque designs have now become familiar,[1] and there has been a marked tendency among stage decorators to present these dramas either in an 'Inigo Jones' style or in the style of what may be regarded as today's equivalent of the seventeenth-century masque, the modern ballet.

In view of this trend and of its general import, it may be profitable to consider briefly the grounds for the belief that the masque thus influenced Shakespeare at the end of his career. Perhaps there is not much more useful to be done on the larger question of the impress laid by the masque, early and late, upon his writings; that subject has been sufficiently explored; but this particular aspect of the larger theme, the supposition that, after Inigo Jones had startled the Jacobean courtiers by his stage machinery, Shakespeare planned his latest dramas in a manner different from that of his other works, does deserve re-examination.

2

The belief itself, of course, basically starts with the assumption – commonly stated as though it were a fact – that these romances were written for the indoor Blackfriars Theatre at which Shakespeare's company began to act in 1610. Since the assumption has had a good deal of scholarly support, perhaps it may prove salutary, at the very start, to stress that all the available evidence is either completely negative or else runs directly counter to such a supposition. The first Quarto of *Pericles* (1609) specifically states that that play had been 'diuers and sundry times acted . . . at the Globe on the Banck-side'; it was 'at the glob' that Simon Forman saw *The Winter's Tale* on 15 May 1611, and, although he did not definitely name the theatre, he probably saw *Cymbeline* there as well during the preceding month. For *The Tempest* no evidence is forthcoming, but we know that when the first Globe went up in flames on 29 June 1613 *Henry VIII* was the play being presented. Except for the debatable *The Two Noble Kinsmen*, issued eighteen years after Shakespeare's death as by him and Fletcher and as 'presented at the Blackfriars', we have thus absolutely no justification whatsoever for associating Shakespeare with the Blackfriars at all – and even *The Two Noble Kinsmen* presents an element of doubt since a title-page ascription of 1634 need not necessarily apply to the original production of the play. Professor Gerald Bentley has suggested[2] that when, about 1608, the King's Men planned occupancy of this theatre Shakespeare, as dramatist-in-chief, would have been asked by his fellows to prepare some new plays in a style fitting a type of stage with which these actors had not previously had experience: the hypothesis is an attractive one; but it is just as probable that, when the second theatre came into use, he elected to continue his efforts at the Globe, the scene of his greatest successes. The blunt truth is that we simply cannot tell, although the weight of documentary evidence, such as it is, inclines against the commonly held belief and towards the supposition that his affiliations remained to the end with his company's older playhouse.

3

Even, however, if we do opine that Shakespeare wrote some of his last plays for the Blackfriars, we are still faced by a serious difficulty. The usual assumption is that the Blackfriars, being a roofed building and appealing to a better-class public, was fitted for the display of scenic effects impossible of achievement at the Globe and that these scenic effects were modelled largely on the settings of the contemporary court masques. Now, while it is true that a few stage-directions in plays from 1611 onwards do tentatively suggest that occasionally some set-pieces may have been introduced on the professional stage during the second decade of the seventeenth century, such evidence as there is neither gives any authority for a belief that the King's Men utilized stage decorations when they started playing at the Blackfriars in 1610 nor contradicts other later evidence which seems to prove definitely that 'scenes' (in the sense of complete settings) entered the London theatres for the first time during the twenties and thirties of the century. Fundamentally, it is true, scholars are agreed about this; but unfortunately some of them, in their enthusiasm, have allowed themselves by implication or even directly to suggest the opposite or to give hints of a misleading kind liable to create a false impression. An early statement by A. H. Thorndike,[3] for example, to the effect that in *The Tempest* there was 'an effort to satisfy the craving for spectacular novelties' was later expanded by this author into a statement concerning the same play that

On the Elizabethan stage, as in all subsequent eras, its performance must have been spectacular ... Doubtless even in Blackfriars the Enchanted Island was given a setting to capture the eye as well as the fancy of the spectator.[4]

For such a suggestion, as has been indicated, there is positively no basis in proof.

With this may be taken a further statement by Professor T. M. Parrott:

Even though Forman saw *The Winter's Tale* at the Globe in May, there can be no doubt that the play was written for Blackfriars and shifted to the Globe when, in the warm spring weather, the actors returned to their open-air playhouse. Even if there were no other reason, the last scene of *The Winter's Tale*, the unveiling of the statue, was evidently planned for the indoor theatre where the possibility of brilliant lighting on the inner stage of a darkened house would make the discovery most effective.[5]

No comment need be made regarding the wholly unsupported remark about the playhouse for which *The Winter's Tale* was written; but we may well draw attention to a basic fallacy in the speculation concerning the statue scene. There was no 'brilliant lighting' in the early theatres: the sole means of illumination was by candlelight. No doubt the playhouses were all a-spangle and a-glitter; but if we may judge from what we know of the Restoration theatres, the auditorium was probably as fully lit as the stage. Presumably it would have been possible, in the statue scene, to place concealed vertical strips of candles at each side of Hermione; but such a device may hardly be called 'brilliant lighting', nor is it permissible either to postulate the use of the device itself as a certainty or to assume that Shakespeare penned his scene with such a theatrical prospect in view.

4

Amid all this unsubstantiated speculation there is one clear fact and one strong probability. The fact is that the Jacobean masque was ushered in at Whitehall by Ben Jonson's *The Masque of Blackness* on 1 January 1605; and the probability is that Shakespeare, as one

of that group of King's Servants responsible for dramatic performances at court, would have been able to see some at least of the
similar productions which extended through *Hymenaei* (1606), *The
Masque of Beauty* (1608), *Hue and Cry after Cupid* (1608) and *The
Masque of Queens* (1609) on to *Oberon* (1611). The questions arise:
what impact did these have on his mind and what use, if any, did he
make of them?

More than half a century ago, A. H. Thorndike sought to demonstrate that the dance of satyrs in *The Winter's Tale* was taken from
the masque of *Oberon*.[6] After pointing out the kinship of the
episodes in masque and play, he emphasized the significance of the
Servant's words in the latter:

> Master, there is three carters, three shepherds, three neat-herds,
> three swine-herds, that have made themselves all men of hair. . . . One
> three of them, by their own report, sir, hath danced before the King.
> IV.4.322–4, 334–5

It is Thorndike's contention that use was here being made on the
professional stage both of the dance itself and of three among the
original performers. It may be so; but perhaps attention should be
called to a textual peculiarity in this scene which raises at least a
slight element of doubt. At the sheep-shearing festival Dorcas,
Mopsa, and Autolycus have just sung the first stanza of a 'passing
merry' ballad; we now know that there was a second stanza to
this,[7] but in the play the Clown interrupts:

> We'll have this song out anon by ourselves: my father and the gent-
> lemen are in sad talk, and we'll not trouble them IV.4.307–9

whereupon he and the girls go out, while Autolycus leaves the
stage with his

> Will you buy any tape,
> Or lace for your cape,
> My dainty duck, my dear-a? IV.4.313–15

We might well have expected this exit to be the cue for Polixenes's
words to the Shepherd:

> O, father, you'll know more of that hereafter IV.4.340

and for his following lines addressed to Camillo:

> Is it not too far gone? 'Tis time to part them.

This is, in fact, the conclusion of the 'sad talk' to which the Clown refers. Rather to our surprise, however, the going out of the Clown and Autolycus is separated from Polixenes's remarks by a passage of some fifteen lines, when suddenly the unnamed Servant announces the arrival of the 'men of hair' and when the *Dance of twelve Satyrs*' is executed. The whole disposition of this part of the scene is clumsy, and there seems good reason for supposing that the Servant's announcement and the dance were an interpolation. Now, if so, the interpolation might easily have been made for the professional stage, but maybe it is more probable that it was inserted for the court performance of *The Winter's Tale* which took place on 5 November 1611. Thus, we need not necessarily assume that here in his original conception and handling of his theme Shakespeare was being directly influenced by the masque.

Other masque-like elements of course, are to be found among these dramas, but beyond the dance of satyrs there do not seem to be any other direct parallels. Ceres, Juno, and the Nymphs appear in both masques and plays; but Shakespeare clearly did not have to go to Whitehall to learn about the classical deities. In any case he had made use of such masque-like material before: there is almost an anti-masque flavour about the show of the Worthies in *Love's Labour's Lost* and the Pyramus and Thisbe playlet in *A Midsummer Night's Dream*, while Hymen in person makes entry at the close of *As You Like It*. Had these been late plays, unquestionably the commentators would have been pointing to such episodes as examples of a Jacobean masque influence upon Shakespeare's dramatic style.[8]

Once more we are confronted by evidence of a negative or contradictory kind, and, even if we accept the dance of satyrs in *The Winter's Tale*, the vision of Posthumus in *Cymbeline*, and the airy deities of *The Tempest* as being inspired by court masques, we are still concerned only with the introduction of a few incidental persons and situations, not with a general dramatic planning or with scenic embellishments.

5

The planning of most of these plays is, in fact, thoroughly un-masque-like. *Pericles* and *The Winter's Tale* depend in different ways upon a narrative technique, and the masque is character-istically independent of narrative. The one play uses Gower as presenter and, as it were, simply displays in action divers episodes from the story he sings, while the other, with Time as chorus in the middle, stretches its adventures over many years; in its title and passingly in its dialogue it never allows the audience to forget that here is a 'romance' in the limited sense of the word, a 'tale'. *Cymbeline*, too, has the same far-extended structure, and if *The Tempest* seems more compact, it is so only because here all that the dramatist presents to us is the conclusion, the final chapter, in a narrative which has summarily been expounded to Miranda (and to the audience) in the long second scene of the first act. It has been asserted that *The Tempest* has a masque-like structure, with Caliban, Stephano, and Trinculo forming the persons of an anti-masque; but there is nothing different in this play from the artisans of *A Midsummer Night's Dream*, the Dogberry and Verges of *Much Ado About Nothing*, the fantastics and the clowns of *Love's Labour's Lost*.

In none of these latest plays is there any particular reliance upon scenery. In them of course, are the usual allusions to localities, but none of these allusions are different in kind from what is generally familiar in other plays of Shakespeare, or indeed from what prevails in the plays of his companions. All the spectators need to know about *The Tempest* is that, save for the first scene, it takes place in an enchanted isle; all they need to know about *The Winter's Tale* is that it starts in the Bohemian palace of Leontes, that in the middle there is a desert coast, that in Sicilia we move from Poli-xenes's palace to the surroundings of a shepherd's cottage, and that, at the end, we return to Leontes's palace in Bohemia. None of these require or are given any particular description. The plays depend on their narrative, their strange adventures, not on their localities.

6

Only in one feature, perhaps, may we, very tentatively, suggest an influence upon Shakespeare exercised by the masque. If indeed Shakespeare did attend some of these performances at Whitehall, it is difficult to believe that the novel experience should not have made some impress on his mind. He may have found little or nothing there which he could effectively use in the planning of his plays, but he may equally well have walked out of Whitehall with visions teeming in his brain.

The appeal of these masques was new, and we may do well to inquire wherein precisely, apart from Inigo Jones's artistic excellence, their novelty consisted. Shakespeare and other Londoners must have been well acquainted with painted scenes. These certainly had for long been known in court productions, and it is probable that they were used at least by some among the children's companies. The simple fact of scenery, therefore, would not have made much impress on the poet's mind, even if that scenery, created by Jones's skill, possessed a beauty completely lacking in earlier efforts. Nor, perhaps, would Jones's unified set have seemed so very important. Undoubtedly much of the earlier painted canvaswork must have been presented in 'simultaneous' manner, with one flat representing one locality and another, another; whereas Inigo Jones sought, in the best Italian manner, to make sidewings, back shutters, and borders all parts of a single design, revealed through the opening of the proscenium frame. This must have had a certain novelty and delight for contemporaries unused to the familiar methods of much continental stagecraft: but again we must confess that it would not have been likely to make any very deep impression on Shakespeare's mind.

Far other must be our judgement when we consider what is essentially the fundamental novelty of Jones's method – the changeability of his scenes. From *The Masque of Beauty* onwards it was on this quality that he concentrated his efforts. And here perhaps we may recognize something new and hitherto unimagined which could have aroused and stimulated Shakespeare's imagination. More and more one becomes convinced that from watching these alterations of scenes at Whitehall the poet may have derived a vision inexperienced before.[9] When we remember that Jones's scenes were most usually of rich palaces, temples, towers, that it was his object to make one of these change suddenly into another, and that beyond all he lavishes his artistry on a delicate cloud-work, can we refrain from believing that Prospero's most famous speech derived its inspiration from this source?

Let us imagine ourselves in Whitehall when Somnus waved a wand 'and so made them seem to see there' the Temple of Peace,[10] when there appeared 'a bright and glorious Palace, whose gates and walls were transparent',[11] when a Globe in midstage turned softly and as softly vanished,[12] when a scene of clouds was made to open and reveal vistas beyond – let us imagine, too, that we had never seen such things before, that our surprise and eagerness were akin to that of the Edwardian child seeing his first transformation scene in a pantomime – and can we not imagine the whole of our emotional response caught up and enshrined in

> like the baseless fabric of this vision,
> The cloud-capped towers, the gorgeous palaces,
> The solemn temples, the great globe itself,
> Yea, all which it inherit, shall dissolve,
> And, like this insubstantial pageant faded,
> Leave not a rack behind? *The Tempest*, IV.1.151–6

Even Somnus is not forgotten, for

> We are such stuff
> As dreams are made on; and our little life
> Is rounded with a sleep. IV.1.156–8

If there be truth in this suggestion, then we should look in these last plays, not for dramatic or theatrical devices taken from what may be called the body of the masque, but rather for imaginative vistas inspired by its soul. The actual execution of Jones's designs in practical form might well have seemed to critical eyes crude and at times absurd; but the masque's soul, expressed in its continually changing, fleeting spectacles, probably would have charmed even our modern eyes satiated by scenic effects of which Jones could not dream. If anything in the masque worked on Shakespeare, it was this magic.

7

Emphasis on the soul inspiring the masque is in harmony with the whole atmosphere of these last plays. Often in them we have the impression that we are floating away into a realm of the spirit and are coming very close to the world of the gods. The supernatural strains heard by Pericles, the vision witnessed by the entranced Posthumus, the celestial majesty of Apollo's temple as described by the rapt Dion and Cleomenes, the wonders of Prospero's enchanted isle are all things outside the world of rationality and the 'real' of the senses. And from this follows a serious and basic conclusion: – if any of Shakespeare's dramas need to be divorced from the actuality of the scenic, these plays are his last works. The shipwreck which opens *The Tempest* is no longer emotionally effective if the actors are set on a mechanically tossing boat or if the billows, ballet-wise, are simulated by flimsy draperies tossed up and down by a bevy of supernumerary maidens. Notoriously, *The Tempest* is a 'difficult' play on the stage, rarely coming up to expectations; and the reason probably is that since it is all spirit, appealing to the imagination, there is a clash between what is shown to our eyes and what Shakespeare intended us to see in the mind only. A stage shipwreck is but a poor, foolish, meaningless thing, when Shakespeare intended a shipwreck in our waking dreams. What can be done with the play was demonstrated years ago, in the twenties, at Lilian Baylis's old Old Vic, when at the beginning of their careers the young John Gielgud, Ralph Richardson, and Leslie French took the parts of Prospero, Caliban, and Ariel in a production which had no more scenery than a box-like structure stage-centre and a few curtains. Here the spectators' imaginations were happily released. But that was before the masque and ballet had laid their hands on the play.

In making a survey of *Shakespeare Today* Miss Margaret Webster, whose own skill in production is unquestioned, has some pertinent remarks on this matter. Speaking of *The Tempest* on the stage, she declares that

the two people who will have the hardest task will be the designer and the actor who plays Ariel. Perhaps the setting should be, essentially, as simple and as indicative as in Thornton Wilder's *Our Town*, when the audience was given a signpost to Grover's Corners, and left to imagine its own niche within 'the Earth, the Universe, the Mind of God.'[13]

Thus, and thus only, can Shakespeare's last plays be truly appreciated on the stage. It were well if our producers could forget these masques which thrilled the courtiers of James's court, except in so far as they made impress on the poet's inner eye and the secret recesses of his mind.

NOTES

1. The basic published collection is, of course, *Designs by Inigo Jones for Masques and Plays at Court* (1924). In *Stuart Masques and the Renaissance Stage* (1937), an endeavour was made to select from the Chatsworth series all others of genuine importance. Individual designs have also been reproduced in dozens of volumes during the past twenty or thirty years.

2. G. E. Bentley, 'Shakespeare and the Blackfriars Theatre', *Shakespeare Survey 1* (1948), pages 38–50. [See pages 143–59 above. – Ed.]

3. 'Influence of the Court-Masques on the Drama, 1608–15', *Publications of the Modern Language Association of America* XV (1900), pages 114–20.

4. Ashley H. Thorndike, *Shakespeare's Theater* (1916), page 197.

5. T. M. Parrott, *Shakespearean Comedy* (1949), page 381.

6. 'Influence of the Court-Masques on the Drama, 1608–15'.

7. J. P. Cutts, 'An Unpublished Contemporary Setting of a Shakespeare Song', *Shakespeare Survey 9* (1956), pages 86–9.

8. Enid Welsford, *The Court Masque* (1927), page 332, does indeed state that 'Bottom and his companions serve the same purpose as the antimasque'. Although she agrees that this play came long before the development of the anti-masque proper, she notes that in the court revels 'from the first grotesque dances were popular, and the principle of contrast was always latent in the masque'.

9. Allardyce Nicoll, *Stuart Masques and the Renaissance Stage* (1937), pages 19–22. The examples given here are taken from that work: they are thus repeated because I am even more assured than I was twenty years ago that to this source we must go for an understanding of Shakespeare's vision. For further comment on the

significance of Prospero's speech see Enid Welsford, *The Court Masque* (1927).

10. *The Vision of the Twelve Goddesses.*
11. *Oberon.*
12. *Hymenaei.*
13. *Shakespeare Today* (1957), page 284.

from *Shakespeare Jahrbuch* 94 (1958), pages 51–62

SUGGESTIONS FOR FURTHER READING

E. C. PETTET: *Shakespeare and the Romance Tradition* (1949). Sets Shakespearian comedy against its background in the romantic literature of the Middle Ages and Renaissance.

NORTHROP FRYE: *A Natural Perspective* (1965). A brilliant discussion of the romance structure which determines the form of Shakespearian comedy. One of the few attempts to provide a synthesis for Shakespearian comedy as a whole.

S. L. WOLFF: *The Greek Romances in Elizabethan Prose Fiction* (1912). A study of the late Greek romances and their Elizabethan imitations, characteristics of which are found in the 'last plays', especially in *Pericles* and *The Winter's Tale*.

LOUIS B. WRIGHT: *Middle-Class Culture in Elizabethan England* (1935). Chapter IV, 'Popular Literary Taste', and Chapter XI, 'Stories for Amusement and Edification', contain much evidence of the popularity of courtly romances among less sophisticated readers.

ENID WELSFORD: *The Court Masque* (1927). The standard account of this spectacular and expensive form of courtly entertainment.

P. EDWARDS: 'Shakespeare's Romances: 1900–1957', *Shakespeare Survey 11* (1958). A concise and sometimes pungent review of modern critical approaches to the 'last plays'.

CLIFFORD LEECH: 'The Structure of the Last Plays', *Shakespeare Survey 11* (1958). An analysis of the structural methods devised by Shakespeare to give dramatic form to the romance material of the 'last plays'.

L. G. SALINGAR: 'Time and Art in Shakespeare's Romances', *Renaissance Drama 9* (1966). A rather diffuse but often suggestive essay on 'the problem of giving imaginative reality to the movement of time' in the 'last plays'.

'PERICLES'

ELEVEN

Pericles, Arcadia, and the Scheme of Romance

J. F. Danby

SHAKESPEARE'S Last Period begins with a storm and ends with *The Tempest*. Storms may be archetypal. They were certainly traditional for all those who knew the *De Consolatione*. For those who did not, but had read Sidney, there was always the ancestral shipwreck of Pyrocles and Musidorus. (Its 'ship, or rather the carcass of a ship' might reappear in Prospero's 'rotten carcass of a butt'.) Intrinsically interesting, it is also important as a pointer to the meaning as well as the provenance of the 'symbols' Shakespeare incorporates into his last plays:

But by that the next morning began a little to make a gilded show of a good meaning, there arose even with the sun, a veil of dark clouds before his face, which, shortly, like ink poured into water, had blacked over all the face of the heaven, preparing as it were a mournful stage for a tragedy to be played on. For forthwith the winds began to speak louder, and, as in a tumultuous kingdom, to think themselves fittest instruments of commandments; and blowing whole storms of hail and rain upon them, they were sooner in danger, than they could almost bethink themselves of change. For then the traitorous sea began to swell in pride against the afflicted navy, under which, while the heaven favoured them, it had lain so calmly, making mountains of itself, over which the tossed and tottering ship should climb, to be straight carried down again to a pit of hellish darkness; with such cruel blows against the sides of the ship that, which way soever it went, was still in his malice, that there was left neither power to stay nor way to escape. And shortly had it so dissevered the loving company, which the day before had tarried together, that most of them never met again, but were swallowed up in his never satisfied mouth. Some indeed, as since was shown, after long wandering, returned into Thessalia, others recovered Byzantium, and served Euarchus in his war. But the ship wherein the princes were, now left as much alone as proud lords be when fortune fails them, though they employed all industry to save themselves, yet what they did was rather for duty to nature than hope to escape, so ugly darkness, as if it would prevent the night's coming, usurped the day's right: which accompanied sometimes with thunders, always with horrible noises of the chafing winds, made the masters and pilots so astonished that they knew not how to direct, and if they knew, they could scarcely, when they directed, hear their own whistle. For the sea strove with the winds which should be louder, and the shrouds of the ship, with a gastful noise to them that were in it, witnessed that their ruin was the wager of the others' contention, and the heaven roaring out thunders the more amazed them, as having those powers for enemies. Certainly there is no danger carries with it more horror than that which grows in those floating kingdoms. For that dwelling place is unnatural to mankind, and then the terribleness of the continual motion, the desolation of the far-being from comfort, the eye and the ear having ugly images ever before it, doth still vex the mind, even when it is best armed against it. But thus the day passed, if that might be called day, while the cunningest mariners were so conquered by the storm that they thought it best with stricken sails to yield to be governed by it: the valiantest feeling inward dismayedness, and yet the fearfullest ashamed fully to show it, seeing that the princes, who were to part from the greatest fortunes, did in their countenances accuse no point of fear, but encouraging them to do what might be done, putting their hands to every most painful office, taught them in one instant to promise themselves the best, and yet to despise the worst. But so were they carried by the tyranny of the wind, and the treason of the sea all that night, which the older it was, the more wayward it showed itself towards them: till the next morning, known to be a morning better by the hour-glass than by the day's clearness, having run fortune so blindly, as itself ever was painted, lest the conclusion should not answer to the rest of the play, they were driven upon a rock, which, hidden with those outrageous waves, did, as it were, closely dissemble his cruel mind, till with an unbelieved violence, but to them that have tried it, the ship ran upon it, and seeming willinger to perish than to have her course stayed, redoubled her blows, till she had broken herself in pieces, and as it were, tearing out her own bowels to feed the sea's greediness, left nothing within it but despair of safety and expectation of a loathsome end. There was to be seen the divers manners of minds in distress: some sat upon the top of the poop weeping and wailing, till the sea swallowed them; some one more able to abide death than the fear of death, cut his own throat to prevent drowning; some prayed: and there wanted not of them which cursed, as if the heavens could not be more angry than they were. . . . But the princes, using the passions of fearing evil, and desiring to escape only to serve the rule of virtue, not to abandon one's self, leaped to a rib of the ship, which broken from his fellows, floated with more likelihood to do service than any other limb of that ruinous body.[1]

Sidney's romance is important because it has such inner coherence – a large, mature, and conscious philosophy. We are protected, with him, from projecting on to him meanings of our own, or finding in him answers to needs of ours he himself did not share and did not intend to answer. In his storm we can confidently follow his own moralizations.

The opening of the passage is conventional enough: morning set out with 'a gilded show of a good meaning' then rapidly changed: appearances are deceitful, and fortune fickle. The sun was veiled, the heavens darkened. Then comes the deliberate suggestion of stage management in the scene – 'as it were a mournful stage for a tragedy to be played on' which works in two ways. Nature behaves in such a theatrical way because nature in fact does have to follow a 'plot': all the happenings in nature are meaningful, obedient to a design which may not be fully apparent. Secondly, by pointing to this element of deliberate manipulation in nature Sidney removes from his highly mannered description of the storm – 'artificial' as it seems – any suggestion of insincerity. The patterned prose that imitates nature imitates her not by external realism but by bringing out the inner design in accordance with which she operates. The spectator of the tragedy is *nearer* to the full reality than the actor in the tragedy itself. The references to the theatre are continued in the next sentence: 'forthwith the winds began to speak louder' like actors in Cambyses' vein, and then quickly the imagery slips into that of the tumultuous kingdoms Elizabethan tragedy celebrates, and the winds become usurping and contentious rebels. The idea of revolt and treachery continues and along with this goes 'pride', the root of all such evil ever since the first revolt. It is only at this point that Sidney then brings in the visualized sea 'making mountains of itself, over which the tossed and tottering ship should climb, to be straight carried down again to a pit of hellish darkness'. The word 'hellish' takes on a livelier meaning for the saturation of the passage in moral suggestion which had preceded it. The personification of the sea we do not object to: the sea, we have already accepted, is itself an agent, the meaning of the total drama in which it plays its part is also a human one – something that the human beings who are at the centre of the storm will only understand in the course of an experience of tempest which fully reveals to them their own nature and that of the designer of the play. Further, the sea can do no more and no worse in the way of destruction than human beings themselves can do. The third sphere of chance misfortunes is not much different in effect from the second sphere of human malice. The sea, in fact, is almost equated with the tyrant or rebel. The princes are cut off from their friends and left in their ship as in a prison, 'as much alone as proud lords be when fortune fails them'. Like Pericles, however,

> galling
> His kingly hands hauling ropes IV.1.55–6

or knowing, like Ferdinand, that

> Some kinds of baseness
> Are nobly undergone, *The Tempest* III.1.2–3

Pyrocles and Musidorus set an example to their crew by 'putting their hands to every most painful office'. But the ship is doomed nevertheless. The tyranny of the wind and the treachery of a rock (the enemy under cover is a permanent agent of disaster for the Elizabethans) finally bring the inevitable upon them. Sidney's concluding sentences are important. A storm reveals the innermost nature of those exposed to it, 'the divers manners of minds in distress'. The princes themselves have been exemplary in their conduct. They act from 'duty to nature' rather than 'hope to escape so ugly a darkness', 'using the passions of fearing evil, and desiring to escape only to serve the rule of virtue'. The rest behave much like those in the first scene of *The Tempest*: some commit suicide, some pray, some curse God. Thus the first and the fourth spheres too are brought into the passage – virtue that will not admit defeat from fortune, and will not submit because of its implicit patience, its confidence that defeat and victory can be married because of the transcendent. By the time the storm has been fully described we are made aware of all the main parts of the Sidneian universe.

Pericles, Shakespeare's first 'romance', clearly follows the established pattern. Gower, summing up at the end of the play, gives a more adequate account of what has taken place than most Epilogues are accustomed to do:

> In Antiochus and his daughter you have heard
> Of monstrous lust the due and just reward:
> In Pericles, his queen, and daughter, seen,
> Although assailed with fortune fierce and keen,
> Virtue preserved from fell destruction's blast,
> Led on by heaven, and crowned with joy at last.
> In Helicanus may you well descry
> A figure of truth, of faith, of loyalty;
> In reverend Cerimon there well appears
> The worth that learned charity aye wears.
> For wicked Cleon and his wife, when fame
> Had spread their cursed deed, and honoured name
> Of Pericles, to rage the city turn,
> That him and his they in his palace burn;
> The gods for murder seemed so content
> To punish – although not done, but meant.
> So, on your patience evermore attending,
> New joy wait on you! Here our play has ending.
>
> V.3.86–103

The play begins with the Prince risking his life for the hand of the Princess. She seems outwardly ideal:

> apparelled like the spring,
> Graces her subjects, and her thoughts the king
> Of every virtue gives renown to men.　　I.1.12–14

But this 'glorious casket' is 'stored with ill'. She is living incestuously with her father, and Pericles reads the riddle. His speech

records the mystique of virginity and the shock of the fall from the
ideal:

> You are a fair viol, and your sense the strings;
> Who, fingered to make man his lawful music,
> Would draw heaven down, and all the gods, to hearken;
> But, being played upon before your time,
> Hell only danceth at so harsh a chime.   I.1.81–5

Pericles is naturally revolted, and he knows he is in possession of
a dangerous secret. Antiochus, having broken one law, will not
stop short of breaking any others. In him law is merely the tyrant's
will. Antiochus knows he has been discovered, but like Cecropia
in the *Arcadia* he will wear the vizor of virtue. Pericles, however, is
aware of his danger:

> How courtesy would seem to cover sin,
> When what is done is like an hypocrite,
> The which is good in nothing but in sight!   I.1.121–3

He determines to save himself by running away:

> Then, lest my life be cropped to keep you clear,
> By flight I'll shun the danger which I fear.   I.1.141–2

Antiochus – again, like Sidney's Plexirtus – procures a convenient
villain-courtier to pursue Pericles and kill him.

Back in his own kingdom, Pericles is still afraid of Antiochus's
vengeance: the more so that his subjects as well as himself will be
drawn into the suffering. He determines on further flight. He calls
for Helicanus, the good servant and no flatterer, and hands over
the kingdom to him, the 'figure of truth, of faith, of loyalty'.
Unlike Antiochus, Pericles recognizes that both princes and
subjects are submitted to virtue, and that kings in this are servants
to those they rule. Helicanus is

> Fit counsellor and servant for a prince,
> Who by thy wisdom mak'st a prince thy servant.   I.2.63–4

This is the ethic of the Arcadian world. Helicanus, too, voices an
Arcadian wisdom. He tells Pericles

> To bear with patience
> Such griefs as you yourself do lay upon yourself   I.2.65–6

just as, later, Leontes will be urged to do as the heavens have
done:

> forget your evil;
> With them forgive yourself.
>
> *The Winter's Tale*, V.1.5–6

And just as the Boatswain knows in *The Tempest* that there is a
proper self-love as an improper. So Pericles is in flight once more.
We next see him landing in famine-stricken Tharsus, relieving
the distress of Cleon and Dionyza, a king and queen in adversity.
Pericles's troubles continue. Having left Tharsus, he is once more
on the sea, and soon shipwrecked. The second act opens with him
walking upon the beach, a sole survivor. In adversity he is studiously correct, resigned rather than rebellious:

> Yet cease your ire, you angry stars of heaven!
> Wind, rain, and thunder, remember earthly man
> Is but a substance that must yield to you;
> And I, as fits my nature, do obey you.
> Alas, the sea hath cast me on the rocks,
> Washed me from shore to shore, and left me breath
> Nothing to think on but ensuing death.
> Let it suffice the greatness of your powers
> To have bereft a prince of all his fortunes;
> And having thrown him from your wat'ry grave
> Here to have death in peace is all he'll crave.   II.1.1–11

Pericles meets the two fishermen who read the moral of the sea –
that it is very like the land, for there too big fish eat the little ones –
and his armour is restored to him, dredged up in the fishermen's
nets. Pericles is now enabled to go to the King's court and take
part in the tourney for the hand of the King's daughter. Simonides
is a good ruler, one of those who are

> A model which heaven makes like to itself.   II.2.11

Subordinate princes

> sit like stars about his throne,
> And he the sun, for them to reverence.   II.3.39–40

He has the king-like reason, too, which remembers the difference between outward show and inward reality:

> Opinion's but a fool, that makes us scan
> The outward habit by the inward man.   II.2.56–7

Pericles wins the tournament and the Princess's love. Thaisa in fact will have Pericles whether her father will or no (a recurrent motif in the romances). Simonides pretends to wrath that she is so wilful and stages an apparent choice for her between love and filial obedience. The anger is, however, only a loving game and all ends happily.

Up to this point we have been following the first two acts of *Pericles* – work only doubtfully Shakespeare's, and almost certainly not of Shakespeare's later period. It is surprising how much of the substance of the late Shakespearian romance these acts contain or adumbrate: how, certainly, they seem to incorporate in coda-form features that could be strictly paralleled in the *Arcadia*. The mystique of virginity; the beautiful appearance and the corrupt heart; the tyrant thrown from the frame of nature and reason by 'blood' or appetite; the tyrant wearing the vizor of kindness, employing a court-henchman to commit his murders; the contrast of the good governor; and of the unfortunate ruler who has, fortunately, a good servant whom he can make vice-regent; the strategy of flight before the 'tempest' of passionate malice; the sea; resignation after shipwreck; the winning of a princess in the end, after the storm and other hard plights; the virgin-boldness of the love which is more absolute and inward than obedience to a father's will; the hinted opposition between the two, and the evasion of any real conflict on this issue – chapter and verse could be given for almost every detail.

If we suppress comparison of these first two acts with the three that follow, we must admit that in their own way they are surprisingly good: good enough, as Shakespeare himself must have considered, to stand as prologue to what he himself would add. What prevents us from admitting they are fully Shakespearian?

First, whatever effectiveness of coherence they have is derivative. They are parasitic on a system which stands behind them.

From this system parts are abstracted and then reassembled. Reports themselves, such as the summary outlines we have made, suggest there is more in the original than in fact is there. For the first two acts suggest more than they can sustain. Secondly, the absence might be noted of any inclusive consciousness in the first two acts – a consciousness centred either in a single character, made capable of investing all the parts with significance, or a consciousness centred in the writer of the acts and made pervasively through the verse or the general moral sensitivity. The first two acts abound in moral precepts which are made to substitute for moral occasions. There is no one capable of embracing the whole, no one who serves to bring together all the parts of the moral universe implied, as Pamela does in the *Arcadia*. There is no one, in fact, who seems as securely centred as are any of the four lovers in the *Arcadia*, or as even Cecropia in her perversity, and Amphialus in his error. Pericles himself is driven by a *vis a tergo*. The mechanics of the moral world are too obvious and too obviously automatic. There is no suggestion here, as there is all the time in the *Arcadia*, of the operative tensions within the sphere of Fortune and Adversity. The copyist of the Sidneian world (assuming that it is with such we have to deal) is insensitive to those things in the Sidneian universe which make it more than a daydream: the pressure of resolution or patience that is resistant to Fortune, the pressure of passion that combines with her irrationals generally, the room for growth and for disastrous collapse that Sidney always retains. The version of the Sidneian world presented in the first two acts is comparatively crude. The whole scheme is rendered inert. At the key points of the action where in Sidney we should expect convincing statements of virtue and patience as apices of the mind – and expect them to be given in those analyses and differentiations Sidney's prose is so capable of – we get instead something surprisingly flat. A good example is Pericles's resignation after his shipwreck. Each of the parts – in this instance the 'angry stars', the imagery of 'Wind, rain, and thunder', the sea that has washed him 'from shore to shore', etc. – seems to recall a prior Shakespearian occasion. But actually, the moral and verbal sensitivity is simply lacking. We are left with the lowest common factors in each case:

verbal formulae instead of poetic statement, the cliché of resignation instead of the vast moment of spiritual forces that turns on 'patience'. In the hands of the writer of the first two acts the romance-world degenerates into one in which nothing can really happen. We are given no sense of the creaturely, of the existential, of being at the centre of organic change. We are left, that is, with no sense of people as people. The use of the traditional scheme can rise only as high as the reporting of moral precepts, and the presentation of what Milton would call 'Apathie' rather than that activation which compels fresh choice and new endeavour.

The late-Shakespearian appears decisively with the first words Pericles utters on his appearance in Act III, scene 1. It is a short scene, but long enough to contain a storm, the announcement of a birth, the death of a wife, her committal to the sea, and three great lyrical speeches by Pericles himself – three purple patches unusual in weight and number even for Shakespeare in so short a space. The technique is typical of the late Shakespeare, however, and worth observing.

The first thing to note is, I think, the way in which the late-Shakespeare can suddenly impose voices upon the stage and upon the audience. 'Suddenly', 'impose', and 'voices' – each of the words is necessary to record the new impression the late-Shakespeare makes. To use his own phrase, Shakespeare can at any moment now *take* us with beauty. If the assault were by something cruder, or if it were less finely managed, it would amount to the employment of shock tactics:

> PERICLES   O, how, Lychorida
> How does my queen? – Thou stormest venomously;
> Wilt thou spit all thyself? The seaman's whistle
> Is as a whisper in the ears of death,
> Unheard, – Lychorida! – Lucina, O
> Divinest patroness, and midwife gentle
> To those that cry by night, convey thy deity
> Aboard our dancing boat; make swift the pangs
> Of my queen's travails!
> > *Enter Lychorida, with an infant*
> >   Now, Lychorida!

184

LYCHORIDA Here is a thing too young for such a place,
Who, if it had conceit, would die, as I
Am like to do. Take in your arms this piece
Of your dead queen.
PERICLES   How, how, Lychorida?
LYCHORIDA Patience, good sir; do not assist the storm.
Here's all that is left living of your queen –
A little daughter. For the sake of it,
Be manly, and take comfort.
PERICLES   O you gods!
Why do you make us love your goodly gifts
And snatch them straight away? We here below
Recall not what we give, and therein may
Use honour with you.
LYCHORIDA   Patience, good sir, even for this charge.

                                                    III.1.6–26

A situation highly charged with feeling is abruptly presented (we
are, for example, put *in the middle* of the storm) and then we are
given a close-up of the character, speaking when feeling is climac-
tically intense. There is swiftness of transition from one tone to
another: Pericles is anxious, apprehensive, and angry within the
space of two lines. Then the swimming suggestion of the 'seaman's
whistle . . . as a whisper in the ears of death, unheard' is floated in,
with its hushing awe, its arrest of passion and tumult, its stillness
in the midst of storm that almost surprises one into contemplation;
and this followed immediately by the loud shout of the nurse, and
this by the plea, compassionate and self-compassionate, to Lucina.
The swimming suggestiveness of phrase is still in evidence – a
manner which brings Shakespeare nearer to the romantics of the
nineteenth century than to his contemporaries in the seventeenth.
The phrase 'those that cry by night' seems to mean more than
merely women in labour. Its resonance covers also all those that
cry for them, and those they are bringing into the world, whose
first sound is a cry. . . . Or does it? For Shakespeare's late verse is
now, comparatively, a friable thing. Its aura of suggestion is
shadowier than can be tabulated in terms of pun, or ambiguity, or
multiple meaning. It is really an expansion of meaning beyond that
which is immediately relevant or required, a constant quickening of

the listener to have feelings immediately available, and a constant sudden overdraft on these. Shakespeare's late verse is a poetry of feeling. For all its richness it is simpler than the verse of the middle period:

> A terrible childbed hast thou had, my dear;
> No light, no fire. Th'unfriendly elements
> Forgot thee utterly; nor have I time
> To give thee hallowed to thy grave, but straight
> Must cast thee, scarcely coffined, in the ooze;
> Where, for a monument upon thy bones,
> And aye-remaining lamps, the belching whale
> And humming water must o'erwhelm thy corpse,
> Lying with simple shells. III.1.56–64

Dr Tillyard has referred to 'that simple, yet strained, remote and magical note that sounds from time to time in the last plays'.[2] The note is sounded, though, very often, together with others – others that are strained and violent, strained in the suddenness of their contrasts. 'Lying with simple shells' gives one note: the adjective dissolving disdain in nostalgic envy. 'Belching whale' gives another – the monstrous, indifferent and bestial life, and yet the mindless, contented coarseness of the creature. 'Humming water' gives yet another – the dizzying depths through which we sink to the 'simple shells', the loss of consciousness, the sound of the distant storm confused to a blind murmur, then the water itself humming as it spins in its vortices, humming like a top, still yet swirling: and as one consciousness is lost we adopt the consciousness of the sea, and death is a sleep and the sound of humming as restful as a lullaby, until we are 'Lying with simple shells' in the absolute 'Apathie' we both long for and disdain.

But in addition to notes like this there is also that of a baroque self-consciousness, the manner daring of 'aye-remaining lamps'. This intrudes, too, between the intimate immediacy and naturalism of the opening lines and the imaginative moment of the closing ones. Something of self-consciousness has to be counted in to complete the description of the late-Shakespearian style: a distance to which Shakespeare projects his creation, a lack of emotional *engagement*, and yet a rich appreciation – an almost indulgent exaggeration – of the opportunity for stance any moment can bring along.

Passages such as this tempt us further than Shakespeare himself seems inclined to go. The immensely suggestive moments can lead out beyond the frame of character and beyond the frame of the theme: into the realm of 'humming water' and 'belching whale'. But Shakespeare had a frame to support him and to keep the moments coherently together. In the case of the last three acts of *Pericles* the frame is supplied by the romance world which had also served the writer of the first two acts.

For *Pericles* is a study of the prince in misfortune. The first two acts show a good man embroiled, swept from security by the tempest of another's wickedness. The misfortunes are external, the loss is the loss of a throne. The second part begins with the more inward loss of a wife, a loss however which brings the gain of a daughter, for Fortune always has a 'doutous or double visage'. Shakespeare is supported by what he has himself learnt about the inner structure of this world as well as guided by what he knows of it from others who have also explored it.

Act III begins with the tempest and ends with Pericles making provision for his daughter, the 'fresh-new seafarer', and bidding a 'priestly farewell' to his wife. Scene 1 is a lyrical Shakespearian handling of the matter of Patience. In his opening speech Pericles addresses the 'god of this great vast' – a deity higher than Fortune. In the first shock of his grief at hearing of Thaisa's death he is in danger of being overthrown. 'Patience, good sir', the nurse calls to him, 'do not assist the storm' –

> Be manly, and take comfort.   III.1.22

The force of Lychorida's last words is apt to be lost on a post-Renaissance audience. 'Manly' implies the summoning up of the full fortitude manhood implies, but also assumes in this context the creaturely dependence of that manhood: virtue cannot be self-sufficient however far it exerts itself, and even though it is asserted to the full. Pericles calls out against the gods, but it is a human bewilderment rather than a passionate revolt. Again Lychorida cries 'Patience, good sir'. Pericles recovers himself and turns to the child. The overflow of compassion is a good augury. Only those can take comfort who can give comfort, and there is immense tenderness in Pericles's words. By the time he is finished he has found a new balance. His reply to the sailor indicates the firm hold he now has on his re-established manliness:

> FIRST SAILOR What courage, sir? God save you!
> PERICLES Courage enough: I do not fear the flaw;
> It hath done to me the worst.   III.1.38–40

When the sailors tell him his wife must be cast overboard he submits to the necessity. In the great speech we have already analysed he fully realizes death's final 'apathie' – away from the storm, on the sea's floor, 'Lying with simple shells': an apathy which is the opposite of patience as death is the opposite of life. He bids Thaisa 'A priestly farewell'.

The difference between the first and the second parts of *Pericles* can now be more clearly seen. Instead of reporting moral precepts Shakespeare is presenting moral occasions. The audience not only has a map to the territory, it can also see the movements of the protagonist across the countryside. In taking over or resuming the play Shakespeare judged rightly that what it needed was a 'voice' – the impression of a living personality, and that personality a centre of sensitive moral consciousness. The unit of communication now is the whole scene. Inside that scene we can see the complete turn or rotation of a person responding to a completely given moral occasion. Lyrically evocative as the scene is, the lyrical imagery would not be sufficient, however, without the clearly mapped territory behind it – which Shakespeare shared with both his audience and his collaborator. 'Belching whale' and 'humming water', overpoweringly suggestive as they are, are not as illuminatingly definitive as the interchange between the sailor and the bereaved husband. 'Imagery' is a deceptive word to use in connexion with occasions such as this. Imagery includes more than metaphor, more even than is usually included in the phrase 'verbal texture'. Shakespeare's main controlling image is the image of a man in certain circumstances speaking from the midst of his situation to another man (Shakespeare, again, gives the Sailor a 'voice'). The flow of meaning that then takes place only has significance within the moral situation that has been presented. The emotive aura of the separable 'images' (what Aristotle called 'diction') is large and maybe vague. The total moral reference of the scene, however, is specific and precise. And the references in this case fall within the field covered by 'patience in adversity'.

The two explaining systems which have been applied recently to the interpretation of the Last Plays miss, I think, the essentially Elizabethan – and for that matter the more deeply human – inwardness of the romance scheme. The first of these has been based on the *Golden Bough* and the fertility cycle and rebirth. The second has been similarly based on the Christian conception of regeneration and resurrection. Neither, I think, is as satisfactory as the contemporary and conventional scheme which Shakespeare used. Anthropology does not take us far enough. By its insidious precipitations it tends to silt over the clear and sharp contours of the Renaissance moral world. The second explaining system errs in the opposite direction. It carries us too far and too fast. It particularizes in a field of meaning beyond Shakespeare's intention – though Shakespeare, I have no doubt, would know St Paul and the burial service, and accepted the New Testament. To theologize the last plays, however, is to distort them. Though patience as Shakespeare conceives it implies St Paul and the New Testament, patience as Shakespeare realizes it in the Last Plays is a familiar and well-walked parish in a wider diocese. Nor is the parish presided over by the Fisher King, and in it St Paul is taken for granted but not allegorized in every Whitsun pastoral. And this brings us to a further distortion which over-anxiety about the greatness of Shakespeare's final plays is sometimes responsible for – a distortion of their tone. Shakespeare's last plays are not conceived at the same level of seriousness as Dante's *Paradiso*. They have an *ironia* of their own. Shakespeare during the last period is comparatively relaxed. He makes a toy of thought. Drawing on the full richness of his inner life, sporadically, as they do, executed with the unanxious brilliance of the maestro who has never lost his flair for improvisation, as they are, the final plays are for all that adjusted to the level of entertainment, controlled by an intention 'which was to please'.

The 'resurrection' scene in *Pericles*, for example, follows immediately on the storm and Thaisa's committal to the sea. The casket in which Thaisa has been placed is washed ashore near the house of Cerimon. Cerimon, as the Epilogue says, is a 'reverend' example of 'learned charity': as Mr Wilson Knight has pointed out, Shakespeare's first sketch for Prospero.[3] Cerimon prefers the power which wisdom gives to that which the mere governor can exercise:

> I hold it ever
> Virtue and cunning were endowments greater
> Than nobleness and riches: careless heirs
> May the two latter darken and expend;
> But immortality attends the former,
> Making a man a god. 'Tis known I ever
> Have studied physic. III.2.26-32

With a kind of endearing *pietas* Shakespeare builds up his scene along lines slightly old-fashioned. We are shown Cerimon first in actual fact helping *'some persons who have been shipwrecked'*. We then see him being greeted by two gentlemen who announce his character:

> Your honour has through Ephesus poured forth
> Your charity, and hundreds call themselves
> Your creatures, who by you have been restored.
> III.2.43-5

Finally Thaisa's coffin is brought in and opened, and the moment of her resuscitation occurs. Again the lyrical note is struck. The verse quickens and pants with wonder:

> Gentlemen,
> This queen will live; nature awakes; a warmth
> Breathes out of her.
>   ... See how she gins to blow
> Into life's flower again!
>   ... She is alive. Behold,
> Her eyelids, cases to those heavenly jewels
> Which Pericles hath lost, begin to part
> Their fringes of bright gold; the diamonds
> Of a most praised water do appear,

> To make the world twice rich. Live, and make
> Us weep to hear your fate, fair creature,
> Rare as you seem to be.
>
> THAISA   O dear Diana, where am I?
> Where's my lord? What world is this?
>
> III.2.97–9, 100–101, 103–11

When thinking of symbolism we must remember that one of the most important things an apple can mean is simply itself. Thaisa's reawakening feels to her like a rebirth – and also like a loss. To the spectators it is wonder enough, the more so that Thaisa is a miracle of beauty. But the moment attains its highest significance, I think, when it is brought into relation with Pericles's great speech before the committal, and into the general romance frame of 'doutous fortune' and the Providence that smiles while it seems to frown. We do not need to make it more important than that – nor less. And indeed, while there is a restoration of the seeming dead to breathing warmth, it is still a world of trial and of separation to which Thaisa is brought back. Cut off from Pericles, she must retire to Diana's temple and endure her exile in patience.

Diana is the tutelary goddess of the Last Plays. She stands for that chastity which puts its seal on romantic love and which is a reflection of the Virtue that controls and transforms 'base affection' in the *Arcadia*. Thaisa herself is never seen in action as the invincible virgin-mind. That role is reserved for her daughter Marina, and Act IV is devoted to its display.

Recent commentators have argued that Shakespeare's technique in the Last Plays can best be regarded as a development towards symbolism. It is more accurate, I think, to regard the development as a move not towards the symbolic but towards the schematic – the schematic with one addition: Shakespeare imposes on the characters schematically conceived what we have called a *voice*. In Act IV the schematic quickly shows itself. Cleon and Dionyza who have been entrusted with the upbringing of Marina have a daughter of their own, and Dionyza, growing jealous of Marina, determines to have her murdered. The conception is a romance commonplace. The 'voice', however, is quickly supplied

– Marina entering *'with a basket of flowers'* on her way to strew her nurse's grave, and saying:

> Ay me! poor maid,
> Born in a tempest, when my mother died,
> This world to me is like a lasting storm,
> Whirring me from my friends   IV.1.18–21

– and Marina speaking to her would-be murderer the almost mono-syllabic language of the heart: 'Why will you kill me?' 'To satisfy my lady'.

> Why would she have me killed?
> Now, as I can remember, by my troth
> I never did her hurt in all my life.
> I never spake bad word, nor did ill turn
> To any living creature. Believe me, la,
> I never killed a mouse, nor hurt a fly;
> I trod upon a worm against my will,
> But I wept for it.   IV.1.72–81

– or Marina again speaking in outraged contempt to the pimp in the brothel to which the pirates who rescued her from her murderer have sold her:

> Thou hold'st a place for which the pained'st fiend
> Of hell would not in reputation change;
> Thou art the damned doorkeeper to every
> Coistrel that comes inquiring for his Tib;
> To the choleric fisting of every rogue
> Thy ear is liable; thy food is such
> As hath been belched on by infected lungs.   IV.6.161–7

Unfortunately for this last voice of strained and schematically violent indignation, Shakespeare suddenly remembers the poor pimp Marina is addressing. He gives him a voice too. Looking out shrewdly from Boult's bleared and piggy eye he makes him say:

> What would you have me do? Go to the wars, would you, where a man may serve seven years for the loss of a leg, and have not money enough in the end to buy him a wooden one?   IV.6.168–71

and at once the scene opens out on to other and larger vistas: on to the world whose presiding deities are Mars and Venus, the world of wars and lechery, glamorizable in *Antony and Cleopatra*, despicable in *Troilus and Cressida*, and (for a moment) arrestingly pitiable now in the plight of this Mytilene stews-attendant. Boult is the only person in the play who asks an awkward question that cannot be answered out of the Arcadian book and for the moment it seems as if Shakespeare has broken his own wicket. Boult's question is out of place in the plays of the Last Period as it would not be earlier. The facts of Mars and Venus cannot be considered in them along with the theories of Diana.

Virginity (it is insisted on again in *Cymbeline*, *The Winter's Tale*, and *The Tempest*) is, however, a subordinate item in the whole system, like marriage against one's parents' wishes. How schematic it is can be realized by comparing the handling in Shakespeare's final plays with the treatment in the *Arcadia*. Sidney's exposition is full and he is at pains to relate it to the main moral issues he is concerned about. Chastity in the *Arcadia* is assailed from within and without. The lovers realize its significance beween themselves, and the princesses maintain it in captivity against both the arguments of Cecropia and the physical assaults of the three brothers who are left in command when Amphialus becomes a casualty. In *Pericles* it is patience in adversity which is the dominating motif, and in Act V patience returns to hold the stage.

The supposed death of his daughter is the second blow Pericles has sustained. It almost exhausts his reserves of 'manliness' but not quite:

> He bears
> A tempest which his mortal vessel tears,
> And yet he rides it out.   IV.4.29–31

Pericles arrives eventually at Mytilene and there, by fortune, his daughter is brought on board his ship in the hope that she will charm him out of his lethargy. Pericles bids her tell her story:

> Report thy parentage. I think thou said'st
> Thou hadst been tossed from wrong to injury,
> And that thou thought'st thy griefs might equal mine,
> If both were opened.

> Tell thy story;
> If thine considered prove the thousand part
> Of my endurance, thou art a man, and I
> Have suffered like a girl. Yet thou dost look
> Like Patience gazing on king's graves, and smiling
> Extremity out of act.   V.1.128–31, 133–8

And from now on the scene begins to move again with the urgent, panting life of restoration, wonderment, and an overflowing joy. Pericles is assured at last that it is Marina indeed:

> O Helicanus, strike me, honoured sir;
> Give me a gash, put me to present pain,
> Lest this great sea of joys rushing upon me
> O'erbear the shores of my mortality,
> And drown me with their sweetness. O, come hither,
> Thou that beget'st him that did thee beget;
> Thou that wast born at sea, buried at Tharsus,
> And found at sea again! O Helicanus,
> Down on thy knees, thank the holy gods as loud
> As thunder threatens us. This is Marina.
>   . . . I embrace you.
> Give me my robes. I am wild in my beholding.
> O heavens bless my girl! But hark, what music?
> Tell Helicanus, my Marina, tell him
> O'er, point by point.   V.1.189–98, 220–24

The speech transforms the 'humming water' into a 'great sea of joys', and the near-loss of consciousness here is the reverse of that in the former speech, an ecstasy instead of an apathy. Nothing remains but for Thaisa to be found too. When this happens (and Shakespeare crowds the second discovery quickly upon the first) the joy is greater, as Chaucer would say, 'than was the revel of hir mariage'. It is a note similar to that at the end of the *Clerkes Tale* which Shakespeare sounds:

> No more, you gods! your present kindness
> Makes my past miseries sports. You shall do well
> That on the touching of her lips I may
> Melt and no more be seen. O, come, be buried
> A second time within these arms!   V.3.41–5

NOTES

1. *The Countess of Pembroke's Arcadia*, edited by Sir Ernest Baker (1907), pages 159–60.
2. E. M. W. Tillyard, *Shakespeare's Last Plays* (1938), page 23.
3. G. Wilson Knight, *The Crown of Life* (1947), page 54.

from *Poets on Fortune's Hill* (1952); revised title: *Elizabethan and Jacobean Poets*) by J. F. Danby, pages 83–103

TWELVE

Themes and Variations in *Pericles*

G. A. Barker

I

Pericles, Prince of Tyre is founded upon one of the most popular stories ever to become the basis for a Shakespearian play. Derived ultimately from the Greek sophistic romance, the Apollonius Saga can be traced through the literature of almost every European language. Yet through a thousand years of dissemination its original form has remained almost unalterably intact.[1] Such stability offers a remarkable opportunity to isolate and examine those instances in which Shakespeare departed from the traditional pattern of the legend. The matter is, however, complicated by the fact that Shakespeare's primary source, probably an earlier dramatic version of the story which is now lost, may itself have varied markedly from the accepted pattern of the saga. George Wilkins's novel, *The Painfull Aduentures of Pericles, Prince of Tyre* (1608), on the other hand, can throw extensive light on the lost source play if we assume that both Shakespeare's play and Wilkins's novel were largely based on the same original play.

By examining those elements common to both Wilkins and Shakespeare but not found in any other version of the legend, we can reconstruct the theme of kingship which dominated the older play. More significantly, we gain an opportunity to study the direction and extent of Shakespeare's revision by isolating those elements in his play which cannot be found in Wilkins's novel or any version accessible to him. It can thus be seen that Shakespeare converted the old play of kingship into a drama of faith and transformed the traditional hero of the legend into a Job-like figure of patience.

While scholars have now in general agreed that Wilkins's novel was based in part upon a play, they have disagreed primarily about whether this play was Shakespeare's *Pericles* or an earlier dramatic version of the Apollonius legend.[2] Although no conclusive evidence has been brought forth to prove either theory, Kenneth Muir has argued persuasively for the possibility of an earlier source play, an Ur-*Pericles*, by isolating a large number of passages in Wilkins which closely resemble blank verse but do not appear in the extant play.[3] If we accept Muir's hypothesis that Wilkins made use of an earlier play which also became the source for Shakespeare's play, Wilkins's novel becomes a link with this lost source play. As we compare it with the extant version of *Pericles*, we gain an insight into Shakespeare's artistic method and purpose, for we begin to see what changes the original play underwent.

2

Perhaps the most significant innovation common to Shakespeare and Wilkins is the change that the character of Helicanus undergoes. In traditional versions of the story, including Gower's[4] and Laurence Twine's,[5] Helicanus is a humble messenger from Tyre, who informs Pericles while he is in Tharsus that King Antiochus has commanded that he be slain. In Wilkins and Shakespeare, Helicanus is turned into Pericles's 'graue Counsellor', who governs Tyre during the Prince's absences and is his closest adviser and confidant.

The new Helicanus, in fact, closely resembles Castiglione's ideal Courtier, whose duties in part are 'not to suffre him [the prince] to be deceived, and to worke that evermore he may understande the truth of everye thinge, and bolster him against flatterers and raylers, and all suche as shoulde endevour to corrupt his minde with unhonest delites.'[6] This is well illustrated in the second chapter of Wilkins's novel when Pericles, worried over the danger that threatens his country because he has guessed Antiochus's secret, is reproved by Helicanus for wasting away his body in sorrow when the welfare of the whole kingdom depends upon his safety: 'That it was ill in him to doe it, and no lesse in his counsell to suffer him, without contradicting it. At which, although the Prince bent his brow stearnely against him, he left not to go forward, but plainly tolde him, it was as fit for him being a Prince to heare of his owne errour as it was lawfull for his authority to commaund, that while he liued so shut vp, so vnseene, so carelesse of his gouernment, order might be disorder for all him.'[7] Pericles accepts the unjust reproof patiently, commends Helicanus for his honesty, and then relates to him the reasons for his fears. The old counsellor begs his pardon for having mistrusted him and then advises him to go on travels to save the country from danger.

The same action is depicted in *Pericles* (I.2). However, the text of this scene is very corrupt. Helicanus's first words are a tirade against flattery:

> Peace, peace, and give experience tongue.
> They do abuse the king that flatter him,
> For flattery is the bellows blows up sin;
> The thing the which is flattered but a spark,
> To which that blast gives heat and stronger glowing;
> Whereas reproof, obedient, and in order,
> Fits kings as they are men, for they may err.
> When Signior Sooth here does proclaim a peace,
> He flatters you, makes war upon your life.
> Prince, pardon me, or strike me if you please;
> I cannot be much lower than my knees. I.2.37–47

Pericles forgives him and praises him for his candour:

> Sit down. Thou art no flatterer.
> I thank thee for't; and heaven forbid
> That kings should let their ears hear their faults hid!
> Fit counsellor and servant for a prince,
> Who by thy wisdom mak'st a prince thy servant,
> What wouldst thou have me do? I.2.60–65

It is significant that someone, presumably the author of the Ur-*Pericles*, has for some purpose grafted a new scene on to the traditional pattern of the legend. Instead of stealthily departing from Tyre in the middle of the night, as in earlier versions, Pericles discusses his dilemma at length with his trusted adviser. It might be argued that this innovation is simply a dramatic expedient, designed to inform the audience of the reasons for Pericles's sudden departure. But this scene accomplishes much more than that. In the traditional story one is little aware of the fact that

Pericles is a reigning monarch – he is simply the hero of a Greek romance who undergoes a series of adventures and hardships and gains possession of several kingdoms by the end of the story. The whole emphasis is upon Pericles the man battered about by fortune – the fact that he is a prince is a mere convention. In the Ur-*Pericles*, however, the hero is seen in a new dimension: he becomes the good king who flees his own kingdom because his presence would endanger his subjects:

> Which care of them, not pity of myself –
> Who am no more but as the tops of trees
> Which fence the roots they grow by and defend them –
> Makes both my body pine and soul to languish,
> And punish that before that he would punish.   I.2.29–33

In older versions, Apollonius departs from Tyre to save his own life, with no apparent concern about his subjects or who will govern them. As we have seen, moreover, Pericles values the frankness and criticism of his counsellor. In many respects, he represents the true King just as Helicanus depicts the true Courtier. As Pericles says to the old counsellor: 'Thou show'dst a subject's shine, I a true prince' (I.2.124).

There is no need to emphasize the importance of the political ideas here expressed – they are in most instances commonplace notions of the time. What does seem significant is that a new thematic structure is being imposed upon the old legend. A whole scene is created in order to discuss a prince's relationship to his counsellor and to depict an ideal king and courtier.

Once the theme of kingship is established, the natural contrasts of the story gain new meaning. King Antiochus and his steward, Thaliard, become the antithesis of Pericles and Helicanus. Antiochus is called a tyrant in both the novel and play. He is guilty of committing incest with his daughter – a heinous sin which subverts the order of nature. Moreover, through long practice Antiochus and his daughter have become unconscious of their crime:

> But custom what they did begin
> Was with long use account no sin.   Prologue, 29–30

Thaliard, in contrast to Helicanus, does not reprove his king, but attempts to carry out his command to kill Pericles. To make the central contrast obvious, the two courts of Tyre and Antioch are effectively juxtaposed in both Wilkins and Shakespeare.

While an inherent contrast exists between these two courts in the tradition of the legend, such is not the case between Tyre and Tharsus. Accordingly, Strangulio, who is traditionally an ordinary citizen of Tharsus, becomes in the novel and play Cleon, its governor. Cleon and his wife, Dionyza, are the usual *false friends* of Greek romance, and in their new role of rulers they add another antithesis to the thematic structure of kingship. Their ingratitude and Pericles's benevolence are enhanced by a new variation from the traditional legend. Traditionally, Pericles bestows his supply of grain upon the famishing town in return for a safe refuge. In Wilkins and Shakespeare, it is made clear that he has come to Tharsus specifically to relieve their famine.

Pericles's third adventure brings him to the court of King Simonides and his daughter Thaisa. Simonides is traditionally a good king and naturally suggests comparison with Pericles, contrast with Antiochus and Cleon. But Simonides's goodness in earlier versions of the story is not so much directly stated as implied by his actions. In Wilkins, however, the king's virtue is directly announced: 'Our countrey heere on the which you are driuen sir, is called *Pentapolis*, and our good king thereof is called *Symonides*: the Good King call you him, quoth *Pericles*? Yea, and rightly so called sir, quoth the poore Fisherman, who so gouernes his king-dome with iustice and vprightnesse, that he is no readier to com-maund, than we his subiects are willing to obey. He is a happy King, quoth *Pericles*, since he gaines the name of Good by his gouernment' (page 34). And almost the very same lines appear in Shakespeare:

FIRST FISHERMAN This is called Pentapolis, and our king the good Simonides.

PERICLES The good Simonides, do you call him?

FIRST FISHERMAN Ay, sir; and he deserves so to be called for his peaceable reign and good government.

PERICLES He is a happy king, since he gains from his subjects the name of good by his government.   II.1.97–103

Simonides becomes an important part in the thematic development of kingship, rivalling Pericles in stature. Moreover, our definition of the true king is amplified. The dialogue between Pericles and Helicanus described the king's relationship with his counsellors. The present scene defines his relationship with his subjects: 'he gains from his subjects the name of good by his government.' It seems clear that through certain modifications of the traditional story a new theme has been imposed upon the legend. By the addition of several scenes, by the aggrandizement of a heretofore minor character, and by exploiting an already inherent antithetical structure, certain ideas on kingship are suggested which find no parallel in earlier versions of the romance. It therefore seems highly probable that, since these modifications appear only in Wilkins and Shakespeare, the theme of kingship itself was derived from the Ur-*Pericles*.

This is not to say that this theme dominates either Wilkins's or Shakespeare's works in the way it may have controlled the original play. There are simply vestiges in both: in the novel they are scattered throughout, while in the play they are limited almost exclusively to the first two acts.

Thus the last scene dealing with kingship and closely resembling the novel occurs towards the end of the second act. Helicanus informs Escanes of the strange death of King Antiochus, which he sees as heaven's just vengeance:

> And yet but justice; for though
> This king were great, his greatness was no guard
> To bar heaven's shaft, but sin had his reward.   II.4.13–15

King Antiochus and his daughter are struck down by lightning as they ride in their chariot. And this example of heavenly retribution may have first led a dramatist interested in the legend to develop the theme of kingship, because it dramatically demonstrates the punishment of an evil king in contrast to the reward that God bestows upon good kings.

Immediately after Helicanus makes his speech, he is beset by the anxious nobles who want him to become king because they assume that Pericles is dead. Helicanus persuades them to wait a year (in the novel it is three months) before they give up hope. The scene, of course, illustrates the complete loyalty of the true counsellor, and, needless to say, it has no source in the traditional legend.

We have said that the theme of kingship continues to appear in the latter parts of the novel, while it largely disappears in the last three acts of Shakespeare's play. This is best seen in scenes which correspond closely to the novel. Lysimachus, the governor of Mytilene, differs from other rulers that appear in the legend. He is neither wholly good nor wholly evil, but simply sins in visiting the brothel where Marina is imprisoned. She, in the tradition of the legend, arouses the pity of the governor by relating her tragic story. In Wilkins's novel, however, Lysimachus is not moved by her fate: 'But the Gouernour suspecting these teares, but to be some new cunning, which her matron the Bawde had instructed her in, to drawe him to a more large expence' (page 88). Therefore, Marina appeals to his position as governor:

If as you say (my Lorde) you are the Gouernour, let not your authoritie, which should teach you to rule others, be the meanes to make you mis-gouerne your selfe: If the eminence of your place came vnto you by discent, and the royalty of your blood, let not your life prooue your birth a bastard: If it were throwne vpon you by opinion, make good, that opinion was the cause to make you great. What reason is there in your Iustice, who hath power ouer all, to vndoe any? . . . It is not good, answered *Marina*, when you that are the Gouernour, who should liue well, the better to be bolde to punish euill, doe knowe that there is such a roofe, and yet come vnder it.   (pages 89–90)

Clearly, Marina is giving Lysimachus a moral lesson on how to be a good ruler – it is a continuation of the same theme of kingship which was developed in the early parts of the novel, and again it is grafted on to the old plot. In Wilkins's novel, Marina's argument is so convincing that Lysimachus is converted: 'I hither came with thoughtes intemperate, foule and deformed, the which your paines so well haue laued, that they are now white' (page 91).

In Shakespeare the same scene of conversion is enacted, but Marina's lengthy argument is reduced to:

> If you were born to honour, show it now;
> If put upon you, make the judgement good
> That thought you worthy of it.   IV.6.91–4

This is clearly a restatement of one point in Marina's argument. The rest of the speech has been discarded. Apparently, Shakespeare is not so concerned with the theme of kingship as was the earlier playwright. In any event, he is ready to sacrifice it when it conflicts with his own artistic purpose.[8] Shakespeare is intent on making Lysimachus into a more desirable suitor for Marina by removing as much of the blemish from him as possible without doing violence to the plot of the old play. We have, therefore, the rather improbable situation of Lysimachus's denying that he came to the brothel with any ill intentions. Consequently, Shakespeare has to strike out most of Marina's argument, since Lysimachus does not need conversion. Yet he can still show his admiration for Marina's speech in words that clearly show Shakespeare's revision:

> Had I brought hither a corrupted mind,
> Thy speech had altered it.   IV.6.103–4

In traditional versions of the legend Pericles strikes his daughter before he recognizes her. The blow usually comes as a result of Marina's reproof: 'O good gentleman, hearken vnto the voice of her that beseecheth thee, and haue respect to the suite of a virgin, that thinking it a far vnworthy thing that so wise a man should languish in griefe, and die with sorrow.'[9] In Wilkins this plea is altered in a way strikingly similar to the revision made of Marina's traditional appeal to Lysimachus. Indeed, it begins with the same idea that a governor must be able to govern himself:

Whereupon she beganne with morall precepts to reproove him, and tolde him, that hee was borne a Prince, whose dignity being to gouerne others, it was most foule in him to misgouerne himselfe. Which while he continued in that sullen estate, he did no lesse, thus to mourne for the losse of a wife and childe, or at any of his owne misfortunes, approoued that he was an enemy to the authoritie of the heauens, whose power was to dispose of him and his, at their pleasure: and that it was as vnfitte for him to repine (for his continuing sorrow shewed he did no lesse) against their determinations and their unaltered willes, as it was for the Giants to make warre against the Gods, who were confounded in their enterprise.   (pages 104–5)

Pericles, upon hearing this reproof, strikes Marina in the face. In Shakespeare, Pericles merely pushes her back, though Marina's words still seem to refer to an earlier version:

> I said, my lord, if you did know my parentage
> You would not do me violence.   V.i.98–9

Pericles, of course, no longer has any motive for striking her because Marina's reproof has been entirely eliminated from the play. And the deletion is highly significant – it clearly reveals the extent of Shakespeare's divergence from the Ur-*Pericles*, for Marina's reproof and Pericles's violence, traditional features of the legend, can no longer be tolerated in Shakespeare's play because the story has undergone a basic transformation.

3

Thus far we have traced a pattern common to both Wilkins and Shakespeare, the theme of kingship, which presumably was an integral part of the Ur-*Pericles*. But we have seen that while this theme weaves its way throughout the novel, in the play it appears prominently only in the first two acts – it holds little concern for the playwright after that because his interest seems to lie elsewhere; in fact, he is willing, as we have seen, to eliminate the theme of kingship entirely when it conflicts with his own purpose.

Scholars have commonly justified Shakespeare's changes in the recognition scene on the ground that he was eliminating an act of outright brutality which seemed out of character in the hero of the play. True as this may be, such an assumption overlooks the equally relevant fact that Marina's reproof, which is the cause of the blow, entirely contradicts Shakespeare's purpose. His Pericles is in no sense 'an enemy to the authoritie of the heauens', nor a prince who misgoverns himself. He is, in fact, as J. M. S. Tompkins has suggested, 'Of all Shakespeare's heroes ... the most patient man'.[10]

The essence of this patience finds expression in Pericles's

acceptance of his fate, his almost complete submission to 'The powers above us':

> We cannot but obey
> The powers above us. Could I rage and roar
> As doth the sea she lies in, yet the end
> Must be as 'tis.   III.3.9–12

This is spoken in grief at the loss of his queen, but it is a tranquil grief that is arrived at only after the immediacy of the event has passed. A greater trial of his faith comes at the instance of the calamity:

> PERICLES   O you gods!
>   Why do you make us love your goodly gifts,
>   And snatch them straight away? We here below
>   Recall not what we give, and therein may
>   Use honour with you.
> LYCHORIDA   Patience, good sir, even for this charge.
> PERICLES Now, mild may be thy life!
>   For a more blusterous birth had never babe;
>   Quiet and gentle thy conditions! for
>   Thou art the rudeliest welcome to this world
>   That ever was prince's child. Happy what follows!
>   Thou hast as chiding a nativity
>   As fire, air, water, earth, and heaven can make,
>   To herald thee from the womb.
>   Even at the first thy loss is more than can
>   Thy portage quit with all thou canst find here.
>   Now the good gods throw their best eyes upon't!
>   III.1.22–37

At the news of Thaisa's death, he bitterly questions the justice of the gods. But he quickly gains control over himself, and his blessing of Marina reveals a resurgent faith, ending with his appeal to 'the good gods'.

We can appreciate the effect that Shakespeare is aiming for by comparing the scene to a parallel passage in Wilkins, who is presumably following the original play more closely. Here the blessing comes before Pericles knows of his wife's death:

Poore inch of Nature (quoth he) thou arte as rudely welcome to the worlde, as euer Princesse Babe was, and hast as chiding a natiuitie, as fire, ayre, earth, and water can affoord thee, when, as if he had forgot himselfe, he abruptly breaks out: but say *Licorida*, how doth my Queene? O sir (quoth she) she hath now passed all daungers, and hath giuen vppe her griefes by ending her life. At which wordes, no tongue is able to expresse the tide of sorrowe that ouer-bounded Pericles, first looking on his Babe, and then crying out for the mother, pittying the one that had lost her bringer ere shee had scarce saluted the worlde, lamenting for himselfe that beene bereft of so inestimable a Iewell by the losse of his wife. (page 59)

Wilkins continues the traditional lamentation scene that follows Thaisa's death. In Gower's *Confessio Amantis*, for example, Apollonius swoons[11] and in the *Gesta Romanorum* 'He tore his garments from his breast, and cast himself with tears and groans upon her inanimate body'.[12] Shakespeare, in contrast, presents a much more subdued mourner, whose personal control is indicative of an inner strength.[13]

It may be argued that Pericles's grief at the supposed death of Marina is inordinate, that his total reclusion from the world does not indicate a submissive acceptance of the ways of the gods; but here again we must realize that Shakespeare did not intend to alter the basic elements of the traditional story – he merely revised the action to gain his own interpretation of the legend. The extent of this revision can be realized only if we try to reconstruct the earlier version he had to work with.

Wilkins follows the traditional legend closely, dividing the lamentation into the grief which Pericles expresses at the news of Marina's death and the outburst which takes place before her supposed tomb:

Which when *Pericles* heard, the very word Death seemed like an edge that cut his heart, his flesh trembled, and his strength failed: yet in that agony a long time standing amased, with his eyes intentiuely fixed on the ground, and at length recouering himselfe, and taking breath, hee first cast his eyes vppe to heauen, saying; O you Gods! extreamity of passion dooth make mee almost ready to accuse you of iniustice . . . . Which [the tomb] when he beheld, and had read the Epitaph, as before written his affection brake out into his eies, and he expressed more actuall sorrow for the losse of her then Inditement can expresse: first, tumbling himselfe vppon her monument, he then fell into a swownd, as if, since he might not leaue all his life with her, yet he would leaue halfe at least, from which trance being at the length recouered, hee apparrelles himselfe in sacke-cloth, running hastily vnto his shippes, desireth the Sea to take him into their wombe, since neither land nor water was fortunate vnto him. (pages 97–9)

Clearly this approaches rebellion against divine providence. Indeed, in both Twine's work and the *Gesta Romanorum*, Pericles entreats his men to cast him into the sea. In contrast, Shakespeare does not dramatize the scene – he chooses to have it related curtly by Gower and a dumb show, although the scene offers natural theatrical possibilities. A short statement describes the lamentation which was detailed in Wilkins: '*Cleon shows Pericles the tomb of Marina, whereat Pericles makes lamentation, puts on sackcloth, and in a mighty passion departs*' (IV.4.22). But there is a more vital difference: there is no hint of rebellion against the gods but only a paroxysm of grief:

> He bears
> A tempest which his mortal vessel tears,
> And yet he rides it out. IV.4.29–31

He makes no attempt to take his own life, though it only prolongs his grief. Shakespeare's artistic skill enables him to impose his own interpretation upon the character of the hero without actually violating the basic tradition. In his hands the theme of kingship is vitalized through the transformation of the hero into an exemplary man and king. Pericles piously submits himself to the will of the gods. His patient endurance is indicative of an inner strength and control. He thus becomes the 'true prince' because by being able to govern himself he is worthy to govern others.

It is interesting to note that Shakespeare's interpretation coincides to some extent with Gower's. In the *Confessio Amantis*, Apollonius, after lamenting the death of his daughter, resigns himself to the ways of God:

> But sithe it may no better be,
> He thonketh god and forth goth he
> Sailende toward Tire ayeine.[14]

There are other striking resemblances which indicate that Shakespeare in rewriting the older play was to some extent influenced by Gower, who, after all, plays a personal role in *Pericles*. Wilkins, for example, in referring to Philoten, Dionyza's daughter, never mentions her name but resorts to such awkward expedients as '*Dyonysa* her daughter' and '*Dyonysaes* daughter', though Philoten is an integral part of the legend, mentioned in most versions. It seems strange that Wilkins, in case the name was missing from the Ur-*Pericles*, could not have obtained this information from some other source – a puzzling question which has been curiously overlooked by scholars. Our interest here lies in the fact that this is one name Shakespeare did not derive from Wilkins's source. The name used by Shakespeare, *Philoten*, resembles most closely Gower's *Philotenne*. (Twine uses *Philomacia*, while *Philomatia* appears in the *Gesta Romanorum*.) Another example of Gower's influence upon Shakespeare is evident in the fact that the feast of Neptune is being celebrated in Mytilene on the day of Pericles's arrival. There is no mention of the feast in Wilkins, Twine, or the *Gesta Romanorum*, but it is described by Gower.

4

Thus far we have examined Shakespeare's reinterpretation of Pericles in the last three acts of the play because it is here that we observe an almost complete absence of the cruder kingship theme that remains so prominent in the first two acts. Moreover, it is generally accepted on the basis of internal evidence that Shakespeare's contribution to *Pericles* is largely limited to the last three acts.[15] This does not mean, however, that Shakespeare did not work on the first part of the play. It seems, rather, that he began by making slight changes in the original play; and, as he progressed, he began to see thematic possibilities in the story of its hero – he began, in short, seriously rewriting later portions of the play. It remains now to be asked whether we can detect evidence in the first two acts of such a thematic revision as we have already traced in the latter part of the play; whether, finally, the play achieves some sense of unity.

At the beginning of Act II, Pericles, shipwrecked on the coast of Pentapolis, addresses the elements:

> Yet cease your ire, you angry stars of heaven!
> Wind, rain, and thunder, remember earthly man
> Is but a substance that must yield to you;
> And I, as fits my nature, do obey you.   II.i.1–4

In contrast, Wilkins relates that Pericles accused 'the Gods of this iniury doone to his innocencie' (page 32). Clearly, we have already here the outline of the submissive, Job-like hero that we encounter later in the play. But does this mean that Shakespeare has simply organized his play around a passive hero, who is buffeted about by adverse fortunes until the gods miraculously restore his losses? It would appear so at first glance; and yet there are scenes in Act I which would seem to imply a far greater unity for the play.

Pericles comes to Antioch and risks his life to solve the riddle because he is enamoured of Antiochus's daughter. He is permitted to see the truth of the riddle, but at what a price:

> O you powers
> That give heaven countless eyes to view men's acts,
> Why cloud they not their sights perpetually,
> If this be true, which makes me pale to read it?   I.i.72–5

The gods have given him power to see the reality behind appearance, to see sin stored within a 'glorious casket':

> Fair glass of light, I loved you, and could still,
> Were not this glorious casket stored with ill.
> But I must tell you now my thoughts revolt;
> For he's no man on whom perfections wait
> That, knowing sin within, will touch the gate.   I.i.76–80

Pericles's awakening is abrupt and shatters his dream of youthful love. He has found sin where all seemed beauty and virtue because his eyes have been opened to a new view of life. And with this vision comes disillusionment and melancholy:

> Why should this change of thoughts,
> The sad companion, dull-eyed melancholy,
> Be my so used a guest as not an hour
> In the day's glorious walk, or peaceful night,
> The tomb where grief should sleep, can breed me quiet?
> Here pleasures court mine eyes, and mine eyes shun them,
> And danger, which I feared, is at Antioch,
> Whose arm seems far too short to hit me here.
> Yet neither pleasure's art can joy my spirits,
> Nor yet the other's distance comfort me.　　　　I.2.1–10

Pericles reasons that his seemingly unjustified fears gain 'after-nourishment' from the cares he has about the safety of his people. And it is this concern for his subjects which, we are told in both the play and Wilkins's novel, causes him to flee Tyre. However, in Shakespeare, as in no other version, we are given another reason for his departure. Helicanus informs the lords that while Pericles was in Antioch

> Royal Antiochus, on what cause I know not,
> Took some displeasure at him; at least he judged so;
> And doubting lest that he had erred or sinned,
> To show his sorrow, he'd correct himself;
> So puts himself unto the shipman's toil,
> With whom each minute threatens life or death.　　I.3.19–24

Helicanus, of course, is hiding the real truth from the nobles, the fact that Pericles knows Antiochus's secret. But this does not fully explain these lines. It appears peculiar to use the term *sin* for an act that may have displeased King Antiochus, and furthermore to do penance for it in a manner that 'each minute threatens life or death'. It seems that these lines are impregnated with theological implications. They suggest that Pericles's fear of Antiochus actually stands for an awareness of sin from which Pericles himself has not remained completely pure. By his own admission, he has been inflamed with desire for Antiochus's daughter; and, though he has not sinned actively, his eyes have been opened by an abrupt contact with evil.[16]

The fact that the above speech does not appear in Wilkins or any other version of the legend does not, of course, prove necessarily that it was added by Shakespeare. Yet if he did not introduce the lines, we are faced by the unlikely possibility that they must have been present in the original play and left out by Wilkins; for, as we have pointed out earlier, the character of Helicanus the Counsellor was superimposed upon the story to develop the theme of kingship. In any case, the scene tends to unify the play by imposing a new interpretation upon the hero's ordeal. King Antiochus is indirectly the cause of all of Pericles's tribulations, for fear of him causes the latter to go to sea in the first place, and news of Antiochus's death results in a second disastrous voyage and the consequent loss of Thaisa and Marina. Yet this makes Antiochus little more than a catalytic agent unless we see him as more than just a tyrant seeking to silence Pericles. In Shakespeare's play, Antiochus is actually the central agent of evil, for he defiles the object of Pericles's love, and opens the Prince's eyes to the reality that lies behind appearance. Pericles's flight from Antiochus thus becomes an escape from evil and his suffering an act of penance for the 'golden fruit' he desired to taste.

He submits himself, as we have seen, completely to the will of the gods and accepts almost passively the tribulations that rain down upon him. In the end, the gods reward him and wondrously restore his daughter and wife to him. But more significantly, Pericles himself is reborn. Marina restores his faith to the point where he is ready to believe what seems impossible:

> Falseness cannot come from thee; for thou lookest
> Modest as Justice, and thou seem'st a palace
> For the crowned Truth to dwell in. I will believe thee,
> And make my senses credit thy relation
> To points that seem impossible; for thou lookest
> Like one I loved indeed.   V.1.119–24

Because he accepts Marina's story on faith, he is spiritually reborn, for he discovers the good that lies beneath apparent evil: the loss of his daughter, which has seemed evil, has turned into good in direct contradiction to the events of the first scene of the play. Indeed, there are other parallels which suggest such a contrast. Marina brings about Pericles's rebirth:

> O, come hither,
> Thou that beget'st him that did thee beget ... V.i.193–4

echoing the incest theme of the riddle:

> He's father, son, and husband mild;
> I mother, wife, and yet his child. I.i.68–9

In contrast to the music that marked the entrance of Antiochus's daughter, music that proved not 'lawful', Pericles now hears the music of the spheres:

> HELICANUS My lord, I hear none.
> PERICLES None?
>   The music of the spheres! List, my Marina.
> LYSIMACHUS It is not good to cross him; give him way.
> PERICLES Rarest sounds! Do ye not hear?
>   *Music*
> LYSIMACHUS My lord, I hear.
> PERICLES Most heavenly music!
>   It nips me unto list'ning, and thick slumber
>   Hangs upon mine eyes: let me rest. V.i.226–33

The music of the spheres, which appears only in Shakespeare's version, suggests a higher reality which Pericles now apprehends. He has been initiated into a vision of experience from which the rest are shut out. Lysimachus can only try to humour his seeming hallucination, but cannot comprehend his experience.

The music of the spheres drowses Pericles's already frenzied senses, and in his sleep Diana appears to him in order to guide him to his lost wife. The appearance of the goddess can be dismissed as a simple *deus ex machina* – it certainly served that purpose in traditional versions of the legend including Wilkins's – but here it is of more significance. Like the music of the spheres, the theophany indicates divine approval of Pericles's spiritual rebirth and points to the heavenly source of his new vision of life. It may be this supernatural element of the legend which first attracted Shakespeare to the Ur-*Pericles* In any case, the theme of death and rebirth, of good behind seeming evil, which Shakespeare developed in *Pericles*, reappears in his later romances. Certainly, we may say that the *Weltansicht* expressed in Shakespeare's tragicomedies, which perhaps first took shape in *Pericles*, is a far departure from the world of his tragedies. To quote Theodore Spencer:

Rebirth, through spring, through woman, acceptance of things as they are, but with glory around them – that is what we find in all the plays from *Pericles* on. In the tragedies the appearance might be good, but the reality – the lust of Gertrude, the faithlessness of Cressida, the hypocrisy of Regan and Goneril, the crown of Scotland, and, to Timon, all mankind – was evil. In the last plays the appearance may be evil, but the reality is good. Marina and Thaisa are alive, not dead, Imogen is faithful, Hermione and Perdita are restored to Leontes, and Miranda's view of man is the opposite of Timon's:

> How beauteous mankind is! O brave new world,
> That has such people in't![17]

I have endeavoured to examine Shakespeare's manner of reshaping the material available to him in preparing *Pericles* for the stage. I have accepted the theory that both he and George Wilkins based their respective works in part at least on a common source, a play now lost. By isolating elements common to both Wilkins and Shakespeare, it became possible to recognize what may have been the dominant theme of the original play, and, more significantly, to understand the direction that Shakespeare's revision took. In his hands, the hero of the Apollonius legend became a Job-like figure, accepting almost passively the tribulations the gods had prepared for him. And the old play of kingship became a drama of faith, in which innocence is penetrated by experience until both merge and are transfigured into a richer vision of life.

NOTES

1. See Albert H. Smyth, 'Shakespeare's Pericles and Apollonius of Tyre', *Proceedings of the American Philosophical Society* 37 (1898), pages 206–312; S. Singer, *Apollonius von Tyrus* (1895).
2. Philip Edwards has suggested that both the novel and the Quarto are reports of a play probably wholly written by Shakespeare ('An

Approach to the Problem of *Pericles*', *Shakespeare Survey 5* (1952), pages 25–49). J. C. Maxwell argues against single authorship for the play, but believes that the novel was dependent upon the existing play rather than upon an earlier version (*Pericles* (New Cambridge Shakespeare, 1956), pages xli–xxv).

3. 'The Problem of Pericles', *English Studies* 30 (1949), pages 65–83. Restated in his *Shakespeare as Collaborator* (1960).

4. *Confessio Amantis* (VIII.271–2008); based primarily on the *Pantheon* of Godfrey of Viterbo.

5. *The Patterne of Painefull Aduentures* (1576, reprinted 1607); derived in general from the *Gesta Romanorum*.

6. Baldassare Castiglione, *The Courtier*, translated by Sir Thomas Hoby (1900), page 337.

7. George Wilkins, *The Painfull Aduentures of Pericles, Prince of Tyre*, edited by Kenneth Muir (1953), page 21. Subsequent references to this edition will appear in the text.

8. Significantly, it is this scene between Lysimachus and Marina that Muir uses as his principal example of 'concealed blank verse' in Wilkins's novel which does not appear in the Quarto (*Shakespeare as Collaborator*, pages 64–9).

9. Laurence Twine, *The Patterne of Painefull Aduentures*, in *Shakespeare's Library*, edited by W. C. Hazlitt (1875), Volume 4, page 311.

10. Professor Tompkins, in her essay 'Why Pericles?', suggests that Shakespeare changed the name of his hero from Apollonius to Pericles because Plutarch stresses the patience of Pericles (*Review of English Studies* 3 (1952), pages 315–24).

I have found further evidence for Tompkins's theory in Wilson's *Arte of Rhetorique* (1553; 1909 edition, page 81). Pericles is here exemplified as a man who patiently endures the suffering of adverse fortune. Interestingly enough the name Simonides also appears in Wilson, though there seems to be no connexion with the King of Pentapolis in Shakespeare (page 212). The *Homily against Contention and Brawling* also cites Pericles (quoting from Plutarch) as an example of patience and restraint (*The Two Books of Homilies* (1859, page 141)).

11. John Gower, *Confessio Amantis*, in *Shakespeare's Library*, Volume 4, page 203.

12. *Gesta Romanorum*, translated by the Reverend C. Swan (1906), page 277.

13. Since this essay was completed, F. D. Hoeniger has corroborated this point in his introduction to the new Arden edition of *Pericles* (1963), pages lxxxvi–lxxxviii.

14. Gower, page 217.

15. Hardin Craig argues that Shakespeare's revision of an earlier play begins extensively only with Act IV ('Pericles and the Painfull Adventures', *Studies in Philology* 45 (1948), pages 600–605).

16. G. Wilson Knight points out that Pericles 'has not actively sinned, except in giving way to a lustful and cheating fantasy, but the result is immersion into an experience of evil with accompanying disgust and danger. It is a fall in the theological sense' (*The Crown of Life* (1947), page 38).

17. 'Appearance and Reality in Shakespeare's Last Plays', *Modern Philology* 39 (1942), page 269.

from *English Studies* 44 (1963), pages 401–14

THIRTEEN

Pericles and the Miracle Play

F. D. Hoeniger

So far, I have stressed the uniqueness of *Pericles*, both in relation to Shakespeare's earlier work and to the play's sources. The interpretation I have offered receives some oblique support from a direction where scholars have so far refused to look. The play is curiously, and I think significantly, like the vernacular religious drama in its later, more developed, and less rigid forms, especially the saint's play. One could argue that from plays of this kind, with which Shakespeare was surely acquainted, most of the broad structural features of *Pericles* are derived. They are at any rate paralleled; among them the device of the choric presenter in the person of a poet, the building up of the action out of a large number of loosely related episodes, the treatment of the play as a 'pageant' rather than a work of highly concentrated action around a central conflict, the tragi-comic development of the action, the large part taken in it by supernatural powers, and the construction of the whole so as to serve an explicit didactic end.

If this observation is sound, it has far-reaching implications for our understanding of *Pericles*. It would mean that not only its story-material and its presenting chorus are medieval, but also its essential dramatic form. And if this is the case, can it perhaps be said to echo the spirit of the bygone age in its underlying thought or purpose also? Earlier, the play's effect was tentatively described as one of wonder at the mysteries and miracles of existence. A look at the play's opening chorus reveals its basic intentions: 'The purchase is to make men glorious'. It seems no accident that this line also describes adequately the basic aim of the legends of the saints and of the Miracle plays derived from them.

An introduction like this is not the place for presenting in great detail all the evidence for the assertion that the structure of *Pericles* closely parallels that of certain Miracle or saint's plays. Here, a few general observations must suffice. English saint's plays have been somewhat ignored because only very few have survived. But it is known that many were performed all over England from about 1100 to 1580, and such a long tradition can hardly have failed to make an impact on the professional writers for the Elizabethan stage. Moreover, much can be inferred about the general nature of many of the lost plays by examining analogous continental plays, such as those in the *Miracles de Notre Dame*. I believe it was J. M. Manly who first recognized the full importance of these Miracle plays for our understanding of Elizabethan drama. Miracle plays, as he defines the term, deal with subjects drawn from the legends of saints and martyrs, and thus can be sharply differentiated from the cyclic plays of Chester, York, and elsewhere, which deal with subjects drawn from Scripture. He claimed that 'these Miracle plays . . . were more important for the development of the drama in England than the great Scripture cycles'.[1]

A qualification applies to those plays based on the Apocrypha, notably the Book of Tobit, which resemble saint's plays rather than cycle plays. But whether drawing for its material on the *Legenda Aurea* or the Apocrypha, 'the most important fact concerning the Miracle play is that its material was essentially romantic'. Their stories were thus essentially like that of *Pericles*. The shift from a religious to a more broadly secular emphasis came easily in the Renaissance.

That Elizabethan secular romantic drama was in large part inspired by continental precedents, especially in Italy, is not in question. Yet one must recognize that this influence had been prepared for natively by the established tradition of the Miracle play. All that was needed in *Pericles* was to carry one step further the process of secularization, already much in evidence in some of the later Miracle plays: to replace God or Christ by Diana or Neptune, and the Christian saint or apocryphal character by a prince or princess; for there is no greater difference between the saint's legends and the romance of Apollonius of Tyre. They are both biographical romances. The fate of Pericles, like that of St Andrew or Mary Magdalene or Tobit, is governed by Providence. Like them, he undergoes manifold adventures, which bring upon him great suffering. Like them, he is lifted out of despair by a miraculous-seeming intervention of a god – a Christ or a Diana.

Of the few surviving English Miracle plays, the one which reminds one most closely of *Pericles* is the Digby play of *Mary Magdalene*. Roughly equal to *Pericles* in length, it divides, like *Pericles*, sharply into two parts, though this is probably pure coincidence. The first part is in twenty scenes. The opening five set forth the tyrannous pride and covetousness of Emperor Tiberius, lord of this world. Under him Satan flourishes. Satan's forces beset the Castle of Maudlyn, and Lechery succeeds in tempting Mary Magdalene, one of its inmates and owners. The later scenes present her redemption and the revival of her brother Lazarus, both by Jesus. Margaret, Martha, and Lazarus return to their castle. The second part is devoted mainly to the role played by Mary Magdalene in the conversion of the king of Marcyll (Marseilles). The final six scenes carry her life to its conclusion, showing how she was sustained in the desert by good from heaven and ending in the burial of her body and the ascension of her soul. But it is the section dealing with Marcyll's conversion that has greatest interest for us. In a vision, Magdalene is commanded by Christ to go by ship to Marcyll in order to convert the Mohammedan king. There she persuades the King and the Queen to cast off their allegiance to the heathen gods. As a consequence, the Queen's desire to be with child is miraculously fulfilled. They prepare for a voyage to the Holy Land, but on the way a violent storm overtakes them, and the Queen dies even while giving birth to her child. Similarly as in III.1 of *Pericles*, the ship's crew demand that both Queen and child be set on a rock. The King himself safely reaches the Holy Land, where he is baptized by Peter. On his return voyage he discovers his babe unharmed on the rock, and his wife suddenly returns to life as if awaking from a trance. They return joyfully, and bless Mary Magdalene, who exhorts them to lead a steadfast Christian life.

It will be seen that in both *Mary Magdalene* and *Pericles* the action is biographical. In both, the protagonist is involved in a series of extraordinary adventures and turns of fortune. Both have a happy ending, largely effected by supernatural intervention. The episodes in both are loosely co-ordinated, and sometimes of a highly spectacular nature. And there are some remarkable correspondences in the detailed incidents.[2] Yet apart from the Christian emphasis of the Digby play, there is of course one further significant difference. The double plot of two generations is not found in the earlier play. Nor is it part of any other Miracle play, with the exception of certain plays based on the apocryphal story of Tobit.[3] We know that the authors of *Pericles* took it over from the narrative source.

And so this discussion has come full circle. However much the structure of *Pericles* may owe to the medieval tradition of Miracle plays, the basic feature of its double plot of two generations can safely be said to be peculiar to it and the other Romances of Shakespeare's last period, and with this plot the theme of loss and restoration. This theme was to be treated by Shakespeare both more clearly and with greater dramatic effectiveness in the plays after *Pericles*, which are of Shakespeare's sole authorship. In them Shakespeare's final vision becomes clearer. And as it becomes clearer, it becomes also something different, as we should expect from Shakespeare, who never simply repeated himself. For instance, there is hardly a hint in *Pericles* of the consciousness of guilt and contrition that haunts certain characters in *Cymbeline* and in *The Winter's Tale*. Yet this does not lessen the extreme interest *Pericles* must have for students of *The Winter's Tale* and *The Tempest*. For in the earlier play Shakespeare can be seen groping for much that was to be given consummate expression in his final work.

NOTES

1. 'The Miracle Play in Mediaeval England', *Essays by Divers Hands*, N.S. VII (1927), pages 133-53.
2. As D. A. Stauffer makes clear in the opening chapter of *English Biography before 1700* (1930), early biography was almost exclusively that of saints or of royal persons, and hagiography exercised a strong influence on the biographies of kings. It is not surprising,

then, that a narrative and biographical drama like *Pericles* should partake of the saint's 'life' and be in the tradition of the saint's play. Pericles, like the converted Marcyll in *Mary Magdalene*, is something of the royal saint, uniting the royal 'life' with the hagiographical 'life'.

3. No early English play on this story is extant but we know of one having been performed at Lincoln (E. K. Chambers, *The Mediaeval Stage* (1903), Volume 2, page 131), and of another referred to in Henslowe's Diary in May and June 1602 (edited by Greg, Volume 1, pages 166–8). A full-length sixteenth-century French play on the story is Mlle de Roches, *Acte de la Tragi-comédie*. Like *Pericles*, it has a double plot of two generations, with loss and restoration.

from Introduction to *Pericles* (new Arden Shakespeare edition, 1963) by F. D. Hoeniger, pages lxxxviii–xci

SUGGESTIONS FOR FURTHER READING

Pericles, edited by F. D. Hoeniger (new Arden Shakespeare, 1963). The most useful edition for a close study of the play, containing, in addition to the editor's Introduction (part of which is reprinted above), ample notes to the text, and an extract from one of the principal sources, Laurence Twine's *The Patterne of Painefull Aduentures* (1607). This and other source material will shortly appear in G. Bullough's *Narrative and Dramatic Sources of Shakespeare*.

KENNETH MUIR: *Shakespeare's Sources*, Volume 1 (1957), and *Shakespeare as Collaborator* (1960). Discuss the complicated problems of the text and authorship of the play, and its relationship to George Wilkins's novel, *The Painfull Adventures of Pericles* (1608), an edition of which Professor Muir published in 1953.

G. WILSON KNIGHT: 'The Writing of *Pericles*', in *The Crown of Life* (1947). An interpretation which emphasizes Shakespeare's reworking of motifs from his previous plays, his increased reliance upon 'poetic magic' rather than 'realistic coherence', and (cutting through the textual difficulties) the unity of conception behind the play.

'CYMBELINE'

FOURTEEN

The Artlessness of *Cymbeline*

Harley Granville-Barker

IF the play's construction is his unfettered work he is at odds with himself indeed. From the beginning he has been a good craftsman, and particularly skilful in the manoeuvring of any two stories into a symmetrical whole. But here the attempt results in a very lop-sided affair. The first scene sees both themes stated: Imogen's marriage to Posthumus, and the strange loss, years before, of her brothers. Then Iachimo's intrigue against her is pursued and completed, most expeditiously; the entire business is done in less than twelve hundred lines, with Cloten and his wooing thrown in. But meanwhile we see nothing, and hear only once, of the young Princes. Certainly Imogen cannot set out on her wanderings and encounter them any sooner than she does; and, once she does, this part of the story – it is the phase of the blending of the two stories, and customarily would be the penultimate phase of the plot as a whole – makes due progress. But what of Posthumus? He is now banished from the scene for the space of another fourteen hundred lines or so. That is bad enough. But when he does return to it, the only contrivances for his development are a soliloquy, a mute duel with Iachimo, a quite undramatic encounter with an anonymous 'Lord', a talk with a gaoler, and a pointless pageant that he sleeps through. This is far worse. He was never much of a hero, but here he becomes a bore. The difficulties are plain. Once his faith in Imogen is destroyed and he has commanded her murder (and we do not need both to see him sending the command and Pisanio receiving it), there is nothing left for him to do till he returns repentant; and once he returns he cannot openly encounter any of the more important characters, or the dramatic effect of his sudden appearance in the last scene (and to that, in its elaboration, every thread, obviously, is to be drawn) will be discounted. But it is just such difficulties as these that the playwright learns to surmount. Can we see Shakespeare, past-master in his craft, making such a mess of a job? If nothing else showed a strange finger in the pie, this letting Posthumus slip from the current of the story, and the clumsiness of the attempt to restore him to prominence in it, should suffice to. Nevertheless, Shakespeare's stamp, or an excellent imitation of it, is on much of the actual writing hereabouts. One would not even swear him entire exemption from the apparitions.

> Poor shadows of Elysium, hence, and rest
> Upon your never-withering banks of flowers.
> Be not with mortal accidents oppressed:
> No care of yours it is; you know 'tis ours.
> Whom best I love I cross; to make my gift,
> The more delayed, delighted.   V.4.97–102

That, though pedestrian, is, for the occasion, good enough.

These structural clumsinesses concern the last two thirds of the play. The passages that Furness gibbets – the most and the worst of them – fall there too; and there we may find, besides, minor banalities of stagecraft, set as a rule in a poverty of writing, the stagecraft and writing both showing a startling change from the opulently thrifty methods that went to the making of *Coriolanus*, *Antony and Cleopatra*, *King Lear*, *Othello*, this play's predecessors.

Are we to debit the mature Shakespeare with the dramatic impotence of Pisanio's soliloquy:

> I heard no letter from my master since
> I wrote him Imogen was slain. 'Tis strange.
> Nor hear I from my mistress, who did promise
> To yield me often tidings. Neither know I
> What is betid to Cloten, but remain
> Perplexed in all. The heavens still must work.
> Wherein I am false I am honest; not true, to be true.
> These present wars shall find I love my country,
> Even to the note o'th'King, or I'll fall in them.
> All other doubts, by time let them be cleared:
> Fortune brings in some boats that are not steered.
>   IV.3.36–46

It is poor stuff; the information in it is hardly needed; it does not seem even meant to provide time for a change of scene or costume. Nor does Shakespeare now use to let his minor characters soliloquize to help his plots along.[1] There are two other such soliloquies: the Queen's rejoicing over Imogen's disappearance, rising to its forcible-feeble climax with

> Gone she is
> To death or to dishonour, and my end
> Can make good use of either. She being down,
> I have the placing of the British crown.   III.5.63–6

This is nearly as redundant in matter; but villainy has its rights, and premature exultation over the misfortunes of the virtuous is one of them. Though it be Shakespeare at his worst, it may still be Shakespeare. So, more certainly, is the Second Lord's soliloquy, with which Cloten's second scene ends. This probably owes its existence to Imogen's need of a little extra time for getting into bed. But it adds information, and, more importantly, reiterates the sympathy of the court for her in her trouble. It falls earlier in the play, in the stretch of the action that few will deny to be wholly Shakespeare's.

But, quality of writing and the unimportance of the speakers apart, is there not a curious artlessness about nearly all the soliloquies in the play? They are so frankly informative. Shakespeare's use of the soliloquy is no more subject to rule than are any other of his methods; but his tendency, as his art matures, is both to make it mainly a vehicle for the intimate thought and emotion of his chief characters only, and to let its plot-forwarding seem quite incidental to this. *Antony and Cleopatra*, a play of action, contains few soliloquies, and they are not of dominant importance; Coriolanus, the man of action, is given hardly one; Hamlet, the reflective hero, abounds in them, but they are germane to idea rather than story. Iago's soliloquies, it may be said, frankly develop the plot. It will be truer to say they forecast it; the dramatic justification for this being that it is a plot, in both senses, hatched in his own brain.[2] And we notice that once it is well under way he soliloquizes little more.

But in *Cymbeline*, what a disintegrating change! Posthumus's soliloquies are reflectively emotional enough. The first is an outburst of rage; it would not, one supposes, have been any differently framed for Othello or Antony. The others contain such simply informative passages as

> I am brought hither
> Among th'Italian gentry, and to fight
> Against my lady's kingdom.
>   ... I'll disrobe me
> Of these Italian weeds, and suit myself
> As does a Briton peasant ...   V.1.17–19, 22–4

as the seemingly needless

> I have resumed again
> The part I came in.   V.3.75–6

And one asks, without being quite sure of the answer, how far is that

> You married ones,
> If each of you should take this course, how many
> Must murder wives much better than themselves
> For wrying but a little! ...   V.1.2–5

meant to be addressed plump to his audience? But the flow of emotion is generally strong enough to sweep any such obstacles along.

Iachimo passes from the dramatic perfection of the soliloquy in the bedchamber to the feebleness of his repentant

> Knighthoods and honours borne
> As I wear mine are titles but of scorn.
> If that thy gentry, Britain, go before
> This lout as he exceeds our lords, the odds
> Is that we scarce are men, and you are gods.   V.2.6–10

– with which we hesitate to discredit Shakespeare in any case.

But what of that not merely ingenuously informative, but so *ex post facto* confidence from Belarius:

> O Cymbeline, heaven and my conscience knows
> Thou didst unjustly banish me! Whereon,
> At three and two years old, I stole these babes,
> Thinking to bar thee of succession as
> Thou refts me of my lands. Euriphile,
> Thou wast their nurse; they took thee for their mother,
> And every day do honour to her grave.
> Myself, Belarius, that am Morgan called,
> They take for natural father.   III.3.99–107

We shall have to search far back in Shakespeare's work for anything quite so apparently artless, and may be doubtful of finding it even there. Furness would make the collaborator responsible for Belarius. But what about the long aside – a soliloquy, in effect – by which Cornelius lets us know that the Queen is not to be trusted, and that the poison he has given her is not poison at all? This is embedded in the admittedly Shakespearian part of the play.

The soliloquies apart, when we find Imogen-Fidele, welcomed by Arviragus-Cadwal with

> I'll make't my comfort
> He is a man. I'll love him as my brother ...   III.6.70–71

then glancing at him and Guiderius-Polydore and exclaiming

> Would it had been so that they
> Had been my father's sons! ...   III.6.75–6

and when the trick by which Cloten must be dressed in Posthumus's garments (so that Imogen waking by his corpse may mistake it) is not glossed over but emphasized and advertised, here, we feel, is artlessness indeed. But it is obviously a sophisticated, not a naïve artlessness, the art that rather displays art than conceals it.[3]

A fair amount of the play – both of its design and execution – is pretty certainly not Shakespeare's. Just how much, it is hard to say (though the impossible negative seems always the easier to prove in these matters), for the suspect stuff is often so closely woven into the fabric. It may have come to him planned as a whole and partly written. In which case he worked very thoroughly over what are now the Folio's first two acts. Thereafter he gave attention to what pleased him most, saw Imogen and her brothers and Cloten through to the end, took a fancy to Lucius and gave him reality, did what more he could for Posthumus under the circumstances, generously threw in the First Gaoler, and rescued Iachimo from final futility. This relieves him of responsibility for the poor planning of the whole; he had been able to refashion the first part to his liking. But why, then, should he leave so many of the last part's ineptitudes in place? Or did the unknown cling affectionately to them, or even put them back again after Shakespeare had washed his hands of the business? We are dabbling now, of course, in pure 'whipping-boy' doctrine, and flaws enough can be found in it. Of the moments of 'unresisting imbecility' Shakespeare must be relieved; careless or conscienceless as he might sometimes be, critical common sense forbids us to saddle him with them. But, trying his hand at a new sort of thing (emulating Beaumont and Fletcher and their *Philaster* – why not? – he had never been above taking a hint), and if, moreover, he was trying it 'by request' in hard-won leisure at Stratford his grip might easily be looser than usual. We find him with a firmer one, that is certain, in *The Winter's Tale* and *The Tempest*. Allowing, then, for some collaboration, and some incertitude besides, at what, are we to suppose, is he aiming, what sort of play is he setting out to write? And if the sophisticated artlessness is his, what end is this meant to serve? These are the practical questions to be answered here.

He has an unlikely story to tell, and in its unlikelihood lies not only its charm, but largely its very being; reduce it to reason, you would wreck it altogether. Now in the theatre there are two ways of dealing with the inexplicable. If the audience are to take it seriously, leave it unexplained. They will be anxious – pathetically anxious – to believe you; with faith in the dose, they will swallow a lot. The other plan is to show one's hand, saying in effect: 'Ladies and gentlemen, this is an exhibition of tricks, and what I want you to enjoy among other things is the skill with which I hope to perform them.' This art, which deliberately displays its art, is very suited to a tragi-comedy, to the telling of a serious story that must yet not be taken too seriously, lest its comedy be swamped by its tragedy and a happy ending become too incongruous. Illusion must by no means be given the go-by; if this does not have its due in the theatre, our emotions will not be stirred. Nor should the audience be overwhelmed by the cleverness of the display; arrogance in an artist antagonizes us. This is where the seeming artlessness comes in; it puts us at our ease, it is the equivalent of 'You see there is no deception.' But very nice steering will be needed between the make-believe in earnest and in jest.

Shakespeare sets his course (as his habit is, and here we may safely assume that it is he) in his very first scene. We have the immediately necessary tale of Posthumus and Imogen, and the more extraordinary one of the abducting of the princes is added. And when the First Gentleman brings the Second Gentleman's raised eyebrows down with

> Howsoe'er 'tis strange
> ... Yet is it true, sir   I.1.65, 67

we of the audience are asked to concur in the acquiescent

> I do well believe you.

For 'this', Shakespeare and the First Gentleman are telling us, 'is the play you are about to hear; and not only these facts, but their rather leisurely amplifying, and that supererogatory tale of Post-humus's birth, should show you the sort of play it is. There is trouble in the air, but you are not to be too strung up about it. Moreover, the way you are being told it all, the easy fall of this verse, with its light endings and spun-out sentences, should be wooing you into the right mood. And this talk about Cassibelan is to help send you back into a fabulous past in which these romantic things may legitimately happen. So now submit your-selves, please, to the illusion of them.'

The beginning, then – quite properly – inclines to make-believe in earnest, rendering to the theatre its normal due. And the play's story will follow its course, nor may any doubt of its likelihood be hinted; that is a point of dramatic honour. But in half a hundred ways, without actually destroying the illusion, Shakespeare can contrive to prevent us taking it too seriously.

Cornelius lets us know at once that the poison is not poison; for, monster though the Queen is, we must not fear tragedy of that stark sort to be impending. We must be interested in watching for the working-out of the trick played upon her, and amused the while that

> She is fooled
> With a most false effect.   I.5.42–3

There is a subtler aim in the artlessness of Belarius's soliloquy. By accepting its frank familiarity we become, in a sense, Shakespeare's accomplices. In telling us the story so simply he is at the same time saying, 'You see what an amusing business this play-writing is; take it, please, no more seriously than I do'. The stressing of the coincidence of the meeting of the sister and her lost brothers has a like effect. We feel, and we are meant to feel, 'What a pretty fairy-tale!' The emphasizing of the artifice, the 'folly of the fiction', by which Cloten's corpse comes to be mistaken for Posthumus's does much to mitigate the crude horror of the business, to bring it into the right tragi-comic key. Keep us intrigued by the preparations for the trick, and we shall gain from its accomplishment a half-professional pleasure; we shall be masters of the illusion, not its victims. And throughout the whole elaborate scene of revelation with which the play ends we are most artfully steered between illusion and enjoyment of the ingenuity of the thing. *We* hold all the clues; the surprises are for Cymbeline, Imogen, Posthumus and the rest, not for us. We soon foresee the end, and our wits are free to fasten on the skill of the approach to it. But there is an unexpected turn or so, to provide excitement; and the situation is kept so fully charged with emotion that our sympathy is securely held.

This art that displays art is a thing very likely to be to the taste of the mature and rather wearied artist. When you are exhausted with hammering great tragic themes into shape it is a relief to find a subject you can play with, and to be safely able to take more interest in the doing than the thing done. For once you can exercise your skill for its own sake. The pretty subject itself seems to invite a certain artlessness of treatment. But the product will have a sophisticated air about it, probably.

NOTES

1. The writing of the rest of this scene is poverty itself (in fact, from Lucius's rescue of Imogen, just before, to the beginning of the long last scene of revelation, there is – except for the character of the Gaoler – marked deterioration of writing). The First Lord's

> So please your majesty,
> The Roman legions, all from Gallia drawn,
> Are landed on your coast, with a supply
> Of Roman gentlemen by the Senate sent

IV.3.23–6

about touches bottom. Sheridan's burlesquing in *The Critic* has more life in it.

2. Edmund's soliloquies in *King Lear* come into the same category.
3. For a similar artlessness of method, compare the Prospero–Miranda, Prospero–Caliban scenes in *The Tempest*, by which the story is told. But *The Tempest* is a Masque rather than a play, and may properly be artificial.

from Prefaces to Shakespeare by Harley Granville-Barker,
Second Series (1930), pages 237–47; 1965 illustrated edition
(2 volumes), Volume 2, pages 77–87

FIFTEEN

History and Histrionics in *Cymbeline*

J. P. Brockbank

THE sources of *Cymbeline* are sufficiently known. What now are we to do with them? Source-hunting offers its own satisfactions and it is an acceptable mode of conspicuous leisure, but it should be possible still to bring it to bear more closely on the problems of literary criticism.[1] Its bearing, however, may differ from play to play. It is salutary, for instance, to recognize that striking debt owed by *The Tempest* to travel literature.[2] When we find that Shakespeare's contemporaries allegorized the historical event we may more readily discount E. E. Stoll's scepticism about allegory in the play. I think, too, that the play sheds a backward light upon its sources, making us more alive to their dramatic and poetic potential.

Cymbeline is a different problem. It is not so self-evident a masterpiece. There is the common passage and there is the strain of rareness. The sources and analogues could be used to explain away whatever fails to make an immediate, effacing impression. But they have too, I think, a more positive value. They can show that many of the play's uniquely impressive effects could have been won only out of that specific area of convention that Shakespeare chose to explore. Within this area we can distinguish something like a dramatic genre, and as a label we might take Polonius's infelicity 'historical-pastoral' or, in deference to received opinion, 'historical romance'. Such labels are useful because they tell us what sort of conventions to look out for, although each play is apt to define its own area, make its own map. My emphasis will be on the 'historical', for there is, I think, a way of reading the sources which lends support to Wilson Knight's claim that *Cymbeline* is to be regarded 'mainly as an historical play'.[3] Criticism may fault his quite remarkable 'interpretation' for trying to evoke a maximum pregnancy from conventions that are insufficiently transmuted from their chronicle and theatrical analogues; but it cannot fault him for recognizing that the fictions of *Cymbeline*, while owing nothing to the factual disciplines commonly called 'historical', seek nevertheless to express certain truths about the processes which have shaped the past of Britain. I shall argue that even the 'romantic significance'[4] of the play is worth mastering, and that we can best master it by way of the chronicle sources.

To initiate the appropriate dialogue between the play and its sources, we might say that *Cymbeline* is about a golden world delivered from a brazen by the agency of a miraculous providence. That archaic formulation would not have startled Shakespeare's contemporaries, and it might equally preface a discussion of the play's alleged transcendent meaning or of its manifest indebtedness to convention. I mean to use it first, however, as a clue to track Shakespeare's reading through the labyrinth of Holinshed.[5]

Holinshed's brief notice of the reign of Kymbeline reads like an old tale, and Shakespeare clearly felt no obligation to treat it as fact. He distinguished firmly between the Tudor material, whose documentary force he retained in the earlier histories, and the Brutan, with which he took the fullest liberties in *Lear* and *Cymbeline*.

There is, however, no obvious reason why he should have turned his attention unhesitatingly to Kymbeline, and since the names of the characters are scattered over a wide span of pages in the second edition of Holinshed, we may be confident that he was widely read in the Brutan phase of the history, that he began at the beginning, and that he read it quite early, culling the name 'Iago' in its course. We may indeed regard *Cymbeline* and *Henry VIII* as the last fruits of the Brutan and Tudor chronicles in Shakespeare's dramatic art. They might be presented as complemental plays – a fantastical history and an historical fantasy, but the exercise would be premature without some excursion into the reading behind *Cymbeline*.

The first chapter of the *Second Booke of the Historie of England* did most, I think, to determine the form and tenor of the play.

It tells of the descent and early life of Brute, and includes this passage:[6]

To this opinion Giouan Villani a Florentine in his vniuersall historie, speaking of Aeneas and his ofspring kings in Italie, seemeth to agree, where he saith: 'Siluis (the sonne of Aeneas by his wife Lauinia) fell in loue with a neece of his mother Lauinia, and by hir had a sonne, of whom she died in trauell, and therefore was called Brutus, who after as he grew in some stature, and hunting in a forrest slue his father vnwares, and therevpon for feare of his grandfather Siluius Posthumus he fled the countrie, and with a retinue of such as followed him, passing through diuers seas, at length he arriued in the Ile of Britaine'.

Concerning therefore our Brute, whether his father Iulius was sonne to Ascanius the sonne of Aeneas by his wife Creusa, or sonne to Posthumus called also Ascanius, and sonne to Aeneas by his wife Lauinia, we will not further stand. But this, we find, that when he came to the age of 15. yeeres, so that he was now able to ride abrode with his father into the forrests and chases, he fortuned (either by mishap, or by God's prouidence) to strike his father with an arrow, in shooting at a deere, of which wound he also died. His grandfather (whether the same was Posthumus, or his elder brother) hearing of this great misfortune that had chanced to his sonne Siluius, liued not long after, but died for verie greefe and sorow (as is supposed) which he conceiued thereof. And the yoong gentleman, immediatlie after he had slaine his father (in maner before alledged) was banished his countrie, and therevpon got him into Grecia, where trauelling the countrie, he lighted by chance among some of the Troian ofspring, and associating himselfe with them, grew by meanes of the linage (whereof he was descended) in proces of time into great reputation among them: chieflie by reason there were yet diuers of the Troian race, and that of great authoritie in that countrie.

There is little here that would be admitted as a 'source' by the criteria of Boswell-Stone, but Shakespeare may well have recognized an opportunity to deploy the conventions of romance in a play made from one or other of the Brutan legends. His story of the lost Princes as it has finally reached us is an invention not owed to, but consonant with, the strange adventures of Brute. And *Cymbeline* touches, in a different order and to changed effect, the motifs of mysterious descent, hunting, murder (a boy killing a prince), banishment, and chance (or providential) encounter with off-spring of the same lineage. There is a kind of obligation here, and in his choice of the names of Posthumus and Innogen (the wife of Brute) Shakespeare seems to offer a playful salute of acknowledgement.

The second chapter offers another piece of ready-made theatrical apparatus. Brute and Innogen 'arrive in Leogitia' and 'aske counsell of an oracle where they shall inhabit'. Brute kneels, 'holding in his right hand a boll prepared for sacrifice full of wine, and the bloude of a white hinde', and after he has done his 'praier and ceremonie ... according to the pagane rite and custome', he falls asleep. The goddess Diana speaks Latin verses (which the chronicle translates) sending him to an isle 'farre by-west beyond the Gallike land'. 'After he awaked out of sleepe', the chronicle goes on, 'and had called his dreame to remembrance, he first doubted whether it were a verie dreame, or a true vision, the goddess hauing spoken to him with liuelie voice'. Once again, the vision is not a source but an occasion. It may have licensed the vision of Posthumus – a stage theophany in a play which, like the myth, is concerned with the ancestral virtue and destiny of Britain. Shakespeare drew of course on his own experience of the theatre and perhaps on a memory of *The Rare Triumphs* for the specific form of the theophany, but whether by chance or design the verse form is oddly consonant with the chronicle.[7]

These early passages are important because they reveal most clearly the romantic, numinous aspect of Geoffrey's myth. But Geoffrey was also something of a tactical political moralist, and for him the high magical destiny of Britain was needlessly thwarted by emulation, 'revenging' and 'dividing'. In the chapters between Brute and Kymbeline Shakespeare would have passed much material already exploited to serve a political moral by the authors of *Locrine, Leir, Gorboduc,* and the pseudo-historical part of *Nobody and Somebody* – reigns which for the most part ask to be treated in the spirit of Richard Harvey's *Philadelphus*, as tracts for the times.[8]

The Third Booke opens with an account of Mulmucius Dun-wallō, the law-giver, named in *Cymbeline* but evidently more fully celebrated in a lost play called after him.[9] Whether he took it from the old play or the chronicle, the name Cloten (given by Harrison to the father of Mulmucius[10]) may have had for Shakespeare a sly historical as well as articulatory propriety. The brassy Cloten and his mother are hypostatized versions of the arbitrary spleen and malevolence that Geoffrey often found antecedent to the rule of law.

Of the fifty or so rulers between Mulmucius and Cassibelane, Holinshed briefly describes a quarter and catalogues the rest. Only one (Elidure) seems to have been touched by the playwrights, but Shakespeare ignored them and his interest was not quickened again until he reached the point where Geoffrey is confronted by Caesar, the old tale foiled by the modern history, fantasy by fact, romance by Rome. Shakespeare accepted the challenge to admit both, and I think J. M. Nosworthy mistaken in wishing he had done otherwise.[11] For had he done otherwise we might never have heard that 'odd and distinctive music' which F. R. Leavis derives from *Cymbeline*'s 'interplay of contrasting themes and modes'.

Kymbeline is named at the centre of a long section dealing with the Roman conquest and the tribute variously yielded and denied by the line from Cassibelane to Arviragus. Shakespeare's readiness to see the tribute as a momentous historical symbol is clear enough from the play, but before we begin to admire and analyse it is worth remarking that he was not alone in trying by supernatural stage machinery and symbolic verse to give something like apocalyptic scale to the tribute settlement. Jasper Fisher's academic play *The True Trojanes*, probably later than *Cymbeline* but apparently independent, testifies equally to a contemporary interest in the conflict and reconciliation of the two 'valorous races' represented by Cassibelane and Caesar.[12] But Shakespeare's treatment yields far more of the potential of Geoffrey's myth than Fisher's.

So far then, Shakespeare's reading offers a paradigm for an action which makes the reconciliation with Rome a high event in the magical movement of British history from the vision of Brute to the golden prospect of the vision of Cadwallader. But it is substance rather for a pageant or a masque than a play. To give it a richer content Shakespeare had to rely in the end on his own resources, but he had scope still to exercise his imagination on other elements in the chronicle. In pursuit of that 'odd and distinctive music' he chose to modulate from the Brutan into the Roman key and from the Roman into the Renaissance Italian. The exercise is exquisitely playful, but what prompted him to attempt it?

Holinshed does not often chime well with Boccaccio; Geoffrey's 'romance' was not the sort which delighted sophisticated Italy. And yet it happens, oddly, that the chronicle can supply a gloss to Iachimo's confession in the last act: the dullness of Britain and the subtlety of Italy are Harrison's themes in Chapter 20 of his *Description of Britaine*. 'For that we dwell northward', he says, 'we are commonly taken ... to be men of great strength and little policie, much courage and small shift'; and after entertaining and dismissing several versions of the same criticism he finishes by giving it a sharp twist to Britain's advantage.[13]

For if it be a vertue to deale vprightlie with singlenesse of mind, sincerelie and plainlie, without anie such suspicious fetches in all our dealings, as they commonlie practise in their affaires, then are our countrimen to be accompted wise and vertuous. But if it be a vice to colour craftinesse, subtile practises, doublenesse, and hollow behauiour, with a cloake of policie, amitie and wisedome: then are Comineus and his countrimen to be reputed vicious.

Harrison would have found Wilson Knight's emphasis on Posthumus as 'the simple islander in danger of moral ruin' entirely congenial.[14] The conventional sentiment of the chronicle is concerned with the national character as well as the national destiny. Shakespeare may have seen in Boccaccio an opportunity to mediate the two.

There may have been a second little motive for calling *The Decameron* and *Frederick of Jennen* into the play. W. W. Lawrence compares Posthumus in Italy with 'a young Englishman making the grand tour at the end of the sixteenth century'[15], and the allegedly absurd anachronism might be lightly excused by a Chronicle passage used for one of Cymbeline's speeches:

it is reported, that Kymbeline being brought vp in Rome, & knighted in the court of Augustus, euer shewed himselfe a friend to the Romans,

& chieflie was loth to breake with them, because the youth of the Britaine nation should not be depriued of the benefit to be trained and brought vp among the Romans, whereby they might learne both to behaue themselues like ciuill men, and to atteine to the knowledge of feats of warre.

Within the spacious perspectives of *Cymbeline* the integrity of Britain is at once nourished and jeopardized by the 'civilizing' impact of ancient Rome and modern Italy upon its heroic and innocent but vulnerable youth.

The play's preoccupation with natural and sophisticated man is, however, something far more searching than anything the sources can suggest to jaded modern eyes. But we can get an inkling of how it might have struck Shakespeare from John Speed's *History* of 1611. Kymbeline himself was not much more for Speed than a name on a coin, but the period of his reign was a theme for rhapsody; it was the time that Christ was born and Augustus ruled in Rome. 'Then were the times that great Kings and Prophets desired to see, but saw them not, when the Wolfe and the Lambe, the Leopard and the Kid, the Calfe and the Lyon fed together.'[16] In a later passage Speed celebrates the marvellous correspondences between Virgilian and Messianic prophecy: 'hee vseth the very words of the *Prophets* in speaking of a *Maid*, and *a Child of a new progenie borne and sent downe from heaven*, by whom the brassy and iron-like world should cease, and a pure *golden age* succeed.' Even had it been published earlier, there would be no reason to suppose that Shakespeare read the *History*. The point is that the sceptical historian was a theologian still and could see fit to display these high conventional sentiments at this moment of his account of Britain. Holinshed's (or Fabyan's) brevities noticing the birth of Christ and the rule of Augustus may have stimulated in Shakespeare's imagination a comparable range of thought; hence what Wilson Knight calls the 'theological impressionism' of *Cymbeline*.

The same part of Speed's *History* offers reflections on the 'Originals of Particular Nations', comparing them on the one hand with 'that first beginning of the universall prosemination of Mankind ... simple and far from those artificiall fraudes, which some call *Wit* and *cunning*', and on the other to 'that first neglective condition' to which men would revolve if 'Lawes, discipline, and Customes' did not restrain them.[17] It is a polarity retained but greatly complicated in the play where the episodes of Cloten and the Princes explore very nicely the possibilities of man exempt from the rule of law.

That fussy phrase 'historical-pastoral' invites in this context a theological exegesis, but Shakespeare tactfully subdues his material to honour the decorum of the theatre rather than that of theological history. Finding that within the span of Kymbeline's reign he could sustain the spell of Brute's, he undertook to charm Boccaccio and Caesar into the same 'system of life'.

It is one of the tasks of criticism to observe the poise of the dialogue, to adapt Derek Traversi's phrase, 'between convention and analysis'. But the poise registers, too, in the handling of stage conventions; the calculated anachronisms of the play as history are matched by a calculated naïvety in its theatrical technique: the 'art that displays art', as Granville-Barker has it. It seems possible that this springs from small beginnings in the chronicle too. An analysis of the peculiar use made of disguise and garments in *Cymbeline* might fairly open with Harrison's observation, 'Oh how much cost is bestowed now adaies vpon our bodies and how little vpon our soules! how manie sutes of apparell hath the one and how little furniture hath the other?'[18] And it might pass to Holinshed's story of Hamo 'apparelling himselfe like a Britaine' to kill Guiderius and of Arviragus who 'caused himselfe to be adorned with the kings cote armour'; and then to the Scottish chronicle where Haie (Shakespeare's model for Belarius and his sons in the battle scene) refused the rich robes that the king offered him and 'was contented to go with the king in his old garments'.[19] Shakespeare could keep one eye here on the chronicle and the other on the fashionable theatre.

In turning from the history to the histrionics in the play, however, we must distinguish between that kind of theatrical virtuosity whose effects are merely startling and arbitrary, and that which serves a responsible purpose. The themes which the chronicle offered are portentous and had Shakespeare engaged with them too profoundly he would have tested the resources of the language and the responsiveness of the audience too severely. He would also have lost touch with the mood of the *Brut*, as he certainly does in *Lear*. He abstains therefore from using his giant's strength and allows certain points to be carried by a conventional gesture. His handling of disguise, soliloquy, stage situations, properties, and even characters secures in turn an apt 'suspension of disbelief' and an equally apt 'suspension of belief'. Cloten and the Queen, for example, may be said to represent a range of complemental vices (roughly speaking, the boorish and sophisticated) which menace the natural integrity of the British court. But this is true only of the conventional configuration; they are never allowed to touch the audience deeply or urgently threaten their composure. 'The evils she hatched were not effected', it is said of the Queen; and they are not effected because Shakespeare uses soliloquies and asides to make her guile transparent, and allows even her gulls to see right through her. *Cymbeline* indeed lets us into all the secrets, even into the secrets of the playmaker's craft. The 'inconsistency' of Cloten and the Queen is not analysed, for example, but simply exhibited; with a faint but distinct irony and a touch of burlesque their vices are made compatible with that minimal virtue of defiant patriotism they display before the Roman ambassador.[20] The tension (such as it is) is kept on the surface, while in that earlier instance of Queen Margaret in *Henry VI* it has to be dug out. If the characters were defined and explored analytically the discordant potential of the material would fracture the play. It is indeed a tribute to the decorum of the piece that Posthumus cannot for long be compared with Othello, nor Iachimo with Iago, the Queen with Lady Macbeth or Margaret, Cymbeline with Lear, nor yet Cloten with Edmund or Faulconbridge. The stresses are less between good and evil characters than between the ingenuous and the disingenuous – the lighter way of putting it is the apter.

The play offers yet more daring sophistications of stage conventions than those deployed in the plots of the disarmed (and disarming) villains. The iteration, for instance, of the phrase 'His meanest garment' leading up to that grotesque mock-recognition scene. In a play which makes so much of deceptive appearances and false judgements, there is sly irony in making the innocent Imogen a false judge and in allowing Cloten's indignation to be vindicated after death. The prevailing transparency of artifice makes one suspect that the 'clotpoll' stage head was deliberately displayed as a hollow property to give bizarre point to the lines introducing it, 'an empty purse; | There was no money in't', and it refines or civilizes the violent pagan force of the symbolic justice administered to 'that harsh, noble, simple nothing' Cloten.

In detail as in large design the mode is self-confessedly artificial. The postulates are openly declared:

> Howsoe'er 'tis strange,
> Or that the negligence may well be laughed at,
> Yet is it true, sir.

> do not play in wench-like words with that
> Which is so serious.

> This was strange chance.

> By accident
> I had a feigned letter of my master's
> Then in my pocket . . . .

> Shall's have a play of this? Thou scornful page,
> There lie thy part.

> Let him show
> His skill in the construction.

Other touches recall *A Midsummer Night's Dream* rather than *Love's Labour's Lost*:

> 'Twas but a bolt of nothing, shot at nothing,
> Which the brain makes of fumes.

> What fairies haunt this ground?

> mine's beyond, beyond.

There are moments too of self-parody: when Cymbeline interrupts a more than usually mannered late-Shakespearian speech from Iachimo with

> I stand on fire.
> Come to the matter;

and again (one suspects) when the gaoler's 'fear no more tavern bills' might be Shakespeare's tongue-in-cheek backward glance at Imogen's obsequies. One needs to step lightly on these points; they are slender platforms for commentary. And much the same applies to the play's imagery; the patterns and iterations traced by Wilson Knight, Traversi, and Nosworthy are undoubtedly there, but they are signs of opportunities lightly taken as occasion offers; they strike as sequences meant to be glimpsed rather than grasped.

All this does not mean that the entertainment is inconsequential. However conventional the frame of *Cymbeline*, it is still meaningful and it sets the more evocative and searching passages in the order of a significant design. But no matter how sharply-cut the stones in the filigree, we are reminded that the skilled craftsman has the strength to crush the fabric at will. 'The best in this kind are but shadows'.

It remains true, however, that *Cymbeline* is not organized from 'a deep centre' like *The Winter's Tale*.[21] We are haunted by intimations of a profound significance, but it is constantly clear that the apocalyptic destiny of Britain cannot be reconciled with the form of pastoral-romance on any but the terms which Shakespeare offers.

We may sum up by taking a last glance at Imogen. Her votaries from Swinburne onwards may be allowed their extravagances and let pass with an ''Ods pittikins' if they will admit that perfection is not, after all, indivisible. Imogen's perfection is playfully extended to her cookery – 'He cut our roots in characters'. But she remains in some sense, still, the centre of the play. It is fitting that she should voice most memorably a version of the Virgil verse transmitted through the chronicle, 'Et penitus toto diuisos orbe Britannos': 'I'th'worlds Volume Our Britaine seemed as of it, but not in't: In a great Poole, a Swannes-nest.'[22] She is a princess of Britain, yet theme for the praise of a Renaissance courtier; a pretty page for the Roman Lucius, yet aptly called a 'heavenly angel'. Her symbolic role is secured both by the dialogue (see the Second Lord's speech just before the bedchamber scene) and by the spectacle:

> And be her sense but as a monument,
> Thus in a chapel lying.

When she lies 'dead' alongside the body of Cloten in the clothes of Posthumus, the spectacle is an evocative symbol of a triple sacrifice (though the word is too strong) – of an innocence that will revive, an animal barbarity which is properly exterminated, and a duplicity (involving Posthumus) which has still to be purged.

Lucius is appropriately named after the first of the Christian kings of the British chronicle, and it happens that the political solution – the tribute allowed from sense of fitness and not won by force of arms – can endorse the ethical in a pageant finale announcing the Golden World with a touch of that 'pagane rite and custome' which opens the *Brut*: 'And let our crooked Smoakes climbe to their Nostrils From our blest Altars ... And in the Temple of great Iupiter Our Peace wee'l ratifie.'

My conclusion perhaps resembles too closely the 'fierce abridgement' of the last act which 'distinction should be rich in'. But I would claim that substantially the same result could be reached through an inquiry into the theatrical analogues, from *The Rare Triumphs* through *Clyomon and Clamydes*, *James IV*, *Edward I*, *Common Conditions*, *The Wounds of Civil War*, *Tancred and Gismunda*, and *The Dumb Knight* to the revived *Mucedorus*, the plays of Field and Beaumont and Fletcher to *The Second Maiden's Tragedy*. It might be shown, I think, that Shakespeare reconciled the conventions of primitive and sophisticated romantic drama to express similar reconciliations accomplished in the substance of the plot.

NOTES

1. I have in mind Hardin Craig's observations in 'Motivation in Shakespeare's Choice of Materials', *Shakespeare Survey 4* (1951). For the *Cymbeline* sources see J. M. Nosworthy's new Arden edition (1955).

2. The material of *The Tempest* is reprinted in Frank Kermode's new Arden edition (1954).

3. G. Wilson Knight, *The Crown of Life*, second edition (1948), page 129.

4. Compare F. R. Leavis, 'Shakespeare . . . has taken over a romantic convention and has done little to give it anything other than a romantic significance' (*The Common Pursuit* (1952; Penguin Books 1962), page 177).

5. I have assumed that Shakespeare used the 1587 Holinshed and have ignored a few passages in lesser-known chronicles which might be faintly nearer to the play. My longer quotations are of material not reprinted by Nosworthy or by W. G Boswell-Stone in *Shakespeare's Holinshed* (1896).

6. Holinshed (1587), Volume 1, H.E., page 7/B.

7. Compare

> An Ile which with the ocean seas
> inclosed is about,
> Where giants dwelt sometime,
> but now is desart ground.
>
> *Holinshed* (1587), Volume 1, H.E., page 9/A

8. Richard Harvey, *Philadelphus, or a defence of Brutus and the Brutan history* (1593). It argues that the Brutans did exist as they show the qualities (mostly bad) that Aristotle leads us to expect from human nature. Harvey took from the history the cautionary politics Geoffrey put into it.

9. Other lost Brutan plays were the *Conquest of Brute* (*Brute Greenshield*) and *Uther Pendragon*. Had they survived we might have been better placed to recognize the conventions behind *Cymbeline*.

10. Holinshed (1587), Volume 1, Description, page 117/A. Boswell-Stone cites a later page where 'Cloten' and 'Clotenus' are named. But Harrison has 'Cloten' with a 'Morgan' near by. Shakespeare may have known Chapter 22 of the 'Description of Britaine'; it gives an abstract of the whole history.

11. New Arden edition of *Cymbeline* (1955), page l.

12. The play is printed in Hazlitt's Dodsley, fourth edition (1875), Volume 12.

13. Holinshed (1587), Volume 1, Description, page 115/A.

14. *The Crown of Life* (1948), page 147. Other points made there could be illustrated from the Description, Book 2, Chapter 7.

15. W. W. Lawrence, *Shakespeare's Problem Comedies* (1931; Penguin Shakespeare Library edition (1969), page 167). The Holinshed passage (Volume 1, H.E., page 33/A) is quoted by Boswell-Stone; compare *Cymbeline* III.1.68.

16. John Speed, *The History of Great Britaine* (1611), page 174. See also page 189.

17. op. cit., page 179.
18. Holinshed (1587), Volume 1, Description, page 172/A.
19. Holinshed (1587), Volume 2, H.S., page 155/B. See also M. C. Bradbrook, 'Shakespeare and the Use of Disguise in Elizabethan Drama', *Essays in Criticism* 2 (1952), pages 159–68.
20. I think Warren D. Smith (*Studies in Philology* 49 (1952), pages 185–94) overstates his claim that Cloten is merely the 'vulgar, ill-mannered villain' in this scene. Shakespeare writes perhaps with some memory of Holinshed's Voadicia (H.E., Book 4, Chapter 11) as well as an eye on Jacobean courtly proprieties.
21. F. R. Leavis, *The Common Pursuit*, page 174.
22. Holinshed (1587), Volume 1, Description, page 2/A.

from *Shakespeare Survey* 11 (1958), pages 42–8

SIXTEEN

Stuart *Cymbeline*

Emrys Jones

I

JOHNSON had this to say about *Cymbeline*:

This play has many just sentiments, some natural dialogues, and some pleasing scenes, but they are obtained at the expense of much incongruity.

To remark the folly of the fiction, the absurdity of the conduct, the confusion of the names and manners of different times, and the impossibility of the events in any system of life, were to waste criticism upon unresisting imbecility, upon faults too evident for detection, and too gross for aggravation.[1]

The editor of the New Cambridge *Cymbeline*, Mr J. C. Maxwell, after quoting this passage, is willing to concede something to Johnson:

Is it enough to say that most of these 'faults' are of the essence of romance and that Johnson did not understand romance? That would be too easy a way out: it is hard to deny an 'incongruity' that goes beyond the mere factual anachronisms and confusions that Johnson refers to; and it is perfectly possible to combine an enthusiastic admiration for others among the Last Plays with strong misgivings about *Cymbeline*.[2]

And he proceeds, in his Introduction, to justify the play in terms of its theatrical effectiveness and to draw upon Granville-Barker's analysis of its tragi-comic mode, its 'sophisticated artlessness'. But Johnson's common-sense objections are not disposed of; they are left hanging in the air, a worrying reminder that present-day scholarship is far from having got *Cymbeline* in focus. The play seems to lack a context which would explain away its wilder incongruities and apparent absurdities, and which would help to place modern readers in the position of its first audiences, for whom, presumably, Johnson's strictures would not have carried so much weight. *Cymbeline* has, after all, a stage history: it seems to have been written between 1608 and 1610; it was still being played in 1634, when it was acted at court before Charles: it was 'well likte by the kinge'.

The most impressive attempt to make sense of the play is Professor Wilson Knight's chapter in *The Crown of Life*: one of his boldest and most original essays. Its main argument is summarized by Mr J. M. Nosworthy in his new Arden edition of *Cymbeline*, which it will be convenient to quote here:

> *Cymbeline* is, in the main, a historical play in which the dramatist blends his two primary historical interests, those of Britain and Rome. Interwoven with national issues is the conflict between Posthumus, who symbolizes what is best in English manhood, and Iachimo, the representative not of Rome but of the corrupt Italy of the Renaissance. National and sexual degeneration are concurrent, but Imogen and the Princes are regenerative forces and the circumstances of the play yield a massive union. The final acceptance of Posthumus's marriage with Imogen typifies the matrimonial peace of the individual, the social integrity of the nation and the union of Britain's best manhood with the essence of royalty, while the Britain-Rome union, which Wilson Knight regards as central, transfers to Cymbeline's kingdom the virtues of Augustus's empire.[3]

Mr Maxwell mentions this study here only to class it as a 'failure': for him *Cymbeline* is characterized by 'the neutralization of strong effects by means of comedy', and he finds it consequently impossible to take the play's 'historical and political side' with anything like Professor Knight's solemnity, although in another context he sides with him over the question of the integrity of the masque of Jupiter. It may be true that Professor Knight treats the play with more moral seriousness than it warrants. He certainly leaves one wishing it were richer than it is. But his essay remains the most painstaking attempt to explain why everything in the play is where it is, and despite what seem to be certain interpretative errors, it deserves to be sifted with a serious regard to what is and what is not valuable in it. The attitude of the New Cambridge editor seems to be: 'Knight's approach is "transcendental", therefore unsound. It's safer to stick to common sense, even if it entails finding *Cymbeline* nearly as unintelligible as Johnson did.'

I think, however, that it is possible to accept a good deal of what Professor Knight has to say about *Cymbeline* without forsaking common sense and an empirical historical approach. Indeed, it is the historical approach that I want to insist on. Professor Knight himself, however, is in my opinion guilty of a certain obscurantism which has had the effect of making his study of *Cymbeline* less complete than it might have been. He makes a clear statement of principle in his first Shakespearian publication, *Myth and Miracle* (1929):

> My method is to regard the plays as they stand in the order to which modern scholarship has assigned them; to refuse to regard 'sources' as exerting any limit to the significance of the completed work of art; to avoid the side-issues of Elizabethan and Jacobean manners, politics, patronage, audiences, revolutions, and explorations; to fix attention solely on the poetic quality and human interest of the plays concerned.[4]

He refers later to, among others, critics using a 'historical' approach:

> ... whenever they find some literary or historical tangent to the fiery circle of poetry, they think, by following its direction into the cold night of the actual, to expose the content of that burning star.[5]

Professor Knight's interpretative work on Shakespeare has been remarkably consistent; and there is no sign of his having modified the principles here outlined. He has, in fact, reissued *Myth and Miracle* as part of *The Crown of Life*. The following remarks will certainly by his standards lead us into 'the cold night of the actual', but they will also, I hope, allow us a better view of that rather dim luminary, the play of *Cymbeline*.

2

Few of the critics who have written about *Cymbeline* seem to have thought about the impression it made on its audiences when, in 1608, 1609, or 1610, it was a new play. One important question that seems not to have been raised concerns the choice of the play's subject: the historical character who gives the play its title. Why did Shakespeare choose that particular king? What interest would King Cymbeline have had for Shakespeare's audiences? I should like to quote Mr Nosworthy again, this time for his account of Shakespeare's handling of the historical material afforded him by Holinshed. (It is perhaps a criticism of the New Cambridge *Cymbeline* that it seems to complement rather than to provide a complete alternative to the new Arden edition. One is compelled to resort to the older edition for a fuller discussion of certain matters; as here for the Holinshed material.) Mr Nosworthy's account is as follows:

> Holinshed supplied Shakespeare with what is, at best, a confused account of a reign so uneventful that it had defeated the inventive powers of generations of quite imaginative chroniclers. Cymbeline, son of Theomantius, became king in 33 B.C., and died after reigning for thirty-five years, leaving two sons, Guiderius and Arviragus. He was brought up in Rome and was absolved, by Augustus Caesar, of obligation to pay tribute. Subsequently tribute was demanded and refused, but Holinshed comments: 'I know not whether Cymbeline or some other British prince refused tribute.' Like the earlier chroniclers, he eventually makes the refusal come from Guiderius, and tells of Caesar's consequent attempts to invade Britain. Still uncertain, he relates how, according to British chroniclers, the Romans were twice defeated in pitched battles, but remarks that Latin sources claimed ultimate victory for the Romans. This generally disjunctive report bristles with glaring inconsistencies of time and circumstance which Holinshed makes no attempt to reconcile.[6]

Mr Nosworthy leaves it at that, and his tone in doing so recalls Johnson's attack on the play's 'unresisting imbecility', for he goes out of his way to suggest that the reign of Cymbeline had no intrinsic interest at all. But it is scarcely wilful perversity that caused Shakespeare to take it as his subject. And even on the basis of Mr Nosworthy's account, one question demands to be raised. In Holinshed it is Guiderius who refuses to pay tribute to Augustus, not Cymbeline. Shakespeare transfers the events of Guiderius's reign to Cymbeline's. Cymbeline's reign was otherwise uneventful.

The main, if not the only, attraction of Cymbeline's reign was its dating. He became king, says Holinshed, in 33 B.C., and died after reigning for thirty-five years. His only importance is that while he was king of Britain, Christ was born. Spenser's account of Cymbeline in his 'chronicle of Briton kings' (*Faerie Queene*, II.10.50–51) brings out his significance unambiguously:

> Next him *Tenantius* raignd, then *Kimbeline*,
> What time th' eternall Lord in fleshly slime
> Enwombed was . . .

(This has already been noted by Mr J. P. Brockbank in an illuminating article, 'History and Histrionics', in *Shakespeare Survey 11*.[7]) Shakespeare wanted an action happening concurrently with this event, so he had to stick to Cymbeline's reign even though it was uneventful. It was in fact a time of peace. In his short account of Cymbeline Holinshed twice mentions the *universal* peace of the time: the *pax Romana* in which Christ was born.

> But whether for this respect or for that it pleased the almightie God so to dispose the minds of men at that present, not onlie the Britains, but in manner all other nations were contented to be obedient to the Romane empire . . .

A little later:

> About the same time also there came unto Kimbaline king of the Britains an ambassador from Augustus the emperor, with thanks, for that entring into the governement of the British state, he had kept his allegiance toward the Romane empire: exhorting him to keepe his subjects in peace with all their neighbors, sith the whole world, through meanes of the same Augustus, was now in quiet, without all warres or troublesome tumults.

A note of transcendental peace is the one on which *Cymbeline* ends; though previously to that there has been no lack of strife. Shakespeare transferred the violent events of Guiderius's reign to his father Cymbeline's because his play needed plot-material of this nature: the action of *Cymbeline* shows division and war giving way to harmony and peace. With the word 'peace' the play ends:

Laud we the gods;
And let our crooked smokes climb to their nostrils
From our bless'd altars. Publish we this peace
To all our subjects. Set we forward; let
A Roman and a British ensign wave
Friendly together. So through Lud's Town march;
And in the temple of great Jupiter
Our peace we'll ratify; seal it with feasts.
Set on there! Never was a war did cease,
Ere bloody hands were washed, with such a peace.

V.5.474–83

This in turn may be compared with a speech of Octavius Caesar in *Antony and Cleopatra*:

The time of universal peace is near.
Prove this a prosp'rous day, the three-nooked world
Shall bear the olive freely.

IV.6.5–7

The question remains: what has this to do with theatre audiences of about 1610, whether at court, or at the Blackfriars, or at the Globe? A great deal, I suggest: it centres on the character and foreign policy of James I. A reading of a history of James's reign or a recent biography such as D. H. Willson's makes it seem likely that the peace-tableau with which *Cymbeline* ends must have a dual reference: it presents dramatically the stillness of the world awaiting the appearance of the Christ-child, but it also pays tribute to James's strenuous peacemaking policy (to which I shall return later). The topical elements of *Cymbeline* have received no scholarly attention, yet they must have contributed to its theatrical success. Relevant here are the works of two scholars in the period: Edwin Greenlaw's *Studies in Spenser's Historical Allegory* (1932) and Miss R. F. Brinkley's *Arthurian Legend in the Seventeenth Century* (1932). Both assemble material that has direct bearing on *Cymbeline*, although neither mentions it explicitly. Miss Brinkley has much to say about the political use made by James of the Tudor-British myth: '... that in James is to be found the consummation of the prophecy of Merlin and Aquila of Shaftesbury to the effect that "the *British Empire* after the *Saxons* and *Normans*, shall return againe to her auncient *Stocke* and *Name*"'.[8] That is to say, England and Scotland will revert to their ancient status of 'Britain' under a single 'British' monarch. In response to the occasion, poets and pamphleteers, the devisers of masques and pageants, as well as dramatists, gave mythological support to James's accession to the English throne. They demonstrated that, far from being a break with the past, the arrival of James in London was the fulfilment of the oldest prophecies of the British people; it was a consummation rather than a violation of England's oldest traditions. The Arthurian matter which Henry VII had used to strengthen the authority of the Tudors was not, as might have been expected, discarded at Elizabeth's death. It was used more intensively than ever during the early years of James's reign. James I claimed that he inherited Henry VII's symbolic role: he too was the second Arthur, called out of the West to restore the nation's fortunes. James was also the second Brute: he was the first since the death of Brute (the legendary eponymous founder of Britain) to unite the whole island under a single monarch. (And in fact James attempted to put a stop to the use of the terms 'English' and 'Scottish' in favour of the comprehensive and – in theory – more ancient term 'British'.) But quite as important as the James/Arthur or James/Brute association was James's favourite self-appointed role of Peacemaker. *Beati pacifici* was his motto; and he loved to be called, and poets duly obliged him, the second Augustus: the pacific emperor under whom Christ was born. In his biography of James, Mr D. H. Willson says of him, in a chapter called 'The Peacemaker' (for James had published a tract called *The Peacemaker or Great Brittaines Blessing*):

Peace had come to England with James king, inherent in some mystic fashion in his royal presence. When, in addressing his first English Parliament, he counted 'the blessings which God hath in my person bestowed upon you', the first of these blessings was peace. 'I have ever, I praise God, kept peace and amity with all, which hath been so far tied to my person, as at my coming here you are witnesses I found the State embarked in a great and tedious war, and only my arrival here, and by the peace in my person, is now amity kept where war was before'. Proud was the King of his peaceful attributes. 'I know not', he wrote, 'by what fortune the dicton of *Pacificus* was added to my title at my coming to England, that of the lion, expressing true fortitude, having been my dicton before. But I am not ashamed of this addition. For King Solomon was a figure of Christ in that he was a king of peace. The greatest gift that our Saviour gave His apostles immediately before His ascension was that He left His peace with them.'[9]

Mr Willson adds: 'And Christ was born under Augustus Caesar, also a king of peace.' It is worth quoting one more paragraph from Mr Willson's biography:

Flowing from James's dominions, peace was going to become universal. He spoke as though he could bestow it where he would, boasting in 1617 that he had established a settled repose in all neighbouring lands. Nations who quarrelled should bring their disputes before him for settlement. 'Come they not hither,' asks *The Peacemaker*, 'as to the fountain from whence peace springs? Here sits Solomon and hither come the tribes for judgement. O happy moderator, blessed Father, not Father of thy country alone, but Father of all thy neighbour countries about thee.'[10]

In an essay on James as a political writer (in *Seventeenth-Century Studies* presented to Sir Herbert Grierson), Professor C. J. Sisson, discussing his pamphlet-war with the Pope, remarks: '... he is haunted by thoughts of the unity of the Christian world under one faith'.[11] For James had written: 'I would with all my heart give my consent that the Bishop of Rome should have the first Seat: I being a Western King would go with the Patriarch of the West.'

For a reading of *Cymbeline* it is, I think, desirable to familiarize oneself with the panegyrical imagery which was frequently applied to James in the early years of his reign. Jonson's *Panegyre* (1603), written for James's first entry into Parliament, announces:

> Again, the Glory of our Western World
> Unfolds himself. ...   3–4

In similar terms a speaker in Dekker's *Magnificent Entertainment* (1603) addresses James:

> Great Monarch of the West, whose glorious Stem,
> Doth now support a triple Diadem,
> Weying more than that of thy grand Grandsire Brute. . . .[12]

This prompts a comparison with a passage towards the end of *Cymbeline* in which Cymbeline's status as a *western* king is similarly stressed; the Roman soothsayer is speaking:

> which foreshowed our princely eagle,
> Th'imperial Caesar, should again unite
> His favour with the radiant Cymbeline,
> Which shines here in the west. V.5.471–4

In panegyrical writing of the time much is made of the fact that Henry VII was James I's great-grandfather. In *The Italians Pageant*, which formed part of Dekker's *Magnificient Entertainment*, the relationship was visually represented in a triumphal arch:

... ouer the Gate, in golden Caracters, these verses (in a long square) were inscribed:

> Tu Regere Imperio populos Iacobe memento,
> Hae tibi erunt Artes, Pacique imponere morem,
> Parcere Subiectis, et debellare Superbos.

And directly aboue this, was aduanc'd the Arms of the kingdome, the Supporters fairly cut out to the life: ouer the Lyon (some prety distance from it) was written:

IACOBO REGI MAGN.

And aboue the head of the *Vnicorne*, at the like distance, this:

HENRICI VII. ABNEP.

In a large Square, erected aboue all these, King *Henry* the seuenth was royally seated in his Imperiall Robes, to whome king *Iames* (mounted on horsebacke) approches, and receyues a Scepter, ouer both their heads these words being written:

HIC VIR, HIC EST.[13]

292 ff.

3

It is in the context of the political use made by James of the Tudor-British myth that the relevance of Milford Haven to *Cymbeline* is to be understood.

Several important scenes in the middle acts of *Cymbeline* take place at or near Milford Haven. The place-name is insistently stressed, yet it does not occur in any of the known sources of the play. (The name Milford occurs seven times, Milford Haven nine times; the only other British place-name mentioned is Lud's town, which occurs four times.) Editors and critics have failed to see the existence of a problem.

I suggest that at the time *Cymbeline* was written Milford Haven was chiefly associated with the landing there in 1485 of Henry Earl of Richmond; with, that is, the accession of Henry VII to the throne. Shakespeare only once elsewhere mentions Milford: this is in *Richard III* (IV.4.534) where a messenger announces

> the Earl of Richmond
> Is with a mighty power landed at Milford.

This is supported by two passages in Drayton's *Polyolbion* (First Part published in 1612) and by the notes written for the poem by Selden. In Song V the following passage occurs:

> A branch sprung out of *Brute*, th' imperiall top shall get,
> Which grafted in the stock of great *Plantaginet*,
> The Stem shall strongly wax, as still the Trunk doth wither:
> That power which bare it thence, againe shall bringe it thither
> By *Tudor*, with faire windes from little *Britaine* driven,
> To whom the goodlie Bay of Milford shall be given;
> As thy wise Prophets, *Wales*, fore-told his wisht arrive,
> And how *Lewellins* Line in him should doubly thrive.   49–56

Another passage concerning Milford occurs at lines 273 ff. in the same Song:

> You goodlie sister Floods, how happy is your state!
> Or should I more commend your features, or your Fate;
> That *Milford*, which this Ile her greatest Port doth call
> Before your equall Floods is lotted to your Fall!
> Where was saile ever seene, or wind hath ever blowne,
> Whence *Penbrooke* yet hath heard of Haven like her owne?

In his note to the first of these passages Selden characterizes Milford as follows:

> At *Milford* haven arrived *Henry* Earle of *Richmont*, aided with some forces and summes of money by the *French Charles* VIII. but so entertained and strengthned by divers of his friends, groaning under the tyrannicall yoake of *Rich* III. that, beyond expectation, at *Bosworth* in *Leicester*, the day and Crowne was soone his.
>
> Every Chronicle tels you more largely.

This association of Milford with the Tudors – and, by extension, with the Stuarts – lends support to Professor Knight's interpretation of *Cymbeline*, with its emphasis on the national theme. Professor Knight himself refers in general terms to the Tudor element in the Welsh scenes: 'probably an Elizabethan would feel a Tudor reference in the royal boys' Welsh upbringing'; but he adds: 'such inquiries into secondary meanings are dangerous and of slight value'. I would object that the audience is no longer Elizabethan: it is important to the play that James is on the throne. I would also contend that the transcendentally national (which is what Professor Knight is concerned with) and the topical are here indivisibly one; the transcendental (as in *Macbeth*, or indeed the Christian interpretation of history generally) is grounded in the particular, and loses by being divorced from it.

By failing to understand the precise symbolic value of Milford Haven, critics can see the play in vague terms only. They rob it of its particularity, which is one kind of strength. Mr D. A. Traversi (in *Shakespeare: The Last Phase*) notices the important part played by Milford in the central action – similar to that of Dover in *King Lear* – but fails, among other things, to explain why the Roman ambassador, returning to Rome from Lud's town, should travel via Milford Haven – not, on the face of it, the directest route. It is to be explained by the fact that Shakespeare's geography in this play is not a literal but a symbolic one. Mr Traversi comments:

> The central part of *Cymbeline* involving the integration of the various symbolic themes is mostly concerned with the events that lead up to the meeting of Imogen, Cloten, and the lost sons of the king at Milford Haven.[14]

But a little later, his failure to see the particular relevance of Milford to the national theme of the play leads him to observe:

... the expression of emotion is reduced ... to something very like a literary quibble in –

> Tell me why Wales was made so happy as
> T'inherit such a haven

when the clearly implied fusion of the ideas of 'heaven' and 'haven' is scarcely justified in terms of intensity of feeling.[15]

Shakespeare, however, is alluding to the same 'haven' as that celebrated by Drayton –

> Where was saile ever seene, or wind hath ever blowne,
> Whence *Penbrooke* yet hath heard of Haven like her owne?

– and it seems probable that Imogen's reference to 'this same blessed Milford' would have been readily interpreted by Shakespeare's audience.

4

It is not my intention to claim that *Cymbeline* is better than most current critical opinion holds. Dr Leavis is clearly right when he relegates the play to an order distinctly below that of *The Winter's Tale*. What I am concerned with is seeing the play in its historical setting, and attempting to locate, in a necessarily imperfect way, the impulses which led to its being written, acted, and applauded. What a historical approach can show, I think, is that *Cymbeline* possesses many of the elements that we usually associate with the Jacobean masque (I do not refer solely to the descent of Jupiter in Act V) and that it is precisely these elements which contribute most decisively to the play's weakness as a whole. It seems to me likely that the character of Cymbeline – at any rate, in the final scene, with its powerful peace-tableau – has a direct reference to James I, before whom it was, presumably, acted. I would also, more tentatively, adduce one or two more facts which may be relevant. Cymbeline (in Shakespeare, though not in Holinshed) has one daughter and two sons; so did James I. James's elder son, Henry, was created Prince of Wales in 1610, and some editors point to 1610 as a likely date for *Cymbeline*; and in connexion with the stress on peace with which the play closes, it is perhaps of interest that 1610 was the only year, of this period, in which all the European states were at peace. Lastly, Cymbeline's final submission to Rome, even after he has won the war against the Romans (which Professor Knight emphasized), might have had some topical value in view of James's efforts to enter into friendly negotiations with Papal Rome. When, towards the end of the play, therefore, Cymbeline emphatically announces: 'Well, | My peace we will begin ...', the audience must have made a complex identification: the peace is both the peace of the world at the time of Christ's birth, in which Britain participates, and also its attempted re-creation at the very time of the play's performance, with Jacobus Pacificus – who was a 'figure' of Augustus – on the throne.

Such allusions to the dramatist's royal patron were not necessarily harmful to the artistic integrity of a drama: *Macbeth*, for instance, does not suffer unduly from them, pervasive though they are. But the reason there is that the compliments are, artistically, at the perimeter of the work, while the centre is occupied by one who was, so to speak, James's personal enemy: Macbeth was the man who had tried to avert the Merlin prophecies and, by trying to avert them, fulfilled them. For Fleance, having fled to Wales, married Princess Nesta, and so ensured one of James's two claims to the English throne. The character of Macbeth can therefore be treated by Shakespeare in a satisfyingly complex way: James can take no offence. But not so with *Cymbeline*, less serious as a work of art for this reason: here evil is quite inadequately treated. Several critics have noticed this: Dr Leavis, for instance, comments: 'Cloten and the Queen are the wicked characters, stepmother and son, of the fairy-tale: they don't strike us as the expression of an adult intuition of evil.' I would add, if we are to take the play as a serious drama, the thoroughly unsatisfactory nature of Cymbeline himself. He is largely neutral and passive while the Queen is alive but comes to no harm, for the author officiously protects him from the consequences of his weak nature and ill-judged actions. The Queen and Cloten are used as scapegoats: they take most of the blame, and are killed off. *The Winter's Tale* is a different matter: Leontes realizes to the full the wickedness of his actions in their lasting consequences. In *Cymbeline*, one may conjecture, the need to avoid giving offence, while simultaneously making extensive use of topical allusion, issues in the mixture of styles in the characterization. It would have been undesirable for Cymbeline's wicked Queen to be approximated, in the minds of the audience, with James's virtuous consort, Anne of Denmark. So the Queen is made conventionally grotesque after a fairy-tale fashion in order to counteract the temptation to find a real-life analogue. At the end of the play, Cymbeline is reinstated; but there is no hint of criticism. He is simply the great Western King, at the centre of things, restored to all his children, and, to close all, magnanimously radiating Peace. The whole play suffers, as *Macbeth* does not, from being too close to its royal audience, and despite some brilliant things there is, imaginatively, a central fumbling, a betrayal of logic.

5

Much of the last paragraph is obviously speculative and, if correct, must await corroboration. Even so, the play remains obscure in places; largely because one is uncertain how far an allegorical reading is pertinent. What seems probable is that *Cymbeline* set Shakespeare's audience no special problem. The dramatist has evoked a body of knowledge, shared by the audience, which doubtless provided a kind of interpretative key to events on the stage which, without such a key, appear insufficiently motivated, almost incoherent. Miss Lilian Winstanley has something similar in mind when she says of Shakespeare: 'he is dealing with the events of most immediate interest to his audience and he is working to a pre-existent unity in the minds of that audience. Events which may not seem connected to us were connected to him and his audience because they were all vividly alive in their minds at the same moment' (*Hamlet and the Scottish Succession*). The play was no doubt *felt* to be right; and no objection would be raised to the apparently illogical position of James I's somehow participating in two roles at once: Cymbeline and Augustus.

'The Tragedie of Cymbeline' is the last play in the first Folio.

Its designation as a tragedy has always been puzzling; and on this point Mr Maxwell makes a useful comment:

Heminge and Condell had denied themselves the convenient category of 'tragi-comedy' and, though *Cymbeline* seems to us to fall naturally into the same class as *The Tempest* and *The Winter's Tale*, it contains weightier public and historical matter, so that it is not inconceivable that the placing of it among the tragedies was the deliberate choice of what seemed the lesser evil.[16]

In one point he departs from editorial tradition: in spelling 'Iachimo' as 'Jachimo'. The innovation seems warranted, since 'Jachimo' (for Italian 'Giacomo') is in accordance with the metre. He might well have made a further departure in spelling 'Cloten' as 'Clotten', which would indicate the correct pronunciation (as in 'clotpoll'). He does in fact point out that the Folio has 'Clotten' up to the fourth act. Brute's wife was Innogen; and Mr Maxwell suggests that the Folio 'Imogen' is probably 'wrong': 'but it would scarcely be tolerable to dislodge the familiar form for anything less than a certainty'. He adduces two facts to support this: '"Innogen" is the name of the (mute) wife of Leonato' in *Much Ado*, and the pair of names is closely approximated in Imogen and Posthumus Leonatus; and Simon Forman, who saw an early performance of *Cymbeline*, mentions 'Innogen' in his report. Although such a mistake on the part of the printer is hard to account for (the name 'Imogen' occurs over twenty times), Mr Maxwell's suggestion is interesting; I almost wish he had boldly emended to 'Innogen'. But he is undoubtedly right to play safe. Still, 'Innogen' should be entertained as a possibility, for something positive is added to *Cymbeline* if we recognize that Shakespeare's heroine shares her name with the legendary first queen of Britain. The name 'Innogen' helps to signalize her role in the play. Professor Knight has remarked that it might be associated with 'innocence'. He has also suggested that she is 'not merely a single lady, but Britain's soul-integrity'; she is an 'essence' of royalty; and with a fine intuition he says of her journey to Milford Haven: 'She is, one feels, magnetized to this, enchanted, spot . . .' She is indeed 'magnetized' to Milford Haven. Without knowing it, she is helping to fulfil a 'prophecy'. But the compelling force is ultimately nothing other than the facts of history:

the Earl of Richmond
Is with a mighty power landed at Milford.

NOTES

1. *Dr Johnson on Shakespeare*, edited by W. K. Wimsatt (1960; Penguin Shakespeare Library edition (1969), page 136).
2. *Cymbeline* (New Cambridge Shakespeare, 1960), edited by J. C. Maxwell, Introduction, page xxviii.
3. *Cymbeline* (new Arden Shakespeare, 1955), edited by J. M. Nosworthy, Introduction, page xlv.
4. G. Wilson Knight, *The Crown of Life* (1947; second edition 1948), page 9.
5. op. cit., page 58.
6. New Arden Shakespeare edition, page xvii–xviii.
7. See above, pages 234–47.
8. *Arthurian Legend in the Seventeenth Century* (1932), page 9.
9. D. H. Willson, *King James VI and I* (1956), pages 271–2.
10. op. cit., page 272.
11. C. J. Sisson, 'King James the First of England as Poet and Political Writer', in *Seventeenth-Century Studies Presented to Sir Herbert Grierson* (1938), page 60.
12. *The Dramatic Works of Thomas Dekker*, edited by Fredson Bowers, Volume 2 (1955).
13. op. cit.
14. D. A. Traversi, *Shakespeare: The Last Phase* (1954), page 63.
15. op. cit., page 65.
16. New Cambridge Shakespeare edition, page 125.

from *Essays in Criticism* 11 (1961), pages 84–99

SEVENTEEN

Cymbeline and Coterie Dramaturgy

Arthur C. Kirsch

IN 1608 the King's Men, of which Shakespeare was a principal shareholder, and for which he was the principal dramatist, acquired the Blackfriars Theatre. *Cymbeline*, *The Winter's Tale*, and *The Tempest* were probably performed there, as well as at the Globe, and the presumption is that at the very least Shakespeare wrote the plays so that they would please both audiences and be suitable to the conditions of both theatres.[1] It is even possible, despite *Pericles*, which antedates the move to Blackfriars and seems designed for the public theatre, that in *Cymbeline* Shakespeare was thinking primarily of the dramatic possibilities of the Blackfriars. It is no doubt a species of folly peculiar to theatre historians to assume that once you explain the conditions of performance and the class of audience you explain the play, but it is surely just as foolish to assume that these things do not count at all, especially since there is so much evidence in Shakespeare's case not only that he was thoroughly professional, but that he was profoundly stirred by the idea and conventions of the theatre itself.

The private playhouses had developed a distinctive idea of theatre by the time Shakespeare became associated with Blackfriars, with a dramaturgy which was recognizably different from that of the Globe. Unfortunately most studies of coterie drama have so exaggerated the differences and so confused dramaturgy with morality that it has been very difficult to have a clear idea either of the nature of this drama or of its possible effects upon the public theatre.[2] There has been, for example, no systematic study of the effect of conditions at Blackfriars upon the dramatic assumptions and structure of plays performed there, although there are studies of the theatre itself and of the boy companies.[3] There have been illuminating studies, however, of individual coterie dramatists, including Beaumont and Fletcher, and it is through Beaumont and Fletcher that the idea of theatre which may have stimulated Shakespeare in *Cymbeline* and the later plays may best be formulated. Beaumont and Fletcher's direct influence upon Shakespeare, though possible, need not be argued, since they did not discover this idea of theatre alone. Whether, therefore, *Philaster* preceded *Cymbeline*, or vice versa, is not at issue.[4] Beaumont and Fletcher's first tragi-comedies are crystallizations of earlier coterie drama as much as they are innovations. Many of the characteristic features of their plays are to be found in Jonson, Marston, and others, and Shakespeare could as easily have learned from these dramatists as he could from Beaumont and Fletcher. What makes Beaumont and Fletcher's tragi-comedies especially useful and revealing is that their dramaturgy is transparent as well as representative.

The most distinguishing feature of this dramaturgy is its deliberate self-consciousness. Beaumont and Fletcher's plays, like all plays, are designed to have an audience, but unlike plays at the Globe their effect depends upon the audience's consciousness of the means by which it is moved. No matter how many surprises they pull out of the plot, no matter how passionate their characters or intriguing their action, the play all the while calls attention to itself as a dramatic fiction. In part this is a natural consequence of the tragi-comic pattern as Fletcher himself defined it in the preface to *The Faithful Shepherdess*: 'A tragicomedie is not so called in respect of mirth and killing, but in respect it wants deaths, which is enough to make it no tragedy, yet brings some near it, which is enough to make it no comedy. . . .'[5] Such a dramatic formulation leads necessarily, as Granville-Barker remarks of *Cymbeline*, to an 'art that rather displays art than conceals it'.[6] In Beaumont and Fletcher this display is manifested in a pervasive emphasis upon the pattern and peripeties of the action rather than upon a continuous (and engaging) story dramatizing a theme, and in a conception of characterization which is discontinuous and deliberately indecorous. Their plays also place great stress upon what Dryden was later to call 'argumentation and discourse', scene after scene of declamatory displays of passion and passionate reasoning. All of it adds up to a drama which is insistently and consciously theatrical in a manner somewhat like opera. James Shirley, in his preface to the 1647 Beaumont and Fletcher folio, described its effect very lucidly:

> You may here find passions raised to that excellent pitch and by such insinuating degrees that you shall not chuse but consent, & go along with them, finding your self at last grown insensibly the very same person you read, and then stand admiring the subtile Trackes of your engagement.[7]

Philaster offers many examples of this technique of engagement and detachment, but one of them is especially suggestive. In Act IV, scene 3, Philaster comes upon his mistress Arathusa in the woods. She is attended by Bellario, his own page. Unaware that Bellario is Euphrasia in disguise (and in love with him), Philaster misinterprets the meeting and launches a passionate diatribe against faithlessness:

> Let me love lightning, let me be embrac't
> And kist by Scorpions, or adore the eyes
> Of Basalisks, rather then trust the tongues
> Of hell-bred women.

At a word from Arathusa, however, he quickly reverses his mood:

> I have done;
> Forgive my passion: Not the calmed sea,
> When *Eolus* locks up his windy brood,
> Is lesse disturb'd then I: I'le make you know't.

He then offers his sword in turn to Arathusa and Bellario to kill him. Both of course refuse and Philaster, in counter-turn, prepares to use the sword to 'performe a peece of Justice' upon Arathusa. He wounds her, but at that moment a 'Countrey Fellow' enters, and the situation changes quite remarkably:

COUNTREY FELLOW Hold dastard, strike a woman! th'art a craven: I warrant thee, thou wouldst bee loth to play halfe a dozen venies at wasters with a good fellow for a broken head.

PHILASTER Leave us good friend.

ARATHUSA What ill-bred man art thou, to intrude thy selfe
Upon our private sports, our recreations?

COUNTREY FELLOW God uds me, I understand you not; but I know
the rogue has hurt you.

PHILASTER Persue thy owne affaires; it will be ill
To multiply blood upon my head, which thou
Wilt force me to.

COUNTREY FELLOW I know not your rethoricke, but I can lay it on
if you touch the woman.

They fight

Philaster is wounded and, hearing the court party approaching, he
runs off. The country fellow demands a kiss from Arathusa, and
only after he learns that she is the Princess does he lose his fine
uncouth country poise. His last words are: 'If I get cleare of this,
I'le goe to see no more gay sights.'[8]

The whole scene is a paradigm of Fletcherian dramaturgy and
was evidently very popular. *Philaster* was often known in the
seventeenth century by its sub-title, 'Loue lyes a Bleeding', and
a most usual illustration on the title-page of the first edition (1620)
shows the 'Cuntrie Gentleman' looking triumphantly at the wounded Princess, with Philaster beating a retreat through the woods.
The sensationalism of Philaster's attack upon Arathusa and the
passion and rhetoric of his diatribes and laments, appropriate to his
feelings but not to the true situation, are obvious hallmarks of
Fletcherian theatre. All his plays are constructed precisely to
produce such situations and such declamatory displays. Less
obvious but even more revealing is the intervention of the country
fellow. In the peculiar dialectic of Fletcherian dramaturgy he would
seem to represent a popular ideal of honour which Philaster at that
point lacks, but at the same time his emphatic outlandishness serves
to qualify any serious apprehensions we may have developed about
Philaster and Arathusa and thus to preserve the 'middle mood'[9]
of the tragi-comedy. His honourable uncouthness, indeed, is an
urbane joke, a conceit which paradoxically insulates the boundaries
of Beaumont and Fletcher's world of gay sights and protects its
private sports and recreations; and his appearance compels us to
take conscious delight in the artifice of the entire scene. In his later
plays Fletcher does not usually employ so stark a device to define
and italicize his theatrical conceits: the juxtapositions of characters

and scenes (or of contrasting emotions within a character) are more integrated with one another and are more elegant; but their purpose and effect are essentially the same.

A similar kind of self-conscious dramaturgy may also be found in Beaumont and Fletcher's earlier plays,[10] but even more important for the present discussion is the whole dramaturgical climate of the private theatres in the first decade of the century. 'Comicall satyre', though first introduced by Jonson's *Every Man Out* at a public theatre, almost immediately became the typical and dominant product of the private playhouses,[11] and the very basis of the form would seem to be a blend of involvement and judgement very much akin, theatrically, to the tragi-comic mixture of Fletcherian drama. Several features of the plays contribute to this blend. As O. J. Campbell pointed out,

the convention that became most distinctive of the new genre was the presence of at least one commentator, and usually two, upon the characters and the dramatic action. . . . These commentators, whether appearing alone or together, stood outside the action, sometimes even directing it as though they were stage managers of a sort. Their function was to keep alive in the spectators a hostile spirit of mockery toward practically all of the other figures in the comedy.[12]

Although the purpose of this spirit is satiric, its dramatic effect is to keep the audience at least partially disengaged from, and consciously aware of, the action and characters. Another contributing factor is what has been called the principle of 'discontinuity'[13]: in Jonson's comical satiric, as well as in many others, there is no continuous plot, but rather a serial arrangement of episodes designed to further various intrigues and expose various characters; and the dramatic effect here too is to keep the spectator simultaneously engaged in the action and aware of its movements and patterns. Moreover the satiric portrayal of character, exemplified by Jonson's humours though by no means limited to them, in many instances encourages a reaction to the character which is both empathetic and critical. Eugene Waith points out a specific example in Jonson's *Poetaster* in which Jonson presents Ovid's emotions at the prospect of banishment in a manner calculated to capture the audience at the same time that it condemns Ovid for capitulating to such emotions.[14] Waith suggests that these techniques in Marston as well as Jonson led to Fletcher's own development of sensationally mingled tones in tragi-comedy.

Jonson's critical self-consciousness alone would have provided an impetus toward the kind of dramaturgy Fletcher developed, but it is Marston especially, I think, who offers the most interesting and significant anticipations of Fletcherian effects. Marston has been freed in recent years from the stigma of coterie nastiness and has emerged as a serious dramatist making most sophisticated and enterprising use of the resources of the private theatre. Although interpretations vary, his most perceptive critics see his plays as operatic: 'the statuesque scenes, simplified characterization, the emotions on stilts – all these point forward to that acceptable form of absurdity we call opera.'[15] This description concerns *Antonio and Mellida*, but it applies equally well to all of Marston's drama and, as far as it goes, to Fletcher's as well. The difference between Marston and Fletcher is that Marston's purpose is more satirical and more searching. Marston constantly, like Fletcher, calls attention to the artificiality of his characters, played by boys, and of their actions, and he has many scenes like the one with the country fellow in *Philaster* which highlight and parody that artifice; but in Marston the result of such scenes is much more like the tragi-comedy to which we are accustomed in the modern theatre of the absurd. His theatrical ambivalence is an expression of an ambivalence he sees in the real world: to use a phrase of G. K. Hunter's, Marston asks us to understand his court intrigues 'as at once passionately serious and absurdly pointless.'[16] I don't think Fletcher does or cares to do this – the worlds of his plays are less significant and more self-contained.

But for all their differences of purpose Marston and Fletcher employ similar theatrical techniques. The similarities can be seen clearly in *The Malcontent*, a play which is particularly significant because Shakespeare's company adapted it for performance at the Globe in 1604. The induction of the adaptation calls especial attention to the play as a play: the actors are introduced by name and discuss the nature of the play in some detail. Together with the additions of the play, the induction seems to be instructing the spectators at the Globe to keep their distance from the action and to remain constantly aware of its transparent theatricality; and the inference is that this kind of dramatic awareness was not customary at the Globe.

But in any event *The Malcontent* itself plainly demands a sophisticated serio-comic response – or, to use Fletcherian terms, a combination of engagement and detachment. The most striking effect of the play is that we are rarely allowed, except perhaps at the very end, to take the action or the feelings of the characters at face value. This is most evident in the case of Malevole. We learn quite early that he has consciously assumed a malcontent role which does not express his real intentions, but since it does express his predicament we can never entirely believe or disbelieve his vituperative rhetoric. This ambivalence spreads out to the whole play once Malevole's beneficent control (and creation) of the action is assured. No matter what happens our reactions are necessarily qualified, if not determined, by his character and intentions, so that in any given situation we are moved by what a character feels at the same time as we are aware that the character is an actor in a carefully directed play within a play. The effect is not simply one of dramatic irony. When, for example, Malevole-Altofront tests the fidelity of his wife, Maria, her response is poignant as well as ironic:

> Captaine, for Gods love save poore wretchednes
> From tyranny of lustfull insolence:
> Inforce me in the deepest dungeon dwell
> Rather then heere; heere round about is hell.[17]

But although such a speech would not fail to move us in the theatre, we would also almost have to be partially conscious of it as a speech, since we would know, quite simply, that 'round about' is no longer the hell Maria sees. The speech is true to her feeling, but not really to her present situation, which has been theatrically contrived – and it is not a very long step from this theatrical contrivance to Fletcher's adroitly engineered occasions for declamatory displays of passion and argument.

Perhaps even closer to Fletcher are the first two acts of *The*

Malcontent, before the comic outcome is guaranteed by the establishment of Malevole's control. In this part of the play Mendoza appears powerful and his intrigues threatening; yet Marston works in a variety of ways to prevent us from becoming fully absorbed in the intrigues or taking their threats too seriously. In the Globe version this disengagement is accomplished in part by the induction and by additions of exaggerated clowning, usually involving Malevole, whose disguise is also made more explicit. The original Blackfriars version, more cogent and more subtle, probably depended heavily upon a sardonic musical accompaniment analogous perhaps to Kurt Weill's scores for Brecht's plays. But both versions also make us keep our distance by an intricate and ever-shifting intrigue, which inevitably draws attention to itself, and by speeches representing studied exaggeration of feelings. Thus, for example, we hear Mendoza deliver an ecstatic encomium upon 'sweet women, most sweete ladies, nay Angells', and, barely a few moments later, an equally passionate diatribe against 'Women? nay furies.'[18] The patently excessive rhetoric of each speech, as well as their deliberate counterpointing, create an awareness of design and style, of theatrical artifice itself.

This awareness is the distinctive mark of Marston's plays, as it is, in a different way, of Fletcher's. Fletcher exploited it virtually for its own sake and developed a pattern of romantic tragi-comedy which depended absolutely upon it; but he did not invent it, nor did he have a monopoly upon the dramatic uses to which it could be put. A self-conscious dramaturgy – including discontinuous action emphasizing scenes rather than plot, and exaggerated characters manipulated for debates and passionate declamations – seems to have been a common denominator of many if not most plays written for the private theatre. Moreover, this dramaturgy was not simply a result of the development of satirical comedy, for satirical comedy itself may be considered an early symptom of the larger movement in the English theatre from the platform to the picture frame stage. There is a pervasive emphasis in satirical comedy upon parody, of traditional theatrical conventions as well as of traditional ideas, and such dramatists as Jonson and Beaumont and Fletcher are patronizing about precisely the public theatre conventions which, like those of the modern movie, require the audience's uncritical involvement in a panoramic, continuous story.[19] But in any case, it is demonstrable that a calculated self-consciousness was characteristic of many plays written for the private theatre in the early seventeenth century and provided a new idea of tragi-comic theatre which subsequently dramatists could exploit, including those, like Shakespeare, whose earlier experience had been primarily in the public theatre.

There are indications that this whole dramaturgical movement in the private theatre was in fact suggestive to Shakespeare in his last plays. *Cymbeline* is the least harmonious of these plays, but, perhaps because Shakespeare's genius is less distractingly present, the play also provides the clearest and strongest evidence of the ways in which the techniques and dramatic implications of coterie drama may have affected him. The salient fact about *Cymbeline*, to begin with, is that it is resistant to any coherent interpretation. The action moves freely through a kaleidoscope of milieux: a primitive British court, a Machiavellian Italy, a Roman Italy, a pastoral cave. Its hero is at best only half-admirable: in the beginning he loves Imogen and values her as 'the gift of the gods' (I.4.81); after Iachimo's deception he orders her death. Its principal villain is similarly only half-sinister: at possibly his most evil moment, when he is attempting to seduce Imogen, Iachimo becomes so intoxicated with his own verbal extravagance that he subverts his own intentions. Cloten, a lesser villain to begin with, is also a clownish boor, as Shakespeare takes pains to establish in the scene with the Second Lord (I.2); the Queen is never more than a cardboard figure; and Cymbeline is not much more than a dupe. Imogen, the principal and unifying figure of interest in the play, is less equivocally portrayed, since in herself she is consistent enough. But on the other hand the play deals with her very strangely. In a scene that is studiously prepared for, the *scène à faire* of the play, she awakens by the headless body of Cloten, who is dressed in Posthumus's garments, and mistaking him for her husband she sings 'an aria of agony'. It is a moving and convincing one, but we cannot help being conscious at the same time, as Granville-Barker remarks, that 'it is a fraud on Imogen; and we are accomplices in it.'[20]

No other heroine in Shakespeare suffers this kind of exploitation.

Faced with such apparent contradictions, most critics have taken refuge in allegory, or in apocalyptic sentimentalizations (of Imogen especially), or in disintegrations of the text. Yet a better answer would seem to be that the play is frankly experimental, a tentative, not always harmonious, attempt to explore the techniques, and implications of the self-conscious dramaturgy that had evolved in the private theatres – and it is a better answer, I think, because it is based on the plausible assumption that Shakespeare is doing what he wants to do (more or less successfully, as the case may be) and that what appear to be contradictions in the play are deliberate and part of its very nature. Most of the features of the play which cause trouble for critics are precisely those which are most typical of self-conscious tragi-comic dramaturgy. Posthumus, in his sudden turn of heart (and subsequent counter-turn), is not unlike countless Fletcherian heroes whose discontinuous characterizations provide the occasions for turns of plot and emotional declamations; and when at the end of the play he strikes his disguised wife to the ground, the theatrical effect is not so very unlike that provided by Philaster's wounding of Arathusa or of the disguised Euphrasia. Fletcher's scenes are not nearly as resonant as Shakespeare's, but the theatrical situations and patterns are nevertheless almost the same. Similarly, Iachimo is very like the villains who abound in Marston's plays – so close to parodies, so consumed with their own flamboyant rhetoric, and so eventually powerless that though they arouse our apprehensions we cannot take them entirely seriously. Granville-Barker says of Iachimo that 'he presents us, in his arrogance, with an approach to a travesty of himself, which is also a travesty of the very medium in which he exists. A subtle and daring piece of craftsmanship, germane to this hybrid tragi-comedy. Instead of opposing the heroic and the comic, Shakespeare blends the two.'[21] There could be no better description of the kind of effect to be found in Marston's satirical comedies, and the notion in particular of Iachimo's 'travesty of the very medium in which he exists' goes to the heart not only of Marston's method but of the method of the private theatre in general.

Imogen, shaped in the more familiar Shakespearian mould,

cannot be explained so easily. She has a pregnancy about her which no character in Marston, and still less in Fletcher, can match. She has a 'tune' of her own (V.5.238), and she is the only character in the play with whom we are really asked to sympathize. There is no emotional indirection or ambivalence, for example, about Imogen's speech immediately after she learns of Posthumus's suspicions about her, nor is there any in our reaction to it:

> False to his bed? What is it to be false?
> To lie in watch there, and to think on him?
> To weep twixt clock and clock? If sleep charge nature,
> To break it with a fearful dream of him,
> And cry myself awake? That's false to's bed,
> Is it?   III.4.38–43

But if Imogen in herself seems remote from coterie drama, the situations in which she is placed are not. She is repeatedly called upon for histrionic displays in much the same way as Marston's heroines or Fletcher's are – through contrived misunderstandings, or mistaken identities, or deceptions. Her grief over the supposed dead body of her husband, moving certainly in itself, is not different in kind from the grief which Maria displays in *The Malcontent* when her disguised husband is supposedly attempting to seduce her. Imogen is made to perform for us, and she is, throughout, exploited not only by plotters but by the plot of the play itself. It is not surprising that there should be a slightly irascible lilt to her tune – Shakespeare's own unconscious reflex perhaps, as well as hers, against the treatment to which she is subjected.

Not only the characters and the plot, moreover, are symptomatic of the play's self-conscious contrivance; everything about *Cymbeline* suggests that Shakespeare 'is somehow *playing* with the play.'[22] Its verse draws attention to itself: a 'new Euphuism', Granville-Barker calls it, where often 'a thought or emotion behind' a speech seems 'too far-fetched for the occasion or the speaker' (again a perfect description of Fletcherian dramaturgy); and its stagecraft consistently requires a style of 'sophisticated artlessness'.[23] Granville-Barker's remarks about the kind of performance the play demands are worth quoting at length:

He has an unlikely story to tell, and in its unlikelihood lies not only its charm, but largely its very being; reduce it to reason, you would wreck it altogether. Now in the theatre there are two ways of dealing with the inexplicable. If the audience are to take it seriously, leave it unexplained. They will be anxious – pathetically anxious – to believe you; with faith in the dose, they will swallow a lot. The other plan is to show one's hand, saying in effect: 'Ladies and gentlemen, this is an exhibition of tricks, and what I want you to enjoy among other things is the skill with which I hope to perform them.' This art, which deliberately displays its art, is very suited to a tragi-comedy, to the telling of a serious story that must yet not be taken too seriously, lest its comedy be swamped by its tragedy and a happy ending become too incongruous. Illusion must by no means be given the go-by; if this does not have its due in the theatre, our emotions will not be stirred. Nor should the audience be overwhelmed by the cleverness of the display; arrogance in an artist antagonizes us. This is where the seeming artlessness comes in; it puts us at our ease, it is the equivalent of 'You see there is no deception.' But very nice steering will be needed between the make-believe in earnest and in jest.[24]

This could serve equally well as a prescription for performance of Marston or of Fletcher, though there would obviously be important differences: in Marston, for example, more burlesque and satiric bite, in Fletcher more *précieux* sophistication. But the styles and basic dramatic patterns in *Cymbeline*, *The Malcontent*, and *Philaster* are significantly analogous, and Shakespeare's characterizations in *Cymbeline*, his plot, his verse, bear so many resemblances to those of Marston or Fletcher that it seems reasonable to conclude that he was in some way adapting their dramaturgy to his own temperament and interests.

In *Cymbeline*, as elsewhere, Shakespeare was open to a host of influences, not least his own earlier work in the public theatre, and the approach to *Cymbeline* that I have suggested is admittedly only a partial perspective. But it is not a shallow one, and it does not necessarily limit us to the kind of comparisons which many critics of Shakespeare find superficial or offensive. On the contrary, an appreciation of the plays of the private theatre can provide insights into the way in which Shakespeare's own public theatre experience was modulated in *Cymbeline* and into some of the more profound themes and effects that are considered to be characteristic not only of *Cymbeline* but of the last plays in general.

Most critics, for example, would agree that the last plays have in common a pattern of action profoundly concerned with rebirth, regeneration, and redemption through suffering in a manner made intelligible by the Christian idea of the paradox of the fortunate fall. The Shepherd in *The Winter's Tale* who finds Perdita states the pattern in its simplest dramatic terms: 'thou met'st with things dying, I with things new-born' (III.3.109–10). This pattern is not obvious in *Cymbeline*, nor fully developed, but it is present. The action of the play turns upon literal or figurative deaths and re-births: a false Posthumus dies so that eventually the true one can resume his identity and place, a disguised Imogen expires unknown before her brothers only to come to life before them as her sister, etc. Act V as a whole is a sustained finale of rebirths. On two occasions, moreover, the loss and sufferings of the central characters are explicitly related to the idea of the fortunate fall: first, in Lucius's words to the disguised Imogen:

> Be cheerful; wipe thine eyes.
> Some falls are means the happier to arise.   IV.2.405–6

and second, in Jupiter's speech in Posthumus's dream:

> Whom best I love I cross; to make my gift,
> The more delayed, delighted.   V.4.101–2

Amidst the various distractions of *Cymbeline* these motifs do not have sustained lucidity or power: *Cymbeline* is a long way from *The Winter's Tale* or even *Pericles*. But that very distance can paradoxically reveal the evolution of Shakespeare's dramatic ideas as the other plays cannot, for *Cymbeline* seems almost to represent the process by which Shakespeare discovered these ideas to be implicit within the conventions and patterns of the tragi-comic theatre of the private playhouses. To begin with, the basic pattern of tragi-comedy, as Fletcher defined it – and as it was in fact practised by earlier coterie dramatists like Marston, even in ostensible comedies – placed primary stress not upon a simple mixture of comedy and tragedy but upon an action which came to a comic resolution despite or even because of tragic possibilities; as Fletcher wrote, 'A tragicomedie is not so called in respect of mirth and killing, but in respect it wants deaths, which is enough to make it no tragedy, yet brings some near it, which is enough to make it no comedy.'[25] For Fletcher this pattern was an end in itself, a means of creating and sustaining peripeties of action and mood. But with a different angle of vision the same pattern becomes almost a perfect theatrical equivalent of the paradox of the fortunate fall, for the Fletcherian peripeties are very easily adaptable to a context in which bad fortune is turned to good, and suffering and sorrow is transformed into joy and forgiveness.

Shakespeare appears to have seen this equivalence and explored it in *Cymbeline*. The play certainly has much of the tone and many of the situations of standard tragi-comic fare, but there is also no question that Lucius's words to Imogen, 'Some falls are means the happier to arise', are apprehended and experienced in the action. The chief means by which Shakespeare dramatizes this Providential paradox is through a characterization of Imogen, a Shakespearian heroine in a Fletcherian world, which is almost comparably paradoxical. We experience Imogen's sufferings, but always with enough dispassion to recognize the pattern which they form. The result is frequently ironical in a way that is difficult for us to accept – Shakespeare's experimentation seems most abrasive with Imogen – but Imogen is still a harbinger of a heroine like Hermione, who has similar Fletcherian predicaments, though more successfully subsumed.

Imogen, moreover, is not the only symptom of the play's metamorphosis of conventional tragi-comic material. The imagery of the play is saturated with inversions and paradoxes. Few of the images alone are without precedent in earlier Shakespearian plays, but cumulatively they seem to be a self-conscious reflection of Shakespeare's preoccupation with the deeper paradoxes of tragi-comic form.

> She is fooled
> With a most false effect; and I the truer
> So to be false with her ...   I.5.42–4

the doctor remarks, after giving the Queen a harmless sleeping potion which she takes to be poison. Iachimo, when he first sees Imogen, explicitly commends her by remarking that she may veritably be the thing she seems:

> All of her that is out of door most rich!
> If she be furnished with a mind so rare,
> She is alone th'Arabian bird, I.6.15–17

and shortly after, of course, she is compelled to disguise that richness. Cloten, the grotesque, instructs Pisanio to accept villainy as good:

> Sirrah, if thou wouldst not be a villain, but do me true service, undergo those employments wherein I should have cause to use thee with a serious industry – that is, what villainy soe'er I bid thee do, to perform it directly and truly – I would think thee an honest man.
> III.5.109–15

Pisanio himself, who is cast in the role of Imogen's executioner and yet is the means of her preservation, speaks constantly in self-conscious paradoxes which mirror his position. After sending Cloten in pursuit of Imogen, he soliloquizes:

> Thou bid'st me to my loss; for true to thee
> Were to prove false, which I never will be,
> To him that is most true. To Milford go,
> And find not her whom thou pursuest. Flow, flow,
> You heavenly blessings, on her! This fool's speed
> Be crossed with slowness! Labour be his meed!
> III.5.157–62

Later, he complains that he remains

> Perplex'd in all. The heavens still must work.
> Wherein I am false I am honest; not true, to be true.
> These present wars shall find I love my country,
> Even to the note o'th'King, or I'll fall in them.
> All other doubts, by time let them be cleared:
> Fortune brings in some boats that are not steered.
> IV.3.41–6

Shortly after, Posthumus joins the British army in the habit of a peasant,

> To shame the guise o'th'world, I will begin
> The fashion – less without and more within ...   V.1.32–3

welcomes his imprisonment:

> Most welcome, bondage! for thou art a way,
> I think, to liberty ...   V.4.3–4

and dreams of Jupiter, whose intervention ultimately provides the heavenly workings, the happier falls, which the play's imagery has consistently anticipated. Act V is a resolution of unresolved paradoxes and a vindication of Providence. Misunderstanding turns to understanding, hate to love, sorrow to joy, and, in a manner characteristic of artful tragi-comedy, our own rejoicing is a function partly of the crosses and griefs which we also have experienced, especially with Imogen, and partly of the triumph of Shakespeare's artifice itself, which we have been made rather consciously to observe.

There is a deeper note to this mixture of involvement and detachment which is just perceptible in *Cymbeline* and which is taken by most recent criticism to represent an essential part of the dramatic effect of the last plays. This note is most clearly felt in the recognition scenes in *Pericles* and *The Winter's Tale*. The First Gentleman thus describes it as he recounts the meeting of Perdita with Leontes and Camillo in *The Winter's Tale*:

but the changes I perceived in the King and Camillo were very notes of admiration. They seemed almost, with staring on one another, to tear the cases of their eyes. There was speech in their dumbness, language in their very gesture. They looked as they had heard of a world ransomed, or one destroyed. A notable passion of wonder appeared in them; but the wisest beholder that knew no more but seeing could not say if th'importance were joy or sorrow: but in the extremity of the one it must needs be.   V.2.10–19

The same extremity and passion appear, less developed, in the final scene of *Cymbeline* as Imogen is discovered:

> POSTHUMUS Shall's have a play of this? Thou scornful page,
>   There lie thy part.
>   *Strikes her. She falls*

PISANIO   O gentlemen, help!
　Mine and your mistress! O, my lord Posthumus!
　You ne'er killed Imogen till now. Help, help!
　Mine honoured lady!

CYMBELINE   Does the world go round?

POSTHUMUS How came these staggers on me?

PISANIO   Wake, my mistress!

CYMBELINE If this be so, the gods do mean to strike me
　To death with mortal joy.   V.5.228–35

It may seem sacrilegious to suggest that the paradox of mortal
joy and its concomitant, the passion of wonder, are intrinsic to the
pattern of drama developed in the private playhouses. Yet in
purely theatrical terms the effects of wonder in Shakespeare and
Fletcher, or Marston, are very close. Philaster wounds Arathusa,
Posthumus strikes Imogen: both are moments of action in which
the extremity of love seems like hate.[26] Similarly, the action as a
whole in *Philaster* or *The Malcontent* constantly joins tragic and
comic possibilities in a manner which encourages a conflation of
emotions resulting in wonder. The wonder in Marston is turned to
satiric detachment, and in Fletcher it terminates in the admiration
of expertise, but the basic theatrical constituents in both cases are
the same as they are in Shakespeare. That Shakespeare has a different and far greater vision – an argument most frequently used
to dismiss such comparisons as nonsense[27] – is not immediately to
the point. Shakespeare throughout his career showed a unique
capacity to find in theatrical conventions themselves the metaphors
for a larger imitation. Few critics, for example, would deny the
relevance of *The Spanish Tragedy* and of revenge play conventions
to an understanding of *Hamlet*, however much different Kyd's
moral vision may be. The Ghost, the play within the play, the
graveyard scene – all staple conventions of the revenge genre –
define a particular world of moral choice for Hamlet at the same
time as they act as theatrical analogues for a more universal human
condition. Though not as comprehensive or clear-cut, a similar
dilation of theatrical convention may be at work in *Cymbeline* and
the last plays. Shakespeare's 'notable passion of wonder', for all its

great reverberations, is theatrically akin to Fletcher's 'middle mood'.

There is, finally, one other central characteristic of the last plays which may have a parallel if not a partial derivation in the dramaturgy of the private theatre. In all the plays the agents or the workings of Providence are made deliberately conspicuous: in *Pericles*, the figures of Gower and Diana; in *Cymbeline*, the highly self-conscious intervention of Jupiter (whose jingle-jangle verse, to the dismay of the disintegrators, may be quite calculated); in *The Winter's Tale*, the figure of Time as well as the diptych construction; and in *The Tempest*, Prospero, who is both a participant and a spectator in a drama which he himself largely creates. The dramatic effect of these characters is to make us conscious not only of a beneficent control of the action but also of the analogue between this control and the dramatist's own artistry. They are all, in other words, 'a projection of the author's craftsmanship',[28] and in that respect represent yet another possible Shakespearian extension of coterie dramaturgy. For, as we have seen, a basic impulse of coterie drama was to make the dramatist's art a subject of his art. In some instances this artistic narcissism led to structures that are significantly similar to Shakespeare's: Malevole's control of the action in *The Malcontent*, for example, is very close to Prospero's role in *The Tempest*; at one point, Malevole, like Prospero, is even explicitly associated with a Providential beneficence.[29] Shakespeare's exploitation of artistic self-consciousness in the last plays is particularly rich, drawing upon the central Renaissance paradox of nature and art and dramatizing, in Northrop Frye's words, 'the sense of nature as comprising not merely an order but a power, at once supernatural and connatural, ... and controlled either by benevolent human magic or by a divine will.'[30] It is impossible, of course, to find such richness or meaning in dramatists like Marston or Fletcher, but once again it is possible and illuminating to see the Shakespearian development as, at least in part, an elaboration of the dramatic self-consciousness they cultivated.

There are other sources and precedents for *Cymbeline*, other approaches to the play, which responsible criticism cannot ignore. Some of them limit or qualify the perspective I have suggested, but none I think invalidate it. Northrop Frye, for example, shows most persuasively that the last plays, *Cymbeline* included, are explorations of comic laws which grow quite naturally out of earlier Shakespearian comedy, and he shows also that many of the characteristics of the last plays, including the blend of detachment and participation, are at the very least implicit in the early comedies.[31] But there is no reason that Shakespeare's exploration of comic form should be incompatible with the possible influence upon him of coterie dramaturgy; in fact, quite the opposite. Frye himself acknowledges that the last plays are self-conscious, that *Cymbeline*, for example, though not a more religious play than *Much Ado*, 'is a more academic play, with a greater technical interest in dramatic structure',[32] and what would be more natural than that given such an interest, however much it were an extension of his earlier experience with comedy, Shakespeare's imagination should have been stimulated by the academic self-consciousness of the contemporary private theatre? There is no need, in this case as with any other, to assume that the interior logic of Shakespeare's artistic development is at odds with his theatrical environment.

The same is true if we regard the heroic romance as the primary or differentiating source for the last plays. Frank Kermode, for example, has suggested that the mood of the last plays is like that of Spenser's *Mutability Cantos*:

> All things stedfastnes do hate
> And changed be: yet being rightly wayd
> They are not changed from their first estate;
> But by their change their being doe dilate:
> And turning to themselues at length againe,
> Doe worke their own perfection so by fate.[33]

This is a fine description of the sense of redeeming time and of Providential design which we experience in the last plays, but it is also, within limits, a good description of the concrete theatrical action not only of Shakespeare's plays but of Fletcher's and many of Marston's as well. Mutability, satirically, even cynically, regarded, is a significant subject of coterie plays, approaching in

Marston the dignity of a theme and employed in Fletcher as a kind of sophisticated premise; and the patterns of action in the plays of both men, with turns and counter-turns that ultimately come to rest where they began, with oscillating rather than developing movements, correspond very closely, in terms of practical play-writing, to the conception of mutability developed verbally in Spenser's verse. And once again it is difficult to imagine that Shakespeare would not have seen this or exploited it. The action is hardly dilated in Fletcher or Marston, and only Shakespeare saw the wonderful possibilities of the eventual return to rest and perfection in the recognition scenes, but the basic theatrical components of the action in all three dramatists are analogous if not identical.

The one intractable stumbling block in the relationship between Shakespeare and the private theatre is *Pericles*. The play preceded the move to Blackfriars, is clearly associated with the public theatre and public theatre dramaturgy, and at the same time presents in almost archetypal form many of the central themes of the last plays, including recognition and the ideas of the fortunate fall and redeeming time.[34] One answer, only partly an evasion, is that even if *Pericles* did initiate the last plays solely within the conventions of the public theatre, Shakespeare's association with Blackfriars none-theless affected the course of development of the subsequent plays. *Cymbeline*, in particular, has too many significant parallels with coterie drama to ignore. But another answer is that neither in *Pericles* nor elsewhere was Shakespeare theatrically insular: a number of his earlier plays, *Troilus and Cressida* especially,[35] show definite evidence of the influence of the private theatre, and *Pericles* itself shows signs of the same influence. Individual scenes, such as the ones dealing with the riddle of incest or with Marina in the brothel, though exploited for different purposes, are discernibly akin to the preoccupations of the private playhouses; and the play as a whole, with its conscious emphasis upon pageantry and an archaic narrator, preserves exactly the blend of involvement and dispassion which is the distinguishing feature of coterie drama-turgy. Neither the sexual focus nor the sense of distancing can as easily be found in the public theatre plays like *The Rare Triumphs of Love and Fortune* or *Mucedorus* which are often regarded as the most important precedents or sources in the genesis of *Pericles*.

There are, then, no insuperable objections to looking at *Cymbeline* and the last plays in the way I have suggested; and there are real advantages. That Shakespeare should have been affected by the dramatic developments in the private theatre is not only possible but probable, given his professional commitments and temperament, and an appreciation of the potentialities of this relationship not only helps explain aspects of *Cymbeline* which are otherwise very difficult to explain, but adds to our understanding of all the last plays without unduly distorting them, which is as much as one can ask of any single approach to Shakespeare.

NOTES

1. The evidence for Shakespeare's association with Blackfriars is discussed by G. E. Bentley, 'Shakespeare and the Blackfriars Theatre', *Shakespeare Survey 1* (1948), pages 38–50 [see pages 143–59 above – Ed.]. I am indebted to Professor Bentley for several suggestions in this article, as well as to Dr James McManaway, Professor Jackson Cope, and, especially, Mr William MacPheron.

2. Alfred Harbage's *Shakespeare and the Rival Traditions* (1952) offends in just this way, though Harbage is also most responsible for establishing differences between the two traditions in the first place.

3. The most recent and thorough treatment of Blackfriars is Irwin Smith's *Shakespeare's Blackfriars Playhouse, Its History and Design* (1964). The boy actors are discussed by H. N. Hillebrand, *The Child Actors* (1926).

4. A. H. Thorndike's *The Influence of Beaumont and Fletcher on Shakespeare* (1901), though still a valuable study, is marred by the unprovable assumption that *Philaster* preceded *Cymbeline*.

5. *The Works of Francis Beaumont and John Fletcher*, edited by A. H. Bullen (Variorum edition), Volume 3 (1908), page 18.

6. *Prefaces to Shakespeare*, Second Series (1930), page 243. [See page 229 above. – Ed.].

7. *Comedies and Tragedies Written by Francis Beaumont and John Fletcher Gentlemen* (1647), sig. A3v. Maynard Mack, 'Engagement and Detachment in Shakespeare's Plays', in *Essays on Shakespeare*

and Elizabethan Drama in Honor of Hardin Craig, edited by Richard Hosley (1962), pages 275–96, uses Shirley's terms to describe the profound capacity of Shakespearian and Elizabethan drama to be at once realistic and symbolic and to make us aware of the analogies between the world and the stage. The sense in which Shirley uses the terms, however, and in which they are applicable to Beaumont and Fletcher (and to coterie drama generally), is essentially different. In Beaumont and Fletcher the balance of engagement and detachment leads to a consciousness of artifice and fiction which exists for its own sake and which ultimately limits rather than exploits the old Elizabethan analogies. For the most thorough discussion of Fletcherian dramaturgy see Eugene M. Waith, *The Pattern of Tragicomedy in Beaumont and Fletcher* (1952); also Arthur Mizener, 'The High Design of *A King and No King*', *Modern Philology* 38 (1940), pages 133–54.

8. *The Dramatic Works in the Beaumont and Fletcher Canon*, edited by Fredson Bowers, Volume 1 (1966), pages 455–9.

9. Una Ellis-Fermor's phrase, *The Jacobean Drama* (1936), page 205.

10. *The Faithful Shepherdess*, though narrower in its range and more awkward in its artifice than *Philaster* and the later plays, depends for its theatrical effect upon similar declamatory displays and upon a similar recognition of artifice on the part of the audience. In a different way, *The Knight of the Burning Pestle* also lays great stress upon conscious theatrical sophistication, since the play's parodic effect clearly depends upon the audience's ability to recognize theatrical conventions at the same time as it is affected by them. The play's apparent failure at Blackfriars may be attributed to the audience's lack of sympathy for the conventions of the public playhouse rather than to any inability to respond to the characteristic Fletcherian blend of engagement and detachment. Finally, *Cupid's Revenge* may be an early play (1607 or 1608), and if so it provides almost a prototype of the use to which this blend would be put in the particular form of tragi-comedy developed in *Philaster* and the subsequent plays (see James Savage, 'The Date of Beaumont and Fletcher's *Cupid's Revenge*', *ELH* 15 (1948), pages 286–94).

11. Harbage, *Shakespeare and the Rival Traditions*, page 71, points out that of the fifty-five extant plays that can be assigned with confidence to the coterie theatres between 1599 and 1613, 'all but a dozen' can be classified as satirical comedies.

12. *Comicall Satyre and Shakespeare's 'Troilus and Cressida'* (1938), page 79.

13. John J. Enck, 'The Peace of the Poetomachia', *Publications of the Modern Language Association of America* 77 (1962), pages 388 ff.

14. 'Characterization in John Fletcher's Tragicomedies', *Review of English Studies* 19 (1943), page 148. See also O. J. Campbell, op. cit., pages 127–8.

15. G. K. Hunter, Introduction to his edition of *Antonio and Mellida* (Regents Drama Series, 1965), page xxi.

16. op. cit., page xvii. See also R. A. Foakes, 'John Marston's Fantastical Plays', in *Studies in English Drama presented to Baldwin Maxwell*, edited by C. B. Woods and C. A. Zimansky (1962), pages 229–39.

17. *The Plays of John Marston*, edited by H. Harvey Wood (1934), Volume 1, page 204.

18. *Plays*, edited by Wood, Volume 1, pages 154, 157.

19. See especially Jonson's 1616 prologue to *Every Man in His Humour*.

20. *Prefaces to Shakespeare*, Second Series (1930), page 340.

21. op. cit., pages 292–3.

22. Frank Kermode, *Shakespeare: The Final Plays* (1963), page 22.

23. op. cit., pages 288, 244. [See page 230 above. – Ed.]

24. op. cit., pages 244–5. [See pages 230–31 above. – Ed.]

25. *The Works of Francis Beaumont and John Fletcher*, edited by A. H. Bullen (Variorum edition), Volume 3, page 18.

26. The analogy is not perfect because Posthumus does not recognize Imogen when he strikes her, whereas Philaster knows Arathusa – the parallel is closer, perhaps, with Perigot's wounding of Amoret in *The Faithful Shepherdess* or with Philaster's wounding of Euphrasia-Bellario. Moreover, since Pericles strikes Marina before he recognizes her in *Pericles*, and *Pericles* antedates both *The Faithful Shepherdess* and *Philaster*, Fletcher, in this instance, may be directly indebted to Shakespeare. But regardless of who is the innovator, what still remains significant is that both dramatists exploit this kind of episode, and for comparable theatrical effects.

27. H. S. Wilson, '*Philaster* and *Cymbeline*', in *English Institute Essays 1951*, pages 146–7, dismisses any Fletcherian influence *or* analogies on essentially this basis. Moreover, even granting with Wilson that Shakespeare is more interested in expectancy than in surprise (page 162) – though the rebirth of Hermione in *The*

Winter's Tale is surely as big a surprise as any in Fletcher – the patterns of dramatic action and characterization in Shakespeare and Fletcher can still be significantly similar.

28. Northrop Frye, *A Natural Perspective* (1965), page 69.

29. Malevole remarks, after Pietro and Ferneze meet and forgive one another:

> Who doubts of providence,
> That sees this change, a heartie faith to all:
> *He needs must rise, who can no lower fall,*
> *For still impetuous* Vicissitude
> *Towzeth the world* . . .

> *The Plays of John Marston*, edited by H. Harvey Wood,
> Volume 1, page 198

30. op. cit., page 71.

31. op. cit., *passim*. For a discussion of Shakespeare's earlier exploitation of ideas of theatre, particularly *theatrum mundi*, see Anne Righter, *Shakespeare and the Idea of the Play* (1962; Penguin Shakespeare Library 1967).

32. op. cit., page 70.

33. Quoted in Kermode, *Shakespeare: The Final Plays*, page 11.

34. See F. D. Hoeniger's introduction to the new Arden edition of *Pericles* (1963), pages lxiii-xci. [See pages 216–20 above. – Ed.] For an illuminating treatment of the dramaturgical innovations of *Pericles*, and their relation to the later plays, see Francis Berry, *The Shakespeare Inset* (1965), pages 148–56.

35. See Robert Kimbrough, *Shakespeare's 'Troilus and Cressida' and its Setting* (1964).

from *ELH: A Journal of English Literary History* 34 (1967),
pages 285–306

Cymbeline, edited by J. M. Nosworthy (new Arden Shakespeare, 1955). The most useful edition for a close study of the play, containing a full discussion of the play in the editor's Introduction, ample notes to the text, and extracts from possible sources. The source of the wager-plot, Boccaccio's 'Story of Bernardo and Genevra', is included in *Elizabethan Love Stories*, edited by T. J. B. Spencer (Penguin Shakespeare Library, 1968). This and other source material will shortly appear in G. Bullough's *Narrative and Dramatic Sources of Shakespeare*.

G. WILSON KNIGHT: *The Crown of Life* (1947). The book contains a notable essay on the play, which emphasizes the theme of national destiny, and defends the 'Vision of Jupiter' as an integral and significant episode in the play.

HAROLD S. WILSON: '*Philaster* and *Cymbeline*', *English Institute Essays 1951*. A comparison of Beaumont's and Fletcher's play with *Cymbeline* shows that, whichever came first, the apparent resemblances are less significant than the fundamentally different levels of seriousness; Beaumont and Fletcher are more interested in superficial theatrical effects than in a profounder imaginative vision.

'THE WINTER'S TALE'

EIGHTEEN

Pandosto and the Nature of Dramatic Romance

John Lawlor

ALTHOUGH *The Winter's Tale* shows in part the influence of other works,[1] its primary source, Greene's *Pandosto*, is echoed more fully than 'any other novel used by Shakespeare as a source'.[2] If 'the playwright has the play-in-performance before his mind's eye while he is transmuting source material'[3] a comparison of the leading differences between Greene's novel and Shakespeare's play may help us towards assessing the characteristics of romance as a dramatic form. In what follows, the emphasis is upon differences of plot and characterization; verbal echoes and image-associations are for the most part ignored.

I

The major differences in the 'story' are readily summarized. As Professor Muir notes,[4] Pandosto's suspicions of Bellaria's behaviour with Egistus are given some groundwork in the novel, including the detail of Bellaria 'oftentimes comming her selfe into his bedchamber, to see that nothing should be amisse to mislike him.'[5] Shakespeare lets us see the whole of the evidence for ourselves in the exchanges between Leontes and his guest, followed by Hermione's success, at Leontes's bidding, in persuading Polixenes to stay. By this means Shakespeare presents a Leontes who begins in isolation, inhabiting a world where everything is to be tested by its appearances. The effect is increased by another change. Greene's Bellaria 'desired the King that for the love hee bare to his young Sonne Garinter' (page 82) he would consult the oracle. But Shakespeare's Leontes sends to Delphos of his own accord – 'for a greater confirmation', his mind being entirely made up:

> Though I am satisfied, and need no more
> Than what I know, yet shall the oracle
> Give rest to th'minds of others, such as he,
> Whose ignorant credulity will not
> Come up to th'truth.   II.1.189–93

Here again the isolation of the central character is intensified; and this is carried to a point of final disaster. When the contents of the oracle are made known to Greene's Pandosto, he is immediately ashamed and asks his nobles to intercede with Bellaria for him (page 85). But Leontes rejects the oracle and thus blasphemes against Apollo:

> There is no truth at all i'th'oracle.
> The sessions shall proceed: this is mere falsehood.
>
> III.2.138–9

So the death of the King's son, reported immediately afterwards, comes as confirmation of the god's anger. Too late, Leontes repents. His Hermione falls before him; and he, with the audience, is bidden, in Paulina's words,

> look down
> And see what death is doing.   III.2.146–7

The scene ends with a chastened Leontes being taken to see the bodies of wife and child. All this is dependent on an oracle whose message remains unknown to the audience until it is read out at the trial. Shakespeare takes the opportunity, rich in theatrical possibility, of showing a queen on trial – a woman who, for once, staunchly defends her reputation against slander – and a king who, setting himself against divine authority, is immediately humbled, and utterly deprived.

A further notable difference is Shakespeare's omitting the crude knockabout of the Shepherd and his wife in Greene. The wife, seeing her husband return with the foundling,

marveling that her husband should be so wanton abroad, sith hee was so quiet at home ... taking up a cudgell (for the most master went breechlesse) sware solemnly that she would make clubs trumps, if he brought any bastard brat within her dores.   (page 89)

This heavy jocularity comes too close to the main theme. Shakespeare's Shepherd is a shrewd but kindly old man; and the dialogue that follows discovery of the child is with his slow-witted son. Greene's Shepherd wins his termagant wife's silence by telling her 'if she could hold her peace, they were made for ever.' But it is Shakespeare's 'Clown' who tells his father 'You're a made old man' – to be answered 'This is fairy gold, boy, and 'twill prove so.' The mercenary motive and the need for silence have been neatly fitted into place. Luck must be recognized – and given its proper scope: 'to be so still requires nothing but secrecy'. Age speaks with an unpretending authority in Shakespeare's old man, who is neither the 'poore mercenarie Shepheard' nor the wary husband of Greene's story. The scene's ending brings the first note of hope in the play: ''Tis a lucky day, boy, and we'll do good deeds on't' (III.3.133–4).

A similar heavy-handedness on Greene's part is felt in his treatment of Dorastus (Shakespeare's Florizel) 'bewitched' by Fawnia's (Perdita's) 'witt and beautie'. He 'all this while road with a flea in his eare'; but, conscious of his station in life,

> began with divers considerations to suppresse his franticke affection, calling to minde, that Fawnia was a shepheard, one not worthy to be looked at of a Prince; much lesse to be loved of such a Potentate: thinking what a discredit it were to himselfe, and what a griefe it would be to his father: blaming fortune, and accusing his own folly that he should be so fond as but once cast a glaunce at such a country slut.
>
> (page 95)

This, with the 'passionate terms' of euphuistic soliloquy that follow, is provoked by the sight of Fawnia 'with the garland on her head' – a country girl who had 'attired her selfe in her best garments,' being 'bidden as the Mistresse of the Feast' to 'a meeting of all the Farmers daughters in Sycilia' (page 93). Nothing so clearly marks an entire divide between Greene's novel and Shakespeare's play as this difference of function for the 'Feast'. The laboured treatment of a rich young man's self-doubts when a poor girl, dressed for the day, has caught his fancy, gives way to the entire acceptance of a Florizel, one who sees beyond the 'Whitsun pastorals' and the 'robe' Perdita wears to the wonder that

> What you do
> Still betters what is done.
>   . . . Each your doing,
> So singular in each particular,
> Crowns what you are doing in the present deeds,
> That all your acts are queens.   IV.4.135-6, 143-6

There is nothing in Florizel of Dorastus's laboured antitheses and subsequent careful cross-examination of Fawnia. The dialogue in Greene lies between prince and peasant and is, appropriately to the genre, upon the virtuous simplicity of the shepherd's life. Fawnia's first 'witty answere' upon this matter 'so inflamed Dorastus fancy, as hee commended himselfe for making so good a choyce.' He therefore 'began to sift her more narrowly' (page 99). We are a world away from the unquestioning devotion of Florizel and the simple return of his love by a Perdita who would reject his 'praises' as 'too large', were he not, palpably, 'an unstained shepherd' (IV.4.147-9).

Again, in Shakespeare's play the 'Feast' is a meeting-place of father and son, court and pastoral, against the background of a natural simplicity and a timeless rite. There, a dialogue upon 'nature' and 'art' is conducted between Perdita and a disguised stranger, Polixenes (accompanied by Camillo), arising from the flowers given to the guests. Shakespeare has turned to good use both the bare hint of disguise in Greene's account of the high-born maid whose beauty is first apparent when she is decked for the feast, and the detail that Fawnia, when Dorastus seeks her out to question her further, is found 'making a Garland of such homely flowers as the fieldes did affoord' (page 98). 'Art' is discussed between Dorastus and Fawnia; but directly, in its relation to the manifest plight of the lovers, when Dorastus, for all his 'Shepheards coat', remains a Prince. Fawnia speaks of the truth behind appearances:

Painted Eagles are pictures, not Eagles: Zeuxis Grapes were like Grapes, yet shaddowes: rich cloathing make not Princes: nor homely attyre, beggers. . . .   (page 103)

Shakespeare's Perdita speaks for nature as against art, in rejecting from her 'rustic garden' the mixed strains advocated by Polixenes. But there is no conscious reference to the situation of the lovers; and in this Shakespeare has taken the decisive step away from a merely dramatized narrative of young love's woes to the true art of the romance play, where the unity to be attained is focused in truths spoken unwittingly by youth and age alike.

This unifying power is evident in the handling of Florizel and Perdita as fugitives to Bohemia. In Greene's account, Dorastus and Fawnia, having set sail from Sicilia, encounter a storm which clears only when the coast of Bohemia is in sight (pages 111–12). It is one more accident. But in Shakespeare's play Camillo's longing to see again his country leads him to counsel Florizel plainly, 'make for Sicilia'. The theme of exile, an inconsolable longing for return, is planted in Act IV, scene 2:

> It is fifteen years since I saw my country. Though I have for the most part been aired abroad, I desire to lay my bones there.

Here, too, Camillo speaks of 'the penitent King, my master'. The tide begins to set towards the shores of Bohemia not by some accident of tempest but in the fulfilment of time, the fifteen years which have confirmed penitence while they have not assuaged longing. Camillo's plan for the young lovers is indeed, in the art of the romance play as against the novel of fortunate accident,

> A course more promising
> Than a wild dedication of yourselves
> To unpathed waters, undreamed shores, most certain
> To miseries enough.   IV.4.562–5

These differences between Greene's novel and Shakespeare's play gain a cumulative force which can be measured in the contrast between Pandosto and Leontes receiving the fugitives. In Greene, 'the fame of Fawnias beautie' reaches a Pandosto 'who then being about the age of fiftie, had notwithstanding young and fresh affections' (page 112). He has the lovers 'apprehended as spyes', and, enraged by Dorastus's standing his ground, imprisons him, while he himself contrarye to his aged yeeres began to be somewhat tickled with the beauty of Fawnia, insomuch that he could take no rest, but cast in his old head a thousand new devises. (page 114)

It is the old Pandosto, irascible ('starting from his seat as one in choler'), malevolent (ready, as Dorastus says, 'upon suspition to inferre beliefe'), and now lustful ('broyling at the heate of unlaw-full lust'); and, as before, prepared to 'forget all curtesie' and resort to 'rigor' against the object of his love (pages 116–17). With the arrival of the Sicilian embassy the truth of Dorastus's parentage is made known. Now, it seems, Pandosto has every justification for railing upon Fawnia; he can vent his own anger at her ob-duracy while apparently reproving her presumption in 'being a beggar, to match with a Prince' (page 119). In the end, there is nothing for it but a farcical volte-face. When the Shepherd speaks of Fawnia's true origins, Pandosto must all in a moment modulate from 'Thou disdainfull vassal, thou currish Kite ...' to 'my Daughter Fawnia, ah my sweet Fawnia, I am thy Father, Fawnia.' We can well believe that 'This suddaine passion of the King drave them all into a maze, especially Fawnia and Dorastus.' It is this Pandosto who, when all have journeyed to Sicilia and the marriage has there taken place, comes to a sad end:

Pandosto (calling to minde how first he betrayed his friend Egistus, how his jealousie was the cause of Bellariaes death, that contrarie to the lawe of Nature hee had lusted after his own Daughter) mooved with these desperate thoughts, he fell in a melancholy fit, and to close up the Comedie with a Tragicall stratageme, he slewe himselfe. ...

(pages 119–21)

Against this unhappy Pandosto we have a Leontes who, as Professor Muir observes, 'receives the lovers with courtesy and affection, and promises to be their advocate with Polixenes'.[6] The 'penitent King' spoken of by Camillo in Act IV, scene 2, is seen at the outset of Act V, one who must be besought

At the last,
Do as the heavens have done, forget your evil;
With them forgive yourself. V.i.4–6

Instead of the 'desperate thoughts' that in the end destroy Pandosto, Shakespeare presents 'A saint-like sorrow' in one who has

> paid down
> More penitence than done trespass. V.1.3-4

After Apollo's sentence, there can be no turning back. While his Queen lies dead there is no escape for Leontes from a death in life. Time himself appears, at the outset of Act IV, to tell the audience of Leontes's remaining in a trance-like, entombed state –

> Th'effects of his fond jealousies so grieving
> That he shuts up himself –

while the action is turning to new life. It is a fulfilment of the oracle's sentence. In Greene the oracle had concluded:

The King shall die without an heire: if that which is lost be not found.

(page 83)

But Shakespeare's alteration is decisive:

> the King shall *live* without an heir. . . .

We turn from punitive death to continuing life. Leontes's is a sentence not to be ended, making a death in life until 'that which is lost' can be found. Pandosto, we recall, had been 'ashamed of his rash folly'; but the mood has not survived in the Pandosto who receives the fugitives. Shakespeare's Leontes, once repentant, remains so – and apparently unalterably so:

> Whilst I remember
> Her and her virtues, I cannot forget
> My blemishes in them, and so still think of
> The wrong I did myself. V.1.6-9

The promise exacted by Paulina that he will marry at her bidding is the first indication that this settled course may have an end. With the entry of the fugitive lovers, we see for the first time in the play a wholly amiable Leontes. There is in his reception of Florizel and Perdita that sense of incalculable loss which is the deepest note in the Shakespearian scale:

> Welcome hither
> As is the spring to th'earth! V.1.150-51

It is the only parallel; a rebirth must take place. Here, again, is the true unity the romance form seeks, if it is to avoid the perils of the merely imposed happy ending. Repentance in action is an open-handed courtesy; Leontes, repenting the offence done to Polixenes, has his opportunity of humility – to plead with the father on behalf of the son. The play itself is achieving its own balance and resolution; the hospitality we had seen violently strained in Act I, scene 2 is now fulfilled. Now it is Leontes who, Polixenes-like, praises another man's beloved, in delicately complimentary terms. Florizel's plea for help –

> at your request
> My father will grant precious things as trifles –

draws the reply:

> Would he do so, I'd beg your precious mistress,
> Which he counts but a trifle.   V.1.220–23

It is Shakespeare's transmutation of Greene's incest-theme (a Pandosto who lusts after his own daughter); and it is at once related to Leontes's sense of unalterable loss. Paulina chides him for the complimentary vein:

> Not a month
> 'Fore your queen died she was more worth such gazes
> Than what you look on now –

and Leontes, in his reply, identifies present courtesy with perpetual longing:

> I thought of her
> Even in those looks I made.   V.1.224–7

Time past is bridged; a youthful Hermione is ever-present to Leontes's mind. For the audience, alerted by Paulina's words, before the arrival of the lovers –

> Unless another,
> As like Hermione as is her picture,
> Affront his eye –   V.1.73–5

the scene is a foretaste of what is to come in greater measure, an evidence of the stirring of new life. Perdita's beauty has moved the recollection of a lost happiness; but although the audience knows that she is the daughter of Leontes, they do not know that her mother lives and will in turn be restored to him.

In the space of one scene (Act V, scene 1) we have travelled all the way from a sadly penitent Leontes to a magnanimous host, taking the part of the young against the old. The following scene reports the rejoicing at the discovery of the daughter; and, too, the marvellous workmanship that has made another Hermione. The last scene opens with Leontes in possession of an unlooked-for happiness, united with Polixenes, his 'crowned brother', and with the lovers, now 'contracted | Heirs' of the two kingdoms. All that can be made well is well. But the statue awakens an impossible longing; and the illusion that it lives is preferable to reality:

> No settled senses of the world can match
> The pleasure of that madness.   V.3.72-3

It is, most movingly, the joyous counterpart of Pandosto's 'desperate thoughts'. When Hermione takes the hand outstretched at Paulina's bidding, Leontes has no further thought of reality. There is the unmatched wonder of his words:

> O, she's warm! –

and with it an entire acceptance of this Hermione, in whatever terms she has come to him:

> If this be magic, let it be an art
> Lawful as eating.   V.3.109-11

Shakespeare's last action is characteristically assured. A Leontes fully restored to life can humorously turn the bargain back on Paulina:

> O peace, Paulina!
> Thou shouldst a husband take by my consent,
> As I by thine a wife.   V.3.135-7

Paulina is mated. The breaches in the human family being restored, the realm of apparent magic falls into place.

To sum up, the decisive changes from Greene are: (1) in the character of Leontes, to begin with the isolation of jealousy; to dispute with Apollo himself on the truth of what is believed; and thereafter to run a settled course of true repentance, shown in action as courtesy to the fugitive lovers. (2) The omission of the crude domestic comedy of Greene's Shepherd and wife, together with other alterations of tone away from the laboured exchanges of the lovers, the lustfulness of the old and the dangerous innocence of the young,[7] and the wry tone of a knowing narrator. (3) The use of the sheep-shearing feast as a meeting-place of youth and age, and the occasion of a dialogue on 'art' and 'nature' which, ostensibly concerned with crossing stocks in plants, is obliquely linked with the marriage of high and low in human society.[8] With these differences go some additions or variations. In place of the Mrs Noah-like Shepherd's wife in Greene, we have a son whose natural simplicity fits him very well to be the gull of a cunning rogue, Autolycus; but who also serves, with rising fortunes, to voice satirical comment on 'gentle' life – 'the kings and the princes' will be claimed as 'our kindred' (V.2.165–9). In romance, courtesy is a dominant theme; and the dullard who is rising in society has a suitable place, if the inwardness of courtesy is to be distinguished from its externals. Altogether outside such a region, and therefore best placed to offset any unrealities of pastoral, stands Shakespeare's creation, Autolycus. If, as has been sometimes supposed,[9] Shakespeare was conscious of absurdities in his story, he deepens a well-tried formula in presenting not only a 'Clown' and a shrewder 'natural', but also a resourceful rogue at loose in Bohemia, ever-ready to turn the situation to his advantage. Some of the tricks of Autolycus, as has often been noted, are set down in the coney-catching pamphlets of Greene. In a dramatist who could adapt both his main plot and one of the main elements in its variation from one and the same author we have a striking instance of what 'the onely Shake-scene in a countrie'[10] could do. Antigonus and Paulina are both new creations,[11] husband and wife, and in a curious way they balance each other – an Antigonus who is somewhat sententious, and is the custodian of Leontes's daughter, is appropriately paired with the authoritative Paulina, on whose stratagem Hermione's 'resurrection' turns.

But the important 'addition' is not in terms of character or episode. It is to take Greene's sub-title 'The Triumph of Time' and invest it with new meaning – a meaning we may catch at in Florizel's rapt wonder at Perdita's perfection, 'I'd have you do it ever'; or in the praise of Giulio Romano's skill – 'who, had he himself eternity and could put breath into his work, would beguile Nature of her custom' (V.2.92–8); or, most movingly, in Leontes's entire readiness to accept 'an art | Lawful as eating'. It is not, indeed, the Triumph of Time, but the human wish to triumph over time, here for once fulfilled. Time is allowed an authentic scope, evident alike in the 'wrinkled' face of Hermione (against the human wish to arrest time in a remembered perfection) and in the grief which Time will not assuage – a sorrow which

> sixteen winters cannot blow away,
> So many summers dry. V.3.50–51

But time has allowed a new generation to grow to maturity; time has taught patience and acceptance. In the end, the ill that mortals would do is prevented; the train of consequence runs all another way. Without unreality, we have both the truth of time and the deeper truth of mortal desiring. We begin to see why *The Winter's Tale* has been regarded as Shakespeare's 'major achievement ... at this time of his life.'[12] If the truth of tragic art turns upon a meeting of the supernatural and the actual, unsearchable mystery for once evident in a pattern of consequence, in dramatic romance at its highest we can have a meeting of the marvellous and the literal – the succession of events falling out in conformity with the deepest wishes of men, whatever the ordinary and apparently inevitable consequence of their acts.

2

The theatre-craft prompting these changes – 'the play-in-performance' before Shakespeare's 'mind's eye' – goes some way to supporting those critics who, like Professor Coghill, have found reason to rescue *The Winter's Tale* from the charge of an ill-made play, where 'dramatic technique' is 'crude and apparently incoherent'.[13] We have seen Shakespeare recasting Greene's Pandosto into a Leontes isolated from his first appearance; and in the course of the play we are to swing from near-demonic possession to a sad resignation. In order that Leontes's passion shall break with full force on the audience, the play opens with a dialogue between Camillo and Archidamus which tells of peace and amity. Camillo's metaphor of husbandry –

They were trained together in their childhoods; and there *rooted* betwixt them then such an *affection*, which cannot choose but branch now –
                                                                    I.1.22–4

is Shakespeare transmuting what Greene says of Egistus, when, finding in Bellaria

a vertuous and courteous disposition, there grew such a secret uniting of their *affections*, that the one could not well be without the companie of the other: insomuch that when Pandosto was busied with such urgent affaires, that he could not be present with his friend Egistus, Bellaria would walke with him into the *garden*.   (pages 69–70)

Shakespeare has transferred to the relationship of Polixenes and Leontes the intimacy between Egistus and Bellaria recorded by Greene. The metaphor, as Professor Mahood notes, looks forward to the talk of grafting in Act IV.[14] The dramatist begins by implanting, so to speak, the idea of inseparable union, under the particular image of natural growth. With it is linked the promise of youth, in the praise of the young Mamillius; and with this, in turn, the notion of age wishing to suspend time:

They that went on crutches ere he was born desire yet their life to see him a man.

But to suspend time is to abolish death; Archidamus replies:

If the King has no son, they would desire to live on crutches till he had one.
                                                          I.1.38–9, 43–4

Here are assembled and interacting the ideas of natural growth (in affection), the promise of a new generation, and the desire of the old to outlive time, if necessary, to see its fulfilment.

The scene that follows is to reverse these expectations: having implanted them, Shakespeare moves immediately to disappoint them. As theatrical art it is truly, as Professor Coghill calls it, the 'technique of the prepared surprise'.[15] But it illustrates an all-important quality of dramatic romance. The audience is given a longer-term expectation which the dramatist can reawaken like the memory of a lost happiness. For the moment, in Act I, scene 2, the reversal is all: and the means to it are twofold – firstly, the contrast between the ceremonious and ornate language of Polixenes and 'the one-syllabled, two-edged utterances of his host'[16]; secondly, the visible presence of a Hermione who bears witness to the theme of growth and seasonal fulfilment:

> Nine changes of the watery star hath been
> The shepherd's note since we have left our throne
> Without a burden.   I.2.1–3

Shakespeare's 'Nine changes of the watery star', placed boldly at the very outset of the scene, is his own variation on the 'suspitious thought' that 'galled a fresh' Pandosto, when, after Egistus's departure, word is brought to him from the prison that his queen is pregnant. The hint for Leontes's passionate outburst lies in Greene's account of Pandosto's behaviour at this later point. Pandosto

no sooner heard the Jaylor say she was with childe, but as one possessed with a phrenzie, hee rose up in a rage. . . .

Here again, true to the nature of narrative, Greene's account has a circumstantial note:

thinking that surely *by computation of time*, that Egistus and not he, was father to the child.
                                                                                (page 78)

Shakespeare makes his Leontes the watchful and suspicious observer of a Hermione visibly pregnant, exchanging pretty courtesies with Polixenes; and at one and the same time to give suspicion the 'proof' it seeks and to declare Leontes's entire ruthlessness, Shakespeare shows him insisting that Hermione shall persuade Polixenes to stay.

On these all-important opening scenes, two points may be added. The contrast of language in Act I, scene 2 has its own part to play in attuning the audience to a set of contrasts between court and country, art and nature. It meets us, as has been noted, with renewed force in the dialogue between Polixenes (disguised) and Perdita, in Act IV, scene 4. There Perdita, as exponent of a natural simplicity, replies to Polixenes's antithetical and complex defence of 'an art | Which does mend Nature' by accepting the proposition that such an art 'itself is Nature' – while steadfastly refusing any application to herself:

> I'll not put
> The dibble in earth to set one slip of them. IV.4.99–100

The plain country words come with unalterable force. Perdita's is a destiny to which she must be brought, not travel of her own volition. We have moved away from the conscious purposes and dilemmas of Greene's story to awareness of a destiny which will bring the persons of the play to ends they cannot foresee. Secondly, the use of the two courtiers, Camillo and Archidamus, in the opening scene, to speak of what they have every reason to expect, is balanced by the coming together of the courtiers in Act V, scene 2 to speak of what was never expected and is now, cumulatively, made known, as each further witness comes to add his knowledge. These 'innominate gentlemen', as Quiller-Couch unkindly called them,[17] are the living proof of what Camillo and Archidamus has told us: that 'a gallant child' 'makes old hearts fresh'; and that life and death are lesser things beside the restoration of a succession to the kingdom. It is a sound instinct that prompts the producer to make these courtiers old, even very old,[18] men. They speak of something which, while true, 'is so like an old tale that the verity of it is in strong suspicion'; and it is well that they should bring a lifetime's experience to bear when proclaiming what is 'Most true, if ever truth were pregnant by circumstance' (V.2.28–31). They speak from within their own experience of past events – the estrangement between the Kings, the loss of the child, the sentence of the oracle; and, looking forward, the resemblance between Giulio Romano's statue and the Hermione of reality. Their rhetoric, it should be noted, is 'the same dialect of early seventeenth-century refinement and wit' as is used by Archidamus and Camillo and by Polixenes in the two opening scenes.[19] In Act V, scene 2 the language of the court is strikingly counterpointed by touches of naturalness, the prosaic questions of 'what next?' neatly interwoven with the flights of delighted hyperbole. To read Greene and Shakespeare side by side is to marvel at the ease with which Shakespeare transmutes the self-conscious rhetoric of 'court' as against 'country'. There is no place for either Dorastus's aristocratic doubts about the propriety of his loving one of low degree, or Pandosto's inflated apostrophes to a daughter turned in an instant from captive to long-lost child. In this latter instance, Shakespeare has neatly avoided the perils of a recognition scene, with its possibilities of 'very tragical mirth', by creating in Act V, scene 2 a scene which mingles tears and laughter, while leaving the deeper emotions of the audience free for a final return of happiness which Leontes will encounter in his own person.

As to this, the last scene of the play, Professor Coghill soundly reminds us of the care taken by Shakespeare to ensure that 'the audience, like Leontes, should believe her dead'.[20] The striking instance of his craft at this point is the failure of the statue to move at Paulina's first bidding. As Professor Coghill notes, the passage is punctuated most heavily:

> Musick; awake her: Strike:
> 'Tis time: descend: be Stone no more: approach:
> Strike all that looke vpon with meruaile: Come:
> Ile fill your Graue vp: nay, come away:
> Bequeath to Death your numnesse: (for from him,
> Deare Life redeemes you). ...   V.3.98–103

There is a fine balance in this. Leontes's first jealous rage had swept aside every consideration, turning the whole world, in an instant, to thriving corruption:

> Goe play (Boy) play, there haue been
> (Or I am much deceiu'd) Cuckolds ere now,
> And many a man there is (euen at this present,
> Now, while I speake this) holds his Wife by th'Arme,
> That little thinkes she ha's been sluyc'd in's absence,
> And his Pond fish'd by his next Neighbor (by
> Sir *Smile*, his Neighbor:) ...   I.2.190–96

The tempo is rapid, the sense contorted as each fresh emphasis comes crowding parenthetically in; the speaker would enfold all men in his savage misery. Now the knot is undone – with slowness, hesitation, almost, it seems, in that tense moment, the most purely theatrical of any in Shakespeare, with a false start – 'stirre: nay, come away.' It is, in this scene as in Act I, scene 2 (with Leontes's 'euen at this present, | Now, while I speake this'), an art that boldly reaches across the play-situation to wrest the spectator from his fancied immunity. An audience that cannot quite believe, in these last moments, that what is hoped for may come true is at one with Leontes himself. However intently the spectator has looked at the 'statue', its first refusal to come alive at Paulina's command must reinforce the certainty that this is plaster or pasteboard, not flesh. When it moves, the last and best trick of all has been accomplished.

There remain to be noticed two points at which the nature of the new thing formed by Shakespeare from Greene's narrative is decisively focused. The first is Act III, scene 3. The previous scene has brought the train of disastrous events to their conclusion. Leontes had blasphemed against Apollo; his son is dead; Hermione, on Paulina's report, is dead, too. Nothing remains but perpetual repentance at their tomb:

> So long as nature
> Will bear up this exercise, so long
> I daily vow to use it. III.2.238–40

Act III, scene 3 takes us at one sweep away from the court, the sphere of imperious authority, and away from purely human agency altogether. Antigonus's instructions were clear: the baby was to be taken

> strangely to some place
> Where chance may nurse or end it.

Echoing this, Antigonus could only ask that

> Some powerful spirit instruct the kites and ravens
> To be thy nurses! Wolves and bears, they say,
> Casting their savageness aside, have done
> Like offices of pity. II.3.181–2,185–8

With Antigonus's farewell to the baby in Act III, scene 3, the last reach of Leontes's power is attained. Now it is time for 'chance' and for bears, if not wolves, to play their part. The old courtier, pursued by the bear, gives way to the old Shepherd; and his acceptance of the child is at one with his acceptance of the 'boiled brains' of elegant youth; he will 'take it up for pity'. As Professor Coghill observes, Antigonus's abrupt removal is 'the moment when the tale, hitherto wholly and deeply tragic, turns suddenly and triumphantly to comedy'.[21] Similarly, the speech of the Shepherd's son that follows, describing the fate of the ship that had brought Antigonus and – 'for the land-service' – Antigonus's own grisly ending, is made comic, in the breathless astonishment of a simple man's effort to tell all, counterpointed by a dutiful but intermittent sense of order in the telling. It is a technique Shakespeare had long before practised as a means of giving theatrical interest to what would otherwise be tediously informative. We may recall, for example, the drunken Borachio's recital in *Much Ado*: 'I tell this tale vilely – I should first tell thee. ...' (III.3.143 ff.). But the function of this Clown's tangled recital goes deeper. The whole world of past disaster is being rapidly packed away. Mr Bethell puts the point well; the technique of laboured and disordered statement in the Clown's mouth is 'not only a means of commanding a special sort of attention, but is also in itself a statement about the nature of reality.'[22] Now the future is to be our entire concern; and this is put with the authority of age to counter the excitement of youth: 'thou met'st with things dying, I with things new-born'. The hinge has turned; from this point onwards there is hope; and, true to the nature of romance, there is room for laughter.

The second point at which the new conception is decisively focused is, of course, the sheep-shearing feast. Here, in structural terms, Shakespeare has learnt a lesson of the greatest importance in dramatic romance. *Pericles* was merely theatrized narrative, successive episodes in a tale that comes to a happy ending through 'the inscrutable workings of Providence'.[23] In *Cymbeline*, we witness something very different, the piling-up of complication, so that in the last act there are six successive disclosures to be made. A recent editor does well to invite us to see *Pericles* and *Cymbeline* in relation to 'a thoroughly disreputable tradition of dramatic romance which could boast no more than a handful of minor inanities'.[24] It is the best of initial approaches to Shakespeare's work in dramatic romance. But we may still differ from Mr Nosworthy's verdict that this play's 'astonishing final scene' is Shakespeare's 'most complete and triumphant *vision* of unity'.[25] The word 'vision' is carefully chosen. No one has shown more clearly than Mr Nosworthy that while a 'formal happy ending should admit an anticipatory spirit of optimism', 'the bulk' of *Cymbeline* is in fact 'over-tragic in tone and conception'.[26] The 'vision' is there certainly; but in structural terms the ending is an imposed unity – a last set of disclosures in which all the separate pieces of the puzzle are sorted and fitted into place. That Shakespeare does this with a truly wonderful skill is not in dispute. The prior consideration in a dramatist's handling of romance is, as Mr Nosworthy himself well shows, the distance which the evil is allowed to travel before it is set to rights. Shakespeare's first cast at dramatic romance had been the successive episodes of the story of *Pericles*, a wanderer who at last achieves the land-fall of happiness. The second, in *Cymbeline*, is the simple formula of a last act which will resolve the mounting complications which have run unchecked to this point.[27] But in *The Winter's Tale* we see a solution which takes us beyond consummate theatre-craft. Now the achievement of unity is not in the last act but in Act IV. There, young and old, planning their separate courses, are brought together; and we see a pattern developing which is not of any man's contriving and which will enfold them all. The dialogue on 'nature' sets the right note, with its obliquity of reference to the crossing of stocks in human society. When the Shepherd, supposedly father of Perdita, has, in reply to Polixenes, father to 'Doricles', made a true judgement of the young man, he has something to say to Perdita; and it is a truth which relates to the whole genre of romance:

> If young Doricles
> Do light upon her, she shall bring him that
> Which he not dreams of.   IV.4.180–82

It is the actual truth of this play that art restores happiness by becoming nature: the statue moves – and descends. In a deeper sense, the truth of the romance-kind, in the theatre, turns directly upon the audience being given not a foresight of events to come – indeed, surprise must play the largest part in the final unfolding – but a foretaste of a happiness which will not finally be withheld. In this we may see the decisive break from that order of comedy in which the audience being in the secret, participates in the working out of an expected design. The crowning surprise of the romance play, if it is not to be mere *coup de théâtre*, must come as fulfilment of a happiness the audience has begun to hope for in despite of probability. Let the last act contain the explanations, with all their dazzling quality of revelation. But the dramatist must have already gathered his persons into a unity, though they knew it not – so that the audience can reach beyond plot-entanglement to a design which sustains all.

In this, Shakespeare has passed beyond external considerations of romance as a dramatic form, and seized upon its distinctive capacity. Properly handled, dramatic romance can enable us to have the best of both worlds of theatrical experience – on the one hand, a continuing sense of act and consequence, acceptance of man as prone to choose the damnation of a merely private world, the region of jealousy, vengefulness, or deep-seated hatred, and thus condemned to learn the bitter lessons of experience; on the other, growing awareness of a train of events that will not be wholly controlled by one man's agency, and may therefore bring about a full reversal of expectation. Mr Eliot once compared the 'meaning' of a poem – the connected 'sense' it in part offers – with the meat which the burglar gives the house-dog, so that he can get on with his job of making an entry.[28] The case is similar. If the writer of dramatic romance is to penetrate our deeper consciousness, he must not allow us to remain merely vigilant about man as agent, alert to connect act and consequence. Against that, he must show us the direction of counter-movement, including the scope of fortunate accident. But, much more important, we must encounter for ourselves the quality of a union between human beings which, cutting across all separate categorizations, is felt as itself an instance, and the highest instance, of 'great creating Nature'. In the stage history of this play it has been the commonest error to deal faithfully with the sad story of Leontes and Hermione on the one hand, and the pastoral tale of Perdita and Florizel on the other, 'without realizing their organic relationship'.[29] Greene's novel, true to type, puts the emphasis all one way; his is 'The Historie of Dorastus and Fawnia'. The real achievement of Shakespeare's play is a 'complex unity';[30] and in casting his story from the novel, Shakespeare moved surely and consistently towards that unity.

NOTES

1. Mr E. Honigmann has suggested that Francis Sabie's blank verse poem, *The Fissherman's Tale* (1595), itself derived from *Pandosto*, is echoed in several passages ('Secondary Sources of *The Winter's Tale*', *Philological Quarterly* 34 (1955), pages 27–38). Professor Kenneth Muir, commenting on possible traces of *The Fissherman's Tale* and its sequel, *Flora's Fortune*, and drawing attention to Greene's coney-catching pamphlets in relation to Autolycus's tricks, also suggests that the dialogue on art and nature in IV.4 may echo a discussion in Puttenham's *Arte of English Poesie*. For Hermione's 'resurrection', Pettie's *Palace of Pleasure* has the stories of Alcestis and Pygmalion, and Pygmalion is also to be found in Marston's verse-rendering and in Ovid's *Metamorphoses*. Professor Muir points out that in *The Tryall of Chevalry* (1605) 'Ferdinand, supposed dead, poses as his own statue'. A clear echo of Golding's Ovid is heard in Perdita's invocation of Proserpine. (See Muir, *Shakespeare's Sources*, Volume 1, Comedies and Tragedies (1957), pages 240–51.) Mr Honigmann, drawing attention to W. F. C. Wigston (*A New Study of Shakespeare*, 1884), stresses the parallel between Hermione's returning from her 'death-sleep', upon the restoration of Perdita, and the myth of Ceres-Proserpine, which is also a 'winter's tale' (op. cit., pages 33–8).

2. Muir, op. cit., page 247.

3. Rudolf Stamm, 'Elizabethan Stage-Practice and the Transmutation of Source Material by the Dramatists', *Shakespeare Survey* 12 (1959), pages 64–70; page 65.

4. op. cit., page 240.

5. The edition of *Pandosto* used is that of 1588, reprinted in *The Descent of Euphues*, edited by James Winny (1957), pages 67–121; page 69.

6. op. cit., page 245.

7. Compare the suspicious anxiety of the Shepherd's neighbours, reporting Dorastus's visits to Fawnia 'for the good will they bare to old Porrus ... wishing him to keepe his daughter at home, least shee went so oft to the field, that she brought him home a young son' (*Pandosto*, page 105).

8. See G. Wilson Knight, *The Crown of Life* (1947), pages 104 ff.

9. For example by Muir (op. cit., page 243); S. L. Bethell, '*The Winter's Tale*': *a Study* (1947), pages 47, 65, etc.

10. *Greene's Groats-worth of Wit* (1596), in *The Shakspere Allusion-Book* (1932), Volume 1, page 2.

11. Muir (op. cit., page 245, note 1) points out that the name Antigonus is to be found in Plutarch (and Autolycus in Ovid and Homer). Professor Wilson Knight suggests that the name Paulina, through the 'New Testament association of "Paul"', may underline her function 'as a personification of Leontes' conscience'. Paulina 'contrasts with the Greek-pagan community of the names around her; and so, for that matter, do the purely Latin names of the two children, Mamillius and Perdita' (*The Sovereign Flower* (1958), page 196).

12. Clifford Leech, 'The Structure of the Last Plays', *Shakespeare Survey 11* (1958), pages 19–30; page 30.

13. Nevill Coghill, 'Six Points of Stage-Craft in *The Winter's Tale*', *Shakespeare Survey 11* (1958), pages 31–41; page 31. The charge is that of S. L. Bethell, op. cit., page 47.

14. M. M. Mahood, *Shakespeare's Wordplay* (1957), pages 147–8. [See pages 347–8 below. – Ed.]

15. Coghill, op. cit., page 32.

16. op. cit., page 33.

17. *The Winter's Tale* (New Cambridge Shakespeare, 1931), page xxiii.

18. As in Peter Wood's production at the Royal Shakespeare Theatre, Stratford-upon-Avon, in 1960.

19. Coghill, op. cit., page 39.

20. op. cit., page 40. Since it is without parallel in Shakespeare's work to withhold this knowledge from the audience, it has been conjectured that he may have originally conceived the play as ending, like the novel, with the finding of Perdita, and that its final form is influenced by recollection of *Pericles*, where both wife and daughter are restored (compare Muir, op. cit., page 251; Leech, op. cit.,

pages 24–5). Whatever the genetic history of the play, it must be noted that the act-structure is 'firmly made and in the traditional mode' (Leech, op. cit., page 25). Mr Honigmann is surely right in contending that the statue scene is acceptable 'not as a makeshift happy ending but as a germinal point in the conception of the play and a carefully planned climax' (op. cit., page 37).

21. op. cit., page 34.

22. op. cit., page 65.

23. Kenneth Muir, *Shakespeare as Collaborator* (1960), page 96.

24. J. M. Nosworthy, *Cymbeline* (new Arden Shakespeare, 1955), page xlix.

25. op. cit., page lxxxi.

26. op. cit., pages l-li.

27. As Professor Leech points out, while in Act IV 'we have careful preparations for the *dénouement* ... there is no new development here, no respite from action'. The last act is truly characterized as 'a separable unit, with its fifth scene a remarkable series of discoveries, reconciliations, and disposals of the inconvenient' (op. cit., page 23).

28. *The Use of Poetry and the Use of Criticism* (1933), page 151.

29. W. Moelwyn Merchant, *Shakespeare and the Artist* (1959), page 209.

30. ibid.

from *Philological Quarterly* 41 (1962), pages 96–113

NINETEEN

The Triumph of Time in *The Winter's Tale*

Inga-Stina Ewbank

IT is often assumed that, while Shakespeare's middle plays and many of his sonnets show a keen awareness of, and even obsession with, the power of time over man, his final plays are not concerned with the themes of time and change. In these plays we are, according to one critic, in 'a fairyland of unrealities' in which 'injurious time plays no controlling part'[1]; and another critic sees Shakespeare as abandoning time-thinking in order to devote himself to 'myths of immortality'.[2] Yet *The Tempest*, for all that it celebrates values which are not subject to time, also balances these against time in its 'injurious' capacity, time which triumphs over

> The cloud-capped towers, the gorgeous palaces,
> The solemn temples, the great globe itself,
> Yea, all which it inherit.   IV.1.152–4

Prospero's island may be a 'fairyland of unrealities', but it is also the land of Petrarch's *Trionfi*:

> Our Tryumphs shal passe our pompes shal decay
> Our lordshyppes our kyngdomes shall all awaye
> And al thynge also that we accompt mortall
> Tyme at the length shal clene deface it al.[3]

And when Shakespeare was looking around for material for the play which was to become *The Winter's Tale*, he chose a story with the sub-title 'The Triumph of Time' and developed it in a fashion which suggests a deepening and enrichment, rather than an abandonment, of time-thinking.

The Time which triumphs on the title-page of Greene's *Pandosto* is not the dreaded *tempus edax* but the beneficent Revealer who shows that 'although by the means of sinister fortune Truth may be concealed, yet by Time in spight of fortune it is most manifestly revealed'.[4] The *Pandosto* story itself fails to work out its motto – *Temporis filia veritas* – for it puts all the emphasis on Fortune, with her wheel, as the ruling agent of human affairs. Shakespeare, on the other hand, makes the Triumph of Time into a controlling theme of his tale; and in doing so he transforms what the conventional motto suggests – a simple victory of Time, the Father of Truth – into a dramatic exploration of the manifold meanings of Time.

The chief evidence of Shakespeare's time-thinking in his middle period lies in the time allusions and time imagery of the plays and sonnets. The chief evidence for assuming a lack of concern with time in the last plays has been, it would seem, their almost total lack of time imagery. But, as I hope to show, while in *The Winter's Tale* time has largely disappeared form the verbal imagery, it is all the more intensely present as a controlling and shaping figure behind the dramatic structure and technique. It is true that certain features of the dramatic technique in *The Winter's Tale* are aimed at achieving an effect of timelessness: S. L. Bethell has shown how Shakespeare uses deliberate anachronisms to create the never-never world of a winter's tale.[5] It would be wrong, however, to conclude that the absence of the objective, social time of history which characterizes the setting of the tale means that in the human issues of the play Shakespeare is unaware of, or uninterested in, man's subjection to time in its various aspects, injurious as well as benevolent.

The most obvious indication of Shakespeare's concern with time is the overall structure of the play. Not only does the action span a long period, so as – and this never happens in the tragedies – to give working-space to time, both as Revealer and as Destroyer; but, through the arrangement of the play into two halves separated by the 'wide gap' of sixteen years, past and present can be emphatically juxtaposed.[6] The structure thus becomes a vehicle for the exploration of the meanings of time – in the sense of what time does to man. The intricacy and complexity of this exploration is revealed, in parts of the play, by subordinated structural features, and it is to these we must first turn if we are to see the full relevance of the larger structure.

The scene of exposition (I.1) is a dialogue between Camillo and Archidamus, which proceeds via a series of references to time seen as natural growth; it places the play in a perspective of naturally ripening time, opening backwards as well as forwards. Camillo describes the span of the relations between the Kings of Sicilia and of Bohemia: from an indicative past 'They were trained together in their childhoods' – to a present consequent upon that past – 'there rooted betwixt them then such an affection, which cannot choose but branch now' – and on to a desired (but soon to be threatened) future – 'The heavens continue their loves!' Similarly he introduces the whole span of human life by way of talking about the little Prince Mamillius: 'They that went on crutches ere he was born desire yet their life to see him a man'; and this subject is expanded to provide, as the scene closes, an ironically foreboding note: 'If the King had no son, they would desire to live on crutches till he had one'. Linking up with this introduction, the beginning of I.2 is a conversation which modulates from one subject to another, with time as the shared note. It opens with the most immediate time-concern, conditioned by plot: how long Polixenes has stayed already and how much longer, if at all, he may be prevailed upon to stay. Even this persuasion (for which there is no source in *Pandosto*) has about it a peculiar urgency, as if love could be measured in time-units:

> When at Bohemia
> You take my lord, I'll give him my commission
> To let him there a month behind the gest
> Prefixed for's parting; yet, good deed, Leontes,
> I love thee not a jar o'th'clock behind
> What lady she her lord.   I.2.39–44

Hermione's fatal victory leads naturally on to remembrances of things past, first of the two Kings' blissful childhood as 'twinned lambs'. Here Shakespeare deliberately juxtaposes time's destruction with things as they were: 'We were', says Polixenes,

> Two lads that thought there was no more behind
> But such a day tomorrow as today,
> And to be boy eternal.　　　　　　　　　I.2.63–5

Polixenes's speeches create a strong sense of time as destructive, as equalling the passing of innocence, making nonsense of the ideals of youth. The transition from this stage of the scene to the next is delicately made via the courtly banter of Polixenes and Hermione. The next remembrance is of the long-seeming courtship of Leontes and Hermione, when finally, so he tells her, after three 'crabbèd months',

> 　　　　　　　　then didst thou utter
> 'I am yours for ever'.　　　　　　　　　I.2.104–5

It is, I think, noteworthy that this recollection of Hermione's forward-looking statement is what triggers off Leontes's first outburst of jealousy. The 'for ever' (which the rest of the play is going to prove true[7]), spoken in innocent remembrance, suddenly becomes tormentingly ironical to Leontes. From his next words, 'Too hot, too hot!', all is feverish haste, in word and deed.

For the action centring on Leontes, from this moment until the end of Act III, is not only a vivid realization of Polixenes's words about the loss of innocence, but it is also a dramatization of the failure to trust Time the Revealer. If Leontes had given himself time to observe the behaviour of Hermione and Polixenes and to listen to his advisers, he would have discovered that his suspicions were rootless. Instead he goes, as it were, against time and is therefore blind to truth; for time, when not allowed to ripen, can only *make*, not *unfold*, error. From now on, speech-patterns, as well as the structure of individual scenes and their combination, are so devised as to bring out the unnatural haste of Leontes's thoughts and acts; and this frenzied hurry is all the more marked for being set against the references to naturally progressing time with which the play opened. The telescoped syntax and half-finished sentences of Leontes's speeches image the frenzy within. His heated imagination fabricates evidence the very nature of which adds to the sense of rush:

> Is whispering nothing?
> Is leaning cheek to cheek? Is meeting noses?
> Kissing with inside lip? Stopping the career
> Of laughter with a sigh? – a note infallible
> Of breaking honesty. Horsing foot on foot?
> Skulking in corners? *Wishing clocks more swift.*
> *Hours minutes? Noon midnight?*   I.2.284–90

and it repeatedly draws time itself into its scope:

> Were my wife's liver
> Infected as her life, she would not live
> The running of one glass.   I.2.304–6

The arrangement of events is partly responsible for the hectic effect of these scenes. Shakespeare here greatly condenses the sequence in the source story. For example, in *Pandosto*, Egistus (Polixenes), having been told of Pandosto's (Leontes's) intention to poison him, waits six days for favourable winds before he sets sail; whereas in *The Winter's Tale* the events up to the end of Act I, when Camillo urges Polixenes

> Please your highness
> To take the urgent hour ...

would seem to happen in as little time as it takes to act them. Camillo's function, in relation to Leontes, is to try to brake the speed:

> Good my lord, be cured
> Of this diseased opinion, and *betimes*,
> For 'tis most dangerous ...   I.2.296–8

and indeed, when brought to insight at the end of III.2, Leontes looks back and sees Camillo as the voice of time whose

> good mind ... *tardied*
> My *swift* command.

But he is not listened to in time; and in a sense he is himself guilty of untimeliness in urging Polixenes to leave at once. Polixenes's hasty departure cannot but tie the knot of error more firmly by confirming Leontes's 'true opinion' (II.1.37).

317

In *Pandosto* Bellaria finds herself quick with child only after Egistus is gone, and she is kept in prison, awaiting trial, till after the child is born. In *The Winter's Tale* Hermione's lying-in is imminent at the outset of the play (Polixenes has been in Sicilia for 'Nine changes of the watery star'), and it is in keeping with the onrush of time in these acts that she is '*something before her time delivered*'. Although at least twenty-three days must have passed during the course of Acts II and III, the structure of events is shaped so as to give the impression that Leontes has not once stopped to think – 'Nor night nor day no rest!' The child is no sooner born than it is doomed to suffer (probable) death. Hermione is rushed into court,

> hurried
> Here to this place, i'th'open air, before
> I have got strength of limit.   III.2.103–5

The verdict of the oracle is no sooner announced than flaunted:

> There is no truth at all i'th'oracle!
> The sessions shall proceed: this is mere falsehood.
>   III.2.138–9

Shortly before, Leontes had hailed the early return of the messengers:

> Twenty-three days
> They have been absent. 'Tis good speed; foretells
> The great Apollo suddenly will have
> The truth of this appear.   II.3.197–200

Indeed Apollo has been 'sudden' in revealing the truth, but Leontes is even more sudden in rejecting it, thereby demonstrating to the full his perversion of truth and justice.

In terms of Elizabethan thought the injustice done to Hermione is linked up with the time theme more closely than a modern reader or audience may realize. Her arraignment can be seen as the epitome of Leontes's rejection of Time, the Father of Truth, for Justice, like her sister virtue Truth, was conceived of as closely associated with Time.[8] Rosalind points to the connexion in her parting words to Orlando after the mock-wooing: 'Time is the old justice that examines all ... offenders, and let Time try' (*As You Like It*, IV.1.184–5). Leontes does not let Time try, despite Antigonus's warning:

> Be certain what you do, sir lest your justice
> Prove violence.
> II.1.127–8

And throughout the court scene (III.2) the word 'justice' rings ironically, coming from Leontes:

> Let us be cleared
> Of being tyrannous, since we so openly
> Proceed in justice, which shall have due course,
> Even to the guilt or the purgation.
> III.2.4–7

Significantly, no one else in this scene uses the word. Hermione never appeals to Leontes's 'justice', for all along is stressed her awareness that she and Leontes – now that time is out of joint – do not use words in the same sense:

> You speak a language that I understand not.
> My life stands in the level of your dreams.
> III.2.79–80

It is, I think, important to notice that it is the first actual death to happen in the play which stops the mad onrush. Previously death has been spoken of, envisaged theoretically, even planned and arranged for; but now Leontes is brought face to face with its actuality. The fact that his son is 'gone', his own issue cut off, his future in terms of the Sonnets' 'lines of life that life repair' interrupted, is what shocks Leontes into seeing in a true perspective the present and the immediate past: 'I have too much believed mine own suspicion'. Too late, this conversion and repentance. The Queen is reported dead, too, and suddenly, in a deliberate contrast to what has gone before, time cannot be long enough:

> A thousand knees,
> Ten thousand years together, naked, fasting,
> Upon a barren mountain, and still winter
> In storm perpetual ...
> III.2.208–11

could not atone for the deeds of a few hectic days of error.

This is the lowest point in the play. The sands have, as it were, rushed through the dramatic hour-glass to measure the decline in Leontes's fortune, his self-inflicted loss of wife and issue. But in the final scene of Act III the finding of the babe replaces things dying with things new-born; and so we are prepared for the visible turning of the hour-glass by 'Time, the Chorus':

> I turn my glass, and give my scene such growing
> As you had slept between.   IV.1.16–17

If we have been aware of the insistence on, and the importance of, the time theme in the first half of the play, we are, I think, prepared to see the introduction of Father Time here as more than a mere stop-gap, a desperate attempt to tidy over the Romance breach of the unities.[9] He has come, at a crucial moment in the play, not merely to substitute for a programme note of something like 'Act IV: Sixteen years later',[10] but to provide a pivotal image, part verbal part visual, of the Triumph of Time. The last fifteen lines of his speech are indeed a résumé of events during the sixteen-year lapse, but they are set in the context of the first fifteen lines, where Time is presented as a principle and power:

> I that please some, try all; both joy and terror
> Of good and bad; that makes and unfolds error. . . .
>   IV.1.1–2

Far from having abandoned time-thinking, Shakespeare presses home the fact that the 'wide gap' of dramatically 'untried growth' is part of the universal process of time who 'makes and unfolds error' in his immutable onward flight. Rather than being timeless, *The Winter's Tale* is thus set in a context of *all* time.

We have seen error being made; now, it is suggested, it is to be unfolded by Time the Revealer. Of course, in a mere plot sense, error had been unfolded at the end of Act III. But truth is more than just getting the facts straight: it is not enough for Leontes to find out that he has been mistaken in his jealousy. He has to become aware of truth in a wider sense, and that can only be achieved through subjection to Time the Revealer – and through grappling with Time the Destroyer. For Time, the Chorus, reminds us of his destructive qualities, too: of his power

> To o'erthrow law, and in one self-born hour
> To plant and o'erwhelm custom.   IV.1.8–9

Above all – anticipating Prospero in his use of the very form of the work of art of which he himself is a part, as an image of transience – he reminds us that 'brightness falls from the air':

> I witness to
> The times that brought them in; so shall I do
> To th'freshest things now reigning, and make stale
> The glistering of this present, as my tale
> Now seems to it.   IV.1.11–15

These lines are less haunting than Prospero's, because they are written in a kind of pageant doggerel, and because the speaker here is the triumphant agent, not the object; so that the element of human nostalgia is lacking. Their effect is to establish the play's connexion with Time's triumph; and the total effect of the choric speech is to invite a dual response to such triumph.

Needless to say, Shakespeare's audience in 1610–11 would have been familiar with the figure of Father Time, from innumerable verbal and pictorial representations and from pageants and masques.[11] Time as the Father of Truth had appeared in the last three royal entries, and Middleton was soon going to use him in the 1613 Lord Mayor's show, *The Triumphs of Truth*. He had become a popular figure in the allegorical masque, because as Revealer he could be used as an effective *deus ex machina* to solve the central conflict and turn anti-masque into masque. Thus he appears, for example, in the fourth of Beaumont and Fletcher's *Four Plays in One*, the masque called *The Triumph of Time*: 'helping triumphantly, | Helping his Master Man'. Yet, to the Elizabethan or Jacobean imagination, Time is never for long allowed to remain a purely beneficent figure. Beaumont and Fletcher's triumphant Time first appears 'mowing mankind down'. When represented iconographically as the Father of Truth, he also has his scythe and his hourglass – an example of this is the emblem of *Veritas temporis filia* in Whitney's *Choice of Emblemes*[12] – and thus remains connected with transience and death. One of the fullest catalogues of the characteristics of Time is Lucrece's diatribe, and there we hear within one stanza that 'Time's glory' is both

> to calm contending kings,
> To unmask falsehood, and bring truth to light

and

> To ruinate proud buildings with [his] hours,
> And smear with dust their glitt'ring golden towers.
>
> *The Rape of Lucrece*, 939–45

Those who tried to put Father Time on the stage in his dual significance often found themselves ending up with an unresolved contradiction, as in Middleton's *Triumphs of Truth*, where Time, the agent of good, suddenly and incongruously turns destructive:

TIME, standing up in TRUTH's Chariot, seeming to make an offer with his sithe to cut off the glories of the day, growing neere now to the season of rest and sleepe, his daughter TRUTH thus meekely stayes his hand.[13]

It was easier for non-dramatic poets to combine destructive and truth-revealing Time, and perhaps the most complete fusion of the two attributes takes place when truth is seen not just as the opposite of falsehood but as, in itself, the realization of the immutable flux of time:

> When *Trewth* (*Tymes daughter*) doth owr triall touch,
> Then take the Glasse and wee shall hardly knowe,
> Owreselves therein we shalbe changed so.[14]

This is the truth connected with time in many of Shakespeare's sonnets on mutability, and indeed in the wrinkled Hermione at the end of *The Winter's Tale*. Shakespeare's choric Time is in a firm Elizabethan tradition when he insists on the multiplicity of his powers – and rather more successful than most pageant Father Times in reconciling his opposed attributes. He needs no disintegrationists or apologists for Shakespeare's 'bad poetry' to justify his appearance in the play, for he is more than a self-contained emblem: he is a concrete image[15] of the multiplicity which the play as a whole dramatizes and which is a leading theme of the second half of the play.

When Act IV opens, sixteen years of time have acted as a healer through the process of growth – natural in the case of Perdita and moral in the case of Leontes. But Leontes himself is withheld from our view till Act V, and two whole scenes precede the appearance on stage of Perdita, thus preparing our acceptance of growth and change before they are actually demonstrated. It is Camillo (just as in I.1) who at the beginning of Act IV brings in the sense of time and puts the immediate action into a time perspective: 'It is fifteen years since I saw my country. . . . I desire to lay my bones there.' We are not, it should be noted, introduced at once to the positive result of the 'wide gap' – the growth into womanhood of the child Perdita – but are first asked to realize what the sixteen years have meant in terms of deprivation for Camillo and, more importantly, of suffering for Leontes: 'that penitent . . . and reconciled king . . . whose loss of his most precious queen and children are even now to be afresh lamented.' This scene, then, as well as preparing for the rest of Act IV, also forms the foundation of the whole of Act V.

The importance of the pastoral scene as an image of regeneration has often been commented on, and even seen as mythical. In the context of the present discussion it is important that Perdita, who is herself almost an image of time seen as natural growth, should first appear in a world where time equals the life of nature and the cycle of the seasons. Perdita's flower-speeches and flower-giving become the epitome of this world. She starts in a vein which may recall Ophelia:

> For you there's rosemary and rue; these keep
> Seeming and savour all the winter long:
> Grace and remembrance be to you both. . . .!   IV.4.74–6

but while Ophelia's flowers are altogether emblematic and dis-tributed according to the emotional significance of the situation and the recipient, Perdita's turn out to be mainly a measure of time and age. Polixenes at once takes her meaning thus:

> well you fit our ages
> With flowers of winter . . .   IV.4.78–9

but Perdita, whether out of courtesy or of chronological accuracy, would assess the ages of Polixenes and Camillo as

> the year growing ancient,
> Not yet on summer's death nor on the birth
> Of trembling winter. ...   IV.4.79–81

The famous discussion on Art versus Nature arises from the 'streaked gillyvors' allegedly representing Polixenes's time of life; and, having agreed to differ, Perdita returns to her identification of time in nature's year with age in man, giving 'flowers | Of middle summer' to 'men of middle age' and lamenting the lack of early spring flowers which would have typified youth, particularly Florizel. Despite their sheer lyrical beauty, these speeches are not just decorative or just meant to create atmosphere: they not only establish a contrast between this world and the world of most of the first three acts, but also define the contrast as being between a world where time is taken for granted as a natural progression and one where time is altogether defied.

Timeless the pastoralism in *The Winter's Tale* is not. Pastoral poets soon discovered that death and transience were in Arcadia, too[16]; and the love of Florizel and Perdita in a central passage pits itself against time and change. Florizel's adoration is formulated as a desire to arrest time, to achieve permanence outside the flux of time:

> When you speak, sweet,
> I'd have you do it ever;
>   ... when you do dance, I wish you
> A wave o'th'sea, that you might ever do
> Nothing but that – move still, still so. ...
>   IV.4.136–7, 140–42

We are reminded of Polixenes's reference, in I.2, to how he and Leontes assumed that 'there was no more behind' than to be 'boy eternal' (and indeed the joint childhood of the two Kings is referred to in pastoral terms); but in Florizel's case the thinking is not naïve, it is wishful, and consciously so. Both Florizel and Perdita are aware of the precariousness of their love in relation to the extra-pastoral world, and throughout the scene the audience sees the threat to it literally present, in the shape of the disguised Polixenes. Before the scene is over, Polixenes has broken up this world of natural time, as Leontes did with the one remembered at the beginning of Act I.

Up till Polixenes's intervention, this scene had presented a structural contrast with the first three acts: long speeches – lyrical, meditative, or descriptive – had set a leisurely pace, relaxed further by singing and dancing. With the King's outburst, the pursuit is on, but instead of our following the hectic activity, as we do in Acts II and III, it takes place off stage; and we are, as Act V opens, finally brought face to face with Leontes.

In V.1 the emphasis is again on the past sixteen years. Time, which we know has to Perdita meant growing up in step with nature, has to Leontes meant unceasing grief over a self-inflicted loss. His sense of time is entirely retrospective; he looks into the future only to lament that it does not exist to him because of

> The wrong I did myself: which was so much
> That heirless it hath made my kingdom, and
> Destroyed the sweet'st companion that e'er man
> Bred his hopes out of.
>
> V.1.9–12

'Heirless' and 'issueless' are thematic words in this scene, made even more poignant (though also ironical in terms of what the audience knows) when Florizel and Perdita arrive to emphasize the difference between what is and what was. It is significant that Hermione is mourned not only for her own sweetness' sake but also as

> the sweet'st companion that e'er man
> Bred his hopes out of.

Leontes has robbed himself not only of love and friendship but also of that other means of defeating time: issue.

After the first acute reminder of loss, the arrival of the young couple (allegedly bearing with them also the loving greetings of Polixenes) strikes a new note in Leontes. The form of his greeting to them –

> Welcome hither
> As is the spring to th'earth! –
>
> V.1.150–51

echoes the many references to 'natural' time in the pastoral scene, and hints at an acceptance of the possibility of time as healing and restoring. Critics of the myth-making school read these lines as a confirmation of the essentially mythical nature of the play: here, they argue, is the first direct sign of the regeneration of the King. But if we see the coming of Perdita and Florizel into Leontes's court as altogether an archetypal situation, then we miss some very human aspects of it which are clearly recognized by Shakespeare. True, the pair are first of all representatives of a second generation, of youth and innocence and regenerative forces – and in being so, they represent to us the beneficial effects of time. But indirectly – through other characters' reaction to her – Perdita also indicates something about time's destructiveness. Paulina is used by Shakespeare in this scene as a choric commentator, turning people's admiration of Perdita into a reminder, though in a muted fashion, that time hath a wallet at his back. Before Perdita appears, the Gentleman's praise of her beauty provokes Paulina to a lamentation much reminiscent of some of the words of Time the Chorus, earlier in the play:

> O Hermione,
> As every present time doth boast itself
> Above a better gone, so must thy grave
> Give way to what's seen now.
>   . . . she had not been,
> Nor was not to be, equalled; thus your verse
> Flowed with her beauty once. 'Tis shrewdly ebbed,
> To say you have seen a better.[17]   V.1.95–8, 100–103

The Gentleman's defence, as concerns Hermione, is a simple 'I have almost forgot'; and at this point it contrasts markedly with Leontes's insistence, a few lines earlier, that *he* cannot forget. But by the end of the scene, in the one possible approach to what in *Pandosto* is a fully developed and elaborated incestuous passion, Leontes himself seems to find the past dimming before the beauty of the present; and again Paulina is there to comment on the treachery:

>   Not a month
> 'Fore your queen died she was more worth such gazes
> Than what you look on now.   V.1.224–6

Perdita's return, then, becomes the occasion for several and varied insights into what time does to man. What it really means to Leontes, when her identity is known, is dramatized in the final scene; for by letting this reunion be merely reported, Shakespeare reserves its impact to combine it with that of the ultimate reunion.

In the last scene the time themes are drawn together and acted out in a unique way. The whole scene has about it a sense of the fullness of time – pointed at the climactic moment by Paulina's ''Tis time: descend' – of stillness and solemnity. Speeches are short, the diction plain, the language almost bare of imagery: as if Shakespeare is anxious not to distract attention from the significance of action and movement. Characters' reactions to the statue are patterned in a fashion which approaches ritual. An unusual number of speeches are devoted just to underlining the emotions and postures of people on stage, as in Paulina's words to Leontes:

> I like your silence: it the more shows off
> Your wonder ...   V.3.21–2

or in Leontes's to the statue:

> O royal piece!
> There's magic in thy majesty, which has
> My evils conjured to remembrance, and
> From thy admiring daughter took the spirits,
> Standing like stone with thee.   V.3.38–42

Verbal repetitions in the first three acts imaged Leontes's obsession and frenzied hurry, as in the 'nothing' speech; here they give the effect of ritual:

> What you can make her do
> I am content to look on; what to speak
> I am content to hear.   V.3.91–3

When the statue comes alive, it is as though we were witnessing the central movement of a masque, with music as accompaniment, Paulina as the presenter and Hermione as the main 'device'. Paulina's commands –

> Music, awake her, strike!
> 'Tis time: descend; be stone no more; approach;
> Strike all that look upon with marvel –   V.3.98–100

are in tone and phrasing very like a presenter's call for the chief figure of the masque to appear.[18]

Into this ritual and revelation Shakespeare has woven the various time-concerns of the play so closely that the scene can be said, in the widest sense, to represent a Triumph of Time. In the widest sense only, for at this stage in the play the simple identification of time as either Revealer or Destroyer has been obliterated. At first the statue seems to bring back the past so vividly that time itself is obliterated:

> O, thus she stood,
> Even with such life of majesty – warm life,
> As now it coldly stands – when first I wooed her!
> V.3.34–6

As on another, fatal, occasion Leontes harks back to his courtship. But the past is present with a difference, for Leontes's reaction also is:

> Hermione was not so much wrinkled, nothing
> So agèd as this seems ...

to which Paulina replies:

> So much the more our carver's excellence,
> Which lets go by some sixteen years and makes her
> As she lived now.   V.3.28–32

The intervening time has meant physical decay, symbolized, as in the Sonnets, by 'necessary wrinkles'. As the sense of the distance between now and sixteen years ago sharpens in Leontes, it again becomes identified with guilt and penance: he speaks of how the statue conjures his evils to remembrance, and Camillo recalls the sorrow

> Which sixteen winters cannot blow away,
> So many summers dry.   V.3.50–51

But the statue comes alive. Paulina's words suggest that Hermione's return is a kind of resurrection:

> Come,
> I'll fill your grave up. Stir; nay, come away.
> Bequeath to death your numbness, for from him
> Dear life redeems you ...   V.3.100–103

and so it is, of course, to Leontes. As he stands there with Hermione and Perdita, many of the Sonnets' resolutions are fused into one dramatic situation. Leontes has defeated time in that his lines of life are stretching into the future. Not only is Perdita restored, but she is in love and about to be married and is herself the potential mother of future generations. Hermione's return represents another form of victory over time; she is a living proof that

> Love's not Time's fool, though rosy lips and cheeks
> Within his bending sickle's compass come.　　　Sonnet 116

These sonnet lines could perhaps also paraphrase the truth that time has finally revealed to Leontes: paradoxically, time has at last in its triumph brought about its own defeat. This does not efface the human suffering that has gone before, however, and that weighs so heavily on the play right till the very end. Rather than a myth of immortality, then, this play is a probing into the human condition, and – as a whole as well as in details – it looks at what time means and does to man.

It would, needless to say, be wrong to think of *The Winter's Tale* as a treatise on time. The play does not state or prove anything. But through its action, its structure, and its poetry, it communicates a constant awareness of the powers of time. Shakespeare, had his small Latin allowed, might well have substituted for the motto of *Pandosto* the words of St Augustine, *Quid est ... tempus? si nemo ex me quaerat, scio; si quaerenti explicare velim, nescio.*[19]

NOTES

1. J. M. Nosworthy, *Cymbeline* (new Arden Shakespeare, 1955), Introduction, page lxiii.
2. G. Wilson Knight, *The Crown of Life* (1947), page 30.
3. *The Tryumphes of Fraunces Petrarcke, translated out of Italian into English by Henrye Parker knyght, Lorde Morley* (1565?), fol. M2ʳ.
4. Greene's *Pandosto*, edited by P. G. Thomas (1907), page xxiii.
5. 'The Winter's Tale': a Study (1947), pages 47 ff.
6. Compare Ernest Schanzer's discussion of how the juxtaposition of the two parts is pointed by structural parallels and contrasts ('The Structural Pattern of *The Winter's Tale*', *A Review of English Literature* 5 (1964), pages 72–82).

7. Leontes is, in a sense, an inverted Troilus. Troilus believes that Cressida's love will last for ever, and is disillusioned by Time. Leontes does not believe in Hermione's 'for ever', and is converted by Time. In each case there is a failure to know the love offered for what it is worth.

8. For a discussion of this association, see S. C. Chew, *The Virtues Reconciled* (1947), pages 90 ff. An example of the close connexion of Time and Justice can be seen in the last of Beaumont and Fletcher's *Four Plays in One*, the masque-play called *The Triumph of Time*. The central Everyman character here abandons false friends, to turn to Time and Justice. The function of Time in this piece is to set things right by unmasking falsehood.

9. See the Introduction to the New Cambridge edition of the play (1931), page xix: '. . . having to skip sixteen years after Act 3, he desperately drags in Father Time with an hour-glass. . . . . Which means on interpretation that Shakespeare . . . simply did not know how to do it, save by invoking some such device.'

10. I cannot agree with Panofsky's criticism of Father Time in this play: 'Sometimes the figure of Father Time is used as a mere device to indicate the lapse of months, years, or centuries, as in Shakespeare's *Winter's Tale*, where Time appears as Chorus before the fifth [*sic*] act' (*Studies in Iconology* (1939), page 81).

11. For examples of these, see, for example, S. C. Chew, 'Time and Fortune', *ELH* 6 (1939), pages 83–113; F. Saxl, 'Veritas Filia Temporis', in *Philosophy and History*; *Essays presented to Ernst Cassirer*, edited by R. Klibansky and H. J. Paton (1936), pages 203 ff.; Rudolf Wittkower, 'Chance, Time and Virtue', *Journal of the Warburg Institute* 1 (1937–8), pages 313–21, and D. J. Gordon, 'Veritas Filia Temporis: Hadrianus Junius and Geoffrey Whitney', *Journal of the Warburg and Courtauld Institutes* 3 (1939–40), pages 228–40.

12. Plate 34b.

13. Nichols, *Progresses of James I* (1828), Volume 2, page 695.

14. Gascoigne, *The Grief of Joye*, edited by J. W. Cunliffe (1910), stanza 52, lines 5–7.

15. Unfortunately in productions of *The Winter's Tale* Father Time often looks like some kind of wizard. The most successful Time I have seen was in a Munich performance in 1959, when he was acted by an octogenarian with little make-up and no paraphernalia other than an hour-glass.

16. See E. Panofsky, 'Et in Arcadia Ego', in *Philosophy and History*; *Essays presented to Ernst Cassirer*.

17. Compare the Chorus lines

> so shall I do
> To th'freshest things now reigning, and make stale
> The glistering of this present ...   IV.1.12–14

18. Compare, to take just one example, the call for Neptune in the masque in *The Maid's Tragedy*, I.1 (edited by A. R. Waller and A. Glover, page 10). Various critics (for example Alice Venezky, *Pageantry on the Shakespearean Stage* (1951), page 128, and T. M. Parrott, *Shakespearean Comedy* (1949), page 386) have suggested that the statue which comes alive is an adaptation of a masque-device; but I have never seen it pointed out that in fact no masque-writer had used this device before *The Winter's Tale* was first performed. Soon after *The Winter's Tale*, however, both Campion and Beaumont in their respective masques for the Princess Elizabeth's wedding made use of statues coming alive. Campion's main masque consists of eight women statues which come to life, four at a time; but in Beaumont's masque the 'statuas' are relegated to the first anti-masque: a variation on the theme is needed by now, and so, 'having but half life put into them, and retaining still somewhat of their old nature', they give 'fit occasion to new and strange varieties both in the music and paces'. It was obviously statues used in this fashion that Bacon had in mind when in his essay 'Of Masques and Triumphs' he placed 'statuas' among the baboons, fools, and other grotesques of the anti-masque. (*A Harmony of the Essays*, edited by E. Arber (1871), pages 539–40. The essay first appeared in the 1625 edition.) It might be noted that the Beaumont masque referred to was in fact 'ordered and furnished' by Bacon.

19. *Confessions*, II.14.

from *A Review of English Literature* 5 (1964), pages 83–100

TWENTY

Recognition in *The Winter's Tale*

Northrop Frye

IN structure *The Winter's Tale*, like *King Lear*, falls into two main parts separated by a storm. The fact that they are also separated by sixteen years is less important. The first part ends with the ill-fated Antigonus caught between a bear and a raging sea, echoing a passage in one of Lear's storm speeches. This first part is the 'winter's tale' proper, for Mamillius is just about to whisper his tale into his mother's ear when the real winter strikes with the entrance of Leontes and his guards. Various bits of imagery, such as Polixenes's wish to get back to Bohemia for fear of 'sneaping winds' blowing at home and Hermione's remark during her trial (reproduced from *Pandosto*) that the Emperor of Russia was her father, are linked to a winter setting. The storm, like the storm in *King Lear*, is described in such a way as to suggest that a whole order of things is being dissolved in a dark chaos of destruction and devouring monsters, and the action of the first part ends in almost unrelieved gloom. The second part is a tragicomedy, where, as in *Cymbeline* and *Measure for Measure*, there is frightening rather than actual hurting. Some of the frightening seems cruel and unnecessary, but the principle of 'all's well that ends well' holds in comedy, however great nonsense it may be in life.

The two parts form a diptych of parallel and contrasting actions, one dealing with age, winter, and the jealousy of Leontes, the other with youth, summer, and the love of Florizel. The first part follows Greene's *Pandosto* closely; for the second part no major source has been identified. A number of symmetrical details, which are commonplaces of Shakespearian design, help to build up the contrast: for instance, the action of each part begins with an attempt to delay a return. The two parts are related in two ways, by sequence and by contrast. The cycle of nature, turning through the winter and summer of the year and through the age and youth of human generations, is at the centre of the play's imagery. The opening scene sets the tone by speaking of Mamillius and of the desire of the older people in the country to live until he comes to reign. The next scene, where the action begins, refers to Leontes's own youth in a world of pastoral innocence and its present reflection in Mamillius. The same cycle is also symbolized, as in *Pericles*, by a mother–daughter relationship, and Perdita echoes Marina when she speaks of Hermione as having 'ended when I but began'. In the transition to the second part the Clown watches the shipwreck and the devouring of Antigonus; the Shepherd exhibits the birth tokens of Perdita and remarks 'thou met'st with things dying, I with things new-born.' Leontes, we are told, was to have returned Polixenes's visit 'this coming summer', but instead of that sixteen years pass and we find ourselves in Bohemia with spring imagery bursting out of Autolycus's first song, 'When daffodils begin to peer'. If Leontes is an imaginary cuckold, Autolycus, the thieving harbinger of spring, is something of an imaginative cuckoo. Thence we go on to the sheep-shearing festival, where the imagery extends from early spring to winter evergreens, a vision of nature demonstrating its creative power throughout the entire year, which is perhaps what the dance of the twelve satyrs represents. The symbolic reason for the sixteen-year gap is clearly to have the cycle of the year reinforced by the slower cycle of human generations.

Dramatic contrast in Shakespeare normally includes a superficial resemblance in which one element is a parody of the other. Theseus remarks in *A Midsummer Night's Dream* that the lunatic, the lover, and the poet are of imagination all compact. Theseus, like Yeats, is a smiling public man past his first youth, but not, like Yeats, a poet and a critic. What critical ability there is in that family belongs entirely to Hippolyta, whose sharp comments are a most effective contrast to Theseus's amiable bumble. Hippolyta objects that the story of the lovers has a consistency to it that lunacy would lack, and everywhere in Shakespearian comedy the resemblance of love and lunacy is based on their opposition. Florizel's love for Perdita, which transcends his duty to his father and his social responsibilities as a prince, is a state of mind above reason. He is advised, he says, by his 'fancy':

> If my reason
> Will thereto be obedient, I have reason;
> If not, my senses, better pleased with madness,
> Do bid it welcome. IV.4.479–82

Leontes's jealousy is a fantasy below reason, and hence a parody of Florizel's state. Camillo, who represents a kind of middle level in the play, is opposed to both, calling one diseased and the other desperate. Both states of mind collide with reality in the middle, and one is annihilated and the other redeemed, like the two aspects of law in Christianity. As the Gentleman says in reporting the finding of Perdita, 'They looked as they had heard of a world ransomed, or one destroyed.' When Leontes has returned to his proper state of mind, he echoes Florizel when he says of watching the statue,

> No settled senses of the world can match
> The pleasure of that madness. V.3.72–3

The play ends in a double recognition scene: the first, which is reported only through the conversation of three Gentlemen, is the recognition of Perdita's parentage; the second is the final scene of the awakening of Hermione and the presenting of Perdita to her. The machinery of the former scene is the ordinary *cognitio* of New Comedy, where the heroine is proved by birth tokens to be respectable enough for the hero to marry her. In many comedies, though never in Shakespeare, such a *cognitio* is brought about through the ingenuity of a tricky servant. Autolycus has this role in *The Winter's Tale*, for though 'out of service' he still regards Florizel as his master, and he has also the rascality and the complacent soliloquies about his own cleverness that go with the role. He gains possession of the secret of Perdita's birth, but somehow or other the denouement takes place without him, and he remains superfluous to the plot, consoling himself with the reflection that doing so good a deed would be inconsistent with the rest of his character. In *The Winter's Tale* Shakespeare has combined the two traditions which descended from Menander, pastoral romance and New Comedy, and has consequently come very close to Menandrine formulas as we have them in such a play as *Epitripontes*. But the fact that this conventional recognition scene is only reported indicates that Shakespeare is less interested in it than in the statue scene, which is all his own.

In *Measure for Measure* and *The Tempest* the happy ending is brought about through the exertions of the central characters, whose successes are so remarkable that they seem to many critics to have something almost supernatural about them, as though they were the agents of a divine providence. The germ of truth in this conception is that in other comedies of the same general structure, where there is no such character, the corresponding dramatic role is filled by a supernatural being – Diana in *Pericles* and Jupiter in *Cymbeline*. *The Winter's Tale* belongs to the second group, for the return of Perdita proceeds from the invisible providence of Apollo.

In *Pericles* and *Cymbeline* there is, in addition to the recognition scene, a dream in which the controlling divinity appears with an announcement of what is to conclude the action. Such a scene forms an emblematic recognition scene, in which we are shown the power that brings about the comic resolution In *The Tempest*, where the power is human, Prospero's magic presents three emblematic visions: a wedding masque of gods to Ferdinand, a disappearing banquet to the Court Party, and 'trumpery' (IV.1.186) to entice Stephano and Trinculo to steal. In *The Winter's Tale* Apollo does not enter the action, and the emblematic recognition scene is represented by the sheep-shearing festival. This is also on three levels. To Florizel it is a kind of betrothal masque and 'a meeting of the petty gods'; to the Court Party, Polixenes and Camillo, it is an illusion which they snatch away; to Autolycus it is an opportunity to sell his 'trumpery' (IV.4.594) and steal purses.

An emblematic recognition scene of this kind is the distinguishing feature of the four late romances. As a convention, it develops from pastoral romance and the narrative or mythological poem. The sheep-shearing festival resembles the big bravura scenes of singing matches and the like in Sidney's *Arcadia*, and *The Rape of Lucrece* comes to an emblematic focus in the tapestry depicting the fall of Troy, where Lucrece identifies herself with Hecuba and

Tarquin with Sinon, and determines that the second Troy will not collapse around a rape like the first one. In the earlier comedies the emblematic recognition scene is usually in the form of burlesque. Thus in *Love's Labour's Lost* the pageant of Worthies elaborates on Don Armado's appeal to the precedents of Solomon, Samson, and Hercules when he falls in love; but his appeal has also burlesqued the main theme of the play. The allegorical garden episode in *Richard II* represents a similar device, but one rather different in its relation to the total dramatic structure.

In any case the controlling power in the dramatic action of *The Winter's Tale* is something identified both with the will of the gods, especially Apollo, and with the power of nature. We have to keep this association of nature and pagan gods in mind when we examine the imagery in the play that reminds us of religious, even explicitly Christian, conceptions. At the beginning Leontes's youth is referred to as a time of paradisal innocence; by the end of the scene he has tumbled into a completely illusory knowledge of good and evil. He says:

> How blest am I
> In my just censure, in my true opinion!
> Alack, for lesser knowledge! How accursed
> In being so blest! II.1.36–9

Or, as Ford says in *The Merry Wives*, 'God be praised for my jealousy!' The irony of the scene in which Leontes is scolded by Paulina turns on the fact that Leontes tries to be a source of righteous wrath when he is actually an object of it. Hermione's trial is supposed to be an act of justice and the sword of justice is produced twice to have oaths sworn on it, but Leontes is under the wrath of Apollo and divine justice is his enemy. The opposite of wrath is grace, and Hermione is associated throughout the play with the word grace. During the uneasy and rather cloying friendliness at the beginning of the play Hermione pronounces the word 'grace' conspicuously three times, after which the harsh dissonances of Leontes's jealousy begin. She also uses the word when she is ordered off to prison and in the only speech that she makes after Act III. But such grace is not Christian or theological grace, which is superior to the order of nature, but a secular analogy of Christian grace which is identical with nature – the grace that Spenser celebrates in the sixth book of *The Faerie Queene*.

In the romances, and in some of the earlier comedies, we have a sense of an irresistible power, whether of divine or human agency, making for a providential resolution. Whenever we have a strong sense of such a power, the human beings on whom it operates seem greatly diminished in size. This is a feature of the romances which often disappoints those who wish that Shakespeare had simply kept on writing tragedies. Because of the heavy emphasis on reconciliation in *Cymbeline*, the jealousy of Posthumus is not titanic, as the jealousy of Othello is titanic; it expresses only a childish petulance about women in general:

> I'll write against them,
> Detest them, curse them. *Cymbeline*, II.5.32–3

Similarly Leontes (as he himself points out) falls far short of being a sombre demonic tyrant on the scale of Macbeth, and can only alternate between bluster and an uneasy sense of having done wrong:

> Away with that audacious lady! Antigonus,
> I charged thee that she should not come about me.
> I knew she would. II.3.42–4

This scaling down of the human perspective is in conformity with a dramatic structure that seems closely analogous to such Christian conceptions as wrath and grace. But the only one of the four romances in which I suspect any explicit – which means allegorical – references to Christianity is *Cymbeline*. Cymbeline was king of Britain at the birth of Christ, and in such scenes as the Gaoler's speculations about death and his wistful 'I would we were all of one mind, and one mind good' (V.4.200), there are hints that some far-reaching change in the human situation is taking place off stage. The play ends on the word 'peace' and with Cymbeline's promise to pay tribute to Rome, almost as though, as soon as the story ended, another one were to begin with Augustus Caesar's decree that all the world should be taxed.

No such explicit links are appropriate to *The Winter's Tale*, though it is true that the story does tell of a mysterious disappearing child born in the winter who has four father-figures assigned to her: a real one, a putative one who later becomes her father-in-law, a fictional one, Smalus of Libya in Florizel's tale, and a shepherd foster-father. This makes up a group of a shepherd and three kings, of whom one is African. The first part of *The Winter's Tale* is, like *Cymbeline*, full of the imagery of superstitious sacrifice. Leontes, unable to sleep, wonders if having Hermione burnt alive would not give him rest. Antigonus offers to spay his three daughters if Hermione is guilty, though he would prefer to castrate himself. Mamillius, whom Leontes thinks of as a part of himself, becomes the victim necessary to save Leontes, and the exposing of Perdita is attended by a sacrificial holocaust. Not only is Antigonus devoured by a bear, but the ship and its crew were 'Wracked the same instant of their master's death, and in the view of the shepherd so that all the instruments which aided to expose the child were even then lost when it was found.' In contrast, the restoring of Perdita to her mother is an act of sacramental communion, but it is a secular communion, and the 'instruments' aiding in it are the human arts. The main characters repair to Paulina's house intending to 'sup' there, and are taken into her chapel and presented with what is alleged to be a work of painting and sculpture. Hermione, like Thaisa in *Pericles*, is brought to life by the playing of music, and references to the art of magic follow. Art, therefore, seems part of the regenerating power of the play, and the imagination of the poet is to be allied with that of the lover as against that of the lunatic.

Apart from the final scene, at least three kinds of art are mentioned in the play. First, there is the art of the gardener who, according to Polixenes's famous speech, may help or change nature by marrying a gentler scion to the wildest stock but can do so only through nature's power, so that 'The art itself is Nature'. This is a sound humanist view: it is the view of Sidney, who contrasts the brazen world of nature with the golden world of art but also speaks of art as a second nature. Sidney's view does not necessitate, but it is consistent with, his ridiculing of plays that show a character as an infant in one act and grown up in the next, and that mingle kings and clowns in the same scene. It is also the view of Ben Jonson who, recognizing a very different conception of nature in Shakespeare's romances, remarked good-humouredly that he was 'loath to make nature afraid in his plays, like those that beget tales, tempests, and suchlike drolleries.' We note that Polixenes's speech entirely fails to convince Perdita, who merely repeats that she will have nothing to do with bastard flowers:

> No more than, were I painted, I would wish
> This youth should say 'twere well, and only therefore
> Desire to breed by me . . .   IV.4.101–3

– a remark which oddly anticipates the disappearance of the painted statue of Hermione into the real Hermione. It also, as has often been pointed out, fails to convince Polixenes himself, for a few moments later we find him in a paroxysm of fury at the thought of his own gentle scion marrying the wild stock of a shepherd's daughter. Whatever its merits, Polixenes's view of art hardly seems to describe the kind of art that the play itself manifests.

Secondly, there is the kind of art represented by Giulio Romano, said to be the painter and sculptor of Hermione's statue, a mimetic realist who 'would beguile Nature of her custom, so perfectly is he her ape' (V.2.97–8). But it turns out that in fact no statue has been made of Hermione, and the entire reference to Romano seems pointless. We do not need his kind of art when we have the real Hermione, and here again, whatever Romano's merits, neither he nor the kind of realism he represents seems to be very central to the play itself. The literary equivalent of realism is plausibility, the supplying of adequate causation for events. There is little plausibility in *The Winter's Tale*, and a great deal of what is repeatedly called 'wonder'. Things are presented to us, not explained. The jealousy of Leontes explodes without warning: an actor may rationalize it in various ways; a careful reader of the text may suspect that the references to his youth have touched off some kind of suppressed guilt; but the essential fact is that the jealousy suddenly appears where it had not been before, like a second subject in a piece of music. 'How should this grow?' Polixenes asks of Camillo, but Camillo evades the question. At the end of the play Hermione is first a statue, then a living woman. The explanations given do not satisfy even Leontes, much less us. He says:

> But how is to be questioned: for I saw her,
> As I thought, dead; and have in vain said many
> A prayer upon her grave.   V.3.139–41

As often in Shakespeare, further explanations are promised to the characters, but are not given to the audience: Paulina merely says 'it appears she lives'.

Thirdly, though one blushes to mention it, there is the crude popular art of the ballads of Autolycus, of which one describes 'how a usurer's wife was brought to bed of twenty money-bags at a burden'. 'Is it true, think you?' asks Mopsa, unconsciously using one of the most frequently echoed words in the play. We notice that Shakespeare seems to be calling our attention to the incredibility of his story and to its ridiculous and outmoded devices when he makes both Paulina and the Gentlemen who report the recognition of Perdita speak of what is happening as 'like an old tale'. The magic words pronounced by Paulina that draw speech from Hermione are 'Our Perdita is found', and Paulina has previously said that the finding of Perdita is 'monstrous to our human reason'. And when one of the Gentlemen says 'Such a deal of wonder is broken out within this hour that ballad-makers cannot be able to express it', we begin to suspect that the kind of art manifested by the play itself is in some respects closer to these 'trumpery' ballads than to the sophisticated idealism and realism of Polixenes and Romano.

My late and much beloved colleague Professor Harold S. Wilson has called attention to the similarity between Polixenes's speech and a passage in Puttenham's *Arte of English Poesie* (1589), which in discussing the relation of art and nature uses the analogy of the gardener and the example of the 'gillyvor'. Puttenham also goes on to say that there is another context where art is 'only a bare imitator of nature's works, following and counterfeiting her actions and effects, as the Marmoset doth many countenances and gestures of man; of which sort are the arts of painting and carving.' We are reminded of Romano, the painter and carver who is the perfect 'ape' of nature. The poet, says Puttenham, is to use all types of art in their proper place, but for his greatest moments he will work 'even as nature her self working by her own peculiar virtue and proper instinct and not by example or meditation or exercise as all other artificers do.' We feel that Puttenham, writing before Shakespeare had got properly started and two centuries earlier than Coleridge, has nonetheless well characterized the peculiar quality of Shakespeare's art.

The fact that Leontes's state of mind is a parody of the imagination of lover and poet links *The Winter's Tale* with Shakespeare's 'humour' comedies, which turn on the contrast between fantasy and reality. Katherina moves from shrew to obedient wife; Falstaff from the seducer to the gull of the merry wives; the King of Navarre and his followers from contemplative pedants seeking authority from books to helpless lovers performing the tasks imposed on them by their ladies. Similarly when Florizel says that his love for Perdita

> cannot fail but by
> The violation of my faith; and then
> Let Nature crush the sides o'th'earth together
> And mar the seeds within!   IV.4.473–6

he is supplying the genuine form of what Camillo describes in parallel cosmological terms:

> you may as well
> Forbid the sea for to obey the moon
> As or by oath remove or counsel shake
> The fabric of his folly, whose foundation
> Is piled upon his faith.   I.2.426–30

Puttenham begins his treatise by comparing the poet, as a creator, to God, 'who without any travail to his divine imagination made all the world of nought.' Leontes's jealousy is a parody of a creation out of nothing, as the insistent repetition of the word 'nothing' in the first act indicates, and as Leontes himself says in his mysterious mumbling half-soliloquy:

> Affection, thy intention stabs the centre.
> Thou dost make possible things not so held,
> Communicat'st with dreams – how can this be? –
> With what's unreal thou coactive art,
> And fellow'st nothing.   I.2.138–42

A humour is restored to a normal outlook by being confronted, not directly with reality, but with a reflection of its own illusion, as Katherina is tamed by being shown the reflection of her own shrewishness in Petruchio. Similarly Leontes, in the final scene, is 'mocked with art', the realistic illusion of Romano's statue which gradually reveals itself to be the real Hermione.

In the artificial society of the Sicilian court there are Mamillius, the hopeful prince who dies, and the infant Perdita who vanishes. In the rural society of Bohemia there are the shepherdess Perdita who is 'Flora | Peering in April's front', and Florizel who, as his name suggests, is her masculine counterpart, and the Prince Charming who later reminds Leontes strongly of Mamillius and becomes Leontes's promised heir. Perdita says that she would like to strew Florizel with flowers:

> like a bank for Love to lie and play on,
> Not like a corse; or if, not to be buried,
> But quick and in mine arms.   IV.4.130–32

The antithesis between the two worlds is marked by Polixenes, who is handed 'flowers of winter' and who proceeds to destroy the festival like a winter wind, repeating the *senex iratus* role of Leontes in the other kingdom. But though he can bully Perdita, he impresses her no more than Leontes had impressed Hermione. Perdita merely says:

> I was not much afeard; for once or twice
> I was about to speak and tell him plainly,
> The selfsame sun that shines upon his court
> Hides not his visage from our cottage, but
> Looks on alike.   IV.4.439–43

There is a faint New Testament echo here, but of course to Perdita the god of the sun would be Apollo, who does see to it that

Polixenes is outwitted, though only by the fact that Perdita is really a princess. As always in Shakespeare, the structure of society is unchanged by the comic action. What happens in *The Winter's Tale* is the opposite of the art of the gardener as Polixenes describes it. A society which is artificial in a limited sense at the beginning of the play becomes at the end still artificial, but natural as well. Nature provides the means for the regeneration of artifice. But still it is true that 'The art itself is Nature', and one wonders why a speech ending with those words should be assigned to Polixenes, the opponent of the festival.

The context of Polixenes's theory is the Renaissance framework in which there are two levels of the order of nature. Art belongs to human nature, and human nature is, properly speaking, the state that man lived in in Eden, or the Golden Age, before his fall into a lower world of physical nature to which he is not adapted. Man attempts to regain his original state through law, virtue, education, and such rational and conscious aids as art. Here nature is a superior order. In poetry this upper level of nature, uncontaminated by the sin and death of the fall, is usually symbolized by the starry spheres, which are now all that is left of it. The starry spheres produce the music of the spheres, and the harmony of music usually represents this upper level of nature in human life.

Most Shakespearian comedy is organized within this framework, and when it is, its imagery takes on the form outlined by G. Wilson Knight in *The Shakespearian Tempest* (1932). The tempest symbolizes the destructive elements in the order of nature, and music the permanently constructive elements in it. Music in its turn is regularly associated with the starry spheres, of which the one closest to us, the moon, is the normal focus. The control of the tempest by the harmony of the spheres appears in the image of the moon pulling the tides, an image used once or twice in *The Winter's Tale*. The action of *The Merchant of Venice*, too, extends from the cosmological harmonies of the fifth act, where the moon sleeps with Endymion, to the tempest that wrecked Antonio's ships. In *Pericles*, which employs this imagery of harmony and tempest most exhaustively, Pericles is said to be a master of music, Cerimon revives Thaisa by music, Diana announces her appearance to Pericles by music, and the final recognition scene unites the music and tempest symbols, since it takes place in the temple of Diana during the festival of Neptune. Music also accompanies the revival of Hermione in the final scene of *The Winter's Tale*. All the attention is absorbed in Hermione as she begins to move while music plays; and we are reminded of Autolycus and of his role as a kind of rascally Orpheus at the sheep-shearing festival: 'My clown ... would not stir his pettitoes till he had both tune and words; which so drew the rest of the herd to me that all their other senses stuck in ears. ... No hearing, no feeling, but my sir's song, and admiring the nothing of it' (IV.4.601–9). Here again Autolycus seems to be used to indicate that something is being subordinated in the play, though by no means eliminated.

In another solstitial play, *A Midsummer Night's Dream*, the cosmology is of this more conventional Renaissance kind. In the middle, between the world of chaos symbolized by tempest and the world of starry spheres symbolized by music, comes the cycle of nature, the world of Eros and Adonis, Puck and Pyramus, the love-god and the dying god. To this middle world the fairies belong, for the fairies are spirits of the four natural elements, and their dissension causes disorder in nature. Above, the cold fruitless moon of Diana, whose nun Hermia would have to be, hangs over the action. While a mermaid is calming the sea by her song and attracting the stars by the power of harmony, Cupid shoots an arrow at the moon and its vestal: it falls in a parabola on a flower and turns it 'purple with love's wound'. The story of Pyramus is not very coherently told in Peter Quince's play, but in Ovid there is a curious image about the blood spurting out of Pyramus in an arc like water out of a burst pipe and falling on the white mulberry and turning it purple. Here nature as a cycle of birth and death, symbolized by the purple flower, revolves underneath nature as a settled and predictable order or harmony, as it does also in a third solstitial play, *Twelfth Night*, which begins with an image comparing music to a wind blowing on a bank of violets.

But in *The Winter's Tale* nature is associated, not with the credible, but with the incredible: nature as an order is subordinated to the nature that yearly confronts us with the impossible miracle of renewed life. In Ben Jonson's animadversions on Shakespeare's unnatural romances it is particularly the functional role of the dance, the 'concupiscence of jigs', as he calls it, that he objects to. But it is the dance that most clearly expresses the pulsating energy of nature as it appears in *The Winter's Tale*, an energy which communicates itself to the dialogue. Such words as 'push' and 'wild' (meaning rash) are constantly echoed; the play ends with the words 'Hastily lead away', and we are told that the repentant Leontes

> o'er and o'er divides him
> 'Twixt his unkindness and his kindness: th'one
> He chides to hell and bids the other grow
> Faster than thought or time. IV.4.548–51

Much is said about magic in the final scene, but there is no magician, no Prospero, only the sense of a participation in the redeeming and reviving power of a nature identified with art, grace, and love. Hence the final recognition is appropriately that of a frozen statue turning into a living presence, and the appropriate Chorus is Time, the destructive element which is also the only possible representative of the timeless.

from *Fables of Identity* (1963) by
Northrop Frye, pages 107–18; first
published in *Essays on Shakespeare and
Elizabethan Drama in Honor of Hardin
Craig* (1962), edited by Richard Hosley,
pages 235–46

TWENTY-ONE

Wordplay in *The Winter's Tale*

M. M. Mahood

I

AT this late hour, it would be a work of supererogation to defend the last plays of Shakespeare against the charges of dullness and incompetence which were once frequent in criticism. On a superficial level, there is little to distinguish such a play as *The Winter's Tale* from the fashionable romances of Beaumont and Fletcher; but as recent writers have demonstrated,[1] Shakespeare's poetry in these last plays is too intense to be read superficially. Each image, each turn of phrase, each play upon a word's meanings, compels us to feel that Shakespeare's total statement adds up to much more than the fairy-tale events of the plot. Yet in the theatre the impetus of the action itself leaves us no time to ponder this deeper significance which remains at or very near the unconscious level, and so inseparable from our theatrical excitement and wonder at Leontes's jealousy, Perdita's preservation, and the return to life of Hermione.

Shakespeare packs meaning into *The Winter's Tale* in a way that might be instanced by the opening words of the second scene. Polixenes, the visiting king, is anxious to get home:

> Nine changes of the watery star hath been
> The shepherd's note since we have left our throne
> Without a burden.

After the naturalistic prose dialogue with which the play began, this orotund phrase achieves one of those swift changes in the pressure of realism – here from contemporary court life to the world of the Player King – which is typical of the dramatic climate of these last plays. But the image accomplishes much more than that. The moon's nine changes imply the themes of pregnancy (helped, perhaps, by 'burden'), of sudden changes of fortune, and of madness, which are all to become explicit in the course of the same scene. The whole image is the first of many taken from country things and the pastoral life, which persist throughout the Sicilian scenes of the play and so help to bridge the 'wide gap' of time and place over which we pass later to the shepherd kingdom of Bohemia. And the leading theme of these scenes in Bohemia, the summer harmony of heaven and earth, is prepared here by mention of the 'watery star' that draws the tides.

For instances of wordplay which, in their economy, match these uses of imagery, we may go back to the opening dialogue between Camillo and Archidamus. Although there are not very many puns in *The Winter's Tale*, the few that are used generate a superb energy. This opening dialogue, for instance, seems no more than the explanatory chat between two minor characters which is part of the competent dramatist's stock-in-trade; but some inquiry into its play of meanings shows it to be much more than this. 'If you shall chance, Camillo,' Archidamus begins, 'to visit Bohemia, on the like occasion whereon my services are now on foot, you shall see, as I have said, great *difference* betwixt our Bohemia and your Sicilia.' This *difference* we shall soon discover to be 'contention' as well as 'dissimilarity'; for *Bohemia* and *Sicily* stand eponymously for the kings as well as the kingdoms – as, after a brief exchange of civilities, Camillo's words indicate:

> Sicilia cannot show himself over-kind to Bohemia. They were *trained* together in their childhoods; and there rooted betwixt them then such an affection, which cannot choose but *branch* now. I.1.21-4

Trained, used of fruit trees as well as of the education of children, introduces an image of two plants united in such a way as to propagate new growth, and this anticipates the talk in Act IV of grafting a noble scion upon the wildest stock, which is symbolic both of the union of court and country in Perdita's upbringing as a shepherd's daughter and of the reunion of the two kings through the marriage of Perdita and Florizel. But *branch*, besides meaning 'throw out new shoots from the family tree', has the sense of 'divide'; and 'Sicilia cannot show himself over-kind' is ambiguous. On the one hand the undertones of the scene prepare us for the fertility legend of a child healing an old man and so bringing prosperity to the land; on the other hand, the secondary meanings of *difference* and *branch*, together with Camillo's ominous insistence upon Mamillius's 'promise', prepare us for the estrangement of the kings and the death of Mamillius which must intervene before a child, Perdita, 'physics the subject, makes old hearts fresh'.

Some of the most richly ambiguous wordplay in all Shakespeare occurs at the beginning of this estrangement, in Leontes's violent seizure of jealousy against Polixenes. It is possible, of course, to read long-standing suspicion into all Leontes's speeches to Polixenes and Hermione, from the first appearance of the three characters.[2] But this impairs the dramatic contrast between the happiness and harmony of the three characters when Polixenes has agreed to stay, and Leontes's subsequent outburst of passion:

> Too hot, too hot!
> To mingle friendship far is mingling bloods.
> I have *tremor cordis* on me: my heart dances,
> But not for joy, not joy.   I.2.108–11

Unlike the Age of the Enlightenment, with its demand for logically clear motivation of character, the pre-Locke and the post-Freud epochs share an acceptance of the seemingly incalculable in human behaviour. The Elizabethans might have put Leontes's outburst down to demonic possession; we should call it a libidinous invasion. The effect in either case is the same – a sudden outburst of normally suppressed feelings, which struggle for their release in savage wordplay. Leontes's puns erupt like steam forcing up a saucepan lid, and by the end of some hundred lines he has fairly boiled over with 'foul imaginings'. There are the conscious puns which release his obscene and aggressive tendencies in

> We must be neat – not neat but cleanly, captain.
> And yet the steer, the heifer, and the calf
> Are all called neat   I.2.123–5

and in

348

> Let what is dear in Sicily be cheap.
> Next to thyself and my young rover, he's
> Apparent to my heart ...   I.2.175–7

where *apparent* means 'seen-through, obvious' as well as 'heir-apparent'. There are unconscious puns on words which remain unspoken: *die*, for example, in

> and then to sigh, as 'twere
> The mort o'th'deer ...   I.2.117–18

and perhaps *stews* in 'his pond fished by his next neighbour'. And there are the innuendoes which Leontes reads into Camillo's innocent use of such words as *business* (line 216) and *satisfy* (line 232). At one point this kind of wordplay becomes threefold, in that it reveals Shakespeare's intentions as well as Leontes's disturbance of mind:

> Go play, boy, play: thy mother plays, and I
> Play too – but so disgraced a part, whose issue
> Will hiss me to my grave.   I.2.187–9

Only the first *play* is used in a single sense. We might paraphrase Leontes's *double entendres* thus: 'Go and amuse yourself; your mother is also pretending to play by acting the kind hostess, but I know that she is a real daughter of the game and up to another sport which makes me act the contemptible role of the deceived husband. So for the moment I'm playing her like a fish ("I am angling now") by giving her line.' This ironic wordplay of Leontes is sustained through *disgraced*, meaning both 'ungraceful' and 'shameful', and *issue* meaning 'exit', 'result', and perhaps also 'Polixenes's bastard child that Hermione now carries'. But *play*, *disgraced*, and *issue* have other functions besides that of rendering Leontes's paroxysm true to life. Shakespeare counters each of Leontes's puns by further meanings which relate the word to the larger context of the play's thought and action. The meaning 'make-believe' is added in this way to all the senses of *play*. Leontes is play-acting in his outburst; it is characteristic of such obsessions as his that the sufferer is deluded yet half knows he is under a delusion – as when we know we are in a nightmare but cannot wake from it. Only the make-believe of Hermione, in playing at being a statue, and the make-believe of Perdita in playing the part of a shepherd's daughter, can restore Leontes to a sane discrimination between illusion and reality. *Disgraced* also has further meanings for the play as a whole: Leontes is without the grace of Heaven in sinning against Hermione; but because the irony of wordplay has a negative as well as a positive force, the word also foreshadows Hermione's symbolic role of Heavenly Grace which never deserts Leontes. *Issue* can, positively, mean Mamillius, whose death drives Leontes to a mortified existence; or it can be Leontes's 'action' (a meaning peculiar to Shakespeare[3]) in defying the oracle and so driving Mamillius to *his* grave. It can also mean the legal issue of Hermione's trial. Perhaps its strongest ironic meaning is 'child', taken negatively; Perdita will, in fact, restore him to life. Perdita is preserved from a death of exposure, Leontes is reclaimed from his life-in-death of grief, and Hermione is called upon to bestow to death her numbness, and all this is in accordance with the oracle of Apollo since 'to the Lord God belong the issues of death'.

2

We can quote the Geneva Bible with no sense of incongruity. The presiding deity of the play may be Apollo, but the Christian scheme of redemption is a leading element, though not by any means the only element, in its pattern of ideas. *Grace*, with *gracious* a keyword of the play, is frequently used in its theological sense of 'the divine influence which operates in men to regenerate and sanctify' (*N.E.D.* II 6b). As Everyman, Humanity, Leontes is able to recall a primeval innocence when he was 'boy eternal':

> We were as twinned lambs that did frisk i'th'sun,
> And bleat the one at th'other. What we changed
> Was innocence for innocence: we knew not
> The doctrine of ill-doing, nor dreamed
> That any did. Had we pursued that life,
> And our weak spirits ne'er been higher reared
> With stronger blood, we should have answered heaven
> Boldly 'Not guilty', the imposition cleared
> Hereditary ours.   I.2.67–75

In the dialogue which follows, the word *grace* is used three times by Hermione, the implication being that she acts the role of regenerative grace to Leontes now he has exchanged Innocence for Experience. But immediately there follows Leontes's rejection of this grace in his outburst against Hermione.

> You'll be found,
> Be you beneath the sky   I.2.179–80

is his threat to Hermione and Polixenes; the words are strong dramatic irony, since it is Leontes himself who is sinning in the sight of Heaven, the single Eye of Apollo made actual to us by the sight images of Leontes's talk with Camillo in the first act – 'your eye-glass | Is thicker than a cuckold's horn' (I.2.268–9); 'a vision so apparent' (line 270); 'To have nor eyes' (line 275); 'And all eyes | Blind with the pin and web but theirs' (lines 290–91); 'Canst with thine eyes at once see good and evil' (line 303); 'servants true about me, that bare eyes' (line 309); 'who mayst see | Plainly as heaven sees earth and earth sees heaven' (lines 314–15). The small but vitally important scene between Cleomenes and Dion, as they return from Delphos at the beginning of Act III, stresses this awesome aspect of the Destroyer Apollo, whose oracle is 'Kin to Jove's thunder'; and the hope that the *issue* of their visit will be *gracious* is not immediately fulfilled. Apollo keeps jealous guard over the fortunes of the gracious Hermione, and her belief that

> powers divine
> Behold our human actions   III.2.27–8

is vindicated when, his oracle defied, Apollo at once smites Leontes with the death of Mamillius:

> Apollo's angry, and the heavens themselves
> Do strike at my injustice.   III.2.144–5

Leontes's change of heart, from a proud defiance of the God to guilt, despair, and finally a sober repentance, is marked by two instances of wordplay. At the beginning of the trial scene he announces that justice shall have

> due course,
> Even to the guilt or the *purgation*.

In the legal sense, human justice will proceed to find Hermione guilty or give her the chance 'of clearing [her]self from the accusation or suspicion of crime and guilt'; in the theological sense, Apollo's justice will establish Leontes's guilt and will also purify him from it by the repentance vowed at the end of the scene:

> Once a day I'll visit
> The chapel where they lie, and tears shed there
> Shall be my *recreation*.   III.2.236–8

Recreation and *re-creation*: the pun is a promise that Leontes is to become 'man new made' at the end of the play, for Apollo offers him grace in the sense of time for amendment (*N.E.D.* II.7) and also hope for the eventual grace of pardon (*N.E.D.* II.8). The King takes to himself the words of Hermione:

> I must be patient till the heavens look
> With an aspect more favourable ...   II.1.106–7

and her withdrawal symbolizes Everyman's patient hope in the return of grace. In the major tragedies of Shakespeare, patience had been a stoical virtue, the capacity to endure. Here it is a Christian virtue, the ability to possess one's soul in patience, which is rewarded when Hermione reappears literally as Patience on a monument, 'smiling' (in the words of *Pericles*) 'Extremity out of act'.

Meanwhile Perdita has 'grown in grace'; as with Tuesday's child, the word has a theological as well as a physical meaning. At the sheep-shearing feast, Leontes's grace of repentance and Hermione's grace of patient forgiveness are kept in mind by Perdita's graceful presentation of flowers to the disguised Polixenes and Camillo:

> Reverend sirs,
> For you there's rosemary and rue; these keep
> Seeming and savour all the winter long:
> *Grace* and remembrance be to you both,
> And welcome to our shearing!   IV.4.73–7

The theological language of the play's first part is revived and intensified when the action returns to Sicily at the beginning of

Act V. The restoration of both the wife and the daughter is spoken of as a regeneration for Leontes. 'Now bless thyself', the old Shepherd had said at the finding of Perdita; 'thou met'st with things dying, I with things new-born'; and the theme is repeated when one courtier tells another how Leontes was reunited with Camillo: 'they looked as they had heard of a world ransomed, or one destroyed'. The ritual-like solemnity of the last scene completes this regeneration. 'It is required', commands Paulina, 'You do awake your faith'; and to music such as accompanied the awakening of Lear and Pericles, Faith, in the person of Hermione, steps off her plinth into Leontes's arms:

> You gods, look down,
> And from your sacred vials pour your *graces*
> Upon my daughter's head.   V.3.121-3

3

So *The Winter's Tale* is a morality play; but its morality is wider, wiser, and more humane than that of a Puritan inner drama of sin, guilt, and contrition. Something is omitted in the attempt made here to allegorize the play. We have had to leave out the sunburnt mirth of the scenes in Bohemia, the Clown, Mopsa, and the rogue Autolycus who made such an impression on Simon Forman when he saw the play in 1611. Worse still, Perdita is really unnecessary if we read *The Winter's Tale* as a kind of *Grace Abounding*, and we are forced to ask why Shakespeare could not have symbolized the spiritual health of the lapsed and forgiven soul by a single figure like Dante's Beatrice or Blake's Jerusalem.

A clue to the answer may perhaps be found if we return to Leontes's outburst in Act I. After 'Go play, boy, play', Leontes abandons the ordinary sense of 'to sport or frolic' for bitterly ironic meanings; and in this wordplay, and the act of dismissing Mamillius, is revealed Leontes's inability to keep himself young, to become as a child again. Polixenes understands the value of play, and Florizel's 'varying childness' keeps him from a spiritual winter. Mamillius also has the power to make old hearts fresh; the sight of him can take twenty-three years off his father's life, and he has a *welkin* eye – the adjective suggesting something providential and life-giving, and not merely 'clear and blue like the sky'. In spite of this, Leontes cannot recapture the non-moral vision of childhood, the state of the 'boy eternal' who had not as yet the knowledge of good and evil. At the beginning of the last act, Cleomenes pleads with Leontes to forgive himself; but this is just what Leontes cannot do until Perdita's return. For if Hermione represents the grace of heaven towards Leontes, Perdita stands for his self-forgiveness, for his recapture of the child's non-moral acceptance of things as they are in Nature. In this way, Perdita plays a role of Nature complementary to Hermione's role of Grace. This moral intransigence in Leontes may have very deep roots. J. I. M. Stewart hints at the transference, in the King's outburst of delusional jealousy, of his guilt at an adolescent relationship with Polixenes for which he cannot forgive himself.[4] Whatever the cause of his fury, his bawdy use of *play* in 'thy mother plays' suggests the moral rigidity born of a moral uncertainty; he cannot see Hermione's real need to play, to the extent perhaps of a harmless flirtation with Polixenes. So a tension is established between two forms of *play*: play as sport, a holiday freedom, and play as Leontes's imprisoning delusion that Hermione is unfaithful to him. Unable to play in the sense of refreshing himself from the non-moral and instinctive life of childhood, Leontes begins to play in the sense of constructing an intensely moral drama in which he enacts the role of the deceived husband. In the opening scene of Act II, these two forms of play, the natural and the unnatural, are literally juxtaposed. On one side of the stage, Mamillius at play produces make-believe shudders with his ghost story; on the other, Leontes's delusion – 'I have drunk, and seen the spider' – communicates a real horror to the audience who are to see him, in the grip of his involuntary make-believe, turn Mamillius's winter's tale into earnest. 'What is this? Sport?' Hermione asks as Mamillius is snatched from her; and once again Leontes perverts the meaning of the most innocent word:

> Away with him, and let her sport herself
> With that she's big with: for 'tis Polixenes
> Has made thee swell thus.   II.1.60–62

The contrast between these two kinds of play is kept up in Leontes's insistence that his delusion is fact:

> No: if I mistake
> In those foundations which I build upon,
> The centre is not big enough to bear
> A schoolboy's top.[5]　　　　　II.1.100–103

So deluded, he is beyond the reach of reason as it is voiced in the well-ordered rhetoric of Camillo or that of Hermione in her formal self-defence at the trial. Hermione is forced to admit that she and Leontes move in different worlds:

> You speak a language that I understand not.
> My life stands in the level of your dreams,
> Which I'll lay down.　　　　　III.2.79–81

With much more irony than he intends, Leontes replies: 'Your actions are my dreams.' Nothing can in fact destroy his confusion of nightmare and reality except the real-life disaster of Mamillius's death.

For two and a half acts of the play the audience has shared an overcharged moral atmosphere, as it has witnessed Leontes's protest against his supposedly impaired honour, shared Paulina's moral indignation at Leontes's treatment of Hermione, and experienced with the whole court a sense of heavenly retribution in the death of Mamillius. Now in the ensuing few scenes, this tension is relaxed and we are transported into a world on holiday. By its remoteness from the real Hermione of the trial scene, Antigonus's vision of Hermione begins the distancing of Sicily and Sicilian attitudes; and the shift from a courtly to a country outlook starts with the old Shepherd's grumbles about the hunt and the coarse kindness with which he dismisses Perdita's begetting as 'behind-door-work. They were warmer that got this than the poor thing is here.' There is a matter-of-fact acceptance of Nature as it is in the Clown's account of the shipwreck and of Antigonus's encounter with the bear. If his vivid descriptions of both seem callous, they are in fact only honest; hogsheads have more reality for him than have Sicilian courtiers, and he sees Antigonus's fate from the bear's point of view. The creature must have its dinner, and 'They are never *curst* but when they are hungry'; his use of the word to imply 'fierce' without any moral nuance contrasts with Leontes's use of it when in the grip of his delusion:

> How blest am I
> In my just censure, in my true opinion!
> Alack, for lesser knowledge! How accursed
> In being so blest! II.1.36–9

In *King Lear* a vision of Nature's cruelty, of man as one of the most savage beasts of prey, was opposed to the traditional notion of Nature as harmony, fecundity, and order. In *The Winter's Tale*, however, Nature is neither morally good nor bad; a bear's appetite and a waiting gentlewoman's lapse are accepted as the way of the world. Animal images are used by Leontes, in the first part of the play, with all the revulsion of Othello's 'Goats and monkeys!' but Antigonus's stud language shows up, by a kind of grotesque parody, the folly of thus regarding everything in Nature as subject to moral judgement; and the scenes in Bohemia restore the child's or the peasant's freedom from morbid preoccupations about good and evil. The wordplay reveals the same change of attitude. *Blood*, for example, when used in the first part of the play, often carries a connotation of 'lust' – its primary meaning in a play like *Othello*. Now, in Autolycus's song about 'the red blood reigns in the winter's pale', it represents a passion as natural and inevitable as the sap that rises in spring, to be accepted as philosophically as the old Shepherd endures the ways of 'these boiled brains of nineteen and two-and-twenty'. For all his classical name, Autolycus is an English coney-catcher, and his daffodil and doxy belong less to the classical Arcadia[6] than to Herrick's Devonshire, where Christianity has absorbed much of an older cult, and if there is a Puritan he too sings psalms to hornpipes. According to Blake's paradox, the return of spiritual vision by which what now seemed finite and corrupt would appear infinite and holy was to be accomplished by 'an improvement of sensual enjoyment'; and such enjoyment is felt throughout the scenes in Bohemia. The sensuous blend of the colourful, the fragrant, the sweet, and the spicy in the Clown's shopping list contrasts sharply with the painful sensibility of some images in the first part of the play – for instance, Leontes's rebuke to Antigonus:

> Cease, no more!
> You smell this business with a sense as *cold*
> As is a dead man's nose ...   II.1.150–52

where the wordplay, by suggesting the touch of death, achieves a *frisson* worthy of a winter's tale.

By the time Autolycus, who has overheard the Clown's list, has caught this particular coney in a travesty of the Good Samaritan story, the holiday mood is complete.[7] Like Florizel, we

> Apprehend
> Nothing but jollity. The gods themselves,
> Humbling their deities to love, have taken
> The shapes of beasts upon them: Jupiter
> Became a bull, and bellowed; the green Neptune
> A ram, and bleated; and the fire-robed god,
> Golden Apollo, a poor, humble swain,
> As I seem now.   IV.4.24–31

These lines, based on a section of Greene's *Pandosto* which Shakespeare did not utilize in any other way, have a particular aptness to the holiday mood of this feast. Even the gods are at play. Jupiter and Neptune become the horned animals in which Leontes saw only the symbol of human bestiality and cuckoldry, and their bellowing and bleating evoke the laughter which is lacking in Leontes, who cannot play. Greene's phrase: 'Neptune became a ram, Jupiter a Bull, Apollo a shepherd' may have recalled to Shakespeare the story told in the second book of the *Metamorphoses* of Apollo's love for the nymph Chione, whom in jealousy he slew with his dart, but whose child he reared to be the life-giving Aesculapius; a parallel to his dual role of destroyer and preserver in *The Winter's Tale*. Apollo's metamorphosis into the shepherd 'Humbling his deity to love' is not incompatible with the presentation of Apollo as the supreme and just God in the first part of the play; it suggests just such a union of Heaven and earth as is implied by Milton's

> Or if Vertue feeble were,
> Heav'n it self would stoop to her.

But in these scenes of the play the reconciliation of heaven and earth is not theological but natural, the fructification of nature by the sun that shines alike upon the good and the evil. In the scenes of sixteen years before, heaven had been at destructive variance with earth in the 'dangerous unsafe lunes i'th'King', in Apollo's thunderbolt, and in the storm's conflict of sea and sky. Now the imagery stresses their harmony:

> for never gazed the moon
> Upon the water as he'll stand and read,
> As 'twere, my daughter's eyes.   IV.4.174–6

And in proof of his constancy, Florizel protests that not

> for all the sun sees or
> The close earth wombs or the profound seas hides
> In unknown fathoms, will I break my oath
> To this my fair beloved.   IV.4.486–9

The image persists after the lovers' voyage to Sicily. Perdita seems to Leontes at his first sight of her

> the most peerless piece of earth, I think,
> That e'er the sun shone bright on ...   V.1.94–5

and he tells how he

> lost a couple that 'twixt heaven and earth
> Might thus have stood, begetting wonder, as
> You, gracious couple, do ...   V.1.131–3

where both the natural and the spiritual union are implied in 'begetting' and 'gracious'. This awareness of the bridal of the earth and sky lends irony to Florizel's bitter assertion (V.1.205) that the stars will kiss the valleys before he and Perdita will be able to marry. The stars do kiss the valleys through those heavenly influences in which most Jacobeans firmly believed; heaven is matched with earth in the life of growth, in the Bohemian shepherds' acceptance of nature's ways, of which Perdita is the symbol.

For Perdita, dressed as the queen of the feast, and acting the part of hostess to her father's guests, represents the natural rightness of play, the renewing power of youth which Leontes once had, and lost, in Mamillius. In her presentation of flowers, time runs back to fetch the age of gold, from winter herbs to August's carnations and stripped gillyflowers, to the June marigold that goes to bed with the sun (another symbol of the union of heaven and earth), and so back to the spring flowers she would give Florizel. The great flower passage is full of what Herrick calls a 'cleanly wantonness': the violets are as sweet as the breath of Venus, the primroses lovesick, the oxlip inviting, and the daffodils *take* the air in a triple sense – enchant, seize, and come out for exercise and pleasure – which suggests all the tentative and yet bold grace of the flower. The daffodil flings itself on the winds of March with that enchanting blend of abandon and modesty that is found in Perdita's wish to strew Florizel with these flowers

> like a bank for Love to lie and play on,
> Not like a corse; or if, not to be buried,
> But quick and in mine arms. Come, take your flowers.
> Methinks I play as I have seen them do
> In Whitsun pastorals: sure this robe of mine
> Does change my disposition. IV.4.130–35

The first *play* here has the same connotation as 'thy mother plays', but it is used with an innocent sexuality which represents that acceptance of the ways of nature that Perdita is to restore to her father. This restoration can be made only when Perdita plays one further role, that of the Libyan princess. For no sooner has she cast aside her disguise with 'I'll queen it no inch farther' than Camillo arranges to see her

> royally appointed as if
> The scene you play were mine IV.4.589–90

and Perdita acquiesces with:

> I see the play so lies
> That I must bear a part. IV.4.651–2

Her part, and that of Florizel also, is to enable Leontes to forgive himself. Looking on them both, the old king feels time unravel until he can understand and accept the excesses of his own youth:

> Were I but twenty-one,
> Your father's image is so hit in you,
> His very air, that I should call you brother,
> As I did him, and speak of something wildly
> By us performed before.
> ... You have a holy father,
> A graceful gentleman, against whose person,
> So sacred as it is, I have done sin:
> For which the heavens, taking angry note,
> Have left me issueless; and your father's blessed,
> As he from heaven merits it, with you,
> Worthy his goodness.   V.i.125–9, 169–75

The irony of this is not only that Leontes's daughter and son-in-law stand before him as he speaks, but that he should call Polixenes 'graceful'. In fact Polixenes, in breaking the match between Florizel and Perdita, has shown a lack of that imaginative vision, symbolized by the two lovers, which Leontes has now acquired and which makes him the lover's advocate, sympathetic to Florizel's plea:

> Remember since you owed no more to Time
> Than I do now.   V.i.218–19

The reunion of Leontes with Perdita concludes this aspect of the play as a defence and justification of play itself. Because Shakespeare is here concerned with recreation as re-creation, much of the play itself seems trifling, a kind of vaudeville: the comic turns of Autolycus, the dances, the Clown's part, the ballads. We must not look closely for wisdom in this fooling; its purpose is to remind Everyman – Leontes and the audience – of his need for folly.

4

Besides this theme of spiritual renewal through the double operation of Grace and Nature, other meanings of the two words are at work in *The Winter's Tale*. It shares with Shakespeare's other late romances a dramatic contrast between Nature and the

Graces of Art. Moreover, the theme of spiritual renewal is closely paralleled by one of social reinvigoration. The question of True Nobility, which Shakespeare had already raised in *All's Well*, is made a concern of *The Winter's Tale* by Shakespeare's play on several words with restrictive social meanings, of which *grace* is one. Leontes carries the title of the King's Grace (*N.E.D.* II 9), but he is none the more gracious, in the sense of being comely or blessed, on that account. Autolycus, a sometime hanger-on of the court pretends to be outraged because the Shepherd should 'offer to have his daughter come into *grace*', but we have already been told that she has 'grown in *grace*' and have taken it to mean her natural dignity of bearing as well as her goodness and beauty. Again, in the use of the word *breeding* there is interplay between the widest meaning of 'begetting', the more limited social meaning of 'a good upbringing', and the most restricted meaning of 'good manners'. Polixenes, slighted by Leontes, is left

> to consider what is *breeding*
> That changes thus his manners ...   I.2.374-5

and in Florizel's

> She is as forward of her *breeding* as
> She is i'th'rear' our *birth*   IV.4.577-8

there is an additional wordplay on *birth*: Perdita's only inferiority is in fact in her age, for she has not only royal birth, but also the natural good breeding of the old Shepherd whose head is nothing turned when he finds himself in high society: 'we must be *gentle*, now we are gentlemen'. The glories of our *blood* and *state* are vanity, because the vaunted blue blood turns out to be the ordinary red stuff in everyone's veins, and however stately our dignity, every man must belong to one or other of the estates which make up the state of society; and Shakespeare makes subtle use of all these meanings in the course of the play.[8] Lastly, there is his use of *free* to mean 'of gentle birth' or 'of noble or honourable character' or 'at liberty'. Hermione in prison remains in her innocence as *free* as the child of whom she is delivered; to Paulina's suggestion that she take the new-born child to the King, Emilia replies:

> Most worthy madam,
> Your honour and your goodness is so evident
> That your *free* undertaking cannot miss
> A thriving *issue* ...   II.2.42–5

and Paulina protests to the court that the queen is

> A gracious, innocent soul,
> More *free* than he is jealous.   II.3.29–30

In these two scenes which close the second act, the point is driven home that the truest courtesy is not a veneer of the court. Leontes's court is a beargarden and the scenes enacted there are farce on the brink of tragedy.[9] Hermione in contrast keeps court in prison with all the ceremony of innocence and so associates herself, before the trial scene, with the gracious ceremonial of Apollo's devotees, as Dion describes them:

> I shall report,
> For most it caught me, the celestial habits –
> Methinks I so should term them – and the reverence
> Of the grave wearers. O, the sacrifice!
> How ceremonious, solemn, and unearthly
> It was i'th'off'ring!   III.1.3–8

At the end of the play, the ceremony which should surround the King's Grace is restored to Leontes; his visit to Paulina is spoken of by her as a surplus of his Grace.

Before this renewal can be achieved, however, the royal grace must replenish itself from the life of nature. When the old Shepherd chides Perdita for her tardiness in welcoming his guests, and compares her reserve with his old wife's joviality, Shakespeare seems at first hearing to be restating the Elizabethan certainty that blood will tell; Florizel and Perdita are merely pretended shepherd and shepherdess, two figures by Fragonard superimposed on a scene by Bruegel. Yet if Perdita is full of grace in every meaning of the word she owes that upbringing to the two old peasants. Polixenes's praise of the custom of grafting 'A gentler scion to the wildest stock' is vivid dramatic irony, not only because he is shortly going to repudiate his theory when his son seeks to marry a shepherdess, but because Perdita's upbringing has been just such a fruitful grafting. The child of a father who has cut himself off from a wholesome rural way of living and thinking is returned by Apollo to the education of Nature, in order that ultimately court and cottage may flourish together under the sun of his favour who 'Looks on alike'.

NOTES

1. Especially S. L. Bethell, *'The Winter's Tale': a Study* (1947); G. Wilson Knight, *The Crown of Life* (1947); F. R. Leavis, 'The Criticism of Shakespeare's Late Plays', *Scrutiny* 10 (1942), reprinted in *The Common Pursuit* (1952; Penguin Books 1962); E. M. W. Tillyard, *Shakespeare's Last Plays* (1938); and D. A. Traversi, *Shakespeare: The Last Phase* (1955).

2. This was done by John Gielgud in his 1951 production at the Phoenix Theatre, London; and there is some warrant for it in Greene's *Pandosto*, from which Shakespeare took the story. But Greene also speaks of a certain melancholy passion *entering* the King's mind.

3. As in *Julius Caesar*, III.1.294: Antony calls Caesar's murder 'The cruel issue of these bloody men'; and *Cymbeline*, II.1.45–6: 'You are a fool granted; therefore your issues, being foolish, do not derogate' – with a pun on the sense of 'offspring'.

4. J. I. M. Stewart, *Character and Motive in Shakespeare* (1948), pages 30–37.

5. This is, I think, echoed in *Comus* when the Elder Brother declares that 'evil on it self shall back recoyl. . . .'

> if this fail,
> The pillar'd firmament is rott'nness
> And earths base built on stubble.

Comus has in common with Shakespeare's last plays more than the family likeness of a pastoral. It has been suggested by J. E. Crofts that Sabrina's role in the masque is very much that of a nature spirit such as Perdita. The Lady remains frozen in a Puritanical disapproval until the nymph releases her.

6. Shakespeare may have changed round the Sicily and Bohemia of his source in order to avoid the literary associations of Sicilian shepherds.

7. S. L. Bethell, in '*The Winter's Tale*': *a Study*, discusses very fully
   the fade-out of Sicilian attitudes. The Biblical parallel, pointed out
   by G. Wilson Knight (*The Crown of Life*, page 101), is given support
   by Autolycus's recall of how he once compassed a motion (that is,
   staged a puppet show) of the Prodigal Son.

8. See especially IV.4.148; IV.4.423, 445.

9. The complexity of Paulina accords with this. She is both magnificent and ludicrous. She has moreover a third aspect, that of
   guardian angel to Hermione and Leontes. She is very like Julia in
   The Cocktail Party – a play which is also about redemption, the eye
   of God and the need for ordinary mortals not to take themselves too
   seriously.

from *Shakespeare's Wordplay* (1957)
by M. M. Mahood, pages 146–63

SUGGESTIONS FOR FURTHER READING

The Winter's Tale, edited by J. H. P. Pafford (new Arden Shakespeare, 1963). The most useful edition for a close study of the play, containing a full discussion of the play in the editor's Introduction, ample notes to the text, and the complete text of the source, Greene's *Pandosto*. The play has also been edited by Ernest Schanzer for the New Penguin Shakespeare (1969), with a concise introductory essay and full commentary.

G. WILSON KNIGHT: *The Crown of Life* (1947). Contains a well-known essay on the play, '"Great Creating Nature"', which emphasizes the thematic unity and profundity of the play, expressing 'a vague, numinous sense of mighty powers'.

S. L. BETHELL: '*The Winter's Tale*': *a Study* (1947). An interpretation of the play as an allegory of the Christian doctrine of the Redemption.

NEVILL COGHILL: 'Six Points of Stage-Craft in *The Winter's Tale*', *Shakespeare Survey 11* (1958). A detailed analysis of particular episodes in the play, including the celebrated pursuit of Antigonus by a bear, to demonstrate their theatrical effectiveness and structural significance.

E. W. TAYLER: *Nature and Art in Renaissance Literature* (1964). A study of the traditional philosophical distinctions between Nature and Art, and their association with the pastoral convention. There is a chapter on *The Winter's Tale*.

FITZROY PYLE: '*The Winter's Tale*': *A Commentary on the Structure* (1969). A careful and detailed consideration of the play in relation to its source, showing how Shakespeare improved upon the articulation and meaningfulness of Greene's romance. An antidote to some of the more transcendental approaches to the play.

'THE TEMPEST'

TWENTY-TWO

'This almost miraculous play'

S. T. Coleridge

... At present I shall only speak of dramas where the ideal is predominant; and chiefly for this reason – that those plays have been attacked with the greatest violence. The objections to them are not the growth of our own country, but of France – the judgement of monkeys, by some wonderful phenomenon, put into the mouths of people shaped like men. These creatures have informed us that Shakespeare is a miraculous monster, in whom many heterogeneous components were thrown together, producing a discordant mass of genius – an irregular and ill-assorted structure of gigantic proportions.

Among the ideal plays, I will take *The Tempest*, by way of example. Various others might be mentioned, but it is impossible to go through every drama, and what I remark on *The Tempest* will apply to all Shakespeare's productions of the same class.

In this play Shakespeare has especially appealed to the imagination, and he has constructed a plot well adapted to the purpose. According to his scheme, he did not appeal to any sensuous impression (the word 'sensuous' is authorized by Milton) of time and place, but to the imagination, and it is to be borne in mind, that of old, and as regards mere scenery, his works may be said to have been recited rather than acted – that is to say, description and narration supplied the place of visual exhibition: the audience was told to fancy that they saw what they only heard described; the painting was not in colours, but in words.

This is particularly to be noted in the first scene – a storm and its confusion on board the King's ship. The highest and the lowest characters are brought together, and with what excellence! Much of the genius of Shakespeare is displayed in these happy combinations – the highest and the lowest, the gayest and the saddest; he is not droll in one scene and melancholy in another, but often both the one and the other in the same scene. Laughter is made to swell the tear of sorrow, and to throw, as it were, a poetic light upon it, while the tear mingles tenderness with the laughter. Shakespeare has evinced the power, which above all other men he possessed, that of introducing the profoundest sentiments of wisdom, where they would be least expected, yet where they are most truly natural. One admirable secret of his art is, that separate speeches frequently do not appear to have been occasioned by those which preceded, and which are consequent upon each other, but to have arisen out of the peculiar character of the speaker.

Before I go further, I may take the opportunity of explaining what is meant by mechanic and organic regularity. In the former the copy must appear as if it had come out of the same mould with the original; in the latter there is a law which all the parts obey, conforming themselves to the outward symbols and manifestations of the essential principle. If we look to the growth of trees, for instance, we shall observe that trees of the same kind vary considerably, according to the circumstances of soil, air, or position; yet we are able to decide at once whether they are oaks, elms, or poplars.[1]

So with Shakespeare's characters: he shows us the life and principle of each being with organic regularity. The Boatswain, in the first scene of *The Tempest*, when the bonds of reverence are thrown off as a sense of danger impresses all, gives a loose to his feelings, and thus pours forth his vulgar mind to the old Counsellor:

Hence! What cares these roarers for the name of king? To cabin! Silence! Trouble us not.

Gonzalo replies

Good, yet remember whom thou hast aboard.

To which the Boatswain answers

None that I more love than myself. You are a councillor. If you can command these elements to silence, and work the peace of the present, we will not hand a rope more. Use your authority. If you cannot, give thanks that you have lived so long, and make yourself ready in your cabin for the mischance of the hour, if it so hap. – Cheerly, good hearts! – Out of our way, I say!   I.1.16–27

An ordinary dramatist would, after this speech, have represented Gonzalo as moralizing, or saying something connected with the Boatswain's language; for ordinary dramatists are not men of genius: they combine their ideas by association, or by logical affinity; but the vital writer, who makes men on the stage what they are in nature, in a moment transports himself into the very being of each personage, and, instead of cutting out artificial puppets, he brings before us the men themselves. Therefore, Gonzalo soliloquizes:

I have great comfort from this fellow. Methinks he hath no drowning-mark upon him: his complexion is perfect gallows. Stand fast, good Fate, to his hanging. Make the rope of his destiny our cable, for our own doth little advantage. If he be not born to be hanged, our case is miserable.

In this part of the scene we see the true sailor with his contempt of danger, and the old counsellor with his high feeling, who, instead of condescending to notice the words just addressed to him, turns off, meditating with himself, and drawing some comfort to his own mind, by trifling with the ill expression of the boatswain's face, founding upon it a hope of safety.

Shakespeare had pre-determined to make the plot of this play such as to involve a certain number of low characters, and at the beginning he pitched the note of the whole. The first scene was meant as a lively commencement of the story; the reader is prepared for something that is to be developed, and in the next scene he brings forward Prospero and Miranda. How is this done? By giving to his favourite character, Miranda, a sentence which at once expresses the violence and fury of the storm, such as it might appear to a witness on the land, and at the same time displays the tenderness of her feelings – the exquisite feelings of a female brought up in a desert, but with all the advantages of education, all that could be communicated by a wise and affectionate father.

She possesses all the delicacy of innocence, yet with all the powers of her mind unweakened by the combats of life. Miranda exclaims:

> O, I have suffered
> With those that I saw suffer! A brave vessel,
> Who had, no doubt, some noble creature in her,
> Dashed all to pieces.   I.2.5–8

The doubt here intimated could have occurred to no mind but to that of Miranda, who had been bred up in the island with her father and a monster only: she did not know, as others do, what sort of creatures were in a ship; others never would have introduced it as a conjecture. This shows, that while Shakespeare is displaying his vast excellence, he never fails to insert some touch or other, which is not merely characteristic of the particular person, but combines two things – the person, and the circumstances acting upon the person. She proceeds:

> O, the cry did knock
> Against my very heart! Poor souls, they perished.
> Had I been any god of power, I would
> Have sunk the sea within the earth, or ere
> It should the good ship so have swallowed and
> The fraughting souls within her.   I.2.8–13

She still dwells upon that which was most wanting to the completeness of her nature – these fellow creatures from whom she appeared banished, with only one relict to keep them alive, not in her memory, but in her imagination.

Another proof of excellent judgement in the poet, for I am now principally adverting to that point, is to be found in the preparation of the reader for what is to follow. Prospero is introduced, first in his magic robe, which, with the assistance of his daughter, he lays aside, and we then know him to be a being possessed of supernatural powers. He then instructs Miranda in the story of their arrival in the island, and this is conducted in such a manner, that the reader never conjectures the technical use the poet has made of the relation, by informing the auditor of what it is necessary for him to know.

The next step is the warning by Prospero, that he means, for particular purposes, to lull his daughter to sleep; and here he exhibits the earliest and mildest proof of magical power. In ordinary and vulgar plays we should have had some person brought upon the stage, whom nobody knows or cares anything about, to let the audience into the secret. Prospero having cast a sleep upon his daughter, by that sleep stops the narrative at the very moment when it was necessary to break it off, in order to excite curiosity, and yet to give the memory and understanding sufficient to carry on the progress of the history uninterruptedly.

Here I cannot help noticing a fine touch of Shakespeare's knowledge of human nature, and generally of the great laws of the human mind: I mean Miranda's infant remembrance. Prospero asks her

> Canst thou remember
> A time before we came unto this cell?
> I do not think thou canst, for then thou wast not
> Out three years old.

Miranda answers

> Certainly, sir, I can.

Prospero inquires

> By what? By any other house or person?
> Of any thing the image tell me, that
> Hath kept with thy remembrance.

To which Miranda returns

> 'Tis far off
> And rather like a dream than an assurance
> That my remembrance warrants. Had I not
> Four or five women once that tended me?   I.2.38–47

This is exquisite! In general, our remembrances of early life arise from vivid colours, especially if we have seen them in motion: for instance, persons when grown up will remember a bright green door, seen when they were quite young; but Miranda, who was somewhat older, recollected four or five women who tended her. She might know men from her father, and her remembrance of the past might be worn out by the present object, but women she only knew by herself, by the contemplation of her own figure in the fountain, and she recalled to her mind what had been. It was not, that she had seen such and such grandees, or such and such peeresses, but she remembered to have seen something like the reflection of herself: it was not herself, and it brought back to her mind what she had seen most like herself.

In my opinion the picturesque power displayed by Shakespeare, of all the poets that ever lived, is only equalled, if equalled, by Milton and Dante. The presence of genius is not shown in elaborating a picture: we have had many specimens of this sort of work in modern poems, where all is so dutchified, if I may use the word, by the most minute touches, that the reader naturally asks why words, and not painting, are used? I know a young lady of much taste, who observed, that in reading recent versified accounts of voyages and travels, she, by a sort of instinct, cast her eyes on the opposite page, for coloured prints of what was so patiently and punctually described.

The power of poetry is, by a single word perhaps, to instil that energy into the mind, which compels the imagination to produce the picture. Prospero tells Miranda

> one midnight
> Fated to th'purpose, did Antonio open
> The gates of Milan; and, i'th'dead of darkness,
> The ministers for th'purpose hurried thence
> Me and thy crying self.   I.2.128–32

Here, by introducing a single happy epithet, 'crying', in the last line, a complete picture is presented to the mind, and in the production of such pictures the power of genius consists.

In reference to preparation, it will be observed that the storm, and all that precedes the tale, as well as the tale itself, serve to develop completely the main character of the drama, as well as the design of Prospero. The manner in which the heroine is charmed asleep fits us for what follows, goes beyond our ordinary belief, and gradually leads us to the appearance and disclosure of a being of the most fanciful and delicate texture, like Prospero, preternaturally gifted.

In this way the entrance of Ariel, if not absolutely forethought by the reader, was foreshown by the writer: in addition, we may remark, that the moral feeling called forth by the sweet words of Miranda,

> Alack, what trouble
> Was I then to you! I.2.151–2

in which she considered only the sufferings and sorrows of her father, puts the reader in a frame of mind to exert his imagination in favour of an object so innocent and interesting. The poet makes him wish that, if supernatural agency were to be employed, it should be used for a being so young and lovely. 'The wish is father to the thought', and Ariel is introduced. Here, what is called poetic faith is required and created, and our common notions of philosophy give way before it: this feeling may be said to be much stronger than historic faith, since for the exercise of poetic faith the mind is previously prepared. I make this remark, though somewhat digressive, in order to lead to a future subject of these lectures – the poems of Milton. When adverting to those, I shall have to explain farther the distinction between the two.

Many Scriptural poems have been written with so much of Scripture in them, that what is not Scripture appears to be not true, and like mingling lies with the most sacred revelations. Now Milton, on the other hand, has taken for his subject that one point of Scripture of which we have the mere fact recorded, and upon this he has most judiciously constructed his whole fable. So of Shakespeare's *King Lear*: we have little historic evidence to guide or confine us, and the few facts handed down to us, and admirably employed by the poet, are sufficient, while we read, to put an end to all doubt as to the credibility of the story. It is idle to say that this or that incident is improbable, because history, as far as it goes, tells us that the fact was so and so. Four or five lines in the Bible include the whole that is said of Milton's story, and the Poet has called up that poetic faith, that conviction of the mind, which is necessary to make that seem true, which otherwise might have been deemed almost fabulous.

But to return to *The Tempest*, and to the wondrous creation of

Ariel. If a doubt could ever be entertained whether Shakespeare was a great poet, acting upon laws arising out of his own nature, and not without law, as has sometimes been idly asserted, that doubt must be removed by the character of Ariel. The very first words uttered by this being introduce the spirit, not as an angel, above man; not a gnome, or a fiend, below man; but while the poet gives him the faculties and the advantages of reason, he divests him of all mortal character, not positively, it is true, but negatively. In air he lives, from air he derives his being, in air he acts; and all his colours and properties seem to have been obtained from the rainbow and the skies. There is nothing about Ariel that cannot be conceived to exist either at sunrise or at sunset: hence all that belongs to Ariel belongs to the delight the mind is capable of receiving from the most lovely external appearances. His answers to Prospero are directly to the question, and nothing beyond; or where he expatiates, which is not unfrequently, it is to himself and upon his own delights, or upon the unnatural situation in which he is placed, though under a kindly power and to good ends.

Shakespeare has properly made Ariel's very first speech characteristic of him. After he has described the manner in which he had raised the storm and produced its harmless consequences, we find that Ariel is discontented – that he has been freed, it is true, from a cruel confinement, but still that he is bound to obey Prospero, and to execute any commands imposed upon him. We feel that such a state of bondage is almost unnatural to him, yet we see that it is delightful for him to be so employed. – It is as if we were to command one of the winds in a different direction to that which nature dictates, or one of the waves, now rising and now sinking, to recede before it bursts upon the shore: such is the feeling we experience, when we learn that a being like Ariel is commanded to fulfil any mortal behest.

When, however, Shakespeare contrasts the treatment of Ariel by Prospero with that of Sycorax, we are sensible that the liberated spirit ought to be grateful, and Ariel does feel and acknowledge the obligation; he immediately assumes the airy being, with a mind so elastically correspondent, that when once a feeling has passed from it, not a trace is left behind.

Is there anything in nature from which Shakespeare caught the idea of this delicate and delightful being, with such child-like simplicity, yet with such preternatural powers? He is neither born of heaven, nor of earth; but, as it were, between both, like a May-blossom kept suspended in air by the fanning breeze, which prevents it from falling to the ground, and only finally, and by compulsion, touching earth. This reluctance of the Sylph to be under the command even of Prospero is kept up through the whole play, and in the exercise of his admirable judgement Shakespeare has availed himself of it, in order to give Ariel an interest in the event, looking forward to that moment when he was to gain his last and only reward – simple and eternal liberty.

Another instance of admirable judgement and excellent preparation is to be found in the creature contrasted with Ariel – Caliban; who is described in such a manner by Prospero, as to lead us to expect the appearance of a foul, unnatural monster. He is not seen at once: his voice is heard; this is the preparation; he was too offensive to be seen first in all his deformity, and in nature we do not receive so much disgust from sound as from sight. After we have heard Caliban's voice he does not enter, until Ariel has entered like a water-nymph. All the strength of contrast is thus acquired without any of the shock of abruptness, or of that unpleasant sensation, which we experience when the object presented is in any way hateful to our vision.

The character of Caliban is wonderfully conceived: he is a sort of creature of the earth, as Ariel is a sort of creature of the air.[2] He partakes of the qualities of the brute, but is distinguished from brutes in two ways: by having mere understanding without moral reason; and by not possessing the instincts which pertain to absolute animals. Still, Caliban is in some respects a noble being: the poet has raised him far above contempt: he is a man in the sense of the imagination: all the images he uses are drawn from nature, and are highly poetical; they fit in with the images of Ariel. Caliban gives us images from the earth, Ariel images from the air. Caliban talks of the difficulty of finding fresh water, of the situation of morasses, and of other circumstances which even brute instinct, without reason, could comprehend. No mean figure is employed, no mean passion displayed, beyond animal passion, and repugnance to command.

The manner in which the lovers are introduced is equally wonderful, and it is the last point I shall now mention in reference to this, almost miraculous, drama. The same judgement is observable in every scene, still preparing, still inviting, and still gratifying, like a finished piece of music. I have omitted to notice one thing, and you must give me leave to advert to it before I proceed: I mean the conspiracy against the life of Alonso. I want to show you how well the poet prepares the feelings of the reader for this plot, which was to execute the most detestable of all crimes, and which, in another play, Shakespeare has called 'the murder of sleep'.

Antonio and Sebastian at first had no such intention: it was suggested by the magical sleep cast on Alonso and Gonzalo; but they are previously introduced scoffing and scorning at what was said by others, without regard to age or situation – without any sense of admiration for the excellent truths they heard delivered, but giving themselves up entirely to the malignant and unsocial feeling, which induced them to listen to everything that was said, not for the sake of profiting by the learning and experience of others, but of hearing something that might gratify vanity and self-love, by making them believe that the person speaking was inferior to themselves.

This let me remark, is one of the grand characteristics of a villain; and it would not be so much a presentiment, as an anticipation of hell, for men to suppose that all mankind were as wicked as themselves, or might be so, if they were not too great fools. Pope, you are perhaps aware, objected to this conspiracy; but in my mind, if it could be omitted, the play would lose a charm which nothing could supply.

Many, indeed innumerable, beautiful passages might be quoted from this play, independently of the astonishing scheme of its construction. Everybody will call to mind the grandeur of the language of Prospero in that divine speech, where he takes leave of his magic art; and were I to indulge myself by repetitions of the kind, I should descend from the character of a lecturer to that of a mere reciter. Before I terminate, I may particularly recall one short passage, which has fallen under the very severe, but inconsiderate, censure of Pope and Arbuthnot,[3] who pronounce it a piece of the grossest bombast. Prospero thus addresses his daughter, directing her attention to Ferdinand:

> The fringèd curtains of thine eye advance,
> And say what thou seest yond.   I.2.409–10

Taking these words as a periphrase of 'Look what is coming yonder', it certainly may to some appear to border on the ridiculous, and to fall under the rule I formerly laid down – that whatever, without injury, can be translated into a foreign language in simple terms, ought to be in simple terms in the original language; but it is to be borne in mind, that different modes of expression frequently arise from difference of situation and education: a blackguard would use very different words, to express the same thing, to those a gentleman would employ, yet both would be natural and proper; difference of feeling gives rise to difference of language: a gentleman speaks in polished terms, with due regard to his own rank and position, while a blackguard, a person little better than half a brute, speaks like half a brute, showing no respect for himself, nor for others.

But I am content to try the lines I have just quoted by the introduction to them; and then, I think, you will admit, that nothing could be more fit and appropriate than such language. How does Prospero introduce them? He has just told Miranda a wonderful story, which deeply affected her, and filled her with surprise and astonishment, and for his own purposes he afterwards lulls her to sleep. When she awakes, Shakespeare has made her wholly inattentive to the present, but wrapped up in the past. An actress, who understands the character of Miranda, would have her eyes cast down, and her eyelids almost covering them, while she was, as it were, living in her dream. At this moment Prospero sees Ferdinand, and wishes to point him out to his daughter, not only with great, but with scenic solemnity, he standing before her, and before the spectator, in the dignified character of a great magician. Something was to appear to Miranda on the sudden, and as unexpectedly as if the hero of a drama were to be on the stage at the instant when the curtain is elevated. It is under such circumstances that Prospero says, in a tone calculated at once to arouse his daughter's attention,

> The fringèd curtains of thine eye advance,
> And say what thou seest yond.

Turning from the sight of Ferdinand to his thoughtful daughter, his attention was first struck by the downcast appearance of her eyes and eyelids; and, in my humble opinion, the solemnity of the phraseology assigned to Prospero is completely in character, recollecting his preternatural capacity, in which the most familiar objects in nature present themselves in a mysterious point of view. It is much easier to find fault with a writer by reference to former notions and experience, than to sit down and read him, recollecting his purpose, connecting one feeling with another, and judging of his words and phrases, in proportion as they convey the sentiments of the persons represented.

Of Miranda we may say, that she possesses in herself all the ideal beauties that could be imagined by the greatest poet of any age or country; but it is not my purpose now, so much to point out the high poetic powers of Shakespeare, as to illustrate his exquisite judgement, and it is solely with this design that I have noticed a passage with which, it seems to me, some critics, and those among the best, have been unreasonably dissatisfied. If Shakespeare be the wonder of the ignorant, he is, and ought to be, much more the wonder of the learned: not only from profundity of thought, but from his astonishing and intuitive knowledge of what man must be at all times, and under all circumstances, he is rather to be looked upon as a prophet than as a poet. Yet, with all these unbounded powers, with all this might and majesty of genius, he makes us feel as if he were unconscious of himself and of his high destiny, disguising the half god in the simplicity of a child.

NOTES *by T. M. Raysor*

1. In making this important distinction between mechanic and organic regularity, Coleridge acknowledged his indebtedness to Schlegel (*Werke*, Volume 6, pages 157–8).

2. Schlegel (*Werke*, Volume 6, pages 236–7) makes exactly the same remark. This probably indicates an influence, though coincidence is possible.

3. *Memoirs of Martinus Scriblerus*, Book II ('The Art of Sinking in Poetry'), Chapter 12.

from 'Lectures of 1811–12, Lecture 9',
Coleridge's Shakespearean Criticism,
edited by T. M. Raysor (2 volumes, 1930), Volume 2,
pages 169–81; 1960 Everyman's Library edition
(2 volumes), Volume 2, pages 130–40

TWENTY-THREE

The Tempest: Conventions of Art and Empire

J. P. Brockbank

THERE is enough self-conscious artifice in the last plays to allow us to suspect that Shakespeare is glancing at his own art when Alonso says:

> This is as strange a maze as e'er men trod,
> And there is in this business more than nature
> Was ever conduct of. Some oracle
> Must rectify our knowledge.   V.1.242–5

And it may be that Prospero quietens the fretful oracles in his first audience with a tongue-in-cheek assurance:

> At picked leisure,
> Which shall be shortly, single I'll resolve you,
> Which to you shall seem probable, of every
> These happened accidents. Till when, be cheerful,
> And think of each thing well.   V.1.247–51

The tense marvellings of the play are oddly hospitable to moments of wry mockery. Things are never quite what they seem.

The play's mysteries, however, are authentic not gratuitous; they touch our sense of wonder and they are accessible to thought; and we need no oracle, skilled in the subtleties and audacities of Renaissance speculation, to rectify our knowledge. We must nevertheless seek to attend with the apt kind of attention, to get the perspectives right, and the tone. For, as often in the comedies, the perspectives and the tone are precisely secured, and it is only too easy to upset the balances of convention, of innocence and scepticism, that keep the allegory of the play at an appropriately un-obtrusive distance.

There is a multiple, complex allegory. It has to do with the social and moral nature of man, with the natural world, with the ways of providence, and with the nature of art. Yet this very complexity is the source of the play's simplicity – of its power to entertain, to move, and to satisfy our playgoing and contemplative spirits.

The Tempest is about a human mess put right by a make-belief magician. Or, to recast the point in the suggestive neo-platonic phrases of Sidney, it is about a golden world delivered from the brazen by providence and miracle. But there remain more specific ways of saying what it is about. In relation to its immediate sources it touches the colonizing enterprise of Shakespeare's England. In relation to one strain of dramatic tradition it is a morality, about the cure of evil and the forgiveness of sin; in relation to another, it is a pastoral entertainment, fit to celebrate the fertility and order of nature; and it owes to the masque its felicitous handling of illusion, spell, and rite. In relation to Shakespeare's own art, it seems to recollect much that has gone before, and to shadow forth (Sidney's phrase) the playwright's role in the theatres of fantasy and reality.

The several kinds of expressiveness found in the play owe much to the fragmentary source material on the one hand and to the tactful management of stage convention on the other. Theatrical techniques are so used that they illuminate an area of Elizabethan consciousness that was expressing itself also in the activities and in the literature of exploration and empire. Long before we pursue 'meanings' (after the play, brooding upon it) we recognize that the allegory is anchored in the instant realities of human experience. Its aetherial affirmations are hard-won, spun out of substantial material. The truths which offer themselves as perennial are made very specifically out of and for the England and the theatre of Shakespeare's own time. The play is as much about colonization as initiation, as much about the intrigues of men as the tricks of spirits.

The principal documents behind *The Tempest* are well known if not wholly easily accessible; they are William Strachey's *True Repertory of the Wreck*, published in *Purchas His Pilgrimes* together with an extract from the anonymous *True Declaration of Virginia*, and Sylvester Jourdan's *A Discovery of the Barmudas*.[1] The uses to which the play puts these materials would have been very different had it not been for the hospitality of the contemporary theatre (whose tastes Shakespeare himself did most to fashion) to the techniques and interest of the late comedies.

Strachey and Jourdan tell how Sir Thomas Gates and Sir George Summers were driven away from the rest of the fleet, bound for Virginia in June 1609, by a storm which finally lodged their ship – the *Sea Venture* – between two rocks off the coast of the Bermudas. After many 'rare and remarkable experiences' they built a new boat, *The Deliverance*, and a pinnace, *Patience*, and set sail for Virginia in May 1610. Their survival (like many another in the pages of Hakluyt) had about it something of the miraculous, and it invited as much comment on the ways of Providence as on the skill and resourcefulness of English sailors.

Shakespeare, with the storms of *Othello*, *The Winter's Tale*, and *Pericles* freshly accomplished for the theatre, would recognize occasion enough for a play in the story of the Bermudas wreck. And the material offers itself most invitingly to a playwright whose interest in the ways of Providence, and in the conversion and salvation of man had matured through long practice in allegoric, romantic comedy. The prose accounts of the wreck are constantly suggestive in ways that would be less noticeable were they read without knowledge of the play. It is often so. The masterpiece illuminates the sources, more than the sources the masterpiece. It is no longer possible to read the collections of Hakluyt and Purchas without recognizing that they offer as much to Shakespeare and to Coleridge as to Captain Cooke.

In the *True Repertory* the storm is both a physical ordeal and a moral:

a dreadfull storme and hideous began to blow from out the North-east, which swelling, and roaring as it were by fits, some houres with more violence than others, at length did beat all light from heaven; which like an hell of darkenesse turned blacke upon us, so much the more fuller of horror, as in such cases horror and feare use to overrunne the troubled, and overmastered sences of all, which (taken up with amazement) the eares lay so sensible to the terrible cries, and murmurs of the windes, and distraction of our Company, as who was most armed, and best prepared, was not a little shaken.   (page 6)

The 'unmercifull tempest' is a terrible leveller; death at sea comes 'uncapable of particularities of goodnesse and inward comforts', and gives the mind no 'free and quiet time, to use her judgement and Empire'. There are hints enough for the play's opening scene in which hope is confounded by the counterpointed roarings of crew, court, and elements; the dignities of seamanship and of prayer are subdued to 'A confused noise within'. For the dignity of Gonzalo's wit (that alone survives the horror and the test) there is no equivalent in the source. But Strachey has his own way of wondering at man's powers of survival:

> The Lord knoweth, I had as little hope, as desire of life in the storme, & in this, it went beyond my will; because beyond my reason, why we should labour to preserve life; yet we did, either because so deare are a few lingring houres of life in all mankinde, or that our Christian knowledges taught us, how much we owed to the rites of Nature, as bound, not to be fasle to our selves, or to neglect the meanes of our owne preservation; the most despaireful things amongst men, being matters of no wonder nor moment with him, who is the rich Fountaine and admirable Essence of all mercy. (page 9)

And it is easy to see in retrospect how, at a touch, the observations, the marvellings and the pieties of Strachey might be transformed into the language of *The Tempest* with its capacity for dwelling upon the preservation of life, the rites of nature, and the 'admirable Essence of all mercy'.

The pieties of the prose accounts are more than conventional; they owe their awed intensity to the sequences of catastrophe and miracle that the voyages endured. We need not hesitate to treat the play as allegory since that is how Shakespeare's contemporaries treated the actual event. After God has delivered the seamen from the 'most dreadfull Tempest' of 'tumultuous and malignant' winds, the authority of the Governor is required to deliver them from what *The True Declaration* calls 'the tempest of Dissention'. Reviewing the mutinies that threatened the survival of the Bermudas party, Strachey writes:

> In these dangers and divellish disquiets (whilest the almighty God wrought for us, and sent us miraculously delivered from the calamities

of the Sea, all blessings upon the shoare, to content and binde us to gratefulnesse) thus inraged amongst our selves, to the destruction each of other, into what a mischiefe and misery had wee bin given up, had wee not had a Governour with his authority to have suppressed the same?   (page 32)

Reading this passage (and some similar ones) with the poet's eye, we can see how Prospero might have taken shape. From his experience of the theatre Shakespeare's imagination and invention readily made a single figure out of the miraculous deliverer from the sea's calamities, and the 'Governour with his authority' stopping the victims of the wreck from killing one another. It is an apt opportunity to take after *Measure for Measure*, which is about the saving powers of a governor, and *Pericles* with its miraculous deliveries from the sea.

A more specific occasion for the play's rendering of the storm as a feat of providential magic is offered by Strachey's description of the St Elmo's fire that danced like Ariel about the rigging:

Onely upon the thursday night Sir George Summers being upon the watch, had an apparition of a little round light, like a faint Starre, trembling, and streaming along with a sparkeling blaze, halfe the height upon the Maine Mast, and shooting sometimes from Shroud to Shroud, tempting to settle as it were upon any of the foure Shrouds: and for three or foure houres together, or rather more, halfe the night it kept with us; running sometimes along the Maine-yard to the very end, and then returning. At which Sir George Summers called divers about him, and shewed them the same, who observed it with much wonder, and carefulnesse: but upon a sodaine, towards the morning watch, they lost the sight of it, and knew not what way it made.
                                                                  (page 11)

The elusive, mockingly playful fire and light in the encompassing total darkness, observed with wonder and carefulness by the crew, is poignantly ironic. Strachey leaves the natural phenomenon very ripe for transmutation into stage symbol. 'The superstitious Seamen', he says, 'make many constructions of this Sea-fire, which neverthelesse is usual in stormes.' The Greeks took it for Castor and Pollux, perhaps, and 'an evill signe of great tempest'. The Italians call it 'Corpo sancto'. The Spaniards call it 'Saint Elmo, and have an authentic and miraculous Legend for it'. The irony is that it could do nothing to help the seamen, but rather quickened their torment:

Be it what it will, we laid other foundations of safety or ruine, then in the rising or falling of it, could it have served us now miraculously to have taken our height by, it might have strucken amazement, and a reverence in our devotions, according to the due of a miracle. But it did not light us any whit the more to our knowne way, who ran now (as doe hoodwinked men) at all adventures. (page 11)

It is one of the play's discoveries that this mocking hell is providentially (and indeed playfully) contrived. While allowing Ariel's tale to mimic the lightning, Shakespeare recalls the sonorous miseries described in an earlier passage:

our clamours drownd in the windes, and the windes in thunder. Prayers might well be in the heart and lips, but drowned in the outcries of the Officers: nothing heard that could give comfort, nothing seene that might incourage hope. It is impossible for me, had I the voice of Stentor, and expression of as many tongues, as his throate of voyces, to express the outcries and miseries, not languishing, but wasting his spirits, and art constant to his owne principles, but not prevailing. (page 7)

By personalizing, in Prospero, the *natural* processes of the storm and its happy outcome, Shakespeare displays theatrically the exacting cruelties of a providence that works to saving purpose:

> PROSPERO   My brave spirit!
> Who was so firm, so constant, that this coil
> Would not infect his reason?
> ARIEL   Not a soul
> But felt a fever of the mad, and played
> Some tricks of desperation.   I.2.206–10

Human reason is 'infected' and human skill disarmed in order that all might be brought to shore safely:

> Not a hair perished.
> On their sustaining garments not a blemish,
> But fresher than before.   I.2.217–29

This allusion to the shipwreck of St Paul at Malta (Acts 27. 34) reminds us that catastrophic voyages and the ways of Providence are readily considered together. God uses shipwrecks. But the play is more insistent than the New Testament upon the waywardness and apparent arbitrariness of Providence (men hood-winked, in a maze, amazed) and it has taken its signals from the prose of the voyagers.

At the utmost point of their despair, when skill and energy can do no more, the sailors are ready to surrender passively to the sea. As Jourdan puts it:

All our men, being utterly spent, tyred, and disabled for longer labour, were even resolved, without any hope of their lives, to shut up the hatches, and to have committed themselves to the mercy of the sea, (which is said to be mercilesse) or rather to the mercy of their mighty God and redeemer. (page 195)

That drift from the commonplace 'mercy of the sea' through 'said to be mercilesse' to 'their mighty God and redeemer' is not inertly conventional. It testifies to the quite palpable presence in both stories (but particularly in the opening paragraphs of Jourdan's) of the sequence – storm, fear, death, miraculous renewal of life. While Shakespeare follows Strachey in his treatment of Ariel's description of the last moments of the wreck, he follows Jourdan where he hints at a ceremonious leave-taking on the stricken ship ('Let's all sink wi'th'King. . . . Let's take leave of him'):

So that some of them having some good and comfortable waters in the ship, fetcht them, and drunke the one to the other, taking their last leave one of the other, untill their more ioyfull and happy meeting, in a more blessed world. (page 195)

The play does not allow too intrusive a ceremonious piety, but rather a wry nostalgia for 'an acre of barren ground' tempering Gonzalo's patient acquiescence: 'The wills above be done, but I would fain die a dry death.' The 'more blessed world' is offered nevertheless when all hope is dead, for, as Strachey reports 'Sir George Summers, when no man dreamed of such happinesse, had discovered, and cried Land'.

After the ordeal by sea, the island inheritance. Both Jourdan and

Strachey are moved by the paradox that made 'The Devils Ilands' (the name commonly given to the Bermudas) 'both the place of our safetie, and meanes of our deliverance'. Jourdan is particularly eloquent in confronting general, superstitious expectations of the islands with his own ecstatic experience of them. 'But our delivery', he says, 'was not more strange in falling so opportunely and happily upon the land, as our feeding and preservation, was beyond our hopes, and all mens expectations most admirable.' It has the quality of Gonzalo's marvellings. Jourdan tells us that the islands were never inhabited by Christian or heathen but were ever esteemed 'a most prodigious and inchanted place affording nothing but gusts, stormes, and foule weather'. 'No man was ever heard, to make for this place, but as against their wils, they have by stormes and dangerousnesse of the rocks, lying seaven leagues into the sea, suffered shipwrack.'

Jourdan's phrases seem to license the play's magical, paradisial, and mysterious atmosphere, and some may be the germ of the rival versions of Shakespeare's island voiced on the one hand by Gonzalo and Adrian, and on the other by Sebastian and Antonio:

Yet did we find there the ayre so temperate and the country so abundantly fruitful of all fit necessaries for the sustenation and preservation of man's life ... Wherefore my opinion sincerely of this Island is, that whereas it hath beene, and is still accounted, the most dangerous, infortunate, and forlorne place of the world, it is in truth the richest, healthfullest, and pleasing land (the quantity and bignesse thereof considered) and merely natural, as ever man set foot upon. (page 197)

Shakespeare intervenes to associate the auspicious vision of the island ('The air breathes upon us here most sweetly') with the innocent courtiers, and the inauspicious ('As if it had lungs, and rotten ones') with the culpably sophisticated. But Strachey and Jourdan are equally clear that 'the foule and generall errour' of the world distorts the truths about the islands which are in time revealed to those who experience it.

In the sources, as in the play, the island deliverance is a beginning and not an end. Once saved from the wreck, the survivors have still to be saved from each other. Strachey tells how Sir Thomas Gates dispatched a longboat (duly modified) to Virginia, moved by 'the care which he took for the estate of the Colony in this his inforced absence' and 'by a long practised experience, foreseeing and fearing what innovation and tumult might happily arise, amongst the younger and ambitious spirits of the new companies'. The Governor's authority, however, proves equally essential to the prosperity of both the communities, of the Bermudas and of Virginia. Strachey writes of the onset of the island mutinies:

And sure it was happy for us, who had now runne this fortune, and were fallen into the bottome of this misery, that we both had our Governour with us, and one so solicitous and carefull, whose both example (as I said) and authority, could lay shame and command upon our people: else, I am perswaded, we had most of us finished our dayes there, so willing were the major part of the common sort (especially when they found such a plenty of victuals) to settle a foundation of ever inhabiting there ... some dangerous and secret discontents nourished amongst us, had like to have been the parents of bloudy issues and mischiefs.   (page 28)

And *The True Declaration* discloses the analogous issues and mischiefs in Virginia:

The ground of all those miseries, was the permissive Providence of God, who, in the fore-mentioned violent storme, separated the head from the bodie, all the vitall powers of Regiment being exiled with Sir Thomas Gates in those infortunate (yet fortunate) Ilands. The broken remainder of those supplyes made a greater shipwracke in the Continent of Virginia, by the tempest of Dissention: every man over-valuing his owne worth, would be a Commander: every man underprizing anothers value, denied to be commanded.   (page 67)

The play's second act does most to explore the mutinous disaffections that attend upon and threaten 'the vitall powers of Regiment'. Its Neapolitan courtiers fittingly convey the temper of Virginia's 'younger and ambitious spirits':

> There be that can rule Naples
> As well as he that sleeps; lords that can prate
> As amply and unnecessarily
> As this Gonzalo. I myself could make
> A chough of as deep chat.   II.1.267–71

'Every man underprizing anothers value, denied to be commanded.'
And the drunken, anarchistic landsmen represent the discontents of
the 'common sort' on the Island. By extending the powers of
Ariel and Prospero over both groups of conspirators, moreover,
Shakespeare allows a fuller expression to the moral ideas that issue
in *The True Declaration*'s reflection on 'the permissive Providence
of God'. The conspiracies are at once permitted and constrained.

It is altogether appropriate that the Governor's authority should
be represented as a care for 'the state of the Colony' and not as a
bent for empire and sovereignty. *The True Declaration* finds for
the word 'colony' its richest meaning and fullest resonance: 'A
Colony is therefore denominated, because they should be Coloni,
the Tillers of the Earth, and Stewards of fertilitie.' 'Should be'; but
are not, for:

> our mutinous Loyterers would not sow with providence, and therefore
> they reaped the fruits of too deere bought Repentance. An incredible
> example of their idlenesse, is the report of Sir Thomas Gates, who
> affirmeth, that after his first comming thither, he hath seen some of
> them eat their fish raw, rather then they would go a stones cast to fetch
> wood and dresse it. (page 68)

The tillers of the earth and the fetchers of wood, runs the argument,
are the heirs of God's plenty: 'Dei laboribus omnia vendunt, God
sels us all things for our labour, when Adam himselfe might not
live in Paradise without dressing the Garden.' It is this thought
that seems to hover mockingly behind the log-bearing labours of
Ferdinand. Prospero, imposing the task, does not do as Sir Thomas
Gates and set his own hand 'to every meane labour' dispensing
'with no travaile of his body'. He rather exercises over the Prince
(himself a potential governor) the rule of Providence's dominant
law; he sells Miranda (the richest of the island's bounties) only in
return for work.

Once the recalcitrant passions of the Virginian colonizers have
been tamed, once they have ceased to 'shark for present booty'
out of idleness and lawlessness, they may hope to enjoy the bounty
of nature. This idea is in itself almost enough to suggest the invention of Caliban. Strachey speaks of the 'liberty and fulness of
sensuality' that drew the 'idle, untoward and wretched' to mur-

uring discontent, and 'disunion of hearts and hands' from labour
age 28). The grotesque, spectacular figure of Caliban, and his con-
piracy with the butler and the jester, enable Shakespeare to make
Strachey's point within the conventions of masque and comedy.

Caliban, however, seems like Prospero to be doubly fashioned
from the travel literature. Not only is he a theatrical epitome of the
animal, anarchic qualities of the colonizers, he is also the epitome
of the primitive and uncivilized condition of the native American.
Strachey tells how the Virginian Indians severely tested the
magnanimity of the Governor 'who since his first landing in the
Countrey (how justly soever provoked) would not by any meanes
be wrought to a violent proceeding against them'. But, like Caliban,
they have natures on which nurture cannot stick; pains humanely
taken are quite lost. One of the Governor's men – alas for tractable
courses – is carried off into the woods and sacrificed; and the
Governor 'well perceived, how little a faire and noble intreatie
workes upon a barbarous disposition, and therefore in some
measure purpose to be revenged' (page 62).

But when Caliban consorts with Trinculo and Stephano the play
expresses, with joyous irony, both the common appetites and the
distinctive attributes of man primitive and man degenerate.
Caliban's scorn of Trinculo's tipsy acquisitiveness, 'Let it alone,
thou fool! It is but trash', measures the distance between them.
Fittingly, the strictures of *The True Declaration* fall most heavily
upon those delinquent colonizers who 'for their private lucre
partly imbezeled the provisions', spoiling the market by leaving
the Virginians 'glutted with our Trifles' (page 70).

As witnesses both to the fine energies of Caliban and to his
truculence, the first audience of *The Tempest* might well have asked
for themselves the questions that Purchas sets in the margin of
The True Repertory:

Can a Savage remayning a Savage be civill? Were not wee our
selves made and not borne civill in our Progenitors dayes? and were
not Caesar's Britaines as brutish as Virginians? (page 62)

To this last question *Cymbeline* had already supplied something
resembling Purchas's own answer, 'The Romane swords were best

teachers of civilitie to this & other Countries neere us.' *The Tempest*
leaves us to wonder at a range of possible answers to the first. For
Shakespeare's understanding of Caliban is not co-extensive with
Prospero's. 'Liberty' and 'fulness of sensuality' (to recall Strachey's terms) are auspicious when opposed, not to temperance, but
to constraint and frigidity. Hence Caliban's virtue and dignity, and
the quickness of his senses accords with his love of music – an
Indian and a Carib characteristic remarked by the voyagers.

As his name may be meant to remind us,[2] Caliban is conceived
as much out of the reports of the Caribana as of those of the
Bermudas and Virginia. *Purchas his Pilgrimage*[3] tells of the *Caraibes*,
the priests of the Cannibal territory in the north of Brazil, to whom
'sometimes (but seldome) the Divell appears', and of their witches
'called *Carayba*, or holiness'. There is here just enough pretext for
associating Caliban with the blacker kind of sorcery that Shakespeare allows to Sycorax.

Sycorax represents a natural malignancy ('with age and envy . . .
grown into a hoop') consonant with her negative and confining
skills. Unlike the Carayba of Purchas's account, however, she does
not embody a native devilry and priestcraft, but is a disreputable
exile from Argier with only a casual claim to dominion over the
island. Thus the play qualifies the righteousness of Caliban's
resentment and complicates the relationships between native and
colonial endowments. We are left to wonder about the ultimate
sources of the moral virus that has infected what might have been a
golden world, and Prospero's account of Caliban's genesis ('got
by the devil himself | Upon thy wicked dam') may be taken either
as imprecation or as a fragment of bizarre biography.

When Shakespeare confronts Prospero with Caliban he does not
restrict the range of his implications in the theatre to the command
that a colonial governor might seek by kindness and by torment
to secure over a native. That relationship itself is only one expression of what Montaigne, in a passage familiar to Shakespeare from
the 'Essay on Cannibals', called the bastardizing of original
naturality by human wit. Shakespeare's scepticism, like Montaigne's, recoils upon authority itself. Prospero's malice ('tonight
thou shalt have cramps') is a comic instance of the barbarism of

civilization that Montaigne finds more shocking than cannibalism; we mangle, torture, and mammock our living neighbours not from natural perversity but 'under pretence of piety and religion'.

The secret dialogue that, metaphorically speaking, Shakespeare conducts with Florio's Montaigne is an intricate one.[4] Gonzalo's Utopian vision is at its centre. Much of Florio's prose is assimilated into the routine of the verse, but the quiet climax of Gonzalo's musings – to do with the fecundity of the anarchic paradise – is intensely in the mode of the last plays:

> nature should bring forth
> Of it own kind all foison, all abundance,
> To feed my innocent people.   I.1.165–7

Florio says that his admirable savages have no need to gain new lands, 'for to this day they yet enjoy that naturall ubertie and fruitfulnesse, which without labouring toyle, doth in such plenteous abundance furnish them with all necessary things, that they need not enlarge their limits'. Gonzalo is mocked by the sophisticated conspirators for, as it were, his reading of Florio. Shakespeare contrives to vindicate Montaigne's contempt for the 'unnatural opinion' that excuses the 'ordinary faults' of 'treason, treacherie, disloyaltie, tyrannie, crueltie, and suchlike'; for however apt and amusing the taunts of Antonio and Sebastian, their persistent malice is seen for what it is, and Gonzalo's words are never quite out of key with the mood that the island scenes have created in the theatre. At the same time, Montaigne's sanguine vision of un-cultivated innocence is exquisitely, and critically, related to the dreams that a benign but vulnerable ageing courtier might have of sovereignty. Where Montaigne believes (or pretends to believe) that the wild nations in reality 'exceed all the pictures where with licentious Poesie hath proudly imbellished the golden age', Shakespeare leaves the notion to an old man's fantasy. But a significant fantasy, properly entertained by 'Holy Gonzalo, honourable man'.

When 'foison' and 'abundance' are again at the centre of atten-tion we are contemplating the betrothal masque. The masque has several kinds of appropriateness in a play about colonization. It accords with Strachey's concern with bounty and the proper regulation of passion, and it reminds us of the indivisible integrity of the laws of nature and government. Miranda's presence on the island has some occasion, perhaps, in the story of Virginia Dare, grand-daughter of Captain John White, born in 1587 in the first English colony of Virginia and left there in a small party.[5] But it matters more that Purchas comments in his marginal note to Strachey's account of the marriage of one of Sir George Summers's men: *The most holy civill and most naturall possession taken of the Bermudas by exercise of Sacraments Marriage, Childbirth, &c.* (page 38). The sacrament of marriage is looked upon as the perfection of the island's sovereignty. Prospero's admonition that Ferdinand should not break Miranda's

> virgin-knot before
> All sanctimonious ceremonies may
> With full and holy rite be ministered ...   IV.1.15–17

is not only in character (the officiously solicitous father), it is also a full recognition that heaven rains down blessings only upon those who honour the sanctities of its order:

> No sweet aspersion shall the heavens let fall
> To make this contract grow; but barren hate,
> Sour-eyed disdain and discord shall bestrew
> The union of your bed with weeds so loathly
> That you shall hate it both.   IV.1.18–22

The metaphors take life from the island truths about 'the tillers of the earth and the stewards of fertility'; life flourishes best by cultivation and restraint.

The masque decoratively, but with a quick pulse, endorses the sustaining idea; the 'sweet aspersion' that the heavens let fall is recalled by Ceres's

> upon my flowers
> Diffusest honey-drops, refreshing showers.   IV.1.78–9

There is much to remind us of the continuity of the play with pastoral comedy – with *As You Like It* and *The Winter's Tale*. 'So rare a wondered father and a wise', says Ferdinand, 'Makes this place Paradise'.

Purchas almost immediately follows his note on the marriage sacrament with another on a camp atrocity – 'Saylers misorder'. The effect in the narrative is a paler version of that in the play when Prospero suddenly remembers

> that foul conspiracy
> Of the beast Caliban and his confederates.   IV.1.139–40

Strachey tells how a sailor murdered one of his fellows with a shovel, and how others conspired to rescue him from the gallows 'in despight and disdaine that Justice should be shewed upon a Sayler'. The 'mischiefs of mariners' reported by Strachey are intensified by the activities of 'savage spies' from among the disaffected Indians (page 50). The Governor's nerves and moral resolution are, like Prospero's, severely tested.

The Tempest does not, however, return to the moral antinomies of pastoral comedy – opposing the seasonal, fecund processes of nature to human sophistication. Its most memorable nature has little to do with that which fills the garners and brings shepherds and sheep-shearing into *The Winter's Tale*. It is not the 'great creating nature' that Perdita honours in her festive ceremonies. It is an elemental nature, made of the air, earth, and water that meet on a tempestuous coast, and in listening to the play's many mysterious and subtle evocations of the ways of the elements we may be aware still of the poet's transfigurations of the sailors' experience.

Shakespeare is sensitive to the narrative sequence (already noticed) of storm, fear, death, and the miraculous renewal of life in the island's 'temperate air'. Shakespeare's tact sustains the sequence without surrender to superstition (*pace* Gonzalo's marvellings) and without inviting moral exegesis. In Ariel's opening songs and in Ferdinand's exquisitely mannered reception of them, the truth of the sequence becomes lyrical and musical:

> Sitting on a bank,
> Weeping again the King my father's wrack,
> This music crept by me upon the waters,
> Allaying both their fury and my passion
> With its sweet air.   I.2.390–94

The quieting of storm and sorrow have in the theatre become the same process. Grief is transposed into melody. The word 'air', like Ariel's song itself, hovers elusively between atmosphere and melody:

> This is no mortal business, nor no sound
> That the earth owes. I hear it now above me.   I.2.407–8

The island's airs are themselves melodious, and when Ferdinand finds Miranda

>   the goddess
> On whom these airs attend   I.2.422–3

the suggestions of aetherial harmony are perfected.

Ariel's second song offers what is perhaps the play's most eloquent and characteristic symbol:

> Those are pearls that were his eyes;
> Nothing of him that doth fade,
> But doth suffer a sea-change
> Into something rich and strange.   I.2.399–402

The sea-change metaphors are a more searching expression of moral change as *The Tempest* presents it than the overtly pastoral convention could supply, and can touch more closely the mysteries of death.

Its beginnings in Shakespeare are familiar in Clarence's dream in *Richard III* – significantly a *dream*, and a reaching-forward to the mood and tenor of the last plays:

> O Lord! Methought what pain it was to drown!
> What dreadful noise of waters in mine ears!   I.4.21–2

The pain and noise of drowning were still 'beating' in Shakespeare's mind when he wrote *The Tempest*, and consolatory transformations are remembered too:

>   and in the holes
> Where eyes did once inhabit, there were crept,
> As 'twere in scorn of eyes, reflecting gems,
> That wooed the slimy bottom of the deep
> And mocked the dead bones that lay scattered by.
>   *Richard III*, I.4.29–33

It is (as A. P. Rossiter once said) 'submarine Seneca'; but it is ready to become 'Those are pearls that were his eyes'. The marine fantasy seems to owe nothing to seaman's lore (Hakluyt and Purchas collect mostly matter-of-fact accounts of the genesis of pearls) although the travel books have much to say about the 'great store of pearl' to be found in Bermuda seas. It suffices that Shakespeare's early experience in the mode enabled him to refine and to amplify his distinctly surrealist vision of death by water. But Clarence expresses too the continuing physical ordeal:

> but still the envious flood
> Stopped in my soul, and would not let it forth
> To find the empty, vast, and wandering air,
> But smothered it within my panting bulk,
> Who almost burst to belch it in the sea.   I.4.37–41

The sentiments and images are soon quite subdued to the English Senecal conventions – the

> melancholy flood,
> With that sour ferryman which poets write of ...
>   I.4.45–6

but not before Shakespeare had written:

> O then began the tempest to my soul!   I.4.44

The sequence, storm, fear, death, is in Clarence's experience unconsummated by the liberation that the strange word 'belch' seems to promise.

It is otherwise in *Pericles*, another play in which marine nature is more poignantly mysterious, more eternal, and more consolatory than pastoral nature:

> Th'unfriendly elements
> Forgot thee utterly; nor have I time
> To give thee hallowed to thy grave, but straight
> Must cast thee, scarcely coffined, in the ooze;
> Where, for a monument upon thy bones,
> And aye-remaining lamps, the belching whale
> And humming water must o'erwhelm thy corpse,
> Lying with simple shells.   III.1.57–64

In *Timon of Athens* too, the sea retains its cleansing sanctity when the pasture that lards the rother's sides and the sun that breeds roots in the corrupt earth are forgotten:

> Timon hath made his everlasting mansion
> Upon the beachèd verge of the salt flood,
> Who once a day with his embossèd froth
> The turbulent surge shall cover.   V.1.213–16

The sea 'whose liquid surge resolves | The moon into salt tears' is symbol too of a perpetual compassion:

> rich conceit
> Taught thee to make vast Neptune weep for aye
> On thy low grave, on faults forgiven.   V.4.77–9

The prose accounts behind *The Tempest* offer Shakespeare new opportunities for this morally expressive sea-eloquence.[6] Ariel admonishes the courtiers as if their survival from the wreck were owed to their destined unfitness for the sea's digestion:

> You are three men of sin, whom destiny –
> That hath to instrument this lower world
> And what is in't – the never-surfeited sea
> Hath caused to belch up you.   III.3.54–7

But the sea-swell of the rhythm subdues the joke to the solemnity of the occasion. Prospero, in a slow movement of the play (the still figures and the leisured speech) that makes it remarkably fitting, uses the figure of the cleansing, clarifying sea:

> Their understanding
> Begins to swell, and the approaching tide
> Will shortly fill the reasonable shore
> That now lies foul and muddy.   V.1.79–82

The sea is an almost constant presence in the play's verbal music; both the dancing kind:

> And ye that on the sands with printless foot
> Do chase the ebbing Neptune ...   V.1.34–5

and the more sombre:

> Methought the billows spoke, and told me of it;
> The winds did sing it to me; and the thunder,
> That deep and dreadful organ-pipe, pronounced
> The name of Prosper: it did bass my trespass.
> Therefore my son i'th'ooze is bedded, and
> I'll seek him deeper than e'er plummet sounded,
> And with him there lie mudded.   III.3.98–104

The moral sonorities are the sonorities of the sea. The apprehension of final judgement is expressed by way of sea, wind, and thunder; but 'deep and dreadful' and 'bass' are as apt for the sea as they are for the thunder; while the thunder lingers upon the next lines stirring the words 'deeper' and 'sounded' as they are used of the plumb-line, and coming to rest in 'mudded'.

Elsewhere, language used about music and about haunting noises is not directly about the sea, but might well have been:

> Even now, we heard a hollow burst of bellowing.   II.1.316

It might be a breaking wave. Recalling the 'humming water' of *Pericles*, it is apt that Caliban should speak of instruments that 'hum' about his ears. Humming is a common spell of the play's language:

> The noontide sun, called forth the mutinous winds. V.1.42

What is manifest in the detail of the play's accomplishment is manifest still in its large design – which owes more to the literature of sea-survival. The suggestion that the action of *The Tempest* takes place under the sea is witty and illuminating. The first scene is about men drowning, and its conventions are decisively naturalistic – there at least the storm is not merely symbolic. But the second scene changes the mood and the convention; the perspectives shift; time and place lose meaning, and characters and events shed a measure of their routine actuality. The play becomes a masque; and not improbably a masque resembling a masque of Neptune, with Ariel and Caliban seen as mutations of triton and sea-nymph. If contemporary productions, however, had looked for hints for figures and décor in the literature of Virginian colonization, they would have found them in John White's 'True Pictures and Fashions'.[7]

To dwell upon the 'sea-sorrow' and 'sea-change' processes of the play is to recognize the difference from the more usual changes associated with pastoral in other comedies and late plays. Only *Pericles* resembles *The Tempest*. In *The Winter's Tale* moral growth is presented as a seasonal process, enabling Leontes to greet Perdita, when innocence returns to Sicilia in the last act, with the words:

> Welcome hither
> As is the spring to th'earth! V.i.150–51

and

> The blessèd gods
> Purge all infection from our air whilst you
> Do climate here! V.i.167–9

But conversion and repentance are not, in *The Tempest*, simple processes of growth. They are elusive mysteries, requiring strange mutations and interventions; occurring within dream states, under spells, conditionally ruled by laws that Shakespeare is content to offer as 'magical'. But it is the sea, as the Elizabethan imagination dwelt upon it, that supplied the language of moral discovery.

Shakespeare's gift, it might be said of this and other plays, was to allegorize the actual; to conjoin his responsiveness to the moral order with his sense of turbulent, intractable realities. In lesser degree that was Strachey's gift too, and Jourdan's. But to the reconciliations accomplished in this play, Shakespeare's theatrical art brings a severe qualification – one that might be expected at this mature and resourceful phase of English drama. It is brought home to us that harmony is achieved in the human world only by allowing to Prospero and to Providence the powers of a playwright; particularly of a playwright skilled in masque – for the cloud-capped towers and all the things that vanish when the magician forfeits his power are recognizably the paraphernalia of masque. In this sense Prospero is indeed Shakespeare, but not Shakespeare the private man (whether retired or exhausted) but Shakespeare the professional playwright and masque-maker, perceiving that the order he seems to reveal in the world that the voyagers disclose to us is a feat of theatrical illusion. The magic does not work everywhere and for ever. From the poetic world there is the return to Milan where Sebastian and Antonio will keep their hard identities. Prospero returns himself and the audience to vulnerable humanity.

The end of the play, however, does not wholly determine its final impression. The climax of the moral magic discovers Ferdinand and Miranda playing at chess. We may remember that a world chess master, Giacchino Greco (il Calabrese), was much about that time visiting England from Italy. Or we may take it that the game is a proper symbol of comedy – of conflict transposed into play. As T. E. Hulme once said – 'Many necessary conditions must be fulfilled before the chess-board can be poised elegantly on the cinders'. Life is only provisionally, for the span of a play which obeys all the unities, a perfectly coherent moral order; and where there is no art – no play – we have leave to doubt that there can be order. Unless it is to be found among Montaigne's savages.

NOTES

1. Strachey's *True Repertory* circulated in manuscript in 1610, but was not printed until 1625, when it appeared in *Purchas His Pilgrimes*, Volume 4, Chapter 6. Morton Luce's old Arden edition (1901) of *The Tempest* contains an appendix on the Bermuda pamphlets; selections are also included in the new Arden edition (1954, by Frank Kermode), together with selections from Jourdan's *A Discovery* (1610). Fuller selections of both are contained in *The Elizabethans' America* (Stratford-upon-Avon Library, 1965), edited by Louis B. Wright.

   Page references to Strachey's *True Repertory and True Declaration* are to the 1906 edition of *Purchas His Pilgrimes*, Volume 19; page references to Jourdan's *A Discovery* are to the modernized version in *The Elizabethans' America*, but the text quoted is the 1812 edition of *Hakluyt's Voyages*, Volume 5.

2. Gustav H. Blanke, *Amerika im Englischen Schrifttum des 16. und 17. Jahrhunderts* (1962), points out that one Bodley atlas has the version 'Caliban' for 'Cariban'. The genesis of names is always elusive. It is noticeable that Strachey (page 14) names the historian

of the West Indies, Gonzalus Ferdinandus Oviedus, which might have supplied Gonzalo and Ferdinand.

3. op. cit., third edition (1617), Book IX, Chapter 5, page 1039.

4. An extract from Florio's translation of Montaigne's essay 'Of the Caniballes' is in Appendix C of the new Arden edition of *The Tempest*. The whole essay is available in the Everyman's Library edition of Florio's Montaigne (Volume 1).

5. See Wright, *The Elizabethans' America*, page 133.

6. See for example *Purchas his Pilgrimage* (1617), page 654.

7. *The Trve Pictvres and Fashions of the People in ... Virginia ... draowne by Iohn White*, appended to *A briefe and true report of the new found land of Virginia* (Frankfurt, 1590). See particularly the figure of *The Coniuerer* or *The Flyer*.

from *Later Shakespeare* (Stratford-upon-Avon Studies 8, 1966), edited by J. R. Brown and Bernard Harris, pages 183–201

TWENTY-FOUR

The Mirror of Analogy

Reuben A. Brower

The Mind, that Ocean where each kind
Does streight its own resemblance find;
Yet it creates, transcending these,
Far other Worlds, and other Seas . . .

(Andrew Marvell)

OF *The Tempest*, we may say what Ferdinand said of the masque,

This is a most majestic vision, and
Harmonious charmingly.   IV.1.118–19

The harmony of the play lies in its metaphorical design, in the closeness and completeness with which its rich and varied elements are linked through almost inexhaustible analogies. It is hard to pick a speech at random without coming on an expression that brings us by analogy into direct contact with elements that seem remote because of their place in the action or because of the type of experience they symbolize. Opening the play at the second act we read,

Four legs and two voices – a most delicate monster.
                                                                          II.2.88–9

The last phrase is comic enough as used of Caliban and as issuing from the lips of Stephano, a 'most foul' speaker. But 'delicate' evokes a more subtle incongruity by recalling characters and a world we might suppose were forgotten. Stephano is parodying Prospero when he rebukes Ariel as 'a spirit too delicate | To act her [Sycorax's] earthy and abhorred commands' and when he says,

Delicate Ariel,
I'll set thee free for this.   I.2.442–3

We have in Stephano's words not only the familiar Shakespearian balancing of comic and serious, but a counterpointing of analogies that run throughout the play. 'Delicate' as the antithesis of 'earth' points to the opposition of Ariel and Caliban and to the often recurring earth-air symbolism of *The Tempest*. 'Delicate' used of this remarkable island creature echoes also the 'delicate temperance' of which the courtiers spoke and 'the air' that 'breathes . . . here most sweetly'. 'Monster' – almost another name for Caliban – balances these airy suggestions with an allusion to the 'people of the island . . . of monstrous shape' and thereby to the strain of fantastic sea lore in *The Tempest*, which is being parodied in this scene.

So viewed, Shakespeare's analogies may perhaps seem too much like exploding nebulae in an expanding though hardly ordered universe. But Shakespeare does not 'multiply variety in a wilderness of mirrors'; he makes use of a few fairly constant analogies that can be traced through expressions sometimes the same and sometimes extraordinarily varied. And the recurrent analogies (or continuities) are linked through a key metaphor into a single metaphorical design. Shakespeare is continually prodding us – often in ways of which we are barely conscious – to relate the passing dialogue with other dialogues into and through a super-design of metaphor.

In concentrating on how the design is built up, I am not forgetting that it is a metaphorical design in a *drama*, that we are interested in how Shakespeare has linked stages in a presentation of changing human relationships. Toward the end of the chapter I hope to show how wonderfully the metaphorical design is related to the main dramatic sequence of *The Tempest*, especially in the climactic speeches of Acts IV and V.

The play moves forward, we should remember, from a scene of tempest to a final promise of 'calm seas, auspicious gales', and through a series of punishments or trials to a series of reconciliations and restorations. Although, as Dr Johnson might say, there is a 'concatenation of events' running through Prospero's 'project' and though the play has a curiously exact time schedule, there is often little chronological or logical connexion between successive dialogues or bits of action. To be sure Shakespeare has the Elizabethan conventions on his side, but the freedom of his dramatic composition in *The Tempest* never seems merely conventional or capricious because the linkage of analogy is so varied and so pervasive.

The surest proof of the pervasiveness of Shakespeare's design lies in the mere number of continuities that can be discovered in the play. But some are more important than others because they can be traced through more expressions or in more scenes and because they express analogies more closely related to the key metaphor. The six main continuities, roughly labelled to indicate their character, are: 'strange-wondrous', 'sleep-and-dream', 'sea-tempest', 'music-and-noise', 'earth-air', 'slavery-freedom', and 'sovereignty-conspiracy'.

All of these continuities appear during the second scene of Act I, which is an exposition of Shakespeare's metaphorical and dramatic designs for the entire play. Near the close of the scene, Ariel's two songs offer wonderfully concentrated expressions of both designs. 'Come unto these yellow sands' calms the 'fury' of the waves and Ferdinand's 'passion', thus charting in brief the course of the action. 'Full fathom five' is anticipatory in a very different fashion. It presents in miniature the main lines of the metaphorical design and sounds the key note of 'sea-change', Shakespeare's most direct expression of the key metaphor of *The Tempest*.

The central portion of the scene follows:

> *Enter Prospero and Miranda*
> MIRANDA If by your art, my dearest father, you have
>   Put the wild waters in this roar, allay them.
>   The sky it seems would pour down stinking pitch,
>   But that the sea, mounting to th'welkin's cheek,
>   Dashes the fire out. O, I have suffered
>   With those that I saw suffer! A brave vessel,
>   Who had, no doubt, some noble creature in her,
>   Dashed all to pieces. O, the cry did knock
>   Against my very heart! Poor souls, they perished.
>   Had I been any god of power, I would
>   Have sunk the sea within the earth, or ere
>   It should the good ship so have swallowed and
>   The fraughting souls within her.

PROSPERO   Be collected.
No more amazement. Tell your piteous heart
There's no harm done.

MIRANDA   O, woe the day!

PROSPERO   No harm.
I have done nothing but in care of thee,
Of thee, my dear one, thee my daughter, who
Art ignorant of what thou art, naught knowing
Of whence I am, nor that I am more better
Than Prospero, master of a full poor cell,
And thy no greater father.

MIRANDA   More to know
Did never meddle with my thoughts.

PROSPERO   'Tis time
I should inform thee farther. Lend thy hand,
And pluck my magic garment from me. — So,
Lie there, my art. — Wipe thou thine eyes. Have comfort.
The direful spectacle of the wrack, which touched
The very virtue of compassion in thee,
I have with such provision in mine art
So safely ordered, that there is no soul —
No, not so much perdition as an hair
Betid to any creature in the vessel
Which thou heard'st cry, which thou sawst sink. Sit down.
For thou must now know farther.

MIRANDA   You have often
Begun to tell me what I am, but stopped,
And left me to a bootless inquisition,
Concluding, 'Stay: not yet.'

PROSPERO   The hour's now come.
The very minute bids thee ope thine ear.
Obey, and be attentive. Canst thou remember
A time before we came unto this cell?
I do not think thou canst, for then thou wast not
Out three years old.

MIRANDA   Certainly, sir, I can.

PROSPERO By what? By any other house or person?
Of any thing the image tell me, that
Hath kept with thy remembrance.

MIRANDA   'Tis far off,
And rather like a dream than an assurance
That my remembrance warrants. Had I not
Four or five women once that tended me?

PROSPERO Thou hadst, and more, Miranda. But how is it
That this lives in thy mind? What seest thou else
In the dark backward and abysm of time?
If thou rememb'rest aught ere thou cam'st here,
How thou cam'st here thou mayst.

MIRANDA   But that I do not.

PROSPERO Twelve year since, Miranda, twelve year since,
Thy father was the Duke of Milan and
A prince of power.

MIRANDA   Sir, are not you my father?

PROSPERO Thy mother was a piece of virtue, and
She said thou wast my daughter; and thy father
Was Duke of Milan; and his only heir
And princess, no worse issued.

MIRANDA   O the heavens!
What foul play had we, that we came from thence?
Or blessèd was't we did?

PROSPERO   Both, both, my girl.
By foul play, as thou sayst, were we heaved thence,
But blessedly holp hither.

MIRANDA   O, my heart bleeds
To think o'th'teen that I have turned you to,
Which is from my remembrance! Please you, farther.

PROSPERO My brother and thy uncle, called Antonio –
I pray thee mark me, that a brother should
Be so perfidious! – he, whom next thyself
Of all the world I loved, and to him put
The manage of my state, as at that time
Through all the signories it was the first,
And Prospero the prime duke, being so reputed
In dignity, and for the liberal arts
Without a parallel; those being all my study,
The government I cast upon my brother,
And to my state grew stranger, being transported
And rapt in secret studies. Thy false uncle –
Dost thou attend me?

MIRANDA   Sir, most heedfully.

PROSPERO Being once perfected how to grant suits,
How to deny them, who t'advance, and who
To trash for over-topping, new created
The creatures that were mine, I say, or changed 'em,
Or else new formed 'em; having both the key
Of officer and office, set all hearts i'th'state
To what tune pleased his ear, that now he was
The ivy which had hid my princely trunk,
And sucked my verdure out on't. Thou attend'st not!

MIRANDA O, good sir, I do.

PROSPERO   I pray thee, mark me.
I, thus neglecting worldly ends, all dedicated
To closeness and the bettering of my mind
With that which, but by being so retired,
O'er-prized all popular rate, in my false brother
Awaked an evil nature; and my trust,
Like a good parent, did beget of him
A falsehood in its contrary, as great
As my trust was, which had indeed no limit,
A confidence sans bound. He being thus lorded,
Not only with what my revenue yielded,
But what my power might else exact, like one
Who having into truth, by telling of it,
Made such a sinner of his memory
To credit his own lie, he did believe
He was indeed the Duke, out o'th'substitution
And executing th'outward face of royalty,
With all prerogative. Hence his ambition growing –
Dost thou hear?

MIRANDA   Your tale, sir, would cure deafness.

PROSPERO To have no screen between this part he played
And him he played it for, he needs will be
Absolute Milan. Me, poor man, my library
Was dukedom large enough. Of temporal royalties
He thinks me now incapable, confederates –
So dry he was for sway – wi'th'King of Naples
To give him annual tribute, do him homage,
Subject his coronet to his crown, and bend

The dukedom yet unbowed — alas, poor Milan —
To most ignoble stooping.

MIRANDA   O the heavens!

PROSPERO Mark his condition and th'event; then tell me
If this might be a brother.

MIRANDA   I should sin
To think but nobly of my grandmother.
Good wombs have borne bad sons.

PROSPERO   Now the condition.
This King of Naples, being an enemy
To me inveterate, hearkens my brother's suit,
Which was, that he, in lieu o'th'premises
Of homage and I know not how much tribute,
Should presently extirpate me and mine
Out of the dukedom, and confer fair Milan,
With all the honours, on my brother. Whereon,
A treacherous army levied, one midnight
Fated to th'purpose, did Antonio open
The gates of Milan; and, i'th'dead of darkness,
The ministers for th'purpose hurried thence
Me and thy crying self.

MIRANDA   Alack, for pity.
I, not remembering how I cried out then,
Will cry it o'er again. It is a hint
That wrings mine eyes to't.

PROSPERO   Hear a little further,
And then I'll bring thee to the present business
Which now's upon's; without the which, this story
Were most impertinent.

MIRANDA   Wherefore did they not
That hour destroy us?

PROSPERO   Well demanded, wench.
My tale provokes that question. Dear, they durst not,
So dear the love my people bore me; nor set
A mark so bloody on the business, but
With colours fairer painted their foul ends.
In few, they hurried us aboard a bark,
Bore us some leagues to sea, where they prepared
A rotten carcass of a butt, not rigged,
Nor tackle, sail, nor mast. The very rats

Instinctively have quit it. There they hoist us,
To cry to th'sea that roared to us, to sigh
To th'winds, whose pity sighing back again
Did us but loving wrong.

MIRANDA   Alack, what trouble
Was I then to you!

PROSPERO   O, a cherubin
Thou wast that did preserve me. Thou didst smile,
Infusèd with a fortitude from heaven,
When I have decked the sea with drops full salt,
Under my burden groaned, which raised in me
And undergoing stomach, to bear up
Against what should ensue.

MIRANDA   How came we ashore?

PROSPERO By Providence divine.
Some food we had, and some fresh water, that
A noble Neapolitan, Gonzalo,
Out of his charity, who being then appointed
Master of this design, did give us, with
Rich garments, linens, stuffs, and necessaries
Which since have steaded much. So, of his gentleness,
Knowing I loved my books, he furnished me
From mine own library with volumes that
I prize above my dukedom.

MIRANDA   Would I might
But ever see that man!

PROSPERO   Now I arise.
Sit still, and hear the last of our sea-sorrow.
Here in this island we arrived, and here
Have I, thy schoolmaster, made thee more profit
Than other princess can, that have more time
For vainer hours, and tutors not so careful.

MIRANDA Heavens thank you for't! And now, I pray you, sir,
For still 'tis beating in my mind, your reason
For raising this sea-storm?

PROSPERO   Know thus far forth.
By accident most strange, bountiful Fortune,
Now my dear lady, hath mine enemies
Brought to this shore; and by my prescience
I find my zenith doth depend upon

411

> A most auspicious star, whose influence
> If now I court not, but omit, my fortunes
> Will ever after droop. Here cease more questions.
> Thou art inclined to sleep. 'Tis a good dullness,
> And give it way. I know thou canst not choose.   I.2.1–186

As we trace the first two continuities ('strange-wondrous', 'sleep-and-dream') the reader can appreciate how unobtrusively they emerge from the developing dramatic pattern. Prospero's narrative, with which the scene opens, tells us of the past and describes the present situation while symbolizing the quality of *The Tempest* world. Prospero explains that his enemies have come to this shore 'By accident most strange', and Miranda, who falls to sleep at the end of his tale, accounts for her lapse by saying

> The strangeness of your story put
> Heaviness in me.   I.2.306–7

Prospero's tale was strange indeed: it included a ruler 'rapt in secret studies', a 'false uncle' who 'new created | The creatures' of the state, the miraculous voyage of Prospero and Miranda (who was 'a cherubin') and their safe arrival 'By Providence divine'. This 'strangeness' is best defined by Alonso's remarks near the end of the play:

> These are not natural events; they strengthen
> From strange to stranger.
> . . . This is as strange a maze as e'er men trod,
> And there is in this business more than nature
> Was ever conduct of.   V.1.227–8, 242–4

They are 'unnatural' in a broad seventeenth-century sense of the term; that is, outside the order which includes all created things. The theme is almost constantly being played on: 'strange', 'strangely', or 'strangeness' occur altogether some seventeen times and similar meanings are echoed in 'wondrous', 'monstrous', 'divine'.

Of all the analogies of the play this is probably the vaguest, the nearest in effect to the atmospheric unity of nineteenth-century Romantic poetry. But a more precise metaphor of strangeness appears, the 'strangeness' of 'new created . . . creatures.' From the 'accident most strange' of the shipwreck we come to Alonso's ponderous woe:

> O thou mine heir
> Of Naples and of Milan, what strange fish
> Hath made his meal on thee?   II.1.113–15

and then to Trinculo's discovery of Caliban – 'A strange fish!' With a similar comic antiphony, Miranda finds Ferdinand 'A thing divine', and Ferdinand replies 'O you wonder!'; while a little later Caliban hails Trinculo as his god and cries 'Thou wondrous man'. The full significance of these strange births will appear later.

The vague 'strangeness' of the island world is closely allied to a state of sleep, both continuities appearing in Miranda's remark about the 'heaviness' that came over her while listening to Prospero's story. The feeling that we are entering on an experience of sleep-and-dream arises beautifully out of the dramatic and rhythmic texture of the opening dialogue between father and daughter. The movement of these speeches with their oddly rocking repetitions is in key with the sleepy incredibility of the events about to be described: 'Canst thou remember ... thou canst ... I can ... thy remembrance ... my remembrance ... thou rememb'rest ... Twelve year since, Miranda twelve year since ...'. Throughout the story Prospero is continually reminding Miranda to 'attend' to the telling, and it seems perfectly natural that at the end she should be 'inclined to sleep'. (Note in passing how neatly Shakespeare has broken a long narrative into dialogue and also given a distinct impression of Prospero's firmness and of Miranda's innocent dependence.) Miranda's images of the past come back to her 'rather like a dream', and Prospero seems to be drawing their story from a world of sleep, 'the dark backward and abysm of time'.

With the next scene (the mourning King and his courtiers) we meet one of Shakespeare's typical analogical progressions. The sleep which affects the courtiers is, like Miranda's, a strange 'heaviness'. Their dialogue runs down, psychologically and rhythmically, through three echoes of Miranda's words:

> GONZALO Will you laugh me asleep, for I am very heavy? ...
> SEBASTIAN Do not omit the heavy offer of it. ...

ALONSO Thank you. Wondrous heavy.
SEBASTIAN What a strange drowsiness possesses them!

II.1.191–2, 197, 201–2

The conversation that follows between the conspirators shows how Shakespeare uses an analogy to move to a new level of action and experience and to make them harmonious with what precedes and follows. Sebastian and Antonio begin by talking about actual sleep and waking: why are they not drowsy like the others? Then Antonio shifts to talking of sleepiness and alertness of mind, and from that to imagining that he sees 'a crown|Dropping' upon Sebastian's head. The wit becomes more complex as Sebastian describes Antonio's talk as 'sleepy language' – without meaning – though indicating that it does have meaning, 'There's meaning in thy snores'. This dialogue, which readers are liable to dismiss as so much Elizabethan wit, has its place within the play's metaphorical pattern. The plotting takes on a preposterous dreamy-sleepy character like that of Prospero's narrative and Miranda's recollections. Through such verbal trifling Shakespeare maintains the continuous quality of his imagined world.

References to similar wakings and sleepings, to dreams and dreamlike states, abound from here to the end of the play, where the sailors are 'brought moping' ... 'Even in a dream', and the grand awakening of all the characters is completed. But up to that point confusion between waking and sleep is the rule, being awake is never far from sleep or dream. In *The Tempest* sleep is always imminent, and more than once action ends in sleep or trance.

The witty talk of the conspirators glides from conceits of 'sleep' to conceits of 'the sea', to talk of 'standing water' and 'flowing' and 'ebbing'. The 'good Gonzalo', in consoling the King, speaks in similar figures:

It is foul weather in us all, good sir,
When you are cloudy.   II.1.143–4

Recurrent expressions of 'sea and tempest', like those of 'sleep and dream', are numerous and have a similar atmospheric value of not letting us forget the special quality of life on Prospero's island. But they also have far more important effects, for many of them become metaphors which are more precisely and more variously symbolic and which link more kinds of experience together.

By tracing two groups of 'tempest' expressions, metaphors of 'sea-swallowing' and images of 'clouds', we may understand how these more complex analogies are built up. We may also see how Shakespeare moves from narrative fact to metaphor, from image or metaphor referring only to narrative fact to metaphor rich in moral and psychological implications. As in creating the analogies of 'strangeness' and 'sleep', Shakespeare starts from a dramatic necessity: the audience must be told what the situation was in the storm scene with which the play opens, and they must learn through an actor (Miranda) how they are to take it. (See the speech on page 406.) Although there is a hint of magic in Miranda's vision of the tempest, she pictures it as a violent actuality:

> Had I been any god of power, I would
> Have sunk the sea within the earth, or ere
> It should the good ship so have swallowed and
> The fraughting souls within her.

As if there were an inner rhythm in these responses, this metaphor, like others we have been tracing, recurs in the plotting episode. Antonio is speaking of his sister Claribel, left behind in Tunis:

> she that from whom
> We all were sea-swallowed, though some cast again,
> And, by that destiny, to perform an act
> Whereof what's past in prologue, what to come,
> In yours and my discharge.   II.1.254–8

In this new context 'sea-swallowed' does several things at once. It brings back Miranda's horrified impression; but the magical nature of the storm now being known, the phrase reminds us that there was no 'sea-swallowing', no actual sinking of 'fraughting souls'. Next, with a curiously Shakespearian 'glide and a jump' via the pun on 'cast', 'sea-swallowed' merges into another metaphor (they are now 'cast' as actors in destiny's drama). 'Sea-swallowing' has become a metaphor that expresses destiny's extraordinary way of bringing Sebastian to the throne.

The irony of Antonio's words, which is clear to the audience, is made explicit later in the solemn speech in which Ariel explains the purpose of the tempest:

> You are three men of sin, whom destiny —
> That hath to instrument this lower world
> And what is in't — the never-surfeited sea
> Hath caused to belch up you. . . .   III.3.54–7

Few passages could show better how Shakespeare carried his analogies along and at the same time completely renews them. The 'belching up' recalls the wreck and the casting ashore and the earlier connexion with destiny. But the sea's action is now described in much grosser terms and with grim sarcasm, while the oddly compact grammar makes 'the never-surfeited sea' very nearly a synonym for 'destiny'. The violence though increased is now religious and moral; the imagery has become expressive of the strenuous punishment and purification of 'three men of sin'. So by the continuity of his varying metaphor Shakespeare has expressed an unbroken transition from actual storm to the storm of the soul. This sequence, which expresses both physical and metaphysical transformations, points very clearly to the key metaphor of *The Tempest*.

The recurrent cloud images present a similar sequence as they take on various symbolic meanings in the course of the play. 'Cloud' does not actually occur in the opening storm scene, but when Trinculo sees 'another storm brewing' and speaks of a 'black cloud', we are reminded of the original tempest. The cloud undergoes an appropriate change in Trinculo's speech; it 'looks like a foul bombard that would shed his liquor'. This comic cloud is very different from 'the curled clouds' on which Ariel rides, though they too are associated with storms. The clouds of Caliban's exquisite speech are those of Ariel and the deities of the masque:

> and then, in dreaming,
> The clouds methought would open, and show riches
> Ready to drop upon me. . . .   III.2.141–3

Clouds — here linked with magical riches — become in Prospero's 'cloud-capped towers' speech a symbol for the unsubstantial splendour of the world. One of the subordinate metaphors there, the 'melting into air' and the 'dissolving' of the clouds, is picked up in Prospero's later words about the courtiers:

> The charm dissolves apace.
> And as the morning steals upon the night,
> Melting the darkness, so their rising senses
> Begin to chase the ignorant fumes that mantle
> Their clearer reason.   V.1.64–8

This dissolution of night clouds (suggested also by 'fumes') is a figure for the change from madness to sanity, from evil ignorance to the clear perceptions of reason. Although the cloud images of the play are so varied, they have a common symbolic value, for whether they are clouds of tempest or of visionary riches or of the soul, they are always magically unsubstantial. The reader is led to feel some touch of likeness among experiences as different as a storm at sea, a bit of drunken whimsy, a vision of heavenly and earthly beauty, and a spiritual regeneration. The cloud sequence, as an arc of metaphor, is in perfect relation to the gradual dramatic movement from tempest and punishment to fair weather and reconciliation, the images having meanings more and more remote from any actual storm.

The 'cloud-like' change in the distracted souls of the guilty nobles was induced (as if in reminiscence of Plato) by '*Solemn music*' –

> A solemn air, and the best comforter
> To an unsettled fancy. . . .   V.1.58–9

Many of the expressions referring to music, like the stage direction above, are not explicitly metaphorical, but along with the continuities of 'sleep' and 'strangeness' they help maintain the magical character of the action. The music is always the music of spirits and always a sign of more than natural events.

The one fairly constant musical metaphor[1] in *The Tempest* is the symbolic opposition of confused noises, especially storm sounds, and harmonious music. The key word and the central impression of the opening scene is certainly 'noise'[2] in the modern sense. The impression is carried over in the first words of the next scene:

> If by your art, my dearest father, you have
> Put the wild waters in this roar, allay them.

Miranda's request is soon answered by Ariel's first song, 'The wild waves' are 'whist'. The *Solemn and strange music* heard when the *strange shapes* bring a banquet to the courtiers makes Alonso say, 'What harmony is this? My good friends, hark!' Gonzalo replies: 'Marvellous sweet music!' By contrast, when Ariel enters shortly after, in order to inform the 'three men of sin' of their punishment by the storm, there is an off-stage sound of *Thunder and lightning*. The masque vision which Ferdinand finds 'Harmonious charmingly' is rudely interrupted by *a strange, hollow, and confused noise* which symbolizes the stormy anger expressed by Prospero in the speeches that follow. When in the next scene he prepares to forgive his enemies, he abjures the 'rough magic' by which he

> called forth the mutinous winds,
> And 'twixt the green sea and the azured vault
> Set roaring war ...   V.1.42–4

As the *Solemn music* is played the clouds of ignorance 'dissolve' and so the musical metaphor, like the sea metaphor, has moved from outer to inner weather.

The music analogy has some close links with the earth-air continuity which we glanced at in the introductory chapter[3] of the book. Ferdinand, following Ariel's 'yellow sands' song, asks 'Where should this music be? I'th'air, or th'earth?' And a little later:

> This is no mortal business, nor no sound
> That the earth owes. I hear it now above me.   I.2.407–8

The connexion of air and music can never be long forgotten: Ariel and his spirits of 'thin air' are the musicians of the island.

The earth-air, Caliban-Ariel antithesis coincides at points with what we might call a slavery-freedom continuity, for Caliban is in Prospero's words both 'slave' and 'earth'. Ariel too is called a 'slave'[4] by Prospero, and for the time of the play he is as much a slave as Caliban. He is always asking for his freedom, which is at last granted, his release being symbolically expressed in the airy rovings of his final song. He flies into perpetual summer and, like air, becomes merged with the elements. By contrast, the 'High-day, freedom!' of which Caliban sings is ironically enough simply a change of masters.

The 'slaves' and 'servants' of the play suffer various kinds of imprisonment, from Ariel in his 'cloven pine' to Ferdinand's mild confinement, and before the end of Act IV everyone except Prospero and Miranda has been imprisoned in one way or another. During the course of Act V all the prisoners except Ferdinand (who has already been released) are set free, each of them by Prospero's special command.

A sovereignty-conspiracy analogy parallels very closely the slavery-freedom analogy, some of the same persons, for example Ferdinand and Caliban, appearing as both slaves and conspirators. 'That foul conspiracy | Of the beast Caliban and his confederates' is of course a parody version of the 'Open-eyed conspiracy' of Sebastian and Antonio. Ferdinand, too, is charged fantastically by Prospero with plotting against his island rule. Talk of kings and royalty turns up in many scenes, being connected usually with the denial of kingship, as in 'good Gonzalo's' speech on his golden age commonwealth where 'he would be king' and yet have 'No sovereignty'. Though no single explicit metaphor for conspiracy or usurpation is often repeated, Shakespeare rings many changes on the theme as he moves from plot to plot. Prospero's brother, we recall, is said to have 'new created | The creatures' of state. Alonso's seizure of power is called a 'substitution': 'crediting his own lies', he began to believe 'He was indeed the Duke', and from merely playing a part he went on to become 'Absolute Milan'. The figure is picked up in the somnolent dialogue of Sebastian and Antonio:

> I remember
> You did supplant your brother Prospero.   II.1.275–6

In the second of the scenes in which Caliban and his fellows plot to overthrow the island 'tyrant', Sebastian's 'supplant' is recalled with a difference:

CALIBAN I would my valiant master would destroy thee!
   I do not lie.

STEPHANO Trinculo, if you trouble him any more in's tale, by this
hand, I will supplant some of your teeth.   III.2.46–9

The figure recurs a little later in a more serious context:

> you three
> From Milan did supplant good Prospero.   III.3.70–71

In Act V, after various supplantings, serious and comic, accomplished or merely projected, all true kings are restored and all false ones dethroned.

The two continuities, sovereignty-conspiracy and slavery-freedom, are also alike in the fact that their metaphorical force is expressed through scenes that are just one step removed from allegory. The more serious of the restorations and releases convey similar kinds of moral meaning. Ferdinand's release from 'wooden slavery' signifies that he is a true lover and a true prince. In being freed from madness Alonso has escaped from 'heart's sorrow' and regained his rightful rank and a 'clear life ensuing'. Both continuities convey an impression of topsy-turvydom in the order of things, an unnatural interchange of status among creatures of every kind. Both express a return to stability after a disturbance of degree.

What then is the key metaphor through which the various continuities are linked, and how are they connected through it? Shakespeare's most direct expression of his key metaphor is 'sea-change', the key phrase of Ariel's song. But what does Shakespeare mean by 'sea-change'? Ariel sings of 'bones' being made into 'coral' and of 'eyes' becoming 'pearls'. A change 'Into something rich and strange', we now understand, is a change 'out of nature'. 'Sea-change' is a metaphor for 'magical transformation', for metamorphosis. The key metaphor of the play is 'change' in this special sense, and 'change' is the analogy common to all of the continuities we have been tracing. (I am not forgetting that they are also expressive of many other relationships, or that Shakespeare is often playing with two or three metaphors at once, as in the various figures of 'sea-swallowing'. But all are at least expressive of change, or changeableness.)

Through the first rather vague analogies we traced, of 'strangeness' and 'sleep-and-dream', numerous events and persons in the play are qualified as belonging to a realm where anything may happen. Expressions of 'strangeness' and 'sleep', like many of the references to sea and music, suggest 'far other Worlds and other Seas', where magical change is to be expected. A more particular metaphor of change is expressed through the stress on the 'strangeness' of 'new creations' and on the confusion between sleep and dream and waking. The island is a world of fluid, merging states of being and forms of life. This lack of dependable boundaries between states is also expressed by the many instances of confusion between natural and divine. Miranda says that she might call Ferdinand

> A thing divine, for nothing natural
> I ever saw so noble.   I.2.419–20

Ferdinand cannot be sure whether she is a goddess or a maid, and Caliban takes Trinculo for a 'brave god'. There is a further comic variation on this theme in Trinculo's difficulty in deciding whether to classify Caliban as fish or man, monster or devil.

But 'change' is most clearly and richly expressed through the sequence of tempest images (especially 'cloud' and 'sea-swallowed') and through the noise-music antithesis. All kinds of sounds harmonious and ugly, like the manifestations of sea and storm, are expressive of magical transformation. 'The fire cracks | Of sulphurous roaring' (imagery in which both storm and sound analogies are blended) 'infects' the courtiers' 'reason', and *Solemn music* induces the 'clearing' of their understanding. The 'music' and the 'tempest' continuities, taken together as metaphors of 'sea-change', are perhaps the most extensive of all the analogies in their organizing power. They recur often, they connect a wide diversity of experiences, and they express in symbolic form some of the main steps in the drama, in particular, the climactic moments of inner change: Ariel's revelation to the courtiers of their guilt, Alonso's first show of remorse, and the final purification.

The earth-air or Caliban-Ariel antithesis may seem to have very little to do with metamorphosis. But the relation of this theme to the key metaphor is clear and important. Air, Ariel, and his music are a blended symbol of change as against the unchanging Caliban, the 'thing of darkness'. He can be punished, but hardly humanized; he is, says Prospero,

> A devil, a born devil, on whose nature
> Nurture can never stick; on whom my pains,
> Humanely taken, all, all lost, quite lost.   IV.1.188–90

The other continuities parallel to earth-air, of slavery-freedom and conspiracy-sovereignty, are frequently expressive of major and minor changes of status among the inhabitants and temporary visitors on Prospero's island.

But the interconnexion of Shakespeare's analogies through the key metaphor cannot be adequately described, since we are able to speak of only one point of relationship at a time. We can get a better sense of the felt union of various lines of analogy in *The Tempest* by looking at the two passages where Shakespeare expresses his key metaphor most completely, the 'Full fathom five' song and Prospero's 'cloud-capped towers' speech.

Rereading Ariel's song at this point we can see how many of the main continuities are alluded to and related in the description of 'sea-change' and how the song anticipates the metaphorical design that emerges through the dialogue of the whole play. The total metaphorical pattern is to an amazing degree an efflorescence from this single crystal:

> Full fathom five thy father lies,
>   Of his bones are coral made;
> Those are pearls that were his eyes;
>   Nothing of him that doth fade
> But doth suffer a sea-change
> Into something rich and strange.
> Sea-nymphs hourly ring his knell:
> (*Burden*) Ding-dong.
> Hark! Now I hear them – Ding-dong bell.

In addition to the more obvious references to the deep sea and its powers and to the 'strangeness' of this drowning, there are indirect anticipations of other analogies. 'Fade' prefigures the 'dissolving cloud' metaphor and the theme of tempest changes, outer and inner. 'Rich', along with 'coral' and 'pearls', anticipates the opulent imagery of the dream-world passages and scenes, the 'riches | Ready to drop' on Caliban and the expressions of wealth[5] and plenty in the masque. The song closes with the nymphs tolling the bell, the transformation and the 'sea-sorrow' are expressed through sea-music. Ferdinand's comment reminds us that the song has connexions with two other lines of analogy:

> The ditty does remember my drowned father.
> This is no mortal business, nor no sound
> That the earth owes. I hear it now above me.　　I.2.406–8

The song convinces Ferdinand that he is now King of Naples (the first of the interchanges of sovereignty), and it is a 'ditty' belonging not to the 'earth', but to the 'air'.

The sense of relationship between the many continuities is still more vividly felt in the lines of Prospero's most memorable speech:

> You do look, my son, in a moved sort,
> As if you were dismayed. Be cheerful, sir.
> Our revels now are ended. These our actors,
> As I foretold you, were all spirits, and
> Are melted into air, into thin air;
> And, like the baseless fabric of this vision,
> The cloud-capped towers, the gorgeous palaces,
> The solemn temples, the great globe itself,
> Yea, all which it inherit, shall dissolve,
> And, like this insubstantial pageant faded,
> Leave not a rack behind. We are such stuff
> As dreams are made on; and our little life
> Is rounded with a sleep.　　IV.1.146–58

In Prospero's words Shakespeare has gathered all the lights of analogy into a single metaphor which sums up the metaphorical design and the essential meaning of *The Tempest*. The language evokes nearly every continuity that we have traced. 'Melted into air', 'dissolve', 'cloud', and 'rack', bring us immediately to Ariel and tempest changes, while 'vision', 'dream', and 'sleep' recall other familiar continuities. 'Revels', 'gorgeous palaces', and 'pageant' (for Elizabethans closely associated with royalty) are echoes of the kingly theme; and 'solemn' is associated particularly with the soft music of change. The 'stuff' of dreams is at once cloud-stuff (air) and cloth, both images being finely compressed in 'baseless fabric'. Taken with 'faded' these images refer obliquely to the garments so miraculously 'new-dyed ... with salt water', one of the first signs of 'sea-change' noted by Gonzalo. Within the metaphor of tempest-clearing and of cloud-like transformation, Shakespeare has included allusions to every important analogy of change in the play.

But it is through the twofold progress of the whole figure that the change metaphor is experienced and its most general meaning fully understood. We read first: that like the actors and scenery of the vision, earth's glories and man shall vanish into nothingness. Through a happy mistake we also read otherwise. By the time we have passed through 'dissolve', 'insubstantial', and 'faded', and reached 'Leave not a rack behind', we are reading 'cloud-capped towers' in reverse as a metaphor for tower-like clouds. 'Towers', 'palaces', 'temples', 'the great globe', 'all which it inherit' are now taken for cloud forms. Through a sort of Proustian merging of icon and subject, we experience the blending of states of being, of substantial and unsubstantial, or real and unreal, which is the essence of *The Tempest* metamorphosis.

Similar meanings are expressed through the closing dream figure, which grows equally out of the metaphorical context of the speech and the play. 'Rounded', we should take with Kittredge as 'surrounded', but without losing the force of round, as in Donne's 'surrounded with tears'. 'Our little life' is more than sentimental, it is our little life (microcosm) in contrast with 'the great globe' (macrocosm). There may also be an over-image in 'surrounded' of the world in classical myth and geography with its encircling ocean, sleep being the stream that 'rounds' the lesser world. In relation to the metaphorical design of the play, 'rounded with a sleep' and the notion of life ending in dreams express again the sense of confusion between sleep and dream and waking. This metaphor which completes the figure of cloud-change is Shakespeare's most perfect symbol for the closeness of states that to our daylight sense are easily separable. Although the vision here expressed goes far beyond the play, it is still a natural extension of the dramatic moment and a fulfilment of the metaphor that has been implicit since the noisy opening lines of *The Tempest*.

But if Shakespeare's total metaphor is in a sense present everywhere, it is also a design that develops in close relation to the main dramatic movement of the play. As we have noted more than once, a particular metaphor will be varied to fit a new dramatic situation and so serve to express the situation more fully and to anticipate the next step in the development of the drama. The best example of this adaptation of metaphor comes in a speech in which Shakespeare seems to be playing capriciously with his noise-music theme. At first sight the passage seems inconsistent with the symbolic contrast between storm noise and music:

> ALONSO O, it is monstrous, monstrous!
>   Methought the billows spoke, and told me of it;
>   The winds did sing it to me; and the thunder,
>   That deep and dreadful organ-pipe, pronounced
>   The name of Prosper: it did bass my trespass. III.3.97–101

It is admittedly odd that the confused noise of the tempest should, in Alonso's soul, compose a harmony – however gloomy – but the paradox fits in perfectly with the developing structure of the play. Alonso has just been told by Ariel that the storm had a purpose as an instrument of destiny. Since at this moment remorse first appears in the play and the inner clearing begins, it is exactly right that the storm sounds should seem harmonious and so point forward to the events of the fourth and fifth acts. No use of metaphor in *The Tempest* reveals more clearly Shakespeare's exact sense of the movement of his drama, of the changing human relations and feelings he is presenting.

In building up his metaphorical design, Shakespeare prepares us for the moment in *The Tempest* when the major shift in dramatic relationships takes place. The moment comes in the speech in which Prospero describes the behaviour of the King and the courtiers as they slowly return from madness to sanity. The first important step toward this climax, Alonso's acknowledgement of his guilt, was expressed through a metaphor combining both sea and musical changes. The next step, Ferdinand's release from his tempest-trials and from dream-like enchantment, is expressed through the masque, which is an elaborate dramatization of metamorphosis, Ariel's 'meaner fellows', 'the rabble', being now transformed into majestic Olympian goddesses. Once again, familiar continuities appear, and again they are transformed to fit a new occasion. 'Earth' for example, is no longer 'barren place and fertile', but the earth enriched by human cultivation and symbolized now by Ceres – not by Caliban, who is 'nature resisting nurture'. Iris summons this new Earth in the gorgeous speech beginning 'Ceres, most bounteous lady, thy rich leas', lines in which we hear a quite new majesty of tone and movement. The couplet form sets the dialogue apart from human speech, while the longer periods, the added stresses, the phrasal balancings are especially appropriate to 'that large utterance of the early gods'. (Here is one of many instances of how Shakespeare adapts his sound patterns to his metaphorical and dramatic designs.) Prospero's visionary speech that ends the 'revels' is not simply a concentration of metaphor without reference to the dramatic development. It announces the changes to come, it gives a rich expression of their meaning, and it anticipates the dream-like flux of the psychological events of the last act.

If we now read Prospero's words in Act V, in which he describes the great changes as they take place, we see many references back to Shakespeare's metaphorical preparation for this moment. We also realize that various lines of action and various lines of analogy are converging almost simultaneously. The speech opens with Prospero's farewell to his art, after which he turns his thoughts to 'restoring the senses' of the courtiers, whom Ariel has just gone to release:

> A solemn air, and the best comforter
> To an unsettled fancy, cure thy brains,
> Now useless, boiled within thy skull. There stand,
> For you are spell-stopped.
> Holy Gonzalo, honourable man,
> Mine eyes, ev'n sociable to the show of thine,
> Fall fellowly drops. The charm dissolves apace.
> And as the morning steals upon the night,

Melting the darkness, so their rising senses
Begin to chase the ignorant fumes that mantle
Their clearer reason. O good Gonzalo,
My true preserver, and a loyal sir
To him thou follow'st, I will pay thy graces
Home both in word and deed. Most cruelly
Didst thou, Alonso, use me and my daughter.
Thy brother was a furtherer in the act.
Thou art pinched for't now, Sebastian. Flesh and blood,
You, brother mine, that entertained ambition,
Expelled remorse and nature, whom with Sebastian –
Whose inward pinches therefore are most strong –
Would here have killed your king, I do forgive thee,
Unnatural though thou art. Their understanding
Begins to swell, and the approaching tide
Will shortly fill the reasonable shore
That now lies foul and muddy. Not one of them
That yet looks on me, or would know me. Ariel,
Fetch me the hat and rapier in my cell.
I will discase me, and myself present
As I was sometime Milan. Quickly, spirit!
Thou shalt ere long be free.   V.1.58–87

If this is a climactic moment, what changes in dramatic relationships are taking place, what is happening dramatically? The 'men of sin', like Ferdinand, have come to the end of the trials which began with the storm and continued through various 'distractions'. Now, as Prospero explains, they are undergoing a moral as well as a mental regeneration, they are 'pinched' with remorse and are being forgiven. The twofold regeneration is further dramatized in the speeches that follow: 'Th'affliction' of Alonso's mind 'amends', he resigns Prospero's dukedom and 'entreats' him to pardon his 'wrongs'.

But these are the prose facts, the bare bones of the changes in dramatic relationships. We cannot feel the peculiar quality of what is taking place or grasp its meaning apart from the metaphorical language through which it is being expressed. And the expressions acquire their force and precision from the whole metaphorical preparation we have been tracing. The courtiers' senses are restored by an 'airy charm', by magic similar to that which was worked by Ariel and his spirits. The allusions to 'heavenly music' and 'A solemn air', in contrast to the 'rough magic' that Prospero has abjured, remind us that these changes will be musically harmonious, like the songs of Ariel, and not noisy and confused like the storm sent to punish these men and reveal their 'monstrous' guilt. Toward the end of the speech, the imagery recalls the tempest metaphor, but it is altered so as to express the mental and moral change that is taking place. The return of understanding is like an approaching tide that covers the evidence of a storm (both 'foul' and 'muddy' have storm associations from earlier occurrences).

But the metaphor that best expresses this clearing is the one for which the preparation has been most complete:

> The charm dissolves apace.
> And as the morning steals upon the night,
> Melting the darkness, so their rising senses
> Begin to chase the ignorant fumes that mantle
> Their clearer reason.

'Dissolving' and 'melting' and 'fumes' take us back at once to the grand transformations of the masque speech, to the earlier cloud transformations both serious and comic; and they take us back further to the association of clouds with magical tempests, inner storms, and clearing weather. We read of the moral and psychological transformations with a present sense of these analogies. They are qualified for us as a dream-like dissolution of tempest clouds, as events in the 'insubstantial' region where reality and unreality merge.

It is through such links that Shakespeare concentrates at this climactic moment the fullest meaning of his key metaphor. There is of course no separation in the reader's experience between the dramatic fact and the metaphorical qualification. The images that recur in Prospero's speech take us back to felt qualities, but to felt qualities embedded in particular dramatic contexts. 'Melting', for example, carries us to the spirit-like dissolution of 'spirits ... melted, into air, into thin air'; but it also reminds us of the masque pageantry and of Prospero's calming of Ferdinand's fears. We hear

Prospero's soothing and mysterious tone in both the earlier and later uses of the word. The dramatic links and the analogical links are experienced at once, which is to say that metaphorical design and dramatic design are perfectly integrated.

We can now realize that metamorphosis is truly the key metaphor to the *drama*, and not the key metaphor to a detachable design of decorative analogies. Through the echoes in Prospero's speech of various lines of analogy, Shakespeare makes us feel each shift in dramatic relationships, as a magical transformation, whether it is the courtiers' return to sanity, or Prospero's restoration to his dukedom, or Ariel's flight into perpetual summer. While all of the 'slaves' and 'prisoners' are being freed, and while all of the 'sovereigns' are being restored, the sense of magical change is never wholly lost. The union of drama and metaphor in *The Tempest* is nowhere more complete than in the last act of the play.

The larger meaning of Shakespeare's total design, which was anticipated in the cloud and dream metaphor of Prospero's visionary speech, is most clearly and fully expressed in these final transformations. In a world where everything may become something else, doubts naturally arise, and in the swift flow of change the confusion about what is and what is not becomes fairly acute. When Prospero 'discases' himself and appears as Duke of Milan, Gonzalo says with understandable caution:

> Whether this be
> Or be not, I'll not swear.

And Prospero answers:

> You do yet taste
> Some subtleties o'th'isle, that will not let you
> Believe things certain.   V.1.122–5

Whereas in the earlier acts the characters had often accepted the unreal as real (spirits, shipwrecks, drownings, visions), they now find it difficult to accept the real as truly real. The play concludes with their acceptance of the unexpected change to reality. But for the spectator there remains the heightened sense of the 'thin partitions' that 'do divide' these states. The world that common sense regards as real, of order in nature and society and of sanity in the individual, is a shimmering transformation of disorder. 'We shall all be changed, in a moment, in the twinkling of an eye.' (This or something like it is as near as we can come to describing the total attitude conveyed by *The Tempest*.)

Thus *The Tempest* is, like Marvell's 'Garden', a Metaphysical poem of metamorphosis,[6] though the meaning of change is quite different for the two writers. It is worth noting too that Shakespeare 'had Ovid in his eye', a fact that is obvious from the echoes of Golding's famous translation. There could be no better proof of Shakespeare's maturity than the contrast between the 'sweet witty' Ovidianism of *Venus and Adonis* and the metaphorical design of *The Tempest*, which gives philosophic meaning to a drama of Ovidian metamorphosis. We remember 'A lily prisoned in a gaol of snow' as an isolated 'beauty', but hardly as an apt symbol of the amorous relations of Venus and Adonis, or as symbolic of some larger meaning in their story. (Indeed a 'gaol of snow' is rather inept for the fervid goddess of the poem.) 'Those are pearls that were his eyes' revives Ariel's sea-music, Ferdinand's melancholy, and a world of fantasy and transshifting states of being. The increased concentration in meaning of the image from *The Tempest* is a sign of a growth in the command of language which is command of life for a poet. As Arnold said of Wordsworth, Shakespeare now 'deals with more of *life*' and 'he deals with *life*, as a whole, more powerfully'. His maturity and power appear in the variety of experience so perfectly harmonized through the imaginative design of *The Tempest*.

NOTES

1. The music and tempest metaphors have been traced in a very different fashion and with quite different aims by G. Wilson Knight in *The Shakespearian Tempest* (1932). My analysis (which I had worked out before reading Professor Knight's essay) has a more limited purpose: to show a continuity of analogy and a development of metaphor parallel to that of the other continuities I have traced.

2. The scene is full of expressions such as: '*A tempestuous noise of thunder and lightning heard*', 'roarers', 'command these elements to

silence', '*A cry within*', 'A plague upon this howling! They are louder than the weather, or our office', 'insolent noisemaker', '*A confused noise within*', etc.

3. See *The Fields of Light*, pages 13, 14.
4. Both are called 'slaves' in I.2., the scene of metaphorical exposition.
5. 'Rich' and 'riches' occur no less than five times in the masque.
6. See the excellent analysis of the poem in M. C. Bradbrook and M. G. Lloyd Thomas, *Andrew Marvell* (1940), pages 59–64.

from *The Fields of Light* (1951)
by Reuben A. Brower, pages 95–122

TWENTY-FIVE

The Tempest on the Stage

David William

THE stage history of *The Tempest* is one of frequent revivals and invariable popularity. Yet most productions differ little from each other, either in their interpretations of the play, or in methods of staging it. For all its formal simplicity, it is a difficult play, and most producers have taken (and continue to take) the easiest (though not always the least expensive) way with it. We are fairly safe in expecting 'a liberal provision of the scenic and musical embellishments which have long been deemed essential in an efficient representation of the play' – a tradition which a critic of a production in 1871 evidently regarded as already well established.

Whilst modern productions may not quite emulate Charles Kean's in 1857, in which 'the scenic appliances are of a more extensive nature than have been attempted in any theatre in Europe' (though a production at Stratford in 1951 ran it fairly close), the play's visual opportunities are still apt to be the chief priority. Nor, of course, should it be doubted that a play so rich and suggestive in atmosphere warrants the highest possible imaginative treatment by both producers and designers; yet how rarely this is achieved. In no play is the visual trap more tempting or more dangerous. Regardless of what belongs to a frippery, and lacking in confidence in the demands which the play makes on the ear (especially in the big exposition at the beginning), producers offer a visual accompaniment that more often than not distracts from the action instead of illuminating it. This, and a tendency to sentimentality (particularly in the sub-plot) are the most recurrent blemishes in modern productions. Time and again, the strength and violence that lie so near the surface of the play are submerged in layers of charm and hocus-pocus; the urgent directness of action, which moves from beginning to end with such narrative skill, is interrupted and weakened by exaggerated detail and peripheral fuss.[1]

The Tempest is not only a difficult play; it is uniquely beautiful; and its difficulty is that its beauty lies principally in the region of its interior action. The climaxes of *Othello* or *Twelfth Night*, for example, are physically demonstrable; there is explicitly significant action to establish them; but the climax of *The Tempest* is a moral decision. The moment occurs early in Act V. Ariel ends his description of the 'distracted' lords with the strangely personal reflection:

> Your charm so strongly works 'em
> That if you now beheld them your affections
> Would become tender.
> PROSPERO   Dost thou think so, spirit?
> ARIEL Mine would, sir, were I human.
> PROSPERO   And mine shall.
> Hast thou, which art but air, a touch, a feeling
> Of their afflictions, and shall not myself,
> One of their kind, that relish all as sharply,
> Passion as they, be kindlier moved than thou art?
> Though with their high wrongs I am struck to th'quick,
> Yet with my nobler reason 'gainst my fury
> Do I take part. The rarer action is
> In virtue than in vengeance. They being penitent,
> The sole drift of my purpose doth extend
> Not a frown further.   V.1.17–30

The reluctance to see in this the stuff of drama, different in kind, but equal in dramatic effect to, say, the death of Desdemona or the meeting of Viola and Sebastian, narrows the range of available theatrical experience (on both sides of the footlights).

Prospero's renunciation of vengeance is the resolution of the play; everything else leads up to it, and upon it the destinies of all the characters (himself included) depend. The creative objective, therefore – to invoke Stanislavsky's useful terminology – is 'To pardon the deceiver'. Hence, the guiding aim of any responsible production must be to organize the action of the play (main plot and sub-plot) so that it is related, however indirectly, to this moment. Only thus can such a climax achieve its explicit dramatic effect.

Like the great tragic heroes, Prospero is a man of strong passions, but, unlike them, does not yield to their promptings. With his enemies entirely in his power, he discards that power entirely. It is not an easy victory; he knows what must ensue from it – not only the pardoning of the guilty, but his own return to the world of governments and younger brothers. The ending of *The Tempest* is very moving, not least because it is so reticent. Beyond the stated issue lies a sense of deprivation as poignant as it is necessary. The liberation of Ariel seems to involve a contraction of Prospero's personality which he both recognizes and accepts. It is as if the powers of the spirit, vested in him on the island, cannot operate in Milan, for Milan bodies forth the real world, in which the life of the spirit is at all points compromised. For one who has seen through the deceptions of that world, a return to it is indeed a sacrifice, but the rising generation find it beautiful, and while their vision lasts, they must put it to the test of practical experience. Beyond this, there is, perhaps, the more ironic hint that even the life of the spirit is susceptible of corruption, and the 'thing of darkness', which Prospero acknowledges his, may serve as a reminder that, for those seeking the consummation of the spirit of this life, there can be no final satisfaction. So the staff must be broken, the book drowned, and the journey home begun while there is yet promise of calm seas and auspicious gales.

The possibility of some such dramatic experience, then, lies at the heart of this play. Though it eschews the ranges of tragedy, it charts a no less powerful landscape. It is the noblest of the revenge-plays.

The Unfolding of the Play

An analysis of *The Tempest*'s structural craftsmanship may indicate why Shakespeare gave it such a form and how that form determines its theatrical qualities.

With the exception of *The Comedy of Errors*, it is the shortest of the plays. It has fewer scenes than any. The action is continuous and confined; in fact, the unities of time and place are observed more stringently than any formulation demands. These facts alone bespeak a deliberate restriction of subject unusual for Shakespeare. Moreover, nearly a quarter of the play is devoted to exposition. That is a very high proportion – too high for theatrical comfort, if it is *mere* exposition. Fortunately, it is not, for it is animated and sustained by continually inventive characterization, and integrated with the establishment of the physical and moral background of the play.

The play opens with violent action: '*A tempestuous noise of thunder and lightning heard. Enter a Shipmaster and a Boatswain*'. The first four lines tell us where we are. The problems of staging this scene are easily outweighed by its advantages as an opening-scene. Not only is it exciting in itself (what shipwreck would not be?), but its very violence of incident arrests the audience's attention at the outset, so that it is readier for the long exposition than it would have been if the play began at I.2. Shakespeare's method with his audience is akin, in fact, to the schoolmaster's who sends his class twice round the playing-field before a lesson. A further merit of the scene, of course, is the introduction of nearly half the *dramatis personae*. Although Shakespeare allows himself little time for assigning appropriate dialogue to the respective characters, what chances arise are aptly taken. Antonio's arrogant indifference and Gonzalo's humorous fortitude are immediately planted. Even if we are unable to identify the members of the royal party (and if the stage-action is as coherently frantic as it should be, that is very likely), we shall recognize them as soon as they reappear in their next scene.

The temperature of the play, then, at its opening, registers well above normal. The second scene begins at a scarcely lower pitch, with Miranda's impassioned anguish. Prospero's affectionate reassurances begin to relax the tension:

> Be collected.
> No more amazement. Tell your piteous heart
> There's no harm done.   I.2.13–15

But the generous distress needs repeated assurances. These are tenderly forthcoming before Prospero begins to divert her attention to more pressing matter:

> No harm.
> I have done nothing but in care of thee,
> Of thee, my dear one, thee my daughter, who
> Art ignorant of what thou art, naught knowing
> Of whence I am, nor that I am more better
> Than Prospero, master of a full poor cell,
> And thy no greater father.   I.2.15–21

Within the first twenty-five lines of the scene, Shakespeare establishes Miranda's instinctive unselfishness and innocence, and Prospero's love for her, blended with a protective authority (note his eight imperatives in less than twice as many lines), and his magic power.

The temper of the scene is now one of eager moderation. Soon it is to change again. Prospero begins his remarkable story. His sense of the momentousness of the occasion is touchingly attested by the solicitude with which he leads Miranda to the dark backward, gently probing in the recesses of her own memory to assist her response to what must follow. He spares nothing in his care of her, but forgets himself, for, as he draws nearer to the picture of the past, its contents begin to unsettle him:

> The direful spectacle of the wrack, which touched
> The very virtue of compassion in thee,
> I have with such provision in mine art
> So safely ordered, that there is no soul –
> No, not so much perdition as an hair
> Betid to any creature in the vessel
> Which thou heard'st cry, which thou sawst sink.
>
> I.2.26–32

At this point, the editors, quivering with indignant vigilance over so sound a text, scent trouble. A solitary anacoluthon is arraigned, brought to trial, and sentenced as an impostor. Dr Johnson leads the way, emending 'soule' to 'soil'; the editor of the

New Temple Shakespeare, defending, in turn, the acceptance of the emendation by the editors of the New Cambridge Shakespeare, justifies his position as follows: 'there are of course plenty of anacolutha in Shakespeare; *but Prospero is in no sort of excitement or disorder of mind*; on the contrary he is explaining with calm satisfaction how well his schemes have worked; and a violent anacoluthon would be undramatic.' The italics are mine, and I suggest the Prospero therein described is not Shakespeare's.

A little later in the same scene he tells Miranda:

> I find my zenith doth depend upon
> A most auspicious star, whose influence
> If now I court not, but omit, my fortunes
> Will ever after droop.   I.2.181–4

That is to say, the moment is critical, and therefore hardly conducive to a mood of 'calm satisfaction'. Nor is this all. For twelve years Prospero has lived alone with the secret of his dukedom. At last he has resolved to break the long silence, to emerge from the isolation which such a secrecy must impose. His further intentions for Miranda are, for the time being, withheld from her, but they are in his mind: if she is to become the Queen of Naples, she must be shown the darkest corners of the house into which she marries. She must also know her own father. Little wonder, then, if the hand that lifts the family skeleton from its long resting-place begins to tremble. He has made the attempt before, but given up, 'Concluding, "Stay: not yet"'. But 'The hour's now come'. Regaining outward composure, and searching the warranty of her remembrance to its little limit, he begins the brave and painful recapitulation:

> Twelve year since, Miranda, twelve year since,
> Thy father was the Duke of Milan and
> A prince of power.   I.2.53–5

As the story develops, so its narrator's feeling heightens. The pace of the speeches quickens, the syntax twists and turns in abrupt, sharp phrases; inversions and subordinate clauses pile up, as, for the first time, he publishes his remembrance of the old high wrongs.

The agitation and urgency beget an extraordinary compression of diction:

> To have no screen between this part he played
> And him he played it for, he needs will be
> Absolute Milan. Me, poor man, my library
> Was dukedom large enough. Of temporal royalties
> He thinks me now incapable, confederates –
> So dry he was for sway – wi'th'King of Naples
> To give him annual tribute, do him homage,
> Subject his coronet to his crown, and bend
> The dukedom yet unbowed – alas, poor Milan –
> To most ignoble stooping.   I.2.107–16

The actor's task here is to suggest the growing opposition between the rational wish to tell the story with objective truth and the passion which the recollected experience gradually engenders. As the story hastens to its climax, we may trace the emerging paradox which is to exercise Prospero's imagination throughout the play – the dual experience of the blackness of the corrupted nature and the innate goodness of the innocent soul.

Dispatching Miranda to sleep, Prospero summons his servant to continue the work already begun. Even for those who know the play, Ariel's first entrance ought never to fail of its magic in the theatre. Personally, I find myself waiting for it (in all but the dreariest productions) with no less excitement than for the first appearance of the Ghost in *Hamlet*. It is finely situated. The material background of the play has been established: it is now time to extend its spiritual dimensions. Prospero's invocation prepares us for no ordinary creature:

> Come away, servant, come! I am ready now.
> Approach, my Ariel! Come!   I.2.187–8

And back, as if down the wind, comes the unearthly answer, with sustained monosyllables and echoing long vowels (what a contrast to Caliban's response to *his* summons):

> All hail, great master! Grave sir, hail!

If an adequate acoustic perspective can be achieved, these seven words surely warrant an off-stage delivery, for their verbal magic, in the context, will be strongest if the appeal is solely to the ear.

Nothing daunted by having managed nearly two hundred lines of exposition, Shakespeare embarks on more. Ariel's dramatic function is established, and, by means of the violent extremes of love and anger which the relationship of master and servant encompasses, Shakespeare reaches further into the depths of Prospero's nature. It is only the inattentive who will find his treatment of Ariel unduly harsh. Under the circumstances, his reaction to Ariel's display of reluctance is understandable. Exclusively, and for the best of reasons, committed to his zenith, he cannot at this juncture think of anticipating Ariel's liberation. That, and of course the power of his love, stretch his already tensed nerves beyond the limits of moderation. Also, the scene is a fine example of Shakespeare's craftsmanship (never more resourceful than when surmounting technical difficulties). For the reproach of master to servant provides a dramatically legitimate opportunity to tell the audience the story of Ariel's duress. The device, if properly managed by the actors, should be entirely successful. Finally, the tenderness with which Prospero dispatches Ariel leaves no doubt as to the true state of his feelings.

The recapitulatory device is repeated with audacious success in the scene with Caliban. The appearance of a new character (and such a character) revitalizes the audience's attention, so that it may receive the last (and shortest) of the three expositions. Once again, of course, there is much more to the scene than mere narrative. First, there is a finely inventive touch to heighten the very moment of Caliban's approach. We have already heard his voice, terse, savage, and resentful: 'There's wood enough within.' Prospero repeats the summons:

> Come forth, I say! There's other business for thee.
> Come, thou tortoise! When?   I.2.315–16

And suddenly, instead of the lumbering monster we expect, the incarnation of debased nature, there flashes across the stage its very opposite: '*Enter Ariel like a water-nymph*'. He pauses for his master's bidding and is gone. Nothing could more potently charge our first experience of Caliban than this exquisite juxtaposition.

To the social and spiritual picture of the island so far projected Caliban now adds the darker tones of guilt and brutality. It is surely part of Shakespeare's intention that the conflict with Prospero is not one-sided, that there is more to it than one of them being 'right' and the other 'wrong'. As the wrath of Prospero fills the stage once more, an ironic undertone accompanies it. For Caliban is his failure, and he knows it. The account which Prospero now gives of his attempts at regenerating the monster is not unfair, though its blame may seem a trifle over-urged:

> I endowed thy purposes
> With words that made them known. But thy vile race,
> Though thou didst learn, had that in't which good natures
> Could not abide to be with. Therefore wast thou
> Deservedly confined into this rock, who hadst
> Deserved more than a prison.[2]   I.2.357–62

But it is not the full account, and comes the terrible answer to repudiate it:

> You taught me language, and my profit on't
> Is, I know how to curse.   I.2.363–4

To the impotent fury of that accusation the raiser of tempests has no fit answer:

> Hag-seed, hence!
> Fetch us in fuel – and be quick, thou'rt best,
> To answer other business I.2.365–7

Regulated severity masks the remorse and frustration which is to inform his consciousness of Caliban until the final dispensation.

Caliban's exit completes the exposition, leaving Shakespeare free to develop the external action. The mood is immediately lightened. The transition is consummate: as Caliban crawls, muttering, from view, the song of Ariel ushers in the play's ideal of romantic love. The music's effect on Ferdinand – a lyrical dissolvement of his sense of the actual – leads to the haunting poignancy of 'Full fathom five'. As the sea-nymphs add their burden, Shakespeare matches the rapture of the senses with the magic of his language. Prospero bends over the unsuspecting Miranda, and, with exquisite under-statement, delivers her to her destiny:

> The fringèd curtains of thine eye advance,
> And say what thou seest yond.   I.2.409–10

Not since the ball of the Capulets has Shakespeare staged so wonderful a lover's meeting.

Nothing remains of the occasion but for Prospero to impose that test of love, 'lest too light winning | Make the prize light', which calls up the long tradition of patient lovers hallowed in literature since Jacob served seven years for Rachel.

The scene ends with a glimpse of another ideal:

> Thou shalt be as free
> As mountain winds; but then exactly do
> All points of my command.   I.2.499–501

And after, perhaps, a moment's gaze at the vanishing figure, Prospero turns, and with a brave assumption of severity, marshals the lovers on their way.

The next scene reintroduces the royal party. By dramatizing their response to the situation, it establishes both their relationships with each other, and their respective places in the moral pattern of the play. Gonzalo's zealous, if unsuccessful, consolation of the King, coupled with the courteous tolerance with which he endures the insults of his other superiors, endorses the sympathetic disposition of Prospero's account of him in the previous scene. Alonso, accessary before the fact of Prospero's banishment, now comes before us as a bereaved father, and his numbed distress speaks instantly of better scruples, which later scenes are to confirm. Sebastian's spiteful recriminations and the cheapness of his badinage arouse immediate aversion. Adrian and Francisco barely engage attention. The strongest figure in the group is the darkest – Antonio. In him, we are to find the continuing principle of corruption, its appetite having grown by what it has fed on. To usurpation and extrusion he now proposes to add murder. The duologue in which he tempts Sebastian is brilliantly managed –

from the deliberate hesitancy of its inception, through the confident case with which he dismantles the weaker man's objections, to the arrogant indifference of its climax:

> but I feel not
> This deity in my bosom. Twenty consciences
> That stand 'twixt me and Milan, candied be they,
> And melt ere they molest.   II.1.282–5

One last twitch of pusillanimity from Sebastian gives Ariel his cue to wake Gonzalo, and the plot is foiled. The power of the island has declared itself to the purest consciousness among those present, and prompts immediate action. Alonso's assurance of his son's death weakens, and he leads his companions on a further search, whilst Ariel departs to bear fresh evidence for his master's judgement.

The image of corruption in its most sophisticated form now gives place to one in its most primitive. The next scene opens with Caliban's curse on Prospero. Through its blend of hatred and terror we perceive the glimmerings of that frustrated sensibility which adds depth to the perspective of Shakespeare's portrayal.

With Trinculo's entrance the language drops into graphic prose. The gaberdine antics and the reunion with Stephano provide an energetic comic diversion from the sustained seriousness of the main plot, whilst the irony of Caliban's transfer of allegiance and vision of freedom should satisfy the impatient moralist. The business which Shakespeare has in hand for these three does not allow him much time to spare for comic relief; but he does not waste his opportunities, and the physical humour of the scene should be as uninhibited as the text implies.

Between this scene and III.2 Shakespeare interposes the brief idyll of the love-scene. Here, both Prospero and the audience are given honourable guarantee of the worth of Miranda's purchaser. Then we return to the sub-plot, its protagonists now well-advanced in liquor, an easy prey to the temptations of lust and ambition that now confront them. Producers should guard against a tendency to sentimentalize this scene. *Pace* the *mores* of English stage-culture, not all drunkards are endearing: the brutality and cowardice of these are an integral part of their characters, which alcohol merely releases. Not since *Measure for Measure* has Shakespeare given us such morally loaded comedy. While the murderous plot is being formed, the magic of the island intervenes, and Shakespeare draws a powerful irony between the selfish insensitivity of the humans' reaction to the music and the poignant fantasy of the monster's. Fortified by Caliban's example, butler and jester follow the strange taborer, and, like their masters, draw closer to the waiting judgement.

With the next scene, the urgency of the main plot is restored. From now on the play moves in a sublimity of atmosphere which is sustained with very little interruption until the end. As the royal people advance upon the tempting viands, the island puts forth a mightier magic, and the guilty men are served with their tremendous indictment. (That it is only they who hear it is proved by Gonzalo's astonished interrogation of Alonso after the banquet vanishes.) Alonso's reply, attesting the witness which the elements themselves have borne against his guilt, is a magnificent prelude to the high miracle that awaits them. In suicidal despair he rushes from the place. Characteristically, the 'distraction' of Antonio and Sebastian takes a different form. Excluding the slightest hint of remorse, it expresses itself in aggressive defiance, as, with drawn and futile swords, they follow the King. Gonzalo remains to point the moral (more accurately than he suspects) to the attendant lords, and then, fearful of ensuing violence, they hurry in pursuit. The magic circle is not far off.

Here, I suggest, the interval, if there must be one, should come. But with so short a play, it is a questionable amenity. Played with proper pace, the performance should last little over two hours, and the advantages which accrue from such uninterrupted concentration are well worth considering. But if the demands on the audience's powers of attention (not to mention the bar receipts) seem to warrant an interval, this seems the best place. Certainly it can come no later, for two thirds of the play is already done. Some producers put it at the end of III.1, but this breaks the continuity of the sub-plot which – though it can afford the brief intermission of the love-scene – is not strong enough to sustain an additional delay. It also involves opening the second act on a weak note. Another alternative interval – after III.2 – is no less unsatisfactory, as it involves too long a time-lapse between the appearances of the royal party. With so concentrated a play it is important to preserve at least an impression of continuous action, and the least damaging pause seems to be after III.3. Producers, of course, are not above contriving their own artificial intervals. A production at the Old Vic several years ago, for example, transposed III.3.95–111 to follow line 83, and cut the lines:

> And in these fits I leave them while I visit
> Young Ferdinand, whom they suppose is drowned,
> And his and mine loved darling.   III.3.92–5

Then, on the phrase 'my meaner ministers', a few lines earlier in the same speech, Prospero was joined by his 'shapes', who, at the cue 'They now are in my power', shrieked and writhed with felicitatory relish as the curtain fell. The object of this nonsense was to gerrymander an 'effective' act-ending, but its achievement was to diminish the grandeur of the scene, and, in particular, to stress Prospero's prestidigitation at the expense of his humanity.

If, therefore, the first act ends after III.3, the second can begin firmly with the betrothal of Ferdinand and Miranda. From this moment Prospero never leaves the stage. The dramatic demands on him are many and various, and test his power and authority to the utmost. But all through – the betrothal, the invocation of the goddesses, the imminent arrival of his old enemies – everything is encompassed with royal composure. There is a moment's wavering, as he suddenly recalls yet another claim on his attention:

> I had forgot that foul conspiracy
> Of the beast Caliban and his confederates
> Against my life.   IV.1.139–41

But his recovery is prompt and disciplined, and brings with it a touching solicitude for the younger hearts:

> Bear with my weakness; my old brain is troubled.
> Be not disturbed with my infirmity.
> If you be pleased, retire into my cell
> And there repose . . .   IV.1.159–62

And so, with the frustration of Caliban's plot ensured, he is now ready to receive his guests. Perhaps not quite as ready as he seems, for, at Ariel's delicate prompting, he must first make his great renunciation. Up to this moment, there must surely be some doubt in his mind (and hence, the audience's) about the kind of dispensation to be made. In the event, it could not be nobler. Indeed its disinterested magnanimity transcends the barrenness of some of the responses. For although Alonso's penitence is full and imaginative, and Caliban himself at last covets grace and wisdom, no word of remorse falls from the lips of the principal offenders. And this is surely Shakespeare's dramatic intention. The ultimate impenitence of Antonio and Sebastian is all of a piece with their behaviour throughout the play. Even when addressed directly by Prospero, they say nothing in reply, and this final silence, broken elsewhere by no more than an occasional flippancy, has its own dramatic effect. But that effect is largely ironic, and I have seldom seen it expressed on the stage. In the very moment of his spiritual triumph, Prospero is brought face to face with the harsher and irreconcilable values of the world.

But his resolution does not alter. With ineffable tenderness, he gives Ariel a last assignment, and ushers the royal party into his cell. He turns before following them (what better moment for the breaking of the staff?), and then, faced only with the dissolution of the strongest spell of all, comes down to speak the Epilogue.

The end of *The Tempest* is so rich in feeling that it may accommodate many kinds of meaning. Only a perverse response, for instance, can refuse to see, within the orbit of Prospero's abdication, some image of Shakespeare's farewell to the creative life. Yet there is far more to the end of the play than this, and we must be careful how explicitly we state the ideas it seems to contain. Too deliberate an unravelling of the threads of poetic suggestion may result in a dramatized lecture instead of a high imaginative experience. Provided he is sure of his territory, a producer may be wiser to make the appeal to the audience indirectly, and thus, by avoiding too explicit a committal of their sympathies, capture them far more securely. Conversely, the merits of letting the play speak for itself are nullified if the company is unaware of its fundamental utterance.

The vague approach has little chance of arrival. The ideal production is perhaps a rarity we may never encounter, but, at least, an attentive and talented enthusiasm is the indispensable point of departure.

For only thus can an audience discern, through this composition of tempest and calm, anger and gentleness, the remorse of the sovereign intelligence and the tormented aspiration of the spirit imprisoned by the senses, the sacrificial love of the old for the young, and the self-increasing love of the young for one another, the assertion of happiness ever after and the negation of the noblest by the basest – only thus can it apprehend the vision of a great dramatic masterpiece, and the victorious sanity of its creator.

The Verse and its Speaking

Much confusion seems to exist about the speaking of Shakespearian verse. Complaints at the inability of most modern actors to speak it even adequately are frequent, and sometimes justified. But any critical postulates on the matter which imply a distinction between good verse-speaking and good acting are quite adrift. Shakespeare's dramatic poetry is drama at the same time as it is poetry, and any delivery which tends to separate the two is at fault. The self-indulgent arabesques of the 'voice beautiful' are no less deplorable than the rhythmic fractures sustained in the cause of so-called naturalism. The only valid test of good verse-speaking is that, in its dramatic context, it should sound necessary and inevitable.

Hence, there is no one particular 'style' for speaking Shakespeare, any more than there is a fixed style of singing. No soprano in her right musical senses would attempt to sing Mozart as she would sing Wagner; furthermore, the style appropriate to Fiordiligi differs no less significantly from Donna Anna's than Senta's from Brünnhilde's. So it is with Shakespeare. The Oberon style will not suit Othello, nor should a delivery that encompasses the lyrical symmetries of *Richard II* be transferred without appropriate adjustment to the muscular directness of *Julius Caesar*. But whilst, at the moment, no responsible opera companies allow singers to appear as Carmen or Don Giovanni until they are at least familiar with the technical requirements of their art, neophyte Romeos and Titanias are far from rare in the English theatre. This might not be so bad if producers paid some attention to the matter once they were confronted with inadequate delivery. But their irresponsibility is extraordinary. Nor is it as if the problems of speaking Shakespeare were unduly formidable. With adequate training, the technical principles can be learnt by all but the rhythmically insensitive (who should not attempt it anyhow). And it should not be too much to ask that such training should not be carried out quite so haphazardly, or so blatantly *coram populo*, as at present. We have surely earned a respite from those productions of Shakespeare which imply that the use of verse is some kind of defective compromise on the part of the author.

The verse of *The Tempest* bears all the qualities to be expected from Shakespeare at the full flow of his creative maturity. It is very varied, and, as with all good styles, always appropriate to the expressive requirements put on it. In the main, it is energetic, compressed, sparing of imagery (especially sensuous imagery), and rhythmically very flexible. There is the intense, nervous rush of:

> like one
> Who having into truth, by telling of it,
> Made such a sinner of his memory,
> To credit his own lie, he did believe
> He was indeed the Duke; out o'th'substitution
> And executing th'outward face of royalty,
> With all prerogative ...   I.2.99–105

or the graver power of the following, with its adroit combination of ellipsis and accumulated subordinate clauses:

> and do pronounce by me
> Lingering perdition – worse than any death
> Can be at once – shall step by step attend
> You and your ways; whose wraths to guard you from,
> Which here, in this most desolate isle, else falls
> Upon your heads, is nothing but heart's sorrow,
> And a clear life ensuing.   III.3.77–83

In more majestic mood, there is the unmistakable grand manner of:

> I have bedimmed
> The noontide sun, called forth the mutinous winds,
> And 'twixt the green sea and the azured vault
> Set roaring war ...   V.1.41–4

in which Shakespeare could not more plainly be demanding the sonorous exploitation of the expansive internal rhymes. By contrast there is the limpid directness of certain lines which entrance the ear with their rhythmic ease and simplicity of syntax:

> Sit still, and hear the last of our sea-sorrow.   I.2.170

> Be not afeard; the isle is full of noises. III.2.136

> Bravely, my diligence. Thou shalt be free.   V.1.241

For further variation, the rhyming couplets of the masque relieve the bold austerity of the language of the rest of the play; their verbal flavour is of profusion and sensuous bounty:

> Who, with thy saffron wings, upon my flowers
> Diffusest honey-drops, refreshing showers:
> And with each end of thy blue bow dost crown
> My bosky acres and my unshrubbed down,
> Rich scarf to my proud earth.   IV.1.78–82

If Shakespeare avoids delaying the swift flow of the main stream of the dialogue with the decorative metaphors of earlier styles, there is no decrease in the vitality of the language. The play abounds in compounds and coinages. In addition to words already quoted, we may find 'fraughting', 'over-topping', 'sight-out-running', 'still-vexed', 'wave-worn', 'urchin-shows', 'cloud-capped', 'pinch-spotted', 'spell-stopped', all of which colour the vocabulary with an authentic strangeness of tone that is conducive to the character of the play.

The verse-speaking in *The Tempest* requires considerable variety. It is not the easiest of styles to master. The flexibility of its rhythms alone is remarkable, even for Shakespeare. But the text never imposes demands beyond the range of a sensitive and athletic delivery. Thorough familiarity is, of course, the safest method of approach, and this involves a good deal more than merely learning the lines. By becoming properly conscious of all the items in Shakespeare's technical equipment – vocabulary, punctuation, syntax, tempo, rhythm – the actor may discover from the text indications of Shakespeare's dramatic intention no less reliable than the stage directions in a modern script or a composer's markings in a musical score. A fine style is its own interpreter.

Staging, Costume, and Music

On 5 November 1897, William Poel produced *The Tempest* for the Elizabethan Stage Society in the Mansion House. Shaw's review of the production may serve as an apt introduction to the problems of staging the play:

Mr Poel says frankly, 'See that singers' gallery up there! Well, lets pretend that it's the ship.' We agree; and the thing is done. But how could we agree to such a pretence with a stage ship? Before it we should say, 'Take that thing away: if our imagination is to create a ship, it must not be contradicted by something that apes a ship so vilely as to fill us with denial and repudiation of its imposture.' . . . The reason is, not that a man can *always* imagine things more vividly than art can present them to him, but that it takes an altogether extraordinary degree of art to compete with the pictures which the imagination makes when it is stimulated by such potent forces as the maternal instinct, superstitious awe, or the poetry of Shakespear. . . . It requires the nicest judgment to know exactly how much help the imagination wants. There is no general rule, not even for any particular author. You can do best without scenery in *The Tempest* and *A Midsummer Night's Dream*, because the best scenery you can get will only destroy the illusion created by the poetry; but it does not at all follow that scenery will not improve a representation of *Othello*.

Poel's strict Elizabethanism is still unacceptable to most modern producers of Shakespeare. But recently there are signs that Shakespeare behind the proscenium arch is declining in favour. The splendid open-stage at the Mermaid Theatre has as yet only been used for a perversion of Shakespeare, but that, and the modifications to the Stratford-upon-Avon stage are hopeful signs that the ascendancy of pictorial Shakespeare is at least being questioned. Certainly the basic facilities of the Elizabethan stage (provided, for example, in the stage at Stratford, Ontario) are appropriate to all the mechanical requirements of *The Tempest*. The inner-stage for Prospero's cell, the various galleries for Ariel as harpy, the appearance of Juno, the hell-trap for the ship's cabin (and Caliban's rock?), and the platform for the main action. No modern proscenium stage can match its opportunities for swift, continuous action, and that flexibly intimate style of speech which so much of the text requires. The problem of speaking Prospero's text in I.2 is enormously increased by the distances between actor and audience in our proscenium theatres – and the apron-stages at Stratford and the Old Vic are only slight modifications. The Elizabethan stage (or, to be more practical, a stage which preserves its advantages, adding to them needful modern facilities of sound and lighting) rightly throws all stress on the play itself. Anyone who has seen Shakespeare performed in these circumstances, or 'in the round', is struck by the instant gain in intimacy and access to the play.

Given a proscenium-stage, however, producers should aim for a setting which accords as closely as possible with the play's structure. Presumably a basically permanent set will be an initial prerequisite, and no alterations to this during the play should be obtrusive or hold up the action. Designers should be restrained from trying to transgress the play's scenic data ('this bare island') and smothering the play with subaqueous gew-gaws and the rest of the botanical farrago. But gorgeousness and mystery should accompany the masque, and it is up to the collective ingenuities of producer, designer, and choreographer to ensure that the audience shall be no less transported than Ferdinand.

Distinctive costumes can do much to strengthen the play's impact. One should not dogmatize here beyond certain essentials which the text makes plain. The lords are the easiest problem. The prime requisite is clothes that will establish their social identities. Seventeenth-century contemporary style (English or European) would place the real world firmly (and becomingly) in the play's visual scheme. The islanders are less straightforward. We know that among his luggage Prospero was enabled to include:

> Rich garments, linens, stuffs, and necessaries
> Which since have steaded much. I.2.164–5

So, if these are to be seen, they must obviously harmonize in style with what the courtiers wear – though an inventive designer may find it helpful to point the passage of twelve years by changes in fashion for the latest visitors to the island.

For the denouement, Prospero must have a royal robe of Milan. If the transformation from the master of a full poor cell to Duke restored is to have the strongest impact possible, then there is a good argument in favour of Prospero's earlier costume being markedly different in style from the courtiers'. His condition of scholar and recluse may provide the designer with helpful points of departure. And, of course, the magic garment must carry the right associations of power and mystery. Miranda, too, will benefit from whatever appearance of detachment from the style of the 'real' world can be designed that is both apt and becoming.

A good many Ariels resort to varying degrees of undress, offset by bizarre tones of body make-up and sundry articles of vegetation. It is, however, salutary to remember that, nearly always, the more clothes are removed the less spiritual the appearance becomes. Perhaps an apter approach to the very difficult problem of designing for Ariel may be to begin with the salient features of his dramatic condition – 'an airy spirit', once imprisoned in a pine, aspiring towards total liberty, rapid transformation. The elemental associations are air and fire:

> I flamed amazement. Sometime I'd divide,
> And burn in many places. I.2.198–9

> Hast thou, which art but air. . . . V.1.21

The disguises of water-nymph and harpy are explicit and therefore easier to encompass.

Caliban's elements, on the other hand, are earth and water, and the 'savage and deformed slave' of the Folio list of characters should present a credibly grotesque debasement of physical humanity. Caliban is capable of not a few human conditions (e.g. lust, drunkenness, and pleasure in music) so that his appearance, however brutal, must indicate an aspiration towards human nature, whereas Ariel's is away from it.

With the goddesses the play should reach its peak of sumptuousness. All three of them are well contrasted in character and function: Juno, grand, and consummate, the highest queen of state; rich and bounteous Ceres, symbol of nature's bounty; and Iris, about whom Shakespeare has virtually written a note to the designer:

> many-coloured messenger. . . .
> Who, with thy saffron wings. . . .   IV.1.76, 78

The ship's crew, and Stephano and Trinculo, present no great problem. They should wear whatever harmonizes with the other costumes and at the same time suggests their professional occupations.

Music plays a very important part in establishing the successive atmospheres of the play. In no other play of Shakespeare is it so organically integrated. If special composition can be afforded, it should be borne in mind, first and foremost, that whoever hears the music of the island is immediately enchanted by it. Purveyors of *musique concrète* are apt to tax an audience's credulity when Caliban speaks of the sounds and *sweet* airs. Certainly the structure of the songs warrants a melodic setting. If, on the other hand, existing music (recorded or live) has to be used, the more recondite ensembles (including harp and/or harpsichord) are likely to provide the most suitable accompaniment. There is so much wonderful early seventeenth-century music that is almost completely unknown that, if the play is being given a contemporary setting, producers need look no further.

Characters and Casting

Prospero

Prospero so dominates the play both in length and in dramatic function that the choice of actor for the part must largely determine the character of the whole production.

In performance the part presents certain hazards. One is a tendency to stress the magician at the expense of the man. This generally results in a delivery of booming tedium and an appearance of minor prophet, with costume and make-up vaguely after William Blake. The intention is to match the great hieratic moments, but these are only effective if the inner tension of the personal conflict has been first suggested. Sir John Gielgud's performance at Stratford-upon-Avon in 1957 offered an exemplary reassessment of the character. Ascetic, wiry, and middle-aged in appearance, he admirably combined the three identities of father, duke, and magician.

Those who prefer their Prosperos old adduce evidence from the text: 'Bear with my weakness; my old brain is troubled' (IV.1. 159), and 'Every third thought shall be my grave' (V.1.312). But the first of these remarks is addressed to Ferdinand and Miranda under particularly exacting circumstances. It is a common habit of the older generation to exaggerate its age to the younger. Moreover, Shakespeare's contemporaries regard fifty and over as older than we do. The second quotation seems even less convincing. Even to a modern quinquagenarian one thought out of three on any topic as absorbing as the grave may not seem unduly excessive.

Another aspect of Prospero which is apt to worry actors, producers, and, in consequence, the audience is his puritanism. The puritanism of *The Tempest* is similar to that of *Comus*. That is to say, it is both positive and idealistic. Its frankest and fullest expression occurs in Prospero's adjurations to Ferdinand before the masque:

> If thou dost break her virgin-knot before
> All sanctimonious ceremonies may
> With full and holy rite be ministered,
> No sweet aspersion shall the heavens let fall
> To make this contract grow ...   IV.1.15–19

and again:

> Look thou be true. Do not give dalliance
> Too much the rein. The strongest oaths are straw
> To th'fire i'th'blood. Be more abstemious,
> Or else, good night your vow.   IV.1.51–4

To both these injunctions, Ferdinand replies with prompt and ardent acquiescence. The modern error is to present this kind of feeling in the spirit of Thou Shalt Not. There is no space here to go into the spiritual background of the Renaissance ideal of chastity. It must suffice to say that Shakespeare in *The Tempest* is writing in full accord with that ideal. Nowadays our attitude to the matter is supposedly more pragmatic. But in the seventeenth century glandular determinism did not enjoy the cultural ascendancy it does today.

If Prospero's sacramental attitude to sex can be presented as a thing of joy and love rather than as the restrictive suspiciousness of a prurient *voyeur* then it should be dramatically acceptable to all who can respond to the imaginative presentation of ideas different from their own.

'The Lords'

Thus theatrical parlance has named them, and, on the whole, disparagingly. Most actors regard them as unrewarding parts. Yet they are all (even Adrian and Francisco) firmly characterized. Their superficial penalty as parts is that they seem to begin much better than they finish. Antonio and Sebastian, for instance, say very little in the last two acts, and Alonso's and Gonzalo's best scenes occur before the last act. Yet the play requires that these characters become increasingly passive with the approach of the denouement. Viewed as deliberate rather than casual, this tapering of individuation may seem a dramatic advantage if the actors concerned will play their later silences and responses for what they are worth.

More often than not the parts are undercast. What, above all, they must have is an aristocratic quality. If the implicit assumption that what they say and do and think carries public consequences is lacking, then indeed they are insufficient strands in the play's texture. Given this quality, however, they are all good parts, and will repay vigilant interpretation.

Alonso develops most. Beginning as an accessory before the fact of Antonio's usurpation, he subsequently shows that the roots of evil do not lie deep in his nature. A sense of bereavement numbs

him into frigid isolation. The kindly solicitude of Gonzalo merely
jars upon his nerves:

> You cram these words into mine ears against
> The stomach of my sense.   II.1.108–9

Then, increasing awareness of the quality of the island revives his
hopes until the indictment of the banquet-scene brings him his
purgation. It is a sign of the importance Shakespeare attaches to
this moment that he gives Alonso one of the greatest speeches in
the play:

> O, it is monstrous, monstrous!
> Methought the billows spoke, and told me of it;
> The winds did sing it to me; and the thunder,
> That deep and dreadful organ-pipe, pronounced
> The name of Prosper: it did bass my trespass.   III.3.97–101

From this moment he is ready for arraignment and acquittal. Shakespeare adds sympathetic touches to the portrait right up to the end.
There is the poignant honesty of:

> But, O, how oddly will it sound that I
> Must ask my child forgiveness!   V.1.197–8

An even more delicate moment comes a little later. It falls to
Gonzalo to invoke divine blessings on the betrothal of the lovers,
and then his sovereign quietly adds: 'I say amen, Gonzalo' (V.1.
204). The humility of that echo is conclusive guarantee of Alonso's
regeneration. Both Sebastian and Antonio are established with
brilliant clarity.[3] What a wealth of characterization, for instance,
there is in Sebastian's:

> To ebb
> Hereditary sloth instructs me ...   II.1.226–7

with its overtones of decadent complacency and passive arrogance.
He is the perfect victim for Antonio's strength and eloquence. Nor
is Antonio's power over him broken at the end. 'What things are
these, my lord Antonio?' (V.1.264), with its blustering flippancy
expressive of the man's discomfiture but also of his impenitence,
tells us that Antonio is not the only younger brother who Shake-

speare leaves unredeemed. The strength of Antonio's will and the weakness of Sebastian's are what raise their respective resistances to the possibility of spiritual growth.

Gonzalo is a more conventionally drawn character. If, in addition to suggesting the warmth and humour of the man, the actor can match Shakespeare's audacity in allowing him every now and again to slip over the edge of tedium (to his companions, of course, not to the audience), then the part becomes a valuable and restful element in the total composition.

Ferdinand and Miranda

The contemporary theatrical climate is not conducive to the breeding of Shakespeare's golden lads and girls. There is a marked deficiency in young actors and actresses who can encompass the poetic, physical, and social qualities without which such parts become otiose. Yet, when they are well played, both parts emerge with charm and vitality. Miranda is alive and individual from the breathless anxiety of her opening speech. She is never afraid – for all her delicacy of mind – of expressing her feelings, and this candour of soul reaches an exquisite climax with her famous exclamation on first seeing the royal visitors:

> O, wonder!
> How many goodly creatures are there here!
> How beauteous mankind is! O brave new world,
> That has such people in't! V.1.181–4

And, although her father, with his gentle aside, is not slow to point out the irony of her observation, for a moment the audience will do right to see the world through Miranda's eyes. (It seldom happens like this, however, as the speech invariably raises a laugh in the theatre, a depressing reflection on the chances of a reasonable hearing for idealism.)

Ferdinand is a prince charming worthy of such a paragon. Courage, rapture, and nobility are written into the part with enough dramatic *raison d'être* for the right sort of actor to make him a real person as well.

Ariel and Caliban

Ariel is probably the most difficult part in the play to cast satisfactorily. The sheer spirituality of the character puts it beyond the range of most actors (and further still beyond actresses). Add to this the need for extreme physical mobility and grace, a highly developed vocal technique both in speaking and in singing, and it is clear that the demands of the part are indeed difficult to meet. Yet the problem of casting Ariel and Caliban is not made easier by the tendency to conceive both characters in terms that are vague and sentimental. For Ariel this involves overtones of Peter Pan, and for Caliban that of Our Dumb Friends' League.

Perhaps it is a mistake to approach either character in terms solely of itself. In fact, I find it difficult to think of either of them apart from Prospero, and believe that they only make full imaginative sense if apprehended as externalized aspects of Prospero – the one of his spiritual, the other of his sensual appetencies. The conditions of earthly existence do not permit either of these appetencies to over-reach themselves, or gratify themselves at the expense of one another, without some injury to the total organism of the self; in this way, the violence of some of Prospero's encounters with both his servants may find its aptest dramatic manifestation in terms of some such symbol of tension. Moreover, both Ariel and Caliban acquire, at certain moments, phenomenal accesses of energy, and these always occur in sight of their own particular horizon of liberation. 'What shall I do? Say what! What shall I do?' cries Ariel after Prospero has promised to discharge him within two days; and we should feel there is no limit for the answer. Correspondingly, Caliban's 'Freedom, high-day! High-day, freedom! Freedom, high-day, freedom!' is nothing if not the natural and exultant expression of the brute instinct glorying in its sudden discovery of independent vitality, when the social inhibitions laid upon it by authority have been released by alcohol.

It is, of course, very difficult, perhaps impossible, to suggest such ultimately abstract notions at all *specifically* on the stage. But one can suggest their *possibility*. That is to say, the appeal must be made to the imagination rather than to the intellect. One cannot be too careful about introducing such notions into the overall concept of a production, but if such a triune relationship as I have indicated can be encompassed – and it can certainly be *assisted* by discreet costuming as well as casting – then I am sure it can only enhance the extraordinarily powerful impression which the supernatural element in the play is capable of making.

Stephano and Trinculo

Here, again, the watch must be set up against mawkishness, without sacrificing any of the comic opportunities. Both characters are firmly integrated in the sub-plot, and this involves them in a programme, the items of which include rape and murder. Though their plan is abjectly mismanaged, it is still a serious project, and brings out the worst in both of them. Stephano's domination over Trinculo echoes, in cruder terms, Antonio's over Sebastian. His immediate reactions to all predicaments are selfish, greedy and unimaginative. Of all Shakespeare's drunkards, he is the least acquainted with delight. His apology to Trinculo is the only generous action he performs, and that is hardly disinterested.

With the possible exception of Malvolio, Trinculo is the most neurotic of Shakespeare's comic characters. His stage-life is a progress from fear to fear, beginning with the weather. His mind is more sensitive than Stephano's, but its only introductions are to terror and misery. The decadence of the Neapolitan court could receive no more conclusive attestation than when its jester and its butler are rejected by the sea.

NOTES

1. An encouraging step in the other direction was taken by Peter Brook's production at Stratford in 1957. This had the advantages of a most convincing and adventurously conceived Prospero from Sir John Gielgud, and a simple, formal setting, consisting of a parallel series of cut-outs reminiscent of Inigo Jones's designs for the *Salmacida Spolia*. Unfortunately the rest of the production did not measure up to these assets. But there was a splendid shipwreck.